SARTRE
THE NECESSITY OF FREEDOM

This book is a comprehensive study of the writings of Jean-Paul Sartre. As well as examining the drama and the fiction, the book analyses the evolution of his philosophy, explores his concern with ethics, psychoanalysis, literary theory, and biography and autobiography, and includes a lengthy section on the still much-neglected study of Flaubert, *L'Idiot de la famille*. One important aim of the book is to rebut the charges made by many recent theorists and philosophers by revealing that Sartre is in fact a major source for concepts such as the decentred subject and detotalized truth, and for the revolt against individualistic humanism. Dr Howells also takes into account much posthumously published material, in particular the *Cahiers pour une morale*, but also the *Lettres au Castor* and the *Carnets de la drôle de guerre*.

The work is a substantial contribution to Sartre studies, but has been written with the non-specialist in mind; to that end all quotations are translated into English and gathered in an appendix.

BOOKS IN THIS SERIES

SARTRE

THE NECESSITY OF FREEDOM

Christina Howells
Fellow of Wadham College, Oxford

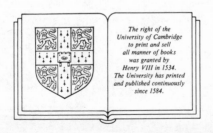

*The right of the
University of Cambridge
to print and sell
all manner of books
was granted by
Henry VIII in 1534.
The University has printed
and published continuously
since 1584.*

CAMBRIDGE UNIVERSITY PRESS

Cambridge

New York   New Rochelle   Melbourne   Sydney

Published by the Press Syndicate of the University of Cambridge
The Pitt Building, Trumpington Street, Cambridge CB2 1RP
32 East 57th Street, New York, NY 10022, USA
10 Stamford Road, Oakleigh, Melbourne 3166, Australia

First published 1988

Printed in Great Britain at
the University Press, Cambridge

British Library cataloguing in publication data
Howells, Christina
Sartre : the necessity of freedom. –
(Major European authors).
1. Sartre, Jean-Paul 2. Sartre, Jean-Paul
– Criticism and interpretation
I. Title II. Series
194   B2430.S34

Library of Congress cataloguing in publication data
Howells, Christina.
Sartre : the necessity of freedom.
(Major European authors)
Bibliography: p.
Includes index.
1. Sartre, Jean-Paul, 1905– – Criticism and
interpretation. 2. Philosophy in literature.
I. Title. II. Series.
PQ2637.A82Z7368   1988   848'.91409   87–15087

ISBN 0 521 23806 4

GG

Contents

General preface to the series

This series was initiated within the Cambridge University Press in the late 1960s, as an at first untitled collection of general critical studies. For convenience it was referred to inside the Press as 'the Major European Authors series', and once the prejudice against the useful cliché 'major' was overcome, the phrase became the official title.

The series was meant to be informal and flexible, and when the books are commissioned no strict guidelines are imposed. The aim has always been to provide critical studies which can justifiably be given a title which starts with the name of the author and is then not too seriously qualified by the subtitle: therefore to be introductory, general and accessible. When the series started the general assumptions were 'New Critical'; there was a strong disinclination to start from a biographical, or even from a more general literary–historical, approach. The general aim was and still is to address the works of the author directly as literature or drama, and to try to give a sense of the structure and effect of novels and poetry, or the way drama works with an audience. More specifically, writers of these studies guide the reader through the whole *œuvre*, being willing to make judgements about importance and quality by selecting which works to dwell on. Readers are helped to form direct impressions by being given liberal quotation and judicious analysis. Little prior knowledge is assumed; in some volumes quotation is entirely in English, and in others translations are given.

The aim is to keep classics of European literature alive and active in the minds of present-day readers; both those pursuing formal courses in literature and educated general readers – a class which still exists, though it is smaller than it ought to be.

Acknowledgements

A version of the second half of Chapter 6 appeared in the *Modern Language Review*, July 1979, vol. 74, no. 3; of Chapter 7 in *French Studies*, April 1979, vol. 33, no. 2; of Chapter 9 in the *Journal of the British Society of Phenomenology*, January 1982, vol. 13, no. 1. Material for Chapters 6 and 7 and the first half of Chapter 8 has been used in my previous study of Sartre: *Sartre's Theory of Literature*, M.H.R.A., 1979, and I am grateful for permission to reprint.

My thanks to the Warden and Fellows of Wadham College, Oxford, for the sabbatical leave which enabled me to finish this book, and for the maternity leave which allowed me to postpone its completion.

And thanks finally to Bernard, my husband, for his unstinting willingness to listen and discuss, for his encouragement, criticism and loving practical feminism; and to Marie-Elise and Dominic for putting the whole enterprise into perspective.

Abbreviations

B	*Baudelaire*
C	*Cahiers pour une morale*
CRD	*Critique de la raison dialectique*
E	*Esquisse d'une théorie des émotions*
EH	*L'Existentialisme est un humanisme*
EN	*L'Etre et le Néant*
I	*L'Imaginaire*
IF	*L'Idiot de la famille*
Im	*L'Imagination*
M	*Les Mots*
Mall	*Mallarmé (Obliques 18–19)*
MS	*Les Mains sales*
OR	*Œuvres romanesques*
SG	*Saint Genet, comédien et martyr*
Sit I–X	*Situations*, vols I–X
TE	*La Transcendance de l'Ego*
TS	*Un Théâtre de situations*

References throughout are to the French edition.
Translations are my own.

Chronological biography

1905	*21 June*. Birth of Jean-Paul-Charles-Aymard Sartre in Paris, 13, rue Mignard, XVIᵉ.
1906	Father dies.
1906–11	Lives with mother and grandparents in Meudon.
1911–15	Moves to Paris, 1, rue Le-Goff, vᵉ.
1913	Lycée Montaigne.
1915	Lycée Henri IV.
1917	Mother remarries (Joseph Mancy). The family moves to La Rochelle where Sartre is unhappy at school.
1920	Returns to Lycée Henri IV.
1921/2	Baccalauréat.
1922–4	Lycée Louis-Le-Grand to prepare entrance to Ecole Normale Supérieure.
1923	Publishes short story 'L'Ange du morbide' and several chapters of 'Jésus la Chouette' in *La Revue sans titre*.
1924–9	Ecole Normale Supérieure.
1928	Fails *agrégation*.
1929	Meets Simone de Beauvoir. Passes *agrégation* in first place, having reconciled himself to presenting more traditional philosophical ideas.
1929–31	Military service.
1931–6	Teaches philosophy at *lycée* in Le Havre. Starts first version of *La Nausée*.
1933–4	Obtains grant to study at the French Institute in Berlin where he discovers phenomenology, writes *La Transcendance de l'Ego* and a second version of *La Nausée*.
1935	Tries mescalin which produces depression and hallucinations.
1936	Publication of *L'Imagination* (Alcan). He and Simone de Beauvoir incorporate Olga Kosakiewicz into their life together to form a *ménage*

à trois. Its failure is recounted in de Beauvoir's novel *L'Invitée*.

Gallimard refuse *Melancolia* (*La Nausée*).

1936–7	Teaches in Laon.
1937	*La Nausée* accepted by Gallimard after some pressure.
1937–9	Teaches in Lycée Pasteur in Paris.
1938	Writes *La Psyché* from which *L'Esquisse d'une théorie des émotions* is drawn.

Publication of *La Nausée*.

1939   Publication of *Le Mur* and *L'Esquisse*.

Conscripted on 2 September to 70th Division in Nancy, later transferred to Brumath and then Morsbronn.

Meanwhile working on *L'Age de raison* and *L'Etre et le Néant*.

1940   Publication of *L'Imaginaire*.

Prix du Roman Populiste for *Le Mur*.

Imprisoned in Padoux, then Nancy, then Stalag XII D in Trèves.

Teaches Heidegger to fellow-prisoners.

Writes and directs *Bariona* in prisoner-of-war camp.

1941   Obtains his freedom from prisoner-of-war camp by dint of posing as a civilian.

Founds a short-lived intellectual Resistance group, Socialisme et Liberté, with Merleau-Ponty.

Teaches in Lycée Condorcet until 1944.

1943   Publication of *Les Mouches* and *L'Etre et le Néant*.

Writes articles of literary criticism on, amongst others, Camus, Blanchot and Bataille.

1944   Meets Genet.

Sets up editorial board for *Les Temps modernes*.

1945   Publication of *Huis clos*, *L'Age de raison*, *Le Sursis*.

Refuses Legion of Honour.

Goes to the United States as a special representative of *Combat* (Camus's journal) and *Le Figaro*, and again later in the year to give a series of lectures in American universities.

The first number of *Les Temps modernes* appears.

Gives the (in)famous lecture on 'L'Existentialisme est un humanisme'. This is at the start of the great vogue for existentialism and of Sartre's notoriety.

1946   Publication of *L'Existentialisme est un humanisme*, *Morts sans sépulture*, *La Putain respectueuse*, *Réflexions sur la question juive*, *Les Jeux sont faits*.

First quarrel with Camus.

1947   Publication of *Situations I, Baudelaire, Théâtre I*.
Qu'est-ce que la littérature? is serialized in *Les Temps modernes*.

1948   Publication of *Les Mains sales, Situations II, L'Engrenage*.
Participates in the founding of the Rassemblement Démocratique Révolutionnaire (R.D.R.)
The Catholic Church puts all Sartre's works on the Index.
Sartre is working on his *Morale* and a long study of Mallarmé (parts of both will be published posthumously).

1949   Publication of *La Mort dans l'âme, Situations III, Entretiens sur la politique*.
Disaffection with and abandonment of R.D.R.
Controversy with Mauriac.
Visits Guatemala, Panama, Curaçao, Haiti, Cuba and Havana.

1950/1   Publication of *Le Diable et le Bon Dieu* (1951). Studies history and economy and rereads Marx.
Part of the study of Genet is published in *Les Temps modernes*.
Sartre and Merleau-Ponty denounce the Soviet concentration camps.
Travels in Sahara and Black Africa.
Significant differences of opinion with Merleau-Ponty over the Korean war.

1952–5   Publication of *Saint Genet, comédien et martyr* (1952), *Kean* (1954).
For the next four years Sartre's concerns are primarily political; he writes *Les Communistes et la paix*; signs a manifesto against the Cold War; forbids a production of *Les Mains sales* in Vienna; speaks on behalf of the peace movement; visits Heidegger; protests against the execution of the Rosenbergs (1953); participates in an extraordinary meeting of the World Council for Peace in Berlin (1954); visits the Soviet Union and describes his experiences there in *Libération* and *L'Unità*; is named vice-president of the France–U.S.S.R. association; visits China (1955); returns to the Soviet Union.

1956   Publication of *Nekrassov*.

The Soviet intervention in Hungary is condemned by Sartre who leaves the France–U.S.S.R. association, writes *Le Fantôme de Staline* and produces a special number of *Les Temps modernes* devoted to the Hungarian question.

1957	Begins writing the *Critique de la raison dialectique*. Protests against the Algerian war and torture.
1958–9	Writes a commentary on Henri Alleg's *La Question* for *L'Express* and the journal is seized. Various subsequent issues of *Les Temps modernes* are also seized.

Participates in demonstrations against de Gaulle; speaks at an anti-fascist rally; gives a press conference on the violation of human rights in Algeria.

1960–6	Publication of *Les Séquestrés d'Altona* and *Critique de la raison dialectique*. Visits Cuba, meets Castro and Che Guevara.

Gives lecture on theatre in the Sorbonne.

Visits Yugoslavia, meets Tito, gives a lecture in Belgrade.

Participates in further debates on Algeria, signs manifestos, gives press conferences.

1962	Further political activity. Visits Poland and the Soviet Union; meets Khrushchev.

John Huston's film *Freud* is released. Sartre's scenario has been changed and he withdraws his name from the titles.

1963	Publication of *Les Mots*.

Participates in political press conferences, gives an anti-apartheid lecture, visits Czechoslovakia.

1964	Publication of *Situations IV, V* and *VI*.

Speaks at U.N.E.S.C.O. Kierkegaard conference and at Conference on Ethics in Gramsci Institute in Rome.

Is awarded and refuses the Nobel Prize (about £25,000).

1965	Publication of *Situations VII, Les Troyennes*.

Refuses to lecture in Cornell University in States. Visits the U.S.S.R.

Supports Mitterrand as presidential candidate.

1966	Publishes extracts from his study of Flaubert in *Les Temps modernes*.

Joins the Russell Tribunal investigating American war crimes in Vietnam.

Gives series of lectures in Japan.

1967 Lectures in Egypt, meets Nasser, visits refugee camps.
Travels in Israel in a less formal capacity.
Correspondence with de Gaulle over the Russell Tribunal.
Sartre and Aragon refuse to participate in the Tenth Congress of Soviet Writers in protest against the Sinyavsky–Daniel trial.
Supports Israel over opening of the Gulf of Aqaba.
Gives lecture on Vietnam in Brussels.

1968 Supports student movement in May uprising.
Accuses Communist Party of betraying the May revolution.
Condemns intervention of Soviet troops in Czechoslovakia.

1969 Sartre's mother dies.
Protests against expulsion of 34 students from University of Paris.
Asks for release of Régis Debray.
Gives T.V. interview on Vietnam War.

1970 Signs declaration on Biafra.
Takes over as editor of *La Cause du peuple*, whose previous two editors have been imprisoned.
Meets Pierre Victor, with whom he later collaborates in ethical discussions.
Participates in founding of Secours Rouge.
Is made nominal director of several minor publications of the extreme Left.
Blames the State as employer for fatal accidents at Lens colliery.

1971 Publication of *L'Idiot de la famille*, vols I and II.
Has mild heart attack.
Supports a hunger strike in favour of political prisoners. Participates in abortive occupation of Sacré Cœur.
Breaks off relations with Cuba over Padilla affair.
Demonstrates against racism.
Signs petition asking for right to emigrate for Soviet citizens.

1972 Publication of *Situations VIII* and *IX* and of *L'Idiot de la famille*, vol. III.
Start of film on his life and works by Astruc and Con-

tat. Disaffection with over-simple line of class-hatred of *La Cause du peuple*.

Agrees to edit new daily paper, *Libération*.

1973   Further, more serious heart attack.

Moves from boulevard Raspail to bd Edgar-Quinet.

Semi-blindness after two haemorrhages in his good eye.

Pierre Victor reads to Sartre who can no longer see sufficiently well.

Takes side of Israel in war of Yom Kippur.

1974   Publication of *On a raison de se révolter*.

Abstains in presidential elections.

Gives up editorship of various left-wing journals on health grounds.

Meets Marcuse for discussion about the situation of the intellectual.

Starts autobiographical dialogues on tape with S. de Beauvoir.

With three others Sartre prepares a series of television programmes on the last seventy years of history. The project is never produced.

Dissociates from U.N.E.S.C.O. as a protest in defence of the State of Israel.

Goes to Stuttgart to meet the terrorist A. Baader and denounces his conditions of imprisonment.

1975   Visits Portugal.

Signs petitions condemning Soviet repression.

In an interview with M. Contat declares himself in favour of 'libertarian socialism'.

Decides to reduce his public activities and spend more time on the preparation for the book on ethics, *Pouvoir et liberté*, with Pierre Victor.

1976   Publication of *Situations X*.

Sartre par lui-même (film) appears.

Accepts doctorate from University of Jerusalem.

Signs various political petitions and articles.

1977   Publication of *Sartre* − text of the film.

Takes up position against the 'nouveaux philosophes', and also declares 'Je ne suis plus Marxiste' (in an interview in *Lotta continua*).

Calls on Israel to respond to President Sadat's peace initiative.

1978	Goes to Israel to try to further the peace initiative. Participates in film on S. de Beauvoir. Appeals for return to France of D. Cohn-Bendit.
1979	Participates in Israeli–Palestinian conference organized by *Les Temps modernes* in Foucault's house. Extract from *Mallarmé* appears in *Obliques.* Participates in press conference for Boat People from Vietnam.
1980	Continues interviews with Pierre Victor. Supports boycott of Olympic Games in Moscow. *20 March.* Hospitalized for oedema of the lungs. *13 April* goes into a coma and dies on *15 April.* *19 April.* Funeral procession from hospital to cemetery of Montparnasse where his ashes are buried.

Further biographical details may be obtained from the seventy-page chronology introducing the Pléiade edition of Sartre's *Œuvres romanesques*; *Les Ecrits de Sartre*, ed. M. Contat and M. Rybalka; F. Jeanson, *Sartre dans sa vie*, Seuil, 1974; S. de Beauvoir, *La Force de l'âge*, *La Force des choses*, *Tout Compte fait*, *La Cérémonie des adieux*; A. Cohen-Solal, *Sartre 1905–1980*; R. Hayman, *Writing Against: A Biography of Sartre*, 1986.

1

The early philosophy: the necessity of freedom

As philosopher, dramatist, novelist, critic and moralist Sartre's major preoccupation was, throughout his life, always the same – freedom, its implications and its obstacles. It is a critical cliché – and Sartre himself contributed to its dissemination – to view the progression of his thought as moving away from a conception of absolute freedom towards a mature position which takes into account the constraints and conditioning of the external world. But such a picture is over-simple. Sartre was concerned from the outset with the relation between freedom and non-freedom, whether the latter be seen in terms of destiny or alienation or simply human finitude, the inescapable conditions of life, that is to say death, work, language. The early Sartre (for convenience, up to the mid-1950s) is concerned primarily with the individual, his situation and his facticity[1]; the later Sartre with society, 'pre-destination' and the 'practico-inert'[2] – in all cases it is against a background of inalienable ontological liberty that these limiting concepts operate. Depending on the perspective chosen, philosophical or political, Sartre may be viewed as an optimist converted to pessimism (this picture of his evolution focusses on individual freedom and its apparent progressive erosion), or as a pessimist converted to optimism (this view centres rather on Sartre's early passive descriptions of freely alienated liberty and his later activist stance which strove to 'change the world'). In fact, however, Sartre's thought does not develop in a linear fashion: freedom is posited initially as both a fact and a goal, and from 1936 to his death in 1980 he was concerned both to define more closely the significance of the fact and to explore the conditions of possibility for the achievement of the goal.

Freedom, then, is the pivot of Sartre's writings, not simply in the domain of psychology or ethics where the question is most explicitly elaborated, but also in his aesthetics and literary criticism whose central focus is the creative imagination as synonymous with the freedom of human consciousness; in the paradoxes of his ontology: man's essence is defined as his liberty; and in his epistemology where he seeks to avoid both idealism and realism and to establish

1

an interdependence of man and the world without privileging either a constituting subject or a pre-constituted universe.

The self

The first area in which Sartre reveals freedom in action is not the outside world but rather the more intimate area of the self. His earliest published works show the way in which we choose not only our actions but also our characters and even our emotions. It is perhaps in our *self*-constitution that we are necessarily most free but feel it least: the resistance of the outside world or other people to our projects is somehow experienced as an external constraint which leaves our freedom unharmed in its essence; the resistance of our own personalities to change may be lived as an internal necessity over which we have little or no control. This, Sartre would say, is because we *desire* to experience our characters as stable: psychological essentialism is reassuring and obviates the effort which would be required to transform the patterns of behaviour and response which we have already established. The idea of an inner self – source of action, feeling, thought and emotion – is deep-rooted and intuitive: it is nonetheless, or perhaps consequently, the first butt of Sartre's existential attack. In *La Transcendance de l'Ego* (1936) Sartre will argue that rather than innate, the self is an imaginary construct, outside consciousness, object not subject of consciousness, a continuous creation held in being by belief. The self or ego , the 'I' and the 'me', are synthetic products of consciousness, unified not unifying, transcendent not immanent. A potential terminological confusion may be forestalled at this stage. Sartre is arguing against Husserl that the ego is transcendent not transcendental. A *transcendental* ego would be a personal core of consciousness, an original unitary subject, source of meaning, centre of personality, interior foundation for my sense of self. For Sartre only consciousness is transcendental, and it is, properly speaking, originally impersonal or at least pre-personal.[3] (In his later writings Sartre will drop the term 'transcendental' entirely, possibly because of its Kantian overtones.) The *transcendent* ego, on the other hand, is external to consciousness, an ideal totality of states, qualities and actions, a construct which I tend to imagine as a source of my feelings and behaviour but which is in fact rather a synthesis. The ego is transcendent in the same way as so-called 'states' such as love or hatred, which are, as we shall see, illusory unities imposed on the perpetual flux of consciousness in our desire to give 'depth' and 'durability' to our feelings.

The 'I', then, is not a unifying force; it is rather consciousness which makes the unity and personality of the 'I' possible (*TE*, 23). Indeed, not only is the ego external to consciousness, it is not even permanently present to consciousness. Sartre's essay starts by agreeing with Kant that 'le Je Pense *doit pouvoir* accompagner toutes nos représentations'[4] (*TE*, 13), which he interprets as meaning that consciousness can always become reflexive, or in other words that self-consciousness is a perpetual possibility, the condition of possibility of experience. But it is the reflexive act itself which, for Sartre, brings the ego into being: 'il n'y a pas de *Je* sur le plan irréfléchi' (*TE*, 32): when I am reading or running for a train I am conscious of the book or the train to be caught, not of myself reading or running, though I may become self-conscious at any moment. Consciousness is always intentional,[5] that is to say it always has an object; much of the time its object is the outside world, but occasionally I will turn my attention on myself. If this is momentary or incidental ('What are you doing?' – 'I'm reading'), the ego will appear fleetingly in the act of reflexion. But if I want to capture that Ego and analyse it I am doomed to disappointment. The self may be an object in the world, but unlike other objects it can be perceived only obliquely, I cannot ever observe my own ego at work: 'L'Ego n'apparaît jamais que lorsqu'on ne le regarde pas . . . par nature l'Ego est fuyant' (*TE*, 70). Since my self is not *in* consciousness I cannot discover it by looking inwards – introspection meets only a frustrating emptiness and opacity. By attempting to focus on the ego, consciousness passes necessarily from the simple reflexive mode in which the ego appears ('I'm reading'), to a complex but nonetheless *non*-reflexive mode which tries vainly to concentrate on an object which has already disappeared. This means that I can never *know myself* in any real sense (*TE*, 69); I have no privileged knowledge of myself: my self-knowledge is exactly equivalent to my knowledge of other people – that is to say a result of observation and interpretation of behaviour. And moreover, to take an external view of myself is necessarily to take a false perspective, to try to believe in a self which I have myself created: 'aussi l'intuition de l'Ego est-elle un mirage perpétuellement décevant' (*TE*, 69). I may be an object for others, I can never be an object for myself. In fact, of course, a fixed, objective self would entail 'la mort de la conscience' (*TE*, 23). Instead of being a source of riches, an inner life would weigh

3

down my consciousness, deny its freedom. But total freedom is disquieting, awareness of spontaneous *ex-nihilo* existence causes anguish and is perpetually refused in the name of permanent (imaginary) structures of personality. I surprise myself when I do not act in accordance with my self-image: 'Moi, j'ai pu faire ça!' (*TE*, 62). It is more comforting to see myself as acting 'out of character' than to recognize my perpetual potential for change. Sartre is laying here the foundations for the study of bad faith which he will elaborate further in *L'Etre et le Néant*.

The emotions

It is also in *La Transcendance de l'Ego* that the study of emotion to be developed in *Esquisse d'une théorie des émotions* (1939)[6] is begun. Sartre's major interest is in our freedom or lack of it with respect to our emotions, and he distinguishes between emotion, sentiment and passion in terms not so much of the strength of feeling as of the reflexive attitude towards that feeling. Emotion differs from sentiment in so far as the latter involves a state of equilibrium when the feeling experienced is adapted to the reality to which it responds. Emotion on the other hand is not a rational response to a situation, it is a way of apprehending the world which aims to *transform* it. Sartre's examples are predominantly negative: hatred, anger and fear. What does it mean to claim that I hate Pierre? All I can really maintain with certainty is that I feel repugnance for Pierre at this moment, but this does not satisfy me: I want to commit myself for the future too.[7] A decision always to find Pierre repugnant would be transparently fragile and unstable, so I invert the process and envisage my hatred as the source of my feeling of repulsion. In my anger I believe I hate Pierre because he is hateful; only an act of purifying reflexion (difficult in the throes of bad temper) would rectify the picture: I see Pierre as hateful *because* I am angry (*TE*, 48).

A problem arises when we compare Sartre's analysis of hatred with his brief discussion of love in his essay on Husserl in 1939: 'Une idée fondamentale de la phénoménologie de Husserl: l'intentionnalité'.[8] There Sartre argues in apparently contradictory fashion that if I love a woman it is because she is lovable. Part of the answer would seem to lie in Sartre's polemical strategy: in the *Transcendance de l'Ego* and the *Esquisse d'une théorie des émotions* he is contesting the traditional conception of emotions as a passive (and causally determined) response to stimuli; in the essay on intentionality he is expounding the theses of Husserl and refuting (Proustian) subjectivism, dismissed as 'la philosophie digestive de l'empirico-criticisme, du néo-kantisme' (*Sit I*, 29). In fact, in Sartre's view, neither love nor hatred are independent of their object, but nor are they *caused* by it: 'La conscience et le monde sont donnés d'un même coup: extérieur par essence à la conscience, le monde est, par essence, relatif à elle' (*Sit I*, 30).[9]

In fact, love and hatred are not properly speaking *emotions* at all (the emotions involved are affection and desire or anger and repulsion), they are rather a synthesis of repeated experiences, a *choice* of attitude. Like the ego they are transcendent. Emotions proper, then, are not enduring sentiments nor states adapted to reality. Emotion is compared by Sartre to magic: it is a temporary response to a situation which I am unable to deal with in real terms. The examples given are familiar: I cannot outwit an opponent in an argument but rather than admit defeat I become angry; I cannot solve a mathematical problem so I tear up the piece of paper on which it is written; I cannot bring myself to confess a misdemeanour so I burst into tears (*E*, 30–1). The reality has not altered, but I have the illusion of escaping from it momentarily. Sartre's examples may suggest that he sees emotional behaviour as insincere, but this is not the case. There are, he recognizes, false emotions when I perhaps feign a joy I do not feel or exaggerate my distress (*E*, 51). But real emotion *believes* in the transformed world it has created for itself. It is not self-conscious: this is not to say that it is unconscious[10] but rather that it is unreflexive, or, in Sartre's terminology, 'consciente d'elle-même non-thétiquement' (*E*, 42). This means that although the object of consciousness is the world it has subjectively transformed, a reflexive consciousness which would recognize itself as source of its own degradation in emotion is always possible. 'C'est dans cette mesure et dans cette mesure seulement qu'on peut dire d'une émotion qu'elle n'est pas sincère' (*E*, 54). If emotion is a game, it is a game in which I believe (*E*, 44). The qualities I project onto objects are not recognized as my projections: 'les qualités intentionées sur les objets sont saisies comme vraies' (*E*, 52). This also throws further light on the *boutade* already referred to: 'Si nous aimons une femme, c'est parce qu'elle est aimable' (*Sit I*, 32). Emotion may be chosen, it is nonetheless undergone. 'L'émotion est subie. On ne peut pas en sortir à son gré, elle s'épuise d'elle-même mais nous ne pouvons l'arrêter' (*E*, 52). We are enthralled: 'envoûtés, débordés, par notre propre émotion' (*E*, 52). Consciousness becomes its own captive, victim of its own trap as in dreams or hysteria (*E*, 55).

All this provides an important corrective to a certain facile view of Sartrean freedom which attributes to him an implausible ideal conception of liberty quite at odds with our experience. Sartre has indeed a radical view of human freedom and responsibility: this does not mean that he analyses consciousness as if it were disembodied and unsituated. Indeed the body is described as representing 'le *sérieux* de l'émotion' (*E*, 52). Real emotion involves not only a certain kind of behaviour, but also physiological changes; the former may be revoked by an effort of will, the latter escape my control: 'On peut s'arrêter de fuir; non de trembler' (*E*, 52); 'Mes mains resteront glacées' (*E*, 53); 'La conscience ne se borne pas à projeter des significations affectives sur le monde qui l'entoure: elle *vit* le monde nouveau qu'elle vient de constituer' (*E*, 53). The bodily transformations form part of a significant behavioural whole without which they would be meaningless, but they constitute a hard-core of somatic response irreducible to interpretation in terms of the freedom of consciousness. Sartre will elaborate his conception of the relation of the body to consciousness in *L'Etre et le Néant*; for the moment he merely alludes to the dual nature of the body, 'd'une part un objet dans le monde et d'autre part le vécu immédiat de la conscience' (*E*, 53).

The origin of emotion may, then, be spontaneous, the experience of it is passive: 'L'origine de l'émotion c'est une dégradation *spontanée* et *vécue* de la conscience en face du monde' (*E*, 54). Emotion necessarily tends towards its own self-perpetuation, in part for physiological reasons, but more importantly because I cannot *simultaneously* posit the world as, say, fearful or hateful and as neutral or positive. 'Il ne faut pas imaginer la spontanéité de la conscience en ce sens qu'elle serait toujours libre de nier quelque chose au moment même où elle poserait ce quelque chose' (*E*, 55). 'La conscience s'émeut sur son émotion, elle renchérit' (*E*, 55). Nonetheless, there is still room for manoeuvre. Since I am my own captive I can release myself, but not without a struggle: 'la libération doit venir d'une réflexion purifiante ou d'une disparition totale de la situation émouvante' (*E*, 55). Purifying reflexion would recognize that it is I who have constituted the emotional world in which I find myself trapped. But this kind of reflexion is rare. Reflexive consciousness is more often *complice* than *purifiante*, inclined to justify my emotions by looking for fresh evidence in the object which has 'provoked' them, rather than recognizing their affective, value-laden charge as a projection. Indeed, Sartre concludes, *réflexion complice* may transform emotion into passion (*E*, 63). This allusive comment seems to dismiss passion as an intense, unadapted emotional state prolonged indefinitely by irrational, indulgent reflexion. As a conclusion it is resolutely anti-Romantic.[11]

The *Esquisse* clearly represents a careful and subtle attempt to account for a complex phenomenon. It would be easy to extract from it apparently contradictory statements concerning the status of emotional behaviour with respect to human freedom, in so far as it is *both* actively chosen *and* passively undergone. But Sartre manages to avoid both incoherence and compromise in his description of a psychological state which may initially produce bodily reactions but which is in its turn perpetuated by them. In his later writings Sartre will enjoy the effects of paradox and self-contradiction which he can obtain by playing with and subverting the binary oppositions of analytic reason and its permanent ally, common sense;[12] in 1939 his philosophical strategy is perhaps more conventional, and he prefers to explain and reconcile the problematic rather than using its full potential to shake the reader from her complacent confidence in the capacity of analytic reason to explain the world.

Phenomenology

The subtitle of *La Transcendance de l'Ego* is *Esquisse d'une description phénoménologique*; the subtitle of *L'Imaginaire* (which we shall examine shortly) is *Psychologie phénoménologique de l'imagination*; that of *L'Etre et le Néant* is *Essai d'ontologie phénoménologique*.

There is plenty here to puzzle the reader: not only the unfamiliar notion of 'phenomenological ontology' to which we shall return, but also the unexpected synthesis implied in 'phenomenological psychology'. Sartre gives a useful brief definition of phenomenology:

La phénoménologie est une description des structures de la conscience transcendentale fondée sur l'intuition des essences de ces structures.[13]

That is, a description of transcendental consciousness investigated through an intuition of essences. The terminology of phenomenology is perhaps more disorientating than its practice. Unlike psychology, which takes as its object situated consciousness, or the individual *psyche*, phenomenology aims to give an account of consciousness stripped of its empirical, personal irrelevancies. The object of phenomenology is *transcendental*, not in any mystical sense but rather in so far as it is not identified with any particular individual. And transcendental consciousness is reached by what is known as the *epoche*, or phenomenological reduction: that is to say the putting aside or 'bracketing off' of the contingent and personal to reveal the underlying universal structures.[14] The phenomenological method is intuition — not in the general sense of insight, but in the philosophical sense of what is apprehended by the mind as immediate evidence. It studies phenomena in the literal sense of ' "ce qui se dénonce soi-même"; ce dont la réalité est précisément l'apparence' (*E*, 15). Intuition differs radically from psychological introspection: introspection is the examination of one's own mental processes — it is necessarily personal, it is also, in Sartre's view, necessarily in-authentic, in so far as it attempts to objectify what is not properly speaking an *object* at all. (We have already seen the inability of introspection to observe the ego since the ego is not *in* consciousness.) Phenomenological intuition[15] seeks to determine the essence of the structures of (transcendental) consciousness — the essence not in any Platonic sense but simply in the sense of the necessary conditions of, say, an image or an emotion. The opposed attitudes of psychologists and phenomenologists towards the role of experimentation and example may usefully elucidate their differences. For the psychologist, experiments provide individual items of evidence which may cumulatively convince him of a particular theory. The phenomenologist works very differently — she seeks the essential conditions of a particular structure such as an image through an intuitive examination of a single example. The same essence necessarily underlies each of its manifestations. The empirical inductive psychologist can only ever reach *probable* conclusions — fresh evidence could always falsify his theories. The phenomenologist works in the domain of the certain — her object is immediately given to her, her material is always ready to hand, it is present in an experience which precedes all ratiocination or experimentation. Sartre pinpoints the difference by playing on the two senses of *expérience* in French: he argues that phenomenological enquiry, being directly concerned with the conditions of experience (*expérience*), has logical and methodological precedence over psychological experiment (*expérience*). 'Ainsi Husserl sait tirer parti de cette proximité absolue de la conscience par rapport à elle-même, dont le psychologue n'avait pas voulu profiter' (*E*, 13). But the phenomenological method sounds deceptively simple: to describe, without preconception, what appears to consciousness. For in fact our ways of thinking are so permeated by what we have always taken for granted that it is no easy task to learn to reflect or observe, as it were, naïvely. In the case of imagination, for example, Sartre writes:

La méthode est simple: produire en nous des images, réfléchir sur ces images, les décrire, c'est-à-dire tenter de déterminer et de classer leurs caractères distinctifs.[16]

If phenomenological reduction were as natural and straightforward as this suggests, the numerous 'false' theories of the image which Sartre decries would surely not have held sway for so long – they would have been seen to be at odds with immediate experience.

How then does Sartre propose to link phenomenology and psychology?

Les sciences psychologiques . . . étudient la conscience de l'être humain, indissolublement liée à un corps et en face d'un monde . . . La réfléxion phénoménologique . . . cherche à saisir les essences. C'est-à-dire qu'elle débute en se plaçant d'emblée sur le terrain de l'universel.   (*I*, 139–40)

The object of psychology is man-in-the-world, not (transcendental) consciousness *per se*; what Sartre has against it is that it is a positivistic science and the truth it reveals is scientific not human. (We will return later to this distinction.)[17] It studies man as an object not a subject, evacuates all value and deals only in the hypothetical, the experimental and the *a posteriori*. In so far as it pretends to be objective, psychology, in Sartre's view, ignores the fact that in the so-called 'human sciences' man is both object *and* subject of study.[18]. But if Sartre, in the name of phenomenology, points out the shortcomings of psychology, he is nonetheless not content to remain in the domain of pure phenomenology. Like the psychologist's, Sartre's major preoccupation is man-in-the-world, and this means that both human facticity and the world that has been 'bracketed off' by the *epoche* must be brought back into play. The phenomenological method is used to enrich and transform psychology, it enables the psychologist to interpret his findings in terms of their human significance: to study, for example, the *meaning* of emotional behaviour. Far from being an incoherent hybrid, phenomenological psychology reinstates the object of psychology with the human significance artificially removed from it, and restores to the object of phenomenology the concrete specificity of its individual manifestation.

Imagination

The study of the imagination both inaugurates and closes Sartre's philosophical writings: from *L'Imagination* in 1936 and *L'Imaginaire* in 1940 to *L'Idiot de la famille* in 1971/2, it is Sartre's constant preoccupation. Identified with the freedom of consciousness, it is the imagination which permits Sartre to relate his literary productions and aesthetic theories to his philosophical and political radicalism. But his attitude towards the imagination is from the outset ambivalent: both the essence of freedom and yet a permanent temptation to escape from the real and contingent into a fantasy world which would temporarily allay desire without satisfying it (I, 162). Source of change − moral, social and political − but also potential substitute for change, the imagination is the pivot around which many of Sartre's paradoxes turn and on which his later anti-Hegelian dialectics are arguably founded.

To understand this fundamental ambivalence we must turn to the early theoretical writings. L'Imagination prepares the ground for L'Imaginaire: it is a critique of previous theories of imagination, culminating in Husserl whom Sartre sees as having made a major advance in the field, marred by certain relics of the traditional conception of the image as an 'impression sensible renaissante' (Im, 152). Sartre attacks the pre-phenomenological views of the image as naïve and metaphysical, based on an a priori conception of the image as a copy of an object: a 'chosisme naïf' (Im, 4–5) which necessarily falsifies the interpretation of both experience and experiment. Sartre gives brief accounts of the theories of Descartes, Leibniz and Hume; Taine and the Associationists; Bergson and the Würzburg School. In all he finds the same tendency to conceive of the image as a weak perception, a content of consciousness. Husserl's notion of intentionality according to which consciousness is always of something outside itself, a direction of attention rather than a receptacle, refuses any view of the image as immanent. Imagination does not involve dwelling on a psychic content, it is rather one of the ways in which consciousness relates to the outside world. It is distinct from perception, not merely a poor relation or a weaker version. In L'Imaginaire Sartre will start where Husserl leaves off and elaborate a full-scale phenomenological psychology of the imagination. The work is divided into two sections: 'Le Certain', which establishes the essence of the imagination in so far as it may be determined by eidetic reflexion − this is the progressive phase of pure phenomenology; and 'Le Probable', a complementary regressive phase of experimental psychology which is no longer purely descriptive but rather involves hypotheses and their 'confirmation': 'ces confirmations ne nous permettront jamais de dépasser le domaine du probable' (I, 76).

Sartre's starting point is his opposition to what he calls the 'illusion d'immanence'. There are no images *in* consciousness. Imagining is a type of consciousness, and Sartre suggests that properly speaking we do not *have* images; the image is a relation. 'A vrai dire l'expression d'image mentale prête à confusion. Il vaudrait mieux dire "conscience de Pierre-en-image", ou "conscience imageante de Pierre" ' (*I*, 17). The second major feature of imagination revealed by intuition is that we learn nothing from it. Since the image is not a weak perception I can in no sense *observe* it; all I can 'learn' from the image is what I have put there myself; in this sense we can speak of its 'pauvreté essentielle' when contrasted with perception (*I*, 20). Thirdly, 'la conscience imageante pose son objet comme un néant'(*I*, 23). In imagination I posit the object as absent or even non-existent; the act of imagining is itself permeated by an awareness that its object is *not* present: if I imagine Pierre I know that I do not *see* him: indeed 'je ne vois rien du tout' (*I*, 25). Anyone familiar with the paradoxes spun around the notion of consciousness as a *néant* in *L'Etre et le Néant*[19] will suspect that Sartre is far from dismissing the image when he categorizes it in these terms. Finally, the imagination is spontaneous and creative whereas 'une conscience perceptive *s'apparaît* comme passivité' (*I*, 26; my italics). One of the problems with *L'Imaginaire* is that it opposes imagination and perception without giving even an outline account of the latter. Nonetheless, some remarks are made, and Sartre is far from devaluing perception in the way certain commentators have suggested:[20] it is described in terms of *plénitude* and *richesse* (*I*, 157). Moreover, it is never in fact equated with passive reception of sensory stimuli: 'je *perçois* toujours plus et *autrement* que je ne vois' (*I*, 156). I am aware of many aspects of an object of perception besides those I *see* at a particular moment (for example the back of my interlocutor's head, or the wallpaper behind the wardrobe, *I*, 157): this awareness depends on knowledge and intention but it does *not*, in Sartre's view, involve imagination. Here Sartre is implicitly refuting Kant's view of perception as necessarily implying an element of imagination. Sartre has been criticized for omitting a discussion of Kant from *L'Imagination*:[21] in fact Kant does not analyse image-forming proper, which is the subject of Sartre's study, and Sartre does refer to him on several significant occasions. But the overall omission is nonetheless revealing, and it will become progressively clearer that Kant is an opponent with whom Sartre has a permanent (albeit oblique) battle in the domain not only of aesthetics but also of ethics and arguably epistemology.

An implicit and traditional (Aristotelian) hierarchy seems to underlie much of Sartre's discussion of imagination: that of knowledge, imagination, affectivity. He refers repeatedly to imagination as a form of *savoir dégradé*: whereas *savoir pur* is defined as knowledge of a rule (*I*, 138) or of abstract relations, imagination is rather an intuitive (*I*, 74) form of knowledge which attempts to 'possess' (*I*, 151, 158) its object immediately; it is a kind of *savoir irréfléchi* (*I*, 148). The vocabulary is charged with negative connotations, although Sartre will insist that he does not consider imagination to be necessarily an inferior form of thought (*I*, 148), simply another non-conceptual mode. But in the affective realm also imagination is devalued: its object is unreal and the feelings associated with it share the same poverty and unreality as the image; as an attempt at possession it can never succeed. Just as I learn nothing from images, neither can they affect me except in so far as I am already moved or wish to be moved. Erotic desire produces erotic images, not vice versa. If erotic images appear to produce sexual excitement, or repulsive images nausea, this is because they have permitted me to focus my desire or repulsion on a particular object. 'Je ne les vois pas malgré moi, je les produis' (*I*, 162). There is a kind of affective dialectic (*I*, 180) between desire or repulsion and imagination in which I make more precise, conscious and explicit feelings which were previously only potential or generalized:

Mais, dira-t-on, au moins les vomissements sont subis. Oui, sans doute, dans la mesure où nous subissons nos énervements, nos idées obsédantes . . . C'est une spontanéité qui échappe à notre contrôle. Mais . . . nous nous sommes émus, emportés, nous avons vomi *à cause de rien*. (*I*, 181)

As in the case of obsessions or hallucinations, 'la conscience est en quelque sorte victime d'elle-même' (*I*, 199). Like emotions, then, images are created spontaneously, but may escape to some extent their creator's control.

Since Sartre has made a radical distinction between perception and imagination, the real and the imaginary, he cannot speak of their interaction in any simple or causal sense. Indeed he maintains that images can never be caused though they may be motivated (*I*, 140). I cannot affect the images I produce, nor be affected *by* them, except in the realm of the imaginary:

L'objet en image est un irréel . . . pour agir sur ces objets irréels, il faut que moi-même je me dédouble, que je m'irréalise. (*I*, 162)

L'irréel ne peut être vu, touché, flairé, qu'irréellement. Réciproquement il ne peut agir que sur un être irréel. (*I*, 176)

We shall see at a later stage the implications of such a separation in the aesthetic sphere: it is clear that it must complicate – to say the least – any discussion of art as potentially committed.[22] Within the affective domain it appears as a further diminution of the power of imagination. My love for Annie may lead me to conjure up her image in her absence, but since the image is unreal it cannot *really* affect me. My sentiments will become gradually impoverished if they are not stimulated by the always unpredictable nature of the real person. 'Les images que nous avons d'Annie vont se banaliser' (*I*, 186). 'Le sentiment s'est *dégradé* car sa richesse, sa profondeur inépuisable venaient de l'objet' (*I*, 186). Love for an absent person is *quasi-amour*; it is perhaps easy ('l'objet irréel . . . va devenir beaucoup plus conforme à nos désirs que ne le fut jamais Annie', *I*, 187), but it is empty, *factice* and *figé* (*I*, 189). For Sartre the imaginary is only ever a poor substitute for the real.

But this negative picture of imagination is far from being the end of the story. Imagination is not simply the formation of images, not just a matter of daydreaming. Imagination also allows us to envisage the possible, the unreal, that which is not; in positing the unreal it simultaneously negates the real, and it is this power to negate which is the key to the freedom of consciousness. It is imagination which permits us to stand back and totalize the world *as* a world. 'Poser le monde comme monde ou le "néantir", c'est une seule et même chose' (*I*, 234). 'Il faut considérer que l'acte de poser le monde comme totalité synthétique et l'acte de "prendre du recul" par rapport au monde ne sont qu'un seul et même acte' (*I*, 234). Without the power to imagine, I would be 'embourbé dans le monde' (*I*, 233), 'transpercé par le réel' (*I*, 239), 'totalement englué dans l'existant et sans possibilité de saisir autre chose que de l'existant' (*I*, 237). Imagination is not merely a faculty of consciousness, 'c'est la conscience toute entière en tant qu'elle réalise sa liberté' (*I*, 236). But if the imagining consciousness is free, this does not mean that it is arbitrary. Like all consciousnesses, it is *intentional*, that is to say it is always *of* something, and if it negates the real this can only be from a position *in* the real. The condition for consciousness to imagine is that it be 'en situation dans le monde'. Imagination and perception, the unreal and the real, may be radically distinct, they are nonetheless interdependent. 'Tout imaginaire paraît "sur fond de monde" mais réciproquement toute appréhension du réel comme monde implique un dépassement caché vers l'imaginaire' (*I*, 238). I perceive the world as I do because I can at any moment stand back from it; in so far as I apprehend the world as a meaningful totality, I go beyond the immediate 'given', and this potential *dépassement* is always implicit in my awareness of my situation.

L'Etre et le Néant

In *L'Etre et le Néant* Sartre does not discuss imagination *per se*, but since it is identified with 'la conscience toute entière en tant qu'elle réalise sa liberté' (*I*, 236) it necessarily underlies the entire work. Sartre's study of freedom is centred in psychology, but it is founded in epistemology and ontology and will end in ethics. The work is subtitled 'Essai d'ontologie phénoménologique': a phenomenological account of being, being as it appears, *le phénomène d'être*. Sartre is in full agreement with phenomenology in so far as it attempts to avoid dualism, to refuse any notion of an unknowable essence (the Kantian noumenon) underlying appearances:

Le phénomène . . . n'indique pas, par-dessus son épaule, un être véritable qui serait, lui, l'absolu. Ce qu'il est, il l'est absolument, car il se dévoile *comme il est*.[23]

But he parts company with phenomenology when he believes it slips into a form of idealism and, having identified being with its appearances, makes it relative to and dependent on human consciousness. From an epistemological point of view, Sartre's aim is to determine to what extent the world pre-exists our consciousness of it and to what extent it is constituted by consciousness.[24] In his view, phenomena must have a transphenomenal foundation: in other words, consciousness does not *create* being, 'l'être est . . . il déborde et fonde la connaissance qu'on en prend' (*EN*, 16). Being has no need of consciousness in order to be. At this point Sartre's account may seem to come close to the 'common-sense' or 'realist' position which envisages consciousness as simply responding to a pre-existing world.[25] But this too is rejected in its turn: Sartre's analysis of consciousness reveals it to be spontaneous, uncaused, neither acting *on* phenomena, nor yet acted on *by* phenomena. The task Sartre has set himself is that of elaborating an ontology which will go beyond both realism and idealism (*EN*, 31). But his attempt to avoid these twin pitfalls poses him a serious problem, that of determining what *kind* of relationship is possible between consciousness and phenomena if neither can act on the other. In the first place Sartre will maintain that the problem is improperly formulated: it starts from a false and abstract perspective. In this sense both realism and idealism erect an artificial separation between man and the world which necessarily undermines their analyses. Consciousness and phenomena do not exist in isolation: consciousness is always *of* something; phenomena always appear *to* consciousness. In a sense one could argue that intentionality may be seen as the key to the relationship between subject and object. What is immediately given *before* abstraction[26] is rather the union of man and world: in Heidegger's terminology 'l'être-dans-le-monde' (*EN*, 38). But this union is not one of identity but rather one of opposition or difference – if consciousness is always *in* and *of* the world this is not to say that it is one *with* the world; on the contrary, its relationship with the world is one of negation: consciousness knows that it is not that of which it is conscious.

Sartre's analysis of the negating power of consciousness is complex; his conclusions are simple: consciousness is the source of negation, it derives its power to negate from nowhere outside itself, it is pure negativity and *néant*. His account is elaborated in the main in opposition to Hegel and Heidegger. The details of this polemic need not concern us here: suffice to say that both are criticized as insufficiently radical – Hegel because his dialectical conception of being and non-being allows him to transform the one into the other and thereby ignore their irrreducible heterogeneity (*EN*, 50); Heidegger because he does not recognize negation as the primary structure of consciousness. Neither Hegel nor Heidegger carries his study of negation through to its source in the *néant* of human consciousness (*EN*, 55). Sartre's own position is unequivocal:

L'être par qui le Néant vient au monde doit être son propre Néant. Et par là il faut entendre non un acte néantisant, qui requerrait à son tour un fondement dans l'Etre, mais une caractéristique ontologique de l'Etre requis. Reste à savoir dans quelle région délicate et exquise de l'Etre nous rencontrons l'Etre qui est son propre Néant. (*EN*, 59)[27]

The paradoxes are indeed *délicats et exquis* and they are only just beginning. In defining consciousness as a *néant* Sartre has, of course, put it beyond the reach of attack from materialism: in so doing he is in a sense adopting a strategy similar to that of (contemporary) negative theology which describes God as superessential Nothingness.[28] Consciousness negates not only the world but itself also: in the first place its past self, 'la conscience se vit elle-même comme néantisation de son être passé' (*EN*, 65). Moreover, as an 'être qui est son propre néant' its present 'being' is never stable – it is 'un être qui est ce qu'il n'est pas et qui n'est pas ce qu'il est'

(*EN*, 97);[29] nor can it be identified with its future, 'je ne *suis* pas celui que je serai' (*EN*, 69). It is this impossibility of self-coincidence, of ever *being* identical with oneself in past, present or future, that is the price to pay for freedom of consciousness. Consciousness is entirely spontaneous, caused neither by the world outside nor by its own past. It is defined in radical opposition to the 'being' of things which is solid, self-identical, subject to the laws of causality. The being of things is *en soi* (*EN*, 33), that is to say it is pure positivity, plenitude; indeed even the minimal self-reflexivity implied in the phrase *en soi* is disavowed by Sartre: 'à la limite de la coïncidence avec soi . . . le soi s'évanouit pour laisser place à l'être identique' (*EN*, 118). Consciousness is *pour soi*, the reflexive is fully appropriate, it is not *soi*, it is fundamentally riven, present *to* itself, and therefore always separated *from* itself: 'S'il est présent à soi, c'est qu'il n'est pas tout à fait soi (*EN*, 120); 'Son être est toujours à distance' (*EN*, 167). If consciousness is *pour soi* that is to say that it is always striving to be *soi*. This does not mean that consciousness desires to abdicate its liberty but rather that it wants the best of both worlds − the freedom of the *pour soi* and the identity of the *en soi*; the two are necessarily incompatible. The mode of being suggested in the paradoxical formulation *en soi pour soi* is impossible: it provides an existential definition of the Being of God (traditionally defined as *ens causa sui*), or rather a 'proof' of his non-existence, since the synthesis is purely imaginary (*EN*, 133). Consciousness, then, aspires towards a self-contradictory divine state, and it is this frustrated aspiration which Sartre describes so eloquently as 'une passion inutile' (*EN*, 708).

The reverse side of liberty is thus frustration, or, in Sartre's terms, anguish:

C'est dans l'angoisse que l'homme prend conscience de sa liberté ou, si l'on préfère, l'angoisse est le mode d'être de la liberté comme conscience d'être.

(*EN*, 66)

L'angoisse est . . . la saisie réflexive de la liberté par elle-même.(*EN*, 77)

Like liberty, anguish is inescapable, but it can be to some extent masked. Much of *L'Etre et le Néant* is concerned with a description of the ways in which men try to hide their freedom from themselves. Examples of this inauthenticity had already been given in *La Transcendance de l'Ego* and the *Esquisse*: man's desire to envisage his ego as a source rather than a construct, his emotions as undergone rather than chosen. Such refusals of freedom involve what Sartre now calls *mauvaise foi* or lying to oneself: it is unlike lying to others, however, for I can never convince myself entirely, I see through my own ruse, I am bound to remain uneasy. Bad faith is unstable and self-contradictory, it depends on the creation of a semblance of duality in consciousness, and tends in fact to oscillate between *bonne foi* and cynicism. Bad faith works in several different ways: all involve a rejection of the central paradox of human existence and focus on only one of the opposed modes of being of the *pour soi*, either denying its being entirely and forgetting that 'il est ce qu'il n'est pas' or else ignoring the special fissured nature of that being, 'il n'est pas ce qu'il est'.[30] Sartre's definition may be abstract; his examples are, as always, concrete and familiar: at one extreme bad faith is manifested in a refusal to recognize oneself in one's behaviour — the homosexual or the coward who denies his homosexuality or cowardice (*EN*, 107), the girl who tries to dissociate from her body and to ignore the fact that her companion has taken her hand (*EN*, 95). At the other extreme, so-called 'sincerity' may be a form of bad faith if it entails an unquestioning identification with one's role, or an attempt to make others identify with their roles — the waiter who coincides entirely with his duties (*EN*, 100), or the self-righteous man who tries to make his friend confess that he *is* a homosexual (*EN*, 104).[31] All these acts of bad faith involve a refusal of the total responsibility for oneself that existential freedom necessarily entails. A different kind of flight from freedom is labelled by Sartre *l'esprit de sérieux*. *L'esprit de sérieux* is an attempt to deny the human origin of meaning and value, and to attribute to the subjective an objective status. Values, Sartre maintains, are not inherent in the world, not 'des données transcendantes' (*EN*, 721); a thing has value because I, or others, value it. Human freedom constitutes rather than responds to value; it creates moral criteria rather than obeying pre-existing moral imperatives:

Il y a angoisse éthique lorsque je me considère dans mon rapport originel aux valeurs . . . elle s'oppose à l'esprit de sérieux qui saisit les valeurs à partir du monde et qui réside dans la substantification rassurante et chosiste des valeurs.   (*EN*, 75–7)

But Sartre's conception of the constitutive role of consciousness in the world goes much further than simply stressing the human origin of value. Consciousness may be a *néant*, a *manque d'être*, a *défaut d'être* (*EN*, 128), it may negate being, but without it there would be no world to speak of. We come back now to the distinction between *being* and *world* mentioned earlier.[32] Of being, or the *en soi*, little can be said: 'Il est, il est en soi, il est ce qu'il est'

(EN, 34). Indeed being 'as it is' cannot be known, all that can be known is the human world:

> Pour connaître l'être tel qu'il est, il faudrait être cet être, mais il n'y a de 'tel qu'il est' que parce que je ne suis pas l'être que je connais et si je le devenais le 'tel qu'il est' s'évanouirait et ne pourrait même plus être pensé.
>
> (*EN*, 270)

Sartre will spin a further web of paradoxes around the way in which the *pour soi* interacts with being. As a *néant*, the *pour soi* adds nothing to being (*EN*, 233, 259); nonetheless 'le pour soi doit être le néant par quoi "il y a" de l'être' (*EN*, 230). Sartre is playing here on the opposition he has set up between *être* and *il y a*: on its own 'being *is*', through the *pour soi* '*il y a* de l'être', an untranslatable phrase perhaps best rendered 'being *exists*'. But the *pour soi* does not change or create being, it simply reveals it. Sartre's precarious navigation between the Scylla and Charybdis of realism and idealism may well make the reader dizzy at this point. In short, it is the *pour soi* which both totalizes and differentiates being, 'Reste à expliquer comment le surgissement du pour-soi à l'être peut faire qu'il y ait un *tout* et des ceci' (*EN*, 229). It is the *pour soi* that constitutes a world out of the *en soi*:

> 'Il y a' de l'être parce que je suis négation de l'être et la mondanité, la spatialité, la quantité, l'ustensilité, la temporalité ne viennent à l'être que parce que je suis la négation de l'être . . . Le monde est humain.
>
> (*EN*, 269 – 70)

The *en soi* is: the *pour soi* makes of it a world which is spatially differentiated, which involves distance and multiplicity (London is 400 miles from Edinburgh); the *en soi* is: the *pour soi* makes of it 'un monde de tâches' (*EN*, 250), a world of projects, tools and obstacles (the wood is impenetrable, the mountain hard to climb); the *en soi* is: the *pour soi* makes of it a world permeated by past and future, in which the present is fissured by anticipation and memory (the cloud is a threat of rain, the blossom a promise of fruit). The *en soi* is not even present without the presence of the *pour soi* (*EN*, 165). But this is not to say that time, for example, is a purely subjective phenomenon: it is objective and universal but necessarily dependent on the *pour soi*. Time is a structure of the *pour soi*, of its lack of self-identity, but it can be experienced only within the relationship of the *pour soi* to the world: 'Le Pour-soi . . . est temporalité . . . mais . . . sur le mode irréfléchi il découvre la temporalité sur l'être, c'est-à-dire dehors' (*EN*, 255). Sartre will point out that science itself has rejected the traditional positivist conception of absolute impersonal objectivity: there is no such thing as 'pure' knowledge or 'inhuman' truth (*EN*, 368–70). Nonetheless 'le monde m'*apparaît* comme objectivement articulé' (*EN*, 387; my italics). It is therefore less of a paradox than it might seem when Sartre claims both that 'le temps universel vient au monde par le Pour-soi' (*EN*, 255) and that 'la temporalité universelle est objective' (*EN*, 255). Moreover, *objective* has another dimension: after all, the *pour soi* is not alone in the world, the constitution of time, space, multiplicity and even value are not solipsistic individual enterprises. I may constitute the world, but I am born into a world already constituted by others. Sartre, we have seen, refuses all forms of idealism; but he would consider *subjective* idealism an absurdity.

As one might therefore expect, Sartre has little time for the traditional problem posed by solipsism, often referred to in British philosophy as the question of 'the existence of other minds'. He traces a deliberately anachronistic and non-chronological development of the question from Husserl through Hegel to Heidegger from whom he adopts the notion that just as we are immediately in-the-world, so we are immediately with-others. 'Je saisis l'être-avec-autrui comme une caractéristique essentielle de mon être' (*EN*, 301). The existence of other people is a direct certainty, not a matter of dispute or even of probability. Sartre describes Hegel as having made considerable progress over Husserl in avoiding solipsism, but disagrees with his description of relations with others in terms of mutual *knowledge*. For Sartre, the *pour soi* of the other is unknowable as a *pour soi* (*EN*, 298). Like Heidegger, Sartre envisages human relations as 'une relation d'être à être' (*EN*, 300), concrete rather than abstract, pre-existing any knowledge of the other (*EN*, 295). But he nonetheless prefers Hegel's description of relations as conflict to the optimistic Heideggerian *Mitsein* (*être-avec*) with its emphasis on common experience: 'L'essence des rapports entre consciences n'est pas le Mitsein, c'est le conflit' (*EN*, 502). Sartre's own account, at least in *L'Etre et le Néant*,[33] is irremediably pessimistic. I constitute the world in permanent opposition to the world as it is constituted by others. 'Je suis celui par qui *il y a* un monde' (*EN*, 314), but so is the other. Like me, the other is *spatialisant* and *temporalisant*: on the one hand, as we have seen, this guarantees the objectivity of the world, on the other it limits my autonomy and moreover makes of me an object in the other's world: 'Autrui . . . se présente . . . comme la négation radicale de mon expérience, puisqu'il est celui pour qui je suis non sujet mais objet' (*EN*, 283). 'Autrui c'est d'abord la fuite permanente des choses vers un terme . . . qui m'échappe . . . [Il] m'a volé le monde' (*EN*, 312–13). Moreover, when the other looks at me he changes my relations to the world, I become *self*-conscious rather than conscious of the world outside: 'Nous ne pouvons percevoir le monde et saisir en même temps un regard fixé sur nous' (*EN*, 316). 'Etre vu me constitue comme un être sans défense pour une liberté qui n'est pas ma liberté' (*En*, 326). I become a *transcendance transcendée* (*EN*, 352, 355). On the other hand, in alienating my subjectivity, the other simultaneously guarantees my objectivity: he is 'celui *par qui* je gagne mon objectité' (*EN*, 329). Since my ego is transcendent (in the sense seen in *La Transcendance de l'Ego*) I know it primarily through the reactions of others. For myself I am pure possibility; through others I learn that I am, for example, *méchant*, *jaloux* or *sympathique* (*EN*, 322), and through this I may gain, momentarily, the illusion of identity for which I strive. It is through the other that I become aware of my facticity which is the necessary obverse of my liberty – aware, for example, of my body as an object in the world. Sartre's discussion of the body is resolutely anti-dualist: he starts from the assumption that rather than *having* a body, I *am* my body (*EN*, 391). In this perspective the body is part of the *pour soi*, not primarily that *of* which I am conscious, but that *through* which I am conscious: 'ce par quoi les choses se découvrent à moi' (*EN*, 366), subject rather than object. 'Je suis mon corps dans la mesure où je *suis*; je ne le *suis pas* dans la mesure où je ne suis pas ce que je suis; c'est par ma néantisation que je lui échappe. Mais je n'en fais pas pour cela un objet' (*EN*, 391). For me, my body is the permanent condition of possibility of existence in the world; it makes my liberty possible (there is no such thing as a disembodied liberty) at the same time as limiting it by its finitude. Sartre identifies it with 'la *facticité* du pour-soi' (*EN*, 371)[34] and equates it with my birth, race, class, nationality, physiology, character and past:

Tout cela, en tant que je le dépasse dans l'unité synthétique de mon être-dans-le-monde, c'est *mon corps* comme condition nécessaire de l'existence d'un monde et comme réalisation contingente de cette condition.(*EN*, 393)

And it is the facticity and contingency of the *pour soi* which give rise – in Sartre's view – to nausea. But subject for me, my body is nonetheless an object for others, part of the *en soi* 'insaisissable et aliénée' (*EN*, 421); instead of seeing through it, I will see it from the outside, possibly in shyness, shame or vanity, for example, as *laid* or *beau*.

Sartre's concrete account of relations with others is no more optimistic than its theoretical basis. My ambiguous dependence on and alienation by others is inescapable. 'Autrui me *regarde*, et, comme tel, il détient le secret de mon être, il sait ce que je suis' (*EN*, 430). Whether I try to *be* what he sees me as, or escape it, the picture is equally gloomy: my freedom and his are incompatible; symbolically I am bound to seek his death. Whether I love, hate, desire or feel indifference towards the other, his alienation and mine are inevitable and interdependent. Even love is mutually destructive, and is itself doomed to destruction in what Sartre calls a 'triple destructibilité' (*EN*, 445): when I love I desire to be loved, in other words I desire that the other should desire me to love him, this alienates my freedom and, in Sartre's view, involves *duperie* and an impossible *renvoi à l'infini*; moreover I want to be loved freely, yet the freedom of the loved one can only make me permanently insecure; finally other people relativize my 'love' and destroy its 'absolute' quality. 'Il en résulte que l'amour comme mode fondamental de l'être-pour-autrui a dans son être-pour-autrui la racine de sa destruction' (*EN*, 445).

The conclusion of Sartre's analyses is that there is *no* way of respecting the liberty of the other: 'le respect de la liberté d'autrui est un vain mot' (*EN*, 480); my very existence imposes a limitation on him: La nausée + être de trop

Dès lors que j'existe, j'établis une limite de fait à la liberté d'Autrui . . . la charité, le laisser-faire, la tolérance . . . est [*sic*] un projet de moi-même qui m'engage et qui engage autrui dans son assentiment. (*EN*, 480)

This state of affairs constitutes the Sartrean version of original sin:

Ainsi, le péché originel, c'est mon surgissement dans un monde où il y a l'autre et, quelles que soient mes relations ultérieures avec l'autre, elles ne seront que des variations sur le thème originel de ma culpabilité. (*EN*, 481)

It has become clear that Sartre's conception of human freedom is highly complex. Since it underpins his entire work and its evolution has been much disputed we must look at a further aspect of the question before leaving the early philosophy. Liberty is inescapable: or in Sartre's oft-quoted formula 'je suis condamné à être libre . . . nous ne sommes pas libres de cesser d'être libres' (*EN*, 515). Sartre's theory leaves room for no half-measures, he refuses to attribute freedom to the 'will' for example and to envisage the determined, just as he refuses to split the psyche into and unconscious: 'une pareille dualité tranchée est e au sein de l'unité psychique' (*EN*, 517).[35] There are sitions which are logically tenable: 'Ou bien l'homme nt déterminé (ce qui est inadmissible en particulier parce qu'une conscience déterminée . . . cesse d'être conscience) ou bien l'homme est entièrement libre' (*EN*, 518). One consequence of this rejection of any kind of psychic dualism is Sartre's scepticism about the process of making decisions in the usual sense of the term: when I weigh up the pros and cons of a certain course of action it is *I* who have given them their respective weights:

La délibération volontaire est toujours truquée. Comment, en effet, apprécier des motifs et des mobiles auxquels précisément je confère leur valeur avant toute délibération et par le choix que je fais de moi-même? . . . Quand je délibère, les jeux sont faits.   (*EN*, 527)

Clearly, then, there is a difference between decision-making and choice. Freedom is a totality: consciousness is not split into 'will' on the one hand and 'want' on the other. What moralists have called 'la volonté' consists primarily in the *a posteriori* rationalization with which we try to justify certain of our choices. But this devaluation of 'will' does not imply that freedom is capricious or arbitrary; it is perhaps worth quoting Sartre at length on this important point:

Cela ne signifie aucunement que je sois libre de me lever ou de m'asseoir, d'entrer ou de sortir, de fuir ou de faire face au danger, si l'on entend par liberté une pure contingence capricieuse, illégale, gratuite et incompréhensible. Certes, chacun de mes actes, fût-ce le plus petit, est entièrement libre . . . mais cela ne signifie pas qu'il puisse être *quelconque*, ni même qu'il soit imprévisible.   (*EN*, 530)

But if acts are not 'caused', not determined by either the world or my past, how then may they be predicted or even understood? Sartre's answer is in terms of the future: 'le mobile ne se comprend que par la fin' (*EN*, 512), and with reference to what he calls 'le projet ultime et initial' (*EN*, 540), that is to say the self and world aimed at, but never of course achieved, and the constitution of which underlies all individual projects. But the 'projet ultime' is not to be envisaged as a 'deliberate' choice: we have seen that Sartre's refusal of determinism does not entail a simple 'voluntarism', and his rejection of the unconscious does not imply that all experiences, choices and intentions are immediately and transparently available to consciousness at any moment (it was already clear from the *Esquisse* that *la réflexion purifiante* was not an easy achievement).

In Sartre's terms the *choix profond* is *non-positionnel* (*EN*, 539), that is to say it is not reflexive.

In other words my behaviour is neither arbitrary nor determined: any action or decision can be interpreted in the light of an original project of which it is part. 'Il n'y a point de caractère – il n'y a qu'un projet de soi-même' (*EN*, 637). Unlike a character, conceived as something innate, my project is freely chosen, but this is not to say that I can depart from it piecemeal: to act in a way out of keeping with my project would necessarily entail a transformation of that project. One of Sartre's concrete examples is of a man hiking with friends who gives up after a few hours because he is 'too tired': his stopping forms part of a total world-view and takes its meaning from this:

Cela n'implique pas que je *doive nécessairement* m'arrêter, mais seulement que je ne puis refuser de m'arrêter que par une conversion radicale de mon être-dans-le-monde, c'est-à-dire par une brusque métamorphose de mon projet initial, c'est-à-dire par un autre choix de moi-même et de mes fins. Cette modification est d'ailleurs toujours possible.   (*EN*, 542)

As Sartre puts it unequivocally: 'j'aurais pu faire autrement, soit; mais à quel prix?' (*EN*, 531, 542).

Freedom, then, is not envisaged as the quasi-miraculous ability to do anything one wishes: on the contrary, it is always seen as a response to concrete and constraining circumstances. 'Il ne peut y avoir de pour-soi libre que comme engagé dans un monde résistant' (*EN*, 563). 'Ainsi ne suis-je jamais libre qu'en situation' (*EN*, 591). In this sense my situation is neither subjective or objective: 'c'est une *relation d'être* entre un pour-soi et l'en-soi qu'il néantise' (*EN*, 634) – in other words, my situation is characterized both by the contingent facts of my existence and by my attitude towards them. My past, for example, cannot be changed but its meaning may be: 'en naissant je prends place, mais je suis responsable de la place que je prends' (*EN*, 576). I constitute the world and my place in it, starting from the 'given', but according to my aims, choices and projects: 'Nous choisissons le monde – non dans sa contexture en-soi mais dans sa signification – en nous choisissant' (*EN*, 541). And just as facticity is the obverse of liberty – 'la liberté est l'appréhension de ma facticité' (*EN*, 575) – so finitude is the obverse of choice:

Tout choix . . . suppose élimination et sélection; tout choix est choix de la finitude.   (*EN*, 576)

La finitude est une structure ontologique du pour-soi qui détermine la liberté . . . Etre fini, en effet, c'est se choisir.   (*EN*, 631)

In choosing, we necessarily reject the multiple alternative possibilities which are henceforth no longer open to us: 'De ce point de vue [on] naît plusieurs et se fait un seul' (*EN*, 631). At the end of my life I am entirely responsible for myself, I have made myself what I have become: 'Il n'y a eu aucune contrainte . . . je n'ai eu aucune excuse . . . je suis responsable de tout, en effet, sauf de ma responsabilité même' (*EN*, 640 – 1). In this context, the notion of man as a *passion inutile* may appear as an expression of radical pessimism: in death I have at last the 'self-coincidence' long desired, but it constitutes my final alienation to others who are the only witnesses of it.

In view of Sartre's stress throughout *L'Etre et le Néant* on what he calls the 'limites de fait' (*EN*, 606) on my liberty – the existence of the other, my facticity, body, past, etc. – it may come as a shock to learn that there has been no *contrainte*, and that there is no possibility of excuse. In a sense, what we see here is Sartre struggling with the limits of language: striving to express what language, with its neat binary oppositions, has no words for. As we shall see, his later solution will be to turn to dialectical reason in preference to the analytic: for the moment, his tactics are to use paradox and sometimes ambiguity to force the reader towards a new perception of the world. There have been no *constraints* in the sense of determining causes, but we have seen several in the sense of external limitations; man has no *excuse* in so far as there is no possibility of abdicating responsibility, but there are certainly 'excuses' in the sense of explanations and attenuations. Man is free to change, but he cannot change *à son gré*. ' "Etre libre" ne signifie pas "obtenir ce qu'on a voulu" ' (*EN*, 563).

One of the problems underlying these paradoxes and ambiguities is, of course, that of the relationship between description and prescription, or more abstractly, ontology and ethics. Ethics may depend on ontology, but ontology cannot prescribe ethics: 'L'ontologie ne saurait formuler elle-même des prescriptions morales' (*EN*, 720). In the final two pages of *L'Etre et le Néant*, 'Perspectives morales', Sartre tackles explicitly the problem of founding an existential ethics. There seem to be, implicit in his discussion, three degrees of existential lucidity or lack of it: not simply the good faith/bad faith, *angoisse/esprit de sérieux* polarities but also an intermediary category of what Pascal would call the *demi-habiles*[36] – those who see part of the truth but not enough to understand its full implications. There are, according to Sartre's phenomenological ontology, two major characteristics of the human – an inescapable freedom, and the passionate desire for identity. Most people, he suggests, spend their lives in a vain attempt to flee their freedom and to achieve an impossible self-coincidence. But recognition of the futility of such an aim can, on its own, lead only to despair: all human activities seem equally pointless in so far as they are manifestations of a passion which is doomed to failure from the outset. It is in this context that we find the much-quoted and much-misinterpreted phrase: 'Ainsi revient-il au même de s'enivrer solitairement ou de conduire les peuples' (*EN*, 721). A close reading of the text reveals that this is *not* Sartre's own position, but rather the pessimistic conclusion of those *demi-habiles* who have understood only half the picture: they have, as it were, intuited the existential abyss, but they have not abandoned the *esprit de sérieux* sufficiently to enable them to take the next step and recognize themselves as potential creators of value: 'l'être par qui les valeurs existent' (*EN*, 722). There may be no absolute values, but there are certainly human values. Moreover, Sartre goes on to imply, albeit tentatively, that whilst not prescribing ethics, ontology might at least *suggest* a possible ethical position. In a world where all meaning and value is human and freely created, might this value-making potential, this free creativity, not itself be valued? In this case liberty, and the inevitably riven nature of human consciousness, would be cherished not shunned. Sartre is proposing a paradoxical existential self-acceptance – paradoxical because, of course, it involves accepting that there is no 'self':

Est-il possible . . . que [la liberté] se prenne elle-même pour valeur en tant que source de toute valeur? . . . Une liberté qui se veut liberté, c'est en effet un être-qui-n'est-pas-ce-qu'il-est et qui-est-ce-qu'il-n'est-pas qui choisit, comme idéal d'être, l'être ce-qu'il-n'est-pas et le n'être-pas-ce-qu'il-est. Il choisit donc non de se *reprendre*, mais de se fuir, non de coïncider avec soi, mais d'être toujours à distance de soi . . . S'agit-il de la mauvaise foi ou d'une autre attitude fondamentale? Et peut-on *vivre* ce nouvel aspect de l'être?   (*EN*, 722)

Behind the spinning words two questions are clear: might liberty itself be a value? and is authenticity possible in practice? Sartre's rhetoric may be trying to persuade us that this is indeed the case, but he does not commit himself explicitly at this stage, but rather promises to answer the questions in a 'prochain ouvrage'. Despite three successive drafts of a *Morale*, no full-scale ethical study was ever completed. In the next chapter we will examine the posthumously published *Cahiers pour une morale*, notebooks written in 1946, which contain Sartre's first serious attempt at tackling the paradoxical demands of an existential ethics.

2

Notes for an ethics

'L'ontologie ne saurait formuler elle-même des prescriptions morales'

(*EN*, 720)

'La morale a lieu dans une atmosphère d'échec' (*C*, 19)

Sartre's recognition of the philosophical impasse produced by any attempt to derive prescription from description does not prevent his being tempted by such a move. What *is* may not provide any rules for what *ought* to be, but slippage between the two domains is not only common, it is inscribed in the very terminology of moral debate: both the Greek term (ethics) and the Latin term (morals) register the age-old tendency to slide from a simple statement of affairs to a prescription[1] for conduct: the *ethos* (nature, disposition) and the *mores* (customs) become enshrined not merely *de facto* but also *de jure*.

Sartre is fully conscious of the dangers of such a shift. Moreover his refusal of an essential human nature might seem to render inappropriate, or even impossible, any attempt to ground a universal ethics. Despite this – or perhaps because of it – Sartre's whole work can be read as a long meditation on moral questions and dilemmas. Of course he never published a major ethical study, though three were projected: one to follow *L'Etre et le Néant*, one subsequent to the *Critique de la raison dialectique*, and a final version at the end of his life in conjunction with his friend Benny Lévy.[2] In the film produced three years before his death, Sartre dismisses, perhaps not surprisingly, his early notes for an ethics as a totally mystified enterprise:

J'ai, au fond, écrit deux Morales: une entre 45 et 47, complètement mystifiée, c'était la 'Morale' que je croyais pouvoir donner comme suite à *l'Etre et le Néant* – j'ai des tas de notes, mais je les ai abandonnées; et puis des notes de 65 environ, sur une autre 'Morale', avec le problème du réalisme et le problème de la morale. Alors j'aurais pu faire un livre, mais je ne l'ai pas fait.[3]

None of the projects was ever completed, though the notes for the first version were published in 1983 as *Cahiers pour une morale*; and Benny Lévy has recently brought out the fruits of his side of the series of 'ethical conversations' he had with Sartre in the 1970s.[4] But it would seem to have been in the late 1940s that Sartre came closest to creating an existential ethics, not only in the *Cahiers* but also more obliquely in *L'Existentialisme est un humanisme* and *Qu'est-ce que la littérature?* *Saint Genet, comédien et martyr* (1952), may perhaps be seen as marking the end of Sartre's first attempt at founding a positive moral universe.

I have implied that an existentialist ethics could be seen as a contradiction in terms: if there are no transcendental values, no absolute criteria for judging right and wrong, if man is free and fully and solely responsible for his choices and life, what justification can there be for a formulation of moral principles, what foundation for an ethical treatise? To answer this question we should perhaps situate Sartre's enterprise in a broader historical context. There seem to be several different if interrelated ways of categorizing ethical principles, depending on whether they are envisaged as based on human or divine values; as relative to the individual situation or eternal and 'objective'; as utilitarian or absolute; as privileging good intentions or good results, ends or means. Sartre, in the company of many moralists since Aristotle, claims to espouse a situational ethics according to which there are no moral absolutes, simply circumstances, frequently conflictual, which must be evaluated individually and without preconception. But, in the company of many other ethical thinkers, culminating without doubt in Kant, Sartre seems to hanker after what the latter called the categorical imperative: the moral command which may never be justly overthrown. To put it in practical terms for a moment: for the former group, lying or murder might be morally justified in certain circumstances (e.g. a just war, or a revolution to overthrow a tyrant); for the latter group, lying and murder would always be morally wrong, even if politically expedient. Now Sartre will not commit himself so specifically, in his philosophical writing at least,[5] on particular moral questions, but he is nonetheless tempted to seek a more general formulation of an ethical imperative. As we have seen, he speculates on the possibility of taking freedom as this imperative in the last paragraph of *L'Etre et le Néant*:

Est-il possible que la liberté se prenne elle-même pour valeur en tant que source de toute valeur? . . . Une liberté qui se veut liberté, c'est en effet un être qui . . . choisit donc non de se *reprendre*, mais de se fuir, non de coïncider avec soi, mais d'être toujours à distance de soi. (*EN*, 722)

In this perspective man would both *be* free and have freedom as his goal; he would be paradoxically defined by his refusal of self-definition and identity. But the dual role of freedom (as fact and as aim) is hypothesized rather than proved or even posited. Elsewhere Sartre will be less cautious. In *Qu'est-ce que la littérature?* for example, literature is described as the free product of a free imagination working for the freedom of all men: 'l'œuvre d'une liberté totale s'adressant à des libertés plénières',[6] and it is far from clear whether this definition is, as is implied, purely descriptive, or whether it conceals − as we may suspect − a normative function. Sartre uses his identification of imagination with the freedom of consciousness to argue that since the work of art depends on the reader's (free) imagination to be constituted as an aesthetic object (as opposed to mere words on a page), it thereby works towards the freedom of that reader, and, by extension, of all potential readers. Indeed Sartre takes over the Kantian notion of the categorical imperative and transfers it from the ethical to the aesthetic domain: the work of art has no end outside itself, it is a pure call to be brought into existence through the imagination (*Sit II*, 98):

L'œuvre d'art *n'a pas de* fin, nous en sommes d'accord avec Kant. Mais c'est qu'elle *est* une fin. (*Sit II*, 98)

L'œuvre d'art est gratuite parce qu'elle est fin absolue et qu'elle se propose au spectateur comme un impératif catégorique. (*Sit II*, 261)

But in so far as art involves communication between creator and spectator it cannot be viewed as merely aesthetic: the ethical imperative is reintroduced, albeit radically transformed from its Kantian sense: 'au fond de l'impératif esthétique nous discernons l'impératif moral' (*Sit II*, 111).[7]

Qu'est-ce que la littérature? was, of course, a polemical work first published as a rallying cry in *Les Temps modernes*: it is perhaps unfair to expect it to be rigorous. Moreover, we may suspect that Sartre is using his philosophical expertise to blind the unwary reader with a dazzling display of terminology which cannot stand up to close inspection.[8] Sartre's shifts from descriptive to prescriptive, from art to ethics, from ontology to politics, are suggestive and exciting, but more like the sleight of hand of a conjuring trick than serious philosophical argument. But it is intriguing to observe the pyrotechnics of Sartre's tussle with Kant: it is as if he were concerned to pit himself against the German philosopher's moral absolutism, here by an attack on the separation of ethics and aesthetics in the *Critique of Judgement*, elsewhere by a direct engagement with Kant's ethical pronouncements.

Sartre's uneasy fascination with Kantian ethics manifests itself frequently throughout his writings.[9] The categorical imperative seems to exercise a strong appeal to Sartre's rationalism and moralism, but to be repugnant to his Romantic individualism. The search for a moral imperative which would leave human freedom untouched produces certain paradoxical effects: the imperative must be meaningful without being alienating, but in practice this seems an impossible ideal: if the imperative is specific enough to be applicable in particular cases, it may be seen as limiting freedom (e.g. 'Don't lie'); if it cannot be applied to actual dilemmas it may appear to be useless. *L'Existentialisme est un humanisme* provides a nice example of Sartre's quandary, for in it he implicitly espouses one version of the Kantian imperative, dismisses another as unhelpful, and seems to offer as his final position a remarkably Kantian formulation of the relationship between ethics and liberty. The individual is described as a legislator choosing not only for himself but also for humanity: 'Je construis l'universel en me choisissant'.[10] 'L'homme qui s'engage . . . est . . . un législateur choisissant en même temps que soi l'humanité entière' (*EH*, 28). In other words he decides what Man should be when he decides what he himself will become. Sartre is here formulating as description, the prescription of Kant's imperative of action as universal law:

Act only on that maxim through which you can at the same time will that it should become a universal law.[11]

Elsewhere in the lecture, Sartre refers to an alternative formulation of the Kantian imperative which exhorts men to treat each other always as ends, not merely as means —

Act in such a way that you always treat humanity, whether in your own person or in the person of any other, never simply as a means, but always at the same time as an end[12]

— and argues that it can provide no practical guidance in specific circumstances: treating one person as an end might involve treating others as a means. Nonetheless, this is a notion which continues to exercise a certain appeal to him, for he frequently reformulates it in existential terms (treat men as subjects not merely as objects) and proposes it in *Saint Genet* as an authentic if unrealizable alternative to alienation:

Si nous pouvions être tous, dans une simultanéité et dans une réciprocité parfaites, objets et sujets à la fois, les uns pour les autres et les uns par les autres . . . ou si nous n'étions comme dans la Cité des fins kantienne, que des sujets se reconnaissant comme sujets, les séparations tomberaient.[13]

Later in his lecture, Sartre refers to Kant as a forerunner of his notion of freedom as its own end, arguing that the notion is both logical and coherent but too abstract to found a practical ethics (*EH*, 85). In short, Sartre's position in *L'Existentialisme est un humanisme* seems Kantian in its abstract form, whilst refusing to acknowledge that a concrete ethics can be derived from general principles:

Les valeurs sont vagues . . . et toujours trop vastes pour le cas précis et concret . . .   (*EH*, 43)

Des principes trop abstraits échouent pour définir l'action . . . Il n'y a aucun moyen de juger. Le contenu est toujours concret, et par conséquent imprévisible; il y a toujours invention.   (*EH*, 85–6)

However, Sartre does claim to believe that retrospective moral judgement is possible, even if prospective moral prescription is not, and like Kant[14] he concludes that what makes an action moral is whether or not it is carried out in accordance with the categorical imperative of freedom: 'La seule chose qui compte, c'est de savoir si l'invention qui se fait, se fait au nom de la liberté' (*EH*, 86). At this point Sartre seems surprisingly prepared to judge the morality of an action solely by the intentions of its author, rather than by its results. But we may perhaps suspect that he is in fact simply invoking the rhetoric of liberty in the face of a dilemma he is unable to resolve.

Sartre's repudiation of his lecture as over-simple is well known:[15] it was given at the height of the vogue for existentialism, and in an attempt to refute accusations of immorality. It is already clear that Sartre's relationship with Kant is far more complex than a straightforward opposition between a relative, situated morality and an absolute ethics. It is as if Kant's ethics were the closest Sartre could come to a satisfactory moral position, and were indeed the source he turned to when required to make existentialism appear morally 'respectable', but were nonetheless deemed to be fundamentally flawed, so that he was unhappy to be associated with them other than for strategic purposes. If we look now at the third version of the Kantian imperative, further light is shed on the debate. This is the formulation of the autonomy of the will.

Act in such a way that your 'will can regard itself as at the same time making universal law by means of its maxim'.[16]

It is this which for Kant safeguards human freedom, for the will is its own legislator; indeed, for a perfect 'holy' will, the categorical imperative would be purely descriptive of what the will naturally seeks. This is why Kant claims that freedom is the keystone of his system (*CPR*, 3), the 'condition of the moral law' (*CPR*, 4). Indeed, for Kant 'it is the moral law which leads directly to the concept of freedom' (*CPR*, 29), for 'the moral law expresses nothing else than the autonomy of pure practical reason, i.e. freedom' (*CPR*, 34). But it is this very conception of freedom which Sartre finds ultimately unacceptable, despite its apparent similarity to his own position. In the first place he rejects Kant's identification of human freedom and free will: it is not merely the will that is free but rather the whole of consciousness (*EN*, 529). Locating freedom in the rational will alone would, for example, support the (Cartesian) opposition between free will and determined passions which Sartre sees as introducing an unacceptable dualism into consciousness, and, moreover, as entailing the logically inconceivable notion that the spontaneous will could be affected by the causality of the passions: for how could any mediation between the two be effected?[17] Secondly, Sartre rejects the very notion of the will freely legislating to itself, which he regards as no more than an internalized alienation masquerading with a dangerous power of conviction as a self-given command: 'Le devoir c'est l'Autre au cœur de la Volonté'.[18]

We have seen that Sartre recognizes Kant as coming very close in certain ways to his own conceptions, and may speculate that at times he experiences the proximity as threatening. This will become clearer if we consider briefly the third antinomy of the Transcendental Dialectic in Kant's *Critique of Pure Reason*. This is the antinomy which posits and confronts the thesis of intelligible freedom and the antithesis of natural necessity or causality. Freedom is simultaneously proven and disproven with equal rigour. Absolute spontaneity and transcendental freedom are set off against the regularity and uniformity of natural laws. In this light Sartre's separation of free *pour soi* and determined *en soi* may appear remarkably Kantian; but in fact the differences are as significant as the similarities. For Kant the intelligible, rational (noumenal) world is free, and the empirical, natural (phenomenal) world is determined. But these are not in fact two worlds, but rather two perspectives on the same world. So man as *noumenon* is free, and man as *phenomenon* is part of the causal order of nature.[19] In other words, there are two possible standpoints from which to view human reality, the one revealing absolute freedom, the other absolute necessity. Now for Sartre the free *pour soi* and the determined *en soi* are not merely two perspectives, they are two radically different kinds of reality. Moreover, whereas for Kant it is the (free) noumenon which is unknowable, for Sartre it is the (unfree) *en soi*. And whereas for Kant the relationship between the two realms is inexplicable and unknowable, for Sartre it is relatively clear: our bodies and our past are *en soi*,[20] our consciousness and our present are *pour soi*. Like Kant, then, Sartre argues that man is either entirely determined or entirely free, but unlike Kant (who presents the reader with the 'proven' but incomprehensible antinomy that man is *both*) Sartre opts for freedom on the grounds that determinism is *inadmissible* (*EN*, 518) since it denies the already established freedom of consciousness. Kant's espousal of apparent paradox seems here to outdo even Sartre's, and perhaps this may throw further light on the reasons behind Sartre's ambivalent attitude towards him.[21]

If we turn now to the *Cahiers pour une morale* we can examine Sartre's tussle with Kant and his quest for a non-alienating ethics in more practical terms. In the first five pages of his notebooks Sartre sets himself a formidable task: that of evolving an atheistic ethics which recognizes its own paradoxical nature, eschews permanent enshrinement, and is explicitly historical, situated and concrete. Kant is rejected implicitly in *all* these requirements: the Kantian ethic, for Sartre, depends on a God who guarantees the practice of morality (or duty) for its own sake; it is universal, absolute, eternal and abstract:[22]

Tant qu'on croit en Dieu, il est loisible de *faire* le Bien pour *être* moral . . . Car en *pratiquant* la charité nous ne servons que les hommes, mais en *étant* charitable nous servons Dieu . . . Mais que Dieu meure et le Saint n'est plus qu'un égoïste . . . Il faut que la moralité se dépasse vers un but qui n'est pas elle. Donner à boire à celui qui a soif non pour donner à boire ni pour être bon mais pour supprimer la soif. La moralité se supprime en se posant, elle se pose en se supprimant.   (*C*, 11)

La moralité: conversion permanente.   (*C*, 12)

Immoralité de la morale.   (*C*, 15)

La morale doit être historique.   (*C*, 14)

Problème de la collaboration ou résistance: voilà un choix moral concret. Le kantisme ne nous apprend rien à ce sujet.   (*C*, 14)

Sartre starts from a position of apparent moral pessimism: the ethical quest is essentially doomed to failure: 'La morale a lieu dans une atmosphère d'échec' (*C*, 19) – but this is not to say that it is pointless. Rather it is paradoxical in several senses. For example, Sartre speculates, how can the incompatible claims of moral spontaneity (or instinctive virtue) and moral reflection (or theorized duty) be reconciled?

Problème: je me défie de la moralité immédiate, il y entre trop de mauvaise foi, toutes les tiédeurs de l'ignorance. Mais, du moins, elle a ce caractère essentiel de la moralité: la spontanéité, la subordination à l'objet . . . La réflexion supprime la mauvaise foi et l'ignorance, mais l'objet passe au rang d'inessentiel.   (*C*, 11)

If moral instinct is likely to be lukewarm and inadequate, moral analysis tends to be more interested in itself than its object. Or, to re-express it in a Kantian register: if we depend on natural virtue, or a disposition to do good, we may never act morally; but if we act only in accordance with what we consider to be our duty, our acts may be cold and unfeeling.[23] Moreover, reflexion itself can never produce ethical certainty: 'Comme le savoir absolu est impossible, il faut concevoir la morale comme s'accomplissant par principe dans l'ignorance' (*C*, 19). It is in this sense that Sartre rejects the optimism of Kantian ethics: he argues that although Kant's 'tu dois donc tu peux' (*C*, 249) is intended to reflect freedom from determinism, since for Kant you are free only when doing your duty ('l'obligation implique que tu n'es pas dans les maillons du déterminisme' – *C*, 249), it goes beyond the truly human and appears to postulate a quasi-divine liberty: 'Il y a donc une confiance dans la liberté de l'homme qui la pose comme si c'était la liberté de Dieu. C'est-à-dire la liberté créatrice absolue' (*C*, 249).[24] What Sartre means is that if the absolute freedom which Kant postulates is considered to be operative in the empirical realm, it is clearly unrealistic. In other words, Sartre is again reflecting on the impossibility of translating with any certainty Kant's categorical imperative into concrete terms, of passing from irrefutable universal ends to practical and specific means.

In fact, however, it is this very impossibility which founds moral behaviour in Sartre's view: it is the failure of any quest for ethical certainty that makes human (as opposed to divine) morality possible: 'C'est dans et par cet échec que chacun de nous doit prendre ses responsabilités morales' (*C*, 19). What appears to be radical moral pessimism is revealed as the reverse side of a form of moral optimism. What does this paradox mean in practice? How can moral failure found success? And how are the *Cahiers* related to the ethics announced at the end of *L'Etre et le Néant* which would take liberty itself as the supreme value?

L'Etre et le Néant did not provide a very promising setting for an ethics. Man was described as a 'passion inutile', perpetually frustrated in his desire for self-identity, unable to escape the bad faith which transformed even his most 'sincere' actions into gestures, and doomed to conflict in his relations with others. Of course, Sartre did not entirely exclude the possibility of change, but the prospect was bleak, and authenticity relegated to two brief footnotes:

> S'il est indifférent d'être de bonne ou de mauvaise foi, parce que la mauvaise foi ressaisit la bonne foi et se glisse à l'origine même de son projet, cela ne veut pas dire qu'on ne puisse échapper radicalement à la mauvaise foi. Mais cela suppose une reprise de l'être pourri par lui-même que nous nommerons authenticité et dont la description n'a pas place ici.
>
> (*EN*, 111, note 1)

> Ces considérations n'excluent pas la possibilité d'une morale de la délivrance et du salut. Mais celle-ci doit être atteinte au terme d'une conversion radicale dont nous ne pouvons parler ici. (*EN*, 484, note 1)

The main thrust of Sartre's argument is clear: 'L'essence des rapports entre consciences n'est pas le Mitsein, c'est le conflit' (*EN*, 502). 'L'amour est conflit' (*EN*, 433). 'Le plaisir est la mort et l'échec du désir' (*EN*, 467). 'La haine, à son tour, est un échec (*EN*, 483). 'Aussi ne pouvons-nous jamais sortir du cercle' (*EN*, 431). However, despite the pessimism of Sartre's conclusions, in the detail of his argument we may perceive that the picture is not necessarily entirely negative. Since it is the freedom of the other that invests me with 'objectivity', that founds my 'being', I want to take hold of that freedom *without* removing its essential characteristic as freedom (*EN*, 430):

> Je ne puis, en effet, *éprouver* cette aliénation sans du même coup reconnaître l'autre comme transcendance. Et cette reconnaissance, nous l'avons vu, n'aurait aucun sens si elle n'était libre reconnaissance de la liberté d'autrui . . . Ainsi, je ne puis saisir autrui comme liberté que dans le libre projet de le saisir comme tel . . . et le libre projet de *reconnaissance* d'autrui ne se distingue pas de la libre assomption de mon être-pour-autrui . . . Il n'y a pas de cercle: mais par la libre assomption de cet être-aliéné que j'éprouve, je fais soudain que la transcendance d'autrui existe pour moi en tant que telle. (*EN*, 609–10)

It is this free recognition of the other as transcendence that will be further elaborated and foregrounded in the *Cahiers pour une morale*; and the re-evaluation should not perhaps surprise us unduly, for it is no more than a logical extension of Sartre's transformative paradoxes: is not human freedom itself the reverse side of man's inability to achieve identity, his failure to be what he is? 'C'est parce que la réalité humaine *n'est pas assez* qu'elle est libre' (*EN*, 516). The *qui perd gagne* (loser wins) reversal will become increasingly important in Sartre's ethics and ontology, but it is without doubt present from the outset.

The *Cahiers*, then, envisage failure as a possible route to conversion, to 'la réflexion non complice' (*C*, 486): 'L'échec peut conduire à la conversion' (*C*, 42). This failure may be experienced in diverse fashions. In the first place, 'la conversion . . . est virtuellement possible chez tous les opprimés' (*C*, 488). The oppressed subject may achieve conversion in an unmediated fashion because of his enforced understanding of subjective experience as an absolute. His self-awareness carries with it an awareness of alienation as dependent not only on others but also on his own complicity. But at the same time, the oppressed man, like all men, has an immediate understanding of human freedom in so far as his slightest attempt to assuage his needs and desires reveals to him his own transcendence. Secondly, 'La conversion . . . peut naître de l'échec perpétuel de toute tentative du Pour-soi pour *être*' (*C*, 488). The frustration of our desire to achieve a fixed essence brings us face to face with failure, forces us to question the meaning of our actions and the world in which we live, and leads us to potentially purifying reflexion. Thirdly, 'La conversion . . . naît de l'échec même de la réflexion complice' (*C*, 489). The failure of our attempts to rationalize our psychic and emotional lives, to identify with our 'characters', to recuperate ourselves reflexively may lead us away from the inadequacy of this attempt at self-complicity towards purifying reflexion.

Purifying reflexion may in turn lead to authenticity. And in the *Cahiers* Sartre sketches out some of the conditions and results of the authenticity of which *L'Etre et le Néant* gave only a negative image. In the first instance, the replacement of a quest for *being* with a project for *action* enables the dialectic of sincerity and bad faith to be overcome. So-called 'sincerity' is in 'bad faith' in so far as it involves an attempt to be true to myself − that is, to an essential self which is for Sartre merely an imaginary construct. Authenticity, on the other hand, involves rather a recognition of what I *want*, that is to say, of my project:

La sincérité est donc exclue parce qu'elle portait sur ce que je *suis*. L'authenticité porte sur ce que je veux . . . C'est le refus de me définir par ce que je suis (Ego) mais par ce que je veux (c'est-à-dire par mon entreprise elle-même). (*C*, 496)

In the ethical realm, sincerity is linked to the kind of moral action which has *being* moral as its end: 'Dans la réflexion complice je donne l'eau pour que le Moi soit bienfaisant' (*C*, 497). Purifying reflexion, on the other hand, like instinctive morality, takes the external purpose of the moral act — here to assuage thirst — as its end and explicitly thematizes it. It is in this sense too that man's relation to his project is 'purified' by reflexion: the project is no longer merely spontaneous, but neither is it *justified*, or made *serious* as it might be by *la réflexion complice*. It remains gratuitous, and is reflexively recognized as such: 'C'est ce double aspect simultané du projet humain, gratuit en son cœur et consacré par la reprise réflexive, qui en fait l'*existence authentique*' (*C*, 497). Moreover, authentic reflexion enables me to *embrace* my gratuitousness, finitude and contingency. As Sartre showed already in *L'Etre et le Néant*, my situation and facticity do not so much *restrict* me as permit my existence. In the *Cahiers* these apparent limitations are further recognized as *une chance* (*C*, 509):

Il faut aimer avoir pu ne pas être; être *de trop* etc. . . . . Pour l'homme authentique . . . la grandeur . . . dérive nécessairement de la misère ou contingence. C'est parce qu'il est point de vue, finitude, contingence et ignorance qu'il fait qu'il y a un monde. (*C*, 509)

Sartre is explicitly espousing Pascal's terminology of *grandeur* and *misère* in order to reverse its implications. He inverts the Christian maxim: the authentic man may lose *himself*, but he gains the whole world: 'Plus le monde est multiple pour moi qui me perds pour que cette multiplicité existe, je suis riche' (*C*, 513). And indeed, like Christian conversion, existential conversion entails gains infinitely greater than what is lost.[25] But unlike the Lapsarian Christian myth, the existential paradise is created rather than recovered: inauthenticity (*'L'Enfer'*, *C*, 577) is primary in so far as it is prereflexive; reflexion, and therefore authenticity, are essentially posterior to existence.

In this sense Sartre does not, at least theoretically, have to go back on the pessimistic ethical picture he painted in *L'Etre et le Néant*. It was, as he said, a description of human relations *before* conversion. But conversion seems to have become a distinct possibility in the *Cahiers*, and the vision of potentially fulfilling relations with others is elaborated in some detail. Sartre writes at length about love, joy, generosity and sacrifice in terms that bear little resemblance to his earlier analyses. Indeed, human conflict appears no longer as an *ontological* necessity, but rather as a historical adjunct of alienation. Of man's sado-masochistic relations with others, seen in *L'Etre et le Néant* as an inescapable vicious circle, he now writes:

Sadisme et Masochisme sont la révélation de l'Autre. Ils n'ont de sens – comme d'ailleurs la lutte des consciences – qu'avant la conversion. Si nous avons assumé le fait d'être liberté et objet pour autrui (ex: le Juif authentique)[26] il n'y a plus aucune raison ontologique de rester sur le plan de la lutte. *J'accepte* mon être-objet et je le dépasse. Mais il peut rester des raisons historiques.   (*C*, 26)

The other is described as he who recognizes me in a 'reconnaissance réciproque' (*C*, 76). He is a 'liberté imprévisible' (*C*, 128) through whom I make myself: 'On se crée soi-même en se donnant à l'autre . . . Ainsi dois-je me perdre pour me trouver' (*C*, 136). True freedom involves giving not taking, it implies recognition of the freedom of the Other: 'La vraie liberté *donne* . . . reconnaît les libertés à travers leurs dons . . . la vraie liberté se fait *occasion* pour les autres libertés' (*C*, 146 – 7). It is clear that the *qui perd gagne* pattern has penetrated and transformed Sartre's analysis of human relations;[27] for example, in one of the notes for a plan he writes:

Pour-soi et autrui: le don. Dans le sacrifice je suis et je préfère l'autre. Je préfère ce que je ne préfère pas. Mais je *suis* le don à l'autre. La joie.
                                                                        (*C*, 156)

Sartre acknowledges that *L'Etre et le Néant* was criticized for neglecting the affirmative aspect of existence, but argues that it was not so much denied as situated, that is to say shown as dependent on the nihilating power of consciousness. 'Au reste ce qui s'oppose à la négation (comme jugement) c'est en effet l'affirmation. Mais ce qui correspond à la néantisation comme son dérivé c'est la *création*' (*C*, 156). However, he recognizes that in some areas his earlier analyses were insufficient, even for the present pre-conversion social order; for example, without denying the sado-masochistic dialectic involved in love, he admits that it is only half the picture:

Pas d'amour sans cette dialectique sadico-masochiste d'asservissement des libertés que j'ai décrite. Pas d'amour sans reconnaissance plus profonde et compréhension réciproque des libertés (dimension qui manque dans l'*E.N.*).   (*C*, 430)

Authentic love is seen to involve recognizing the aims of the other
(*C*, 290), celebrating his world-view without attempting to appropriate it, and protecting him with my freedom. When I love, I
will the contingent finitude and vulnerability of the loved one, his
physical being-in-the-world (*C*, 516, 390). Sartre even describes the
classless society in terms of mutual love and recognition:

L'Ego *est pour se perdre*: c'est le Don. La réconciliation avec le destin c'est
la générosité. Dans une société sans classes ce peut être aussi l'amour c'est-
à-dire le projet en confiance que des libertés valorisées comme telles et
voulues comme telles reprennent et transforment mon œuvre et donc mon
Ego qui se perd alors dans la dimension absolue de la liberté. (*C*, 434)

These analyses and implicit definitions (for example of generosity) may help us to understand Sartre's attempt to construct what
he calls a hierarchy of values leading up to freedom. *L'Etre et le
Néant* stressed the way in which liberty creates values, so that
nothing external can justify my choice of value-scheme:

Il s'ensuit que ma liberté est l'unique fondement des valeurs et que *rien*,
absolument rien, ne me justifie d'adopter telle ou telle valeur, telle ou telle
échelle de valeurs. (*EN*, 76)

But this does not, as we have already seen, mean that all values are
equivalent. Traditional values may mask human freedom:

Méthode: les valeurs revêtent la liberté en même temps qu'elles l'aliénent.
Une classification des valeurs doit conduire à la liberté. Classer les valeurs
dans un ordre tel que la liberté y paraisse de plus en plus. Au sommet:
générosité. (*C*, 16)

The attempts at classification are in the main in the second *Cahier*.
Here is the most complete:

Hiérarchie des valeurs montrant qu'elles se rapprochent, comme une
asymptote à une droite, de la liberté. Les valeurs les plus basses écrasent
la liberté sous *l'Etre*:
    pureté, innocence, race, sincérité.
Les valeurs intermédiaires: la notion de vie comme objectivation de la
transcendance:
    noblesse, virilité, valeurs sexuelles et de nouveau *race*.
Les valeurs sociales:
l'Autre comme produit du projet et comme sollicitation extérieure du projet. Déjà intervient l'idée de création.
    Nation, société, etc., le SACRIFICE.
Les valeurs de *subjectivité*:
    passion
    plaisir et instant

critique et exigence d'évidence
responsabilité
création
générosité.

Cette hiérarchie nous amène à apercevoir comme une lumière au-delà du plafond de générosité, la liberté proprement dite.   (*C*, 486)

Despite superficial appearances, Sartre is not in fact placing different values in order of merit (for example, generosity is *better than* sincerity) so that choice may be made in case of clash! Rather he is analysing and classifying traditionally recognized values in terms of their relationship to human freedom. In effect, 'les valeurs les plus basses', such as sincerity and purity, are in fact existential *anti*-values, some of the 'values' of bad faith: part of an attempt to achieve fixed identity with, for example, a pure inner *self*. At the top come 'les valeurs de la *subjectivité*', most of which are examined elsewhere in the *Cahiers*, where their meanings diverge significantly from traditional usage. For example, we have just seen generosity equated with 'réconciliation avec le Destin' (*C*, 434), i.e. acceptance of finitude and dependence on the Other. Elsewhere passion is redefined not as sexual love, nor the useless quest for an essence, as in *L'Etre et le Néant*, but as the reflexive embracing of contingency: 'Par la réflexivité, je consens à être homme, c'est-à-dire à m'engager dans une aventure qui a les plus fortes chances de finir mal, je transforme ma contingence en *Passion*' (*C*, 498). Again, creation will be examined in some detail as the essence of all human action (*C*, 552), be it physical or artistic creation of objects, invention of values and meanings, or *dévoilement* (revelation) of the outside world and other people. In a sense these are all ways in which freedom may take itself − in me and the other − as its own end. Indeed this is one of the definitions Sartre gives of purifying reflexion − the 'constitution d'une liberté qui se prend elle-même pour fin' (*C*, 578).

We have so far left on one side one of the most important questions raised by the *Cahiers*: that of the status Sartre accords to the 'conversion' after which morality will be possible. In the first pages of the *Cahiers* Sartre writes:

On ne peut pas faire la conversion *seul*. Autrement dit la morale n'est possible que si tout le monde est moral.   (*C*, 16)

This already appears rather different from the radical conversion referred to in *L'Etre et le Néant*. Conversion is still identified with a kind of purifying reflexion born of the failure of the *pour soi* to achieve self-identity (*C*, 488). But it is also envisaged as a social, rather than a purely individual, phenomenon with clear political implications:

Sens de la conversion: rejet de l'aliénation. (*C*, 486)

Elle est virtuellement possible chez tous les opprimés. (*C*, 488)

This means that ethics can no longer be considered an individual enterprise: 'La suppression de l'aliénation doit être universelle. Impossibilité d'être moral seul' (*C*, 487). The advent of universal morality is explicitly described as an *imaginary* utopia, and appears to be a version of the Kantian City of Ends:

L'Histoire sera *toujours* aliénée . . . Si toutefois nous imaginons une utopie où chacun traite l'autre comme une fin, c'est-à-dire prend l'entreprise de l'autre comme fin, nous pouvons imaginer une Histoire où l'altérité est reprise par l'unité . . . La révolution historique dépend de la conversion morale. L'utopie c'est que la conversion de tous à la fois, toujours possible, est la combinaison la moins probable (à cause de la diversité des situations). Il convient donc d'égaliser les situations pour rendre cette combinaison moins improbable et donner à l'Histoire une chance de sortir de la pseudo-Histoire. (*C*, 54 – 5)

Historical revolution depends on moral conversion. But moral conversion will not come about in the present historical circumstances: social change must make moral change more likely, so that it may in turn bring about social revolution. Sartre here appears to be refusing to take sides in the debate, exemplified in Rimbaud and Marx, as to the priority of social or moral revolution. ('Rimbaud voulait changer la vie et Marx la société.'[28]) This refusal is encapsulated in his (dialectical) *Histoire ↔ morale* formula:

D'où problème: Histoire ↔ morale. L'Histoire implique la morale (sans conversion universelle, pas de sens à l'évolution ou aux révolutions). La morale implique l'Histoire (pas de moralité possible sans action systématique sur la situation). (*C*, 487)

Despite the connotations of his terminology Sartre may be seen to be distancing himself from both Marx and Kant, and even more forcibly from Hegel. Marx's end of pre-history,[29] Hegel's end of history, and Kant's Kingdom of Ends are all seen to be flawed by a totalizing and universalizing aim which disregards individual specificity:

La fin de l'Histoire ce serait l'avènement de la Morale. Mais cet avènement ne peut être provoqué du sein de l'Histoire . . . la moralité n'est pas d'ailleurs fusion des consciences en un seul sujet, mais acceptation de la Totalité détotalisée et décision à l'intérieur de cette inégalité reconnue de prendre pour fin concrète chaque conscience dans sa singularité concrète (et non dans son universalité kantienne). *(C, 95)*

It would seem to be this that Sartre has in mind when he equates the end of History with death: a truly unified totality would exclude of necessity the subjective and the specific:

Toute morale suppose la fin de l'Histoire (ou plutôt la fin de l'Histoire et [*sic:* est?] l'apparition du règne de la morale). Mais la fin de l'Histoire est aussi la mort. *(C, 149)*

Morality is seen to consist in *preparing* for the impossible Kingdom of Ends or the end of History: 'La *vraie* moralité (concrète): préparer le règne des fins par une politique révolutionnaire, finie et créatrice' (*C*, 487). 'Retournement: que le règne des fins est précisément dans la préparation du règne des fins' (*C*, 487).[30]

Just as *L'Etre et le Néant* makes Sartre appear a resolute pessimist in so far as it describes inauthentic existence, so the *Cahiers* may make him seem an incorrigible optimist whilst he attempts to describe a post-conversion ethics. But morality, like the Kingdom of Ends and the end of History, is perpetually deferred. Indeed there are moments when Sartre seems to suggest that the only possible morality in the present social situation is the espousal of *immorality*: '*Il ne se peut pas* que le révolutionnaire ne viole les règles de la morale' (*C*, 110). And although he describes terrorist violence as 'une voie sans issue', a 'structure de la servitude' (*C*, 420), he also envisages it as a typical example of a particularly pessimistic moral 'law':

En cas *d'impossibilité* le choix du Bien conduit à renforcer l'impossible, il faut choisir le Mal pour trouver le Bien. *(C, 420)*

'Il faut choisir le Mal pour trouver le Bien.' It is this structure of moral inversion, along with Sartre's rejection of a hypostatized ethics – 'immoralité de la morale' (*C*, 15) – which will be taken up and further developed in the paradoxes and *tourniquets* of *Saint Genet*.

Like all Sartre's biographies, including his own, *Saint Genet* is a mythical rather than empirical reconstruction of a choice of self: 'Cela s'est passé ainsi ou autrement . . . Peu importe.'[31] In Sartre's version the child Genet is traumatized at the age of ten by 'un mot vertigineux.' The word is *voleur*: Genet is caught stealing from his foster-parents and stigmatized as a thief, a label he is too young to reject and so internalizes, along with all the contradictions inherent in seeing *oneself* as evil, since 'le Mal c'est l'Autre' (*SG*, 36). Homosexual and thief, the adult Genet is rebaptized by Sartre a saint and martyr: he is moral scapegoat for *l'Homme de Bien*, the Just Man who refuses to recognize either his own potential for immorality or the impossibility of universal ethical norms, and who represses his disquiet by dint of projecting the negative aspect of his moral ambivalence onto the Other: Criminal and Pervert:

Le mal c'est l'unité de toutes ses impulsions à critiquer, à juger, à rejeter en tant qu'il refuse de les *reconnaître*, d'y voir l'exercice normal de sa liberté . . . Les gens de Bien ont forgé le mythe du Mal en privant la liberté humaine de son pouvoir positif et en le réduisant à sa seule négativité.

(*SG*, 35–7)

Saint Genet focusses on the alienating power of absolute ethical demands which do not take account of the incompatibility between their rigid imperatives and the confused and complex society in which we live:

Ainsi toute Morale qui ne se donne pas explicitement comme *impossible aujourd'hui* contribue à la mystification et à l'aliénation des hommes. Le 'problème moral' naît de ce que la Morale est *pour nous* tout en même temps inévitable et impossible.   (*SG*, 212)

'C'est la loi . . . qui crée le péché' (*SG*, 35): Sartre echoes Saint Paul. But it is the Kantian as much as the Jewish or Christian Law that he seems once again to have in mind, for he proceeds immediately to a pastiche of the antinomies: evil both is and is not, it is simultaneously absolute and relative, order and disorder etc. (*SG*, 36 – 8). Sartre takes evident delight in exploring the aporias implicit in any attempt to define evil, 'contradiction pure' (*SG*, 36), and it is at times hard in *Saint Genet* to disentangle Sartre's own position from that of Genet. He seems to revel in the disconcerting effects he can obtain by taking with apparent philosophical seriousness the code of conduct of a den of thieves and pimps. The parody he gives of Kant's categorical imperative is presented as an expression of Genet's position, but its form is of course Sartre's:

Agis de telle sorte que la société te traite toujours comme un objet, un moyen et jamais comme une fin, comme une personne. Agis comme si la maxime de chacun de tes actes devait servir de règle dans la caverne des voleurs.   (*SG*, 83)

But a text of parody and pastiche neither affirms nor negates its object. It reveals rather an uneasy fascination which leaves its own status uncertain. Sartre's evident sympathy for Genet, his contempt for the Just Man's facile ethical self-satisfaction, and his free and disturbing exploration of the paradoxes and *tourniquets* of moral inversion indicate clearly Sartre's distance from the arguably naïve optimism of the *Cahiers*. But just as the *Cahiers* are less utopian than they at first appear, so is *Saint Genet* less iconoclastic. Indeed Sartre still seems tempted by the ideal of creating an existential ethics: he refers to a new table of values (*SG*, 230), and speaks of 'la vraie morale' (*SG*, 211) which may be unrealizable in the present historical climate, but is still an ideal to be espoused, 'l'éthique de la praxis' (*SG*, 212). And in a sense one might argue that this new morality seems remarkably familiar – it is perhaps easier to innovate in the realm of ethical theory than in that of ethical practice. Love is retained as reciprocity (*SG*, 133, 584), an 'entreprise à deux' (*SG*, 366). Beauty, whilst identified with Evil (*le Néant*), is still 'le libre appel qu'une liberté créatrice adresse à toutes les autres libertés' (*SG*, 551). And the work ends with a 'Prière pour le bon usage de Jean Genet' in which the Kantian City of Ends resurfaces as an impossible but desirable dream. It might appear at this point that Sartre's 'bon usage' of Genet is disappointingly conventional: a recuperation of 'evil' within a humanistic tradition which it (ironically) protects from totalitarian complacency. But this reading is over-simple. Sartre is *not* reinscribing Genet within the limits of 'normal' ethical behaviour: he is in fact rejecting both Genet and, even more forcibly, the society that helped produce him.

Sartre uses Genet both as a test-case for his view that conventional morality is alienating, and as a vehicle for the exploration of his interest in ethical inversion and paradox. In a sense Sartre has pitted Genet against Kant in an attempt to reveal the inadequacies of both. Kant's rigour has already been shown to be alienating; Genet's fantasmatic espousal of evil is rejected in its turn as an inversion of the Christian myth of sainthood. Sartre's main criticism of Genet is that he, like the mystic, *sets out* to lose the whole world. As I have already suggested, Sartre's attitude to failure is highly complex. *Qui perd gagne* may mean that the loser wins; it does not mean that he can *espouse* failure, rather that it is both inevitable and salutary (*C*, 454). Failure undermines all my endeavours: 'Il y a échec lorsqu'il y a action . . . Il y a échec lorsque la fin n'est pas réalisée . . . Tout triomphe est échec. Je ne reconnais plus ma fin' (*C*, 450 – 3). But it is failure which saves me from the self-satisfied stagnation of success. It is for this reason that Sartre continues in his own attempts to forge an existential ethics, even in the knowledge that these are bound to fail. Since a universal morality at the end of History would entail death (because the end of concrete human singularity), then the indefinite postponement of such an advent must be a success in human terms. And, in the last analysis, the double *qui perd gagne / qui gagne perd* reversals mean that it is only *I* who can choose to define what I have achieved in terms of failure or success (*C*, 452). And my judgement is subsumed within my progressive project rather than envisaged as part of 'objective' truth. What Sartre's ethical reflections have perhaps in the end revealed is not simply the internal contradictions of an attempt to found an existential ethics, but rather the *necessity* of ethical deferral and difference in a world where an original foundation would mean the end of freedom (*C*, 455), and a pure morality is not only impossible but also unthinkable: 'Le Bien sans le Mal c'est l'Etre parménidien, c'est-à-dire la Mort' (*SG*, 211).

3

The novels

Recent Continental thinking, in particular in the wake of Jacques Derrida, has been keen to contest the traditional distinction between philosophy and literature, and to refuse the truth/fiction opposition which underlies it. Philosophy is no longer envisaged as giving a privileged access to 'objective' truth, but as presenting a partial perspective which creates rather than describes its object. And literature in consequence becomes no *more* fictive, false or imaginary than any other discourse about the world. In this perspective, Plato's poets are no longer seen as 'lying' or even fabricating, they are presenting a 'truth' as valid as that of the philosopher who would seek to banish them.

Sartre would not go so far as those who wish to break down the philosophy/literature distinction entirely, though his work can, as will become clear, be seen as a progressively more concerted attempt to undermine such binary oppositions. Existentialism and phenomenology are essentially concrete, situated philosophies, expressed through example and illustration as much as exposition and analysis. Conversely, in Sartre's view, novels are necessarily expressive of the novelist's world view or philosophy: 'une technique romanesque renvoie toujours à la métaphysique du romancier'.[1] And by metaphysics Sartre does not of course mean an obscure byzantine abstraction,[2] but rather an exploration of man's situation in the world:

Je dirai que nous sommes tous des écrivains métaphysiciens . . . car la métaphysique n'est pas une discussion stérile sur des notions abstraites qui échappent à l'expérience, c'est un effort vivant pour embrasser du dedans la condition humaine dans sa totalité.[3]

'Embrasser *du dedans* la condition humaine': Sartre will dismiss as impossible any attempt to take a totalizing overview of the human condition: moreover this unsituated and external *pensée de survol* would necessarily be limited to the uncomprehending point of view of an uninvolved observer. Only God could achieve the synthesis of immanence and transcendence vital to a thoroughgoing totalization, and He remains a logical impossibility. The perspective of the philosopher is as situated and partial as that of the novelist. But this is not to say that Sartre takes a Nietzschean view of the elusiveness of truth: on the contrary, truth is fully accessible to man precisely because truth is human. As an existentialist, Sartre, as we have seen, proclaims man as the source not only of value, but also of the world *as* a world, and all its truth. Furthermore, as a phenomenologist, Sartre takes an anti-empiricist attitude towards the individual example: rather than one piece of evidence for an inductive method, each example of a phenomenon contains its 'essence' and can be described in its typicality as revealing the structures, qualities and significance of the phenomenon. We have already examined the implications of phenomenology for Sartre's philosophical method: its relevance to his literary production is all the more evident. In his later writings he uses the syntactically ambivalent phrase *universel singulier* (singular universal and/or universal singular) to refer to the way in which an individual instance may express a totality, the part contain implicitly the whole. This dialectical conception of reality has implications for literature in at least three different ways: in the first place, man himself is an *universel singulier* so that any man is literally, not merely metaphorically, representative of all men; secondly, in so far as he is a totality, each element of a man's behaviour or life-style is revealing of him as a whole: 'l'homme est une totalité . . . en conséquence, il s'exprime tout entier dans la plus insignifiante et la plus superficielle de ses conduites' (*EN*, 656). And thirdly, the work of art itself is similarly synecdochic: 'dans l'œuvre d'art, chaque structure partielle indique, de diverses manières, diverses autres structures partielles et la structure totale' (*EN*, 581). Sartre's dialectical understanding of man, the world and the work of art has, necessarily, important consequences for his conception of the way literature should be composed, the most evident of which is the inappropriateness of an omniscient narrator. But more important in the present context, it further undermines the philosophy/literature opposition by suggesting not only that an abstract external totalization is impossible, but that it is only through the example, or the part, that the whole, or universal, can be conceived or expressed at all. In this sense literature is already carrying out the task of philosophy when it concentrates on the individual and the fragmentary. This is perhaps one of the things Sartre had in mind when he described his three-thousand-page historical, psychoanalytic, sociological biography of Flaubert as a *roman vrai*. But we shall return to this point later.[4]

For Sartre, then, literature is not merely fictive, subjective and anecdotal: it is a form of *universel singulier* which reveals the world to its readers:

Ecrire, c'est donc dévoiler le monde . . . C'est bien le but final de l'art: récupérer ce monde-ci en le donnant à voir tel qu'il est, mais comme s'il avait sa source dans la liberté humaine.   (*Sit II*, 109, 106)

Sartre's definition of the aim of art is in one perspective problematic: we have already seen that *Being* 'as it is' is fundamentally unknowable, and that the *world*, on the other hand, *always* has its source in the freedom of consciousness. Taken literally, then, the definition is either impossible or tautological. Sartre is evidently anxious to close the gap between the work of art and the world, and is apparently prepared to imply (at least for the purposes of polemics) that art can communicate a realm arguably inaccessible even to philosophy.[5] But these theoretical objections need not detain us now. Sartre's intention is clear: art can, and should, depict the world as we know it, that is to say, in all its flux and contingency:

Cette pâte molle parcourue d'ondulations qui ont leur cause et leur fin hors d'elles-mêmes, ce monde sans avenir, où tout est rencontre, où le présent vient comme un voleur, où l'événement résiste par nature à la pensée et au langage, où les individus sont des accidents, des cailloux dans la pâte, pour lesquels l'esprit forge, après coup, des rubriques générales.   (*Sit I*, 77)

This is, of course, the very world Roquentin discovers − to his dismay − in *La Nausée*. It is moreover, in Sartre's view, the world of the novel, not of the short story:

Le roman se déroule au présent, comme la vie . . . Dans le roman les jeux ne sont pas faits, car l'homme romanesque est libre. Ils se font sous nos yeux; notre impatience, notre ignorance, notre attente sont les mêmes que celles du héros. Le *récit*, au contraire . . . se fait au passé. Mais le récit explique: l'orde chronologique − ordre pour la vie − dissimule à peine l'ordre des causes − ordre pour l'entendement; l'événement ne nous touche pas, il est à mi-chemin entre le fait et la loi.   (*Sit I*, 15–16)

The distinction is very similar to that between 'story' and 'plot' elaborated by E. M. Forster a decade earlier.[6] And Sartre seems to have constructed his own short stories in *Le Mur* in accordance with this conception of 'plot': they are focussed and centred, recounted in some cases retrospectively ('Le Mur' and 'Erostrate') and always with a certain sense of necessity: Lucien is, from the title of 'L'Enfance d'un chef' alone, destined to become a leader; even in 'Intimité' the astute reader may suspect from the outset that, with her distaste for sex, Lulu does not really intend to leave her impotent husband for her more demanding lover.

But these remarks consider the fictional work very much from the reader's point of view — in what sense can it in fact be claimed that 'l'homme romanesque est libre' and that 'les jeux ne sont pas faits' in a novel any more than in a *récit*? Surely characters and events are no more than puppets and plot of their creator? Roquentin himself is acutely aware of the insidious teleology necessarily entailed in telling a story:

Pour que l'événement le plus banal devienne une aventure, il faut et il suffit qu'on se mette à le *raconter* . . . Il faut choisir: vivre ou raconter . . . Quand on vit, il n'arrive rien. Les décors changent, les gens entrent et sortent, voilà tout. Il n'y a jamais de commencements . . . Il n'y a pas de fin non plus . . . Lundi, mardi, mercredi. Avril, mai, juin. 1924, 1925, 1926.

Ça, c'est vivre. Mais quand on raconte la vie, tout change . . . les événements se produisent dans un sens et nous les racontons en sens in-verse. On a l'air de débuter par le commencement: 'C'était par un beau soir d'automne de 1922. J'étais clerc de notaire à Marommes.' Et en réalité c'est par la fin qu'on a commencé. Elle est là, invisible et présente, c'est elle qui donne à ces quelques mots la pompe et la valeur d'un commence-ment . . . Pour nous, le type est déjà le héros de l'histoire . . . Et nous avons le sentiment que le héros a vécu tous les détails de cette nuit comme des annonciations, comme des promesses . . . Nous oublions que l'avenir n'était pas encore là; le type se promenait dans une nuit sans présages, qui lui offrait pêle-mêle ses richesses monotones et il ne choisissait pas.[7]

We may be sure that Roquentin has no intuitions about the nature of story-telling which are denied to Sartre. Of course 'les jeux sont faits', but the reader must get an impression of open-endedness or she may lose interest and not be prepared to lend her time, emo-tions and impatience to the novel.[8] Sartre criticizes Mauriac because he is too *evidently* in control of what happens: art depends on the illusion of freedom, without it 'le roman s'évanouit sous vos yeux' (*Sit I*, 44). This means of course that the novelist must 'cheat' if he wants to exclude Providence from his novels, as he has exclud-ed it from his world;[9] he must hide his mastery, his control and his transcendent choice from the reader: 'Il faudra alors masquer ce choix par des procédés purement esthétiques, construire des trompe-l'œil et, comme toujours en art, mentir pour être vrai' (*Sit II*, 327 – 8).

On the whole it would seem that Sartre's novels conform fairly well to his own prescription. *La Nausée* is told from day-to-day in the form of a journal, it is the account of an attempt at comprehension of self and world through writing, and if some passages (for example the meeting with Annie, lunch with the Autodidact, the visit to Bouville museum) read suspiciously like anecdotes or *récits*, it is precisely because this is what they are: moments of life transformed by their telling into *stories*; but it is Roquentin himself who is the story-teller, and it forms part of his own dilemma: 'Il faut choisir: vivre ou raconter' (*OR*, 48). At the end we see Roquentin apparently succumbing to the temptation to *raconter* rather than *vivre*. *Les Chemins de la liberté* attempt to counteract even this internally justifiable teleology: the opening of *L'Age de Raison* provides an immediate example:

Au milieu de la rue Vercingétorix, un grand type saisit Mathieu par le bras; un agent faisait les cent pas sur l'autre trottoir.
"Donne-moi quelque chose, patron; j'ai faim."
Il avait les yeux rapprochés et des lèvres épaisses, il sentait l'alcool.

(*OR*, 393)

If the reader, like Roquentin, believes she is reading the opening lines of an 'adventure' she is to be disappointed: nothing happens – Mathieu gives the drunk *cent sous*, is given in return an old stamp from Madrid, and goes on his way, like the reader perhaps, with 'un vague regret', and a certain nostalgia for what might have been. 'Un train siffla et Mathieu pensa: "Je suis vieux" ' (*OR*, 395). This is not, of course, to suggest that the episode has no function in the structure of the novel – the drunkard is significant in reminding Mathieu of his lack of commitment in the Spanish Civil War and of the fact he is getting older – but its purpose is initially masked from the reader, and it is certainly far from being the beginning of an 'adventure'. Throughout *Les Chemins de la liberté* expectations of 'adventure' are systematically frustrated: when Mathieu kisses his student Ivich in a taxi he merely annoys her; having vied with her by sticking a knife into his own palm in a night club, he meekly goes off to the nearest washroom for his hand to be bandaged; when he finds himself in Lola's bedroom, in a position to steal the money he desperately needs for Marcelle's abortion, he lacks the courage to take it – and when he forces himself to return for it, it is too late: Lola has woken up. Similarly, Daniel does not castrate himself nor even drown his cats, and when he decides to marry Marcelle it is as unprepared and startling to him as it is to the reader. As in her own life, the reader cannot predict what will happen to surprise her: the unpredictable is precisely that. Similarly in *Le Sursis*, the triviality, disappointment, foolishness and occasional delight of everyday life continue under the threat of war: the characters may enjoy a brief illusion of destiny, but with Chamberlain's capitulation over Czechoslovakia even that is lost:

Leur destin s'était évanoui, le temps s'était remis à couler au petit bonheur, sans but; le train roulait sans but, par habitude . . . "On dirait un lendemain de fête", pensa Mathieu, le cœur serré. (OR, 1113)

And the impression of living *au jour le jour* with the characters reaches its peak in the second part of *la Mort dans l'âme* and in *Drôle d'amitié* which are told throughout in the present tense.

Sartre's conception of the novel is centred very much around the role of the reader. It is the reader who brings the work into existence, who (re)creates it, who is an essential collaborator in its production. The work is described as a call from writer to reader to participate in the paradox of what Sartre calls 'un rêve libre' (*Sit II*, 100), which appears to be his version of the 'willing suspension of disbelief'. For the reader, causality and finality are inverted: what is experienced in *reading* as causal has been *written* with a certain finality: the reader interprets Daniel's refusal to lend Mathieu money as a gratuitous whim, or as evidence of callousness; for the writer, Daniel's refusal is necessary if Mathieu's quest is not to come to a premature conclusion.[10] Yet the reader trusts implicitly that Daniel's decision is part of some overall authorial design: part of her aesthetic pleasure lies in the tension between the illusion of arbitrariness and the hidden knowledge of purpose, or what Sartre calls the 'sentiment de sécurité' (*Sit II*, 108). It is also in the act of reading that the potential commitment of the novel is realized. In so far as works of art necessarily convey a certain world-view, the reader is drawn into a participation in the creation, not merely the observation, of that world as she reads:

Ecrire, c'est donc à la fois dévoiler le monde et le proposer comme une tâche à la générosité du lecteur . . . L'erreur du réalisme a été de croire que le réel se révélait à la contemplation et que, en conséquence, on en pouvait faire une peinture impartiale. Comment serait-ce possible, puisque la perception même est partiale, puisque, à elle seule, la nomination est déjà modification de l'objet? . . . Tout l'art de l'auteur est pour m'obliger à *créer* ce qu'il *dévoile*, donc à me compromettre. (*Sit II*, 109–10)

The reader of *Le Sursis* may share the fear and anticipation of the characters, may have the illusion of inhabiting 'cette pâte molle parcourue d'ondulations . . . ce monde sans avenir, où tout est rencontre' (*Sit I*, 77); but this very contingency is leading her orably to share Mathieu's (and Sartre's) disgust at the Munich tulation, for the political message is as clear as it is inexplicit. The nique of apparently arbitrary simultaneity on which the work is based permits Sartre to show the rape of Ivich coinciding with the 'rape' of Czechoslovakia:

Et si l'on me donne ce monde avec ses injustices, ce n'est pas pour que je contemple celles-ci avec froideur, mais pour que je les anime de mon indignation . . . et l'indignation généreuse est serment de changer . . . au fond de l'impératif esthétique, nous discernons l'impératif moral.

(*Sit II*, 111)

We have already an idea of the *métaphysique* Sartre wishes to convey; we must look now in more detail at precisely how his fictive world manages to communicate it, concentrating in particular on the interplay of liberty and situation, and the interaction between freedom, facticity and alienation.

For Sartre there is of course no fixed character, no essential self, no immutable ego: the 'I' is merely a synthesis created and held in being through the imagination, consciousness is impersonal or at most pre-personal. Normally we tend, nonetheless, to *experience* ourselves as necessary and determining, for the total freedom involved in a recognition of our radical spontaneity causes us anguish. And this recognition is precisely a constituent factor in Roquentin's nausea: along with the breakdown of the apparently fixed 'laws' of the universe and social values comes an increasing insecurity with respect to his own identity. In the first place he tries to see himself as others see him, attempting an external viewpoint contemplating himself in a mirror. But all he can see is 'une chair fade qui s'épanouit et palpite avec abandon' (*OR*, 23). The humanizing structures of social life have deserted even his own self-image:

Les gens qui vivent en société ont appris à se voir, dans les glaces, tels qu'ils apparaissent à leurs amis. Je n'ai pas d'amis: est-ce pour cela que ma chair est si nue? On dirait – oui, on dirait la nature sans les hommes. (*OR*, 24)[11]

At a later stage he feels alienated not only from his body but also from his thoughts and feelings: the contingency of his own existence fills him with repugnance: 'J'existe parce que je pense . . . si j'existe, *c'est parce que* j'ai horreur d'exister. C'est moi, *c'est moi* qui me tire du néant auquel j'aspire' (*OR*, 119). And finally his sense of self deserts him entirely, leaving only an embodied but impersonal consciousness:

A présent, quand je dis "je", ça me semble creux . . . Et soudain le Je pâlit, pâlit et c'en est fait, il s'éteint.

Lucide, immobile, déserte, la conscience est posée entre des murs; elle se perpétue. Personne ne l'habite plus . . . Mais elle ne s'oublie *jamais*; elle est conscience d'être une conscience qui s'oublie . . . il y a conscience de ce corps qui marche lentement dans une rue sombre . . Il y a conscience de tout ça et conscience, hélas! de la conscience. Mais personne n'est là pour souffrir et se tordre les mains et se prendre soi-même en pitié.

(*OR*, 200–2)

Roquentin, however, is an atypical example. Sartre's characters are not on the whole so analytic about their own ego, or rather its lack, though Mathieu has a similar experience of explicit loss of self after kissing Ivich (*OR*, 683–4). And Roquentin's experience of unselfhood does not seem to bring with it an awareness of freedom, but simply of unease and distress. On the whole the novels present freedom *from* character more indirectly and negatively. There is little or no mention of heredity or family background; the characters tend to be isolated, shown at leisure rather than at work, unstable and unpredictable. And when background is stressed, as in the *récit* 'L'Enfance d'un chef', it is motivated both by the importance attributed to it by Lucien, and by Sartre's desire to make a political or ideological point: the Barresian emphasis on native roots is part of the reactionary world-view of a nascent fascist. Moreover, if the characters are portrayed at moments of crisis – Roquentin disillusioned with his study of Rollebon, Mathieu faced with an undesired prospect of paternity – they are not shown making free, rational decisions with respect to these crises. Roquentin relates how he suddenly realized he was bored with his life in Indo-China: 'La statue me parut désagréable et stupide et je sentis que je m'ennuyais profondément. Je ne parvenais pas à comprendre pourquoi j'étais en Indochine' (*OR*, 10). His loss of interest in Rollebon seems equally irrational: 'Je n'écris plus mon livre sur Rollebon; c'est fini, je ne *peux* plus l'écrire . . . La grande affaire Rollebon a pris fin, comme une grande passion' (*OR*, 113, 116). Sartre's characters do not seem in control of their lives: they are as unpredictable to themselves as they are to us. Mathieu 'decides' to tell Marcelle he loves her and will marry her: he opens his mouth only to admit (and discover) that he does not:

Il s'était levé; il allait lui dire: "Je t'aime." Il chancela un peu et dit d'une voix claire: "Eh bien, c'est vrai . . . je n'ai plus d'amour pour toi."
La phrase était prononcée depuis longtemps qu'il l'écoutait encore, avec stupeur. (*OR*, 704)

Daniel 'decides' to drown his beloved cats in an act of self-punishment, but takes them home again, apparently against his will:

Daniel était dédoublé . . . il pensa à Mathieu avec une sorte d'orgueil: "C'est *moi* qui suis libre", se dit-il. Mais c'était un orgueil impersonnel, car Daniel n'était plus personne . . . Tout d'un coup il sentit qu'il ne faisait plus qu'un. Un seul. Un lâche. Un type qui aimait ses chats et ne voulait pas les foutre à l'eau. Il prit son canif, se baissa et coupa la ficelle. En silence: même au-dedans de lui-même il faisait silence, il avait trop honte pour parler devant soi. Il reprit le panier et remonta l'escalier.

(*OR*, 489–90)

Sartre's characters are as complex as his theory of freedom: 'will', 'decision', 'deliberate' choice are mistrusted as simplifications which tend to involve the masking of genuine project and choice in the bad faith of rationalization. Real choice and apparent decision-making are not identical and may at times be at odds. This is far closer to the reality of experience than the naïve interpretation of freedom as free will which certain of Sartre's commentators tend to foist onto him:[12]

Voulez-vous que vos personnages vivent? Faites qu'ils soient libres. Il ne s'agit pas de définir, encore moins d'expliquer . . . mais seulement de *présenter* des passions et des actes imprévisibles . . . [les personnages romanesques] . . . ont des caractères, mais c'est pour y échapper; libres par-delà leur nature, s'ils cèdent à leur nature c'est encore par liberté. Ils peuvent se laisser happer par les engrenages psychiques, mais ils ne seront jamais des mécaniques. (*Sit I*, 34)

Plus de caractères: les héros sont des libertés prises au piège, comme nous tous. (*Sit II*, 313)

'Des libertés prises au piège.' Sartre's characters are never free in a void: they are situated, limited by their facticity, and alienated by other people. Some, like Brunet, Daniel and the Autodidact, have chosen the 'useless passion' of attempting self-coincidence: they cannot escape the freedom which persistently undermines their projects and allows, for example, Brunet to desert the Communist Party and the prisoner-of-war camp with Vicarios in *Drôle d'amitié*, or the Autodidact to regain his dignity in refusing Roquentin's pity after his humiliation in the library. Conversely, those like Mathieu and Roquentin, who have chosen the equally sterile passion of protecting their liberty at all costs, find it similarly undermined by the brute facts of material life – Marcelle becomes pregnant; and by the uncontrollable decisions of other people – she wants to keep the baby; Annie has lost faith in 'moments parfaits'. As Sartre wrote in his introduction to *Les Chemins de la liberté*:

Cet homme qui est ainsi condamné à la liberté, il doit pourtant se libérer . . . Ce cheminement de l'homme libre vers sa liberté, c'est le paradoxe de la liberté et c'est aussi le thème de mon livre . . . une description des apories de la liberté . . . Mathieu incarne cette liberté totale que Hegel appelle liberté terroriste et qui est véritablement la contre-liberté . . . Mathieu, c'est la liberté d'indifférence, liberté abstraite, liberté pour rien . . . Brunet incarne l'esprit de sérieux, qui croit aux valeurs transcendantes, écrites au ciel, intelligibles . . . Brunet est un militant qui manque sa liberté.   (*OR*, 1915)

Similarly, the complex interrelationship of freedom and non-freedom is shown in the domain of emotional life, or in the sheer physical experience of bodily functions. Sartre may consider that we choose our emotions, he also knows that we suffer them, and, moreover, that they tend towards their own perpetuation through their bodily effects and manifestations. The relationship between body and consciousness is, for Sartre, both alienating and alienated. 'Une nausée discrète et insurmontable révèle perpétuellement mon corps à ma conscience' (*EN*, 404). It is particularly the experience of sexual desire which threatens the freedom of consciousness:

Le désir me compromet . . . dans le désir sexuel la conscience est comme empâtée . . . le plus faible désir est déjà submergeant . . . La conscience alourdie et pâmée glisse vers un alanguissement comparable au sommeil.
(*EN*, 404)

Sometimes Sartre's characters welcome desire precisely because it temporarily obliterates the painful lucidity of everyday existence: 'Boris sentit qu'il désirait Lola et il en fut satisfait: le désir pompait les idées noires, comme d'ailleurs les autres idées' (*OR*, 426–7). More often, however, they see the loss of control as a threat: a little later Boris is already regretting his desire:

Elle gémit bientôt et Boris se dit: "Ça y est, je vais tomber dans les pommes!" Une onde pâteuse montait de ses reins à sa nuque. "Je ne veux pas," se dit Boris en serrant les dents. Mais il lui sembla soudain qu'on le soulevait par le cou, comme un lapin, il se laissa aller sur le corps de Lola et ne fut plus qu'un tournoiement rouge et voluptueux.   (*OR*, 429)

Less 'elevated' bodily activities such as eating or excreting are further cause for human distress: the invalid Charles is so appalled by his need to excrete in the mixed company of a hospital train carriage, that he succeeds, at least for a while, in dominating his desire: 'Il se verrouilla, ses entrailles se fermèrent comme un poing, il ne sentit plus son corps . . . Toutes les envies, tous les désirs s'étaient effacés, il se sentait propre et sec' (*OR*, 958–9). Brunet is ashamed of his hunger and thirst (*OR*, 1355), frightened even of his desire to escape the prisoner-of-war camp and return to normal life: 'Il a peur de cet énorme désir qui le submerge tout à coup, désir de vivre, désir d'aimer, désir de caresser des seins blancs' (*OR*, 1389). In so far as the body is an active agent, lived as a totality, as the normal facticity attendant on being-in-the-world, it passes unnoticed. It is only when it has needs at odds with an individual's project, when it is momentarily experienced as fragmented or isolated, focussed on its own right as flesh, that it becomes alienating or obscure, revealing 'l'inertie de sa chair' (*EN*, 471). When Marcelle tells Mathieu she is pregnant, he becomes aware and ashamed of his penis, 'cette fleur coupable' (*OR*, 406), and imagines Marcelle thinking of the sexual act in terms of infantile incontinence: ' "Le salaud, il m'a fait ça, il s'est oublié en moi comme un gosse qui fait dans ses draps" ' (*OR*, 409).[13] Even, or perhaps especially, at the most extreme moments of emotional trauma the body does not behave as conventionally expected: before he fires on the Germans from the bell-tower Mathieu's fear expresses itself as *douceur*, as a 'rêve pâteux', as an illusion of universal love (*OR*, 1335). When actually shooting he experiences desire (*OR*, 1341), suffocation, the sensation of burning (*OR*, 1340) and loses all sense of time. After kissing Ivich and being rejected by her, Mathieu feels he wants to cry, but instead he laughs, and undergoes a series of apparently meaningless bodily sensations: 'Le corps se remit en marche en traînant des pieds, lourd et chaud avec des frissons, des brûlures de colère, à la gorge, à l'estomac' (*OR*, 684). The alienation involved in the side of emotion which is its facticity is expressed most forcibly in these unexpected, distorting and sometimes antithetical expressions which dehumanize sentiment and stress its incoherence. Passions and virtues alike undergo this radically anti-humanist transformation. Mathieu's love for Ivich is '*âcre*' (*OR*, 708); he feels passionate about the smell of her vomit (*OR*, 672). Daniel's *bonté* towards Marcelle expresses itself as irritation, and a need to violate and humiliate her (*OR*, 570). Since, for Sartre, love, hatred, jealousy etc. are synthetic and transcendent, composite not unified, they are necessarily made up of a series of disconnected feelings, sufficiently constant to be identifiable, but nonetheless unstable.[14] In this sense Sartre has radicalized Proust's *intermittences du cœur*. ('intermittences of the heart').

The dialectic of freedom and facticity is fundamentally incompatible with the *métaphysique* implied by the use of an omniscient narrator whose privileged perspective would be at odds both with our experience of the world and other people, and also with the spontaneity and unpredictability of man as Sartre sees him:

Puisque nous étions *situés*, les seuls romans que nous puissions songer à écrire étaient des romans de *situation*, sans narrateurs internes ni témoins tout-connaissants; bref il nous fallait, si nous voulions rendre compte de notre époque, faire passer la technique romanesque de la mécanique newtonienne à la relativité généralisée, peupler nos livres de consciences à demi lucides et à demi obscures, dont nous considérerions peut-être les unes ou les autres avec plus de sympathie, mais dont aucune n'aurait sur l'événement ni sur soi de point de vue privilégié, présenter des créatures dont la réalité serait le tissu embrouillé et contradictoire des appréciations que chacune porterait sur toutes – y compris sur elle-même – et toutes sur chacune et qui ne pourraient jamais décider du dedans si les changements de leurs destins venaient de leurs efforts, de leurs fautes ou du cours de l'univers. (*Sit II*, 252–3)

This means in practice that the novels will be narrated in the first person, a paradoxical mode in which even the most assured and self-confidently 'objective' descriptions and judgements are radically vitiated by their necessarily 'subjective' horizon: however scrupulous a journal Roquentin may keep, we cannot ultimately trust in his diagnosis of his own disequilibrium. Or they will be narrated, like *Les Chemins de la liberté*, through a succession of individual perspectives: be it section by section in *L'Age de raison* or phrase by phrase in *Le Sursis*; recounted formally in the third person, the viewpoint is nonetheless as strictly subjective as the 'je' form – the reader sees events first through Mathieu's eyes, and later through those of Boris, Marcelle and Daniel. This means that both character and situation are necessarily revealed in a gradual, fragmentary fashion; but since for Sartre each person is a totality, all of his actions, tastes etc. are revealing of the whole: 'il n'est pas un goût, un tic, un acte humain qui ne soit révélateur' (*EN*, 656). In this sense, the interpretation of characters in fiction is a task and activity much as it is in everyday life, and since the author refrains from commenting, the reader may neglect evidence, misinterpret or simply fail to understand. As in existential psychoanalysis proper, 'le travail essentiel est une herméneutique, c'est-à-dire un déchiffrage, une fixation et une conceptualisation' (*EN*, 656). Roquentin's taste for picking up dirty papers may invite a Freudian analysis;[15] it remains on the whole opaque to the reader who may feel it is charged with a significance she fails to appreciate, but who probably follows Roquentin's example in noting it with a certain mystification. Similarly the reader's comprehension of Ivich is no clearer than Mathieu's own, and both tend to share the same mixture of attraction and irritation in the face of someone apparently so enigmatic and yet so superficial. Conversely, we share in Roquentin's increasing understanding of his nausea, and in Mathieu's awareness of certain moments in his past as privileged in the formation of his project of total freedom. Nonetheless, when the seven-year-old Mathieu smashes an ancient Chinese vase of his uncle's, the reader may recognize not only an iconoclastic and gratuitous act, but also hints of the *liberté terroriste*, the futile freedom for nothing, which is to come between Mathieu and any genuine maturity.

The reader's perspective on the world depicted in the novels is then as subjective and fragmented as that of the characters. The way the world appears depends on the characters' projects. Usually, of course, for Sartre, the contingency of the *en soi* is masked by our intentions towards it: the totalizing power of the imagination negates the chaos of matter, patterns and orders existence, and makes from brute being a human world. This totalization depends on a dialectic between perception and imagination and usually passes unnoticed. At certain moments, however, particularly when everyday actions are temporarily suspended, one pole of the dialectic may acquire particular prominence. When this is the imagination, the world appears as a spectacle for contemplation, in a form of the aesthetic attitude, and events may assume an impression of finality and be interpreted in terms of lived adventures. When it is perception which dominates, it produces an awareness of contingency and of 'la pâte même des choses' which makes characters feel 'totalement englué[s] dans l'existant' (*I*, 237). In *La Nausée* Roquentin experiences both modes of consciousness: it is his *perception* of contingency which induces nausea, and his *imaginative* delight in the jazz-tune which transforms life into an art-form, charged with finality and purpose. As he listens to 'Some of these days' his nausea leaves him:

Quand la voix s'est élevée, dans le silence, j'ai senti mon corps se durcir et la Nausée s'est évanouie . . . Moi, j'ai eu de vraies aventures. Je n'en retrouve aucun détail, mais j'aperçois l'enchaînement rigoureux des circonstances . . . J'ai eu des femmes, je me suis battu avec des types; et jamais je ne pouvais revenir en arrière, pas plus qu'un disque ne peut tourner à rebours. Et tout cela me menait *où*? A cette minute-ci, à cette banquette, dans cette bulle de clarté toute bourdonnante de musique.

(*OR*, 29–30)

Roquentin realizes that the feeling of adventure is purely illusory – 'il faut choisir: vivre ou raconter' – but he does not recognize that his nausea is equally misleading. The world is *not* an 'ignoble marmelade' (*OR*, 159), full of 'choses . . . grotesques, têtues, géantes' (*OR*, 148), it is human and significant, and 'l'être tel qu'il est' (*EN*, 270) is in any case unknowable and inaccessible. As Sartre pointed out in his essay on Camus, 'la philosophie contemporaine a établi que les significations étaient elles aussi des données immédiates . . . Tel est le monde humain à l'endroit' (*Sit I*, 108, 118). But having recognized the human origin of meaning and value, Roquentin is no longer able to accept it: in a sense he is nostalgic for the 'être nécessaire et cause de soi' (*OR*, 155) who masks contingency from the believer. Aware of imagination as escape, he does not recognize its importance as freedom.

In *Les Chemins de la liberté* it is less often contingency which impinges on the characters' consciousnesses, though the pregnant Marcelle is aware of it from time to time (*OR*, 464–6), as is Daniel in his moments of self-disgust (*OR*, 484), or more unusually Brunet when war breaks out:

Tout s'était mis à tomber, il avait vu les maisons comme elles étaient pour de vrai: des chutes arrêtées . . . quelques kilos de plus et la chute recommencerait; les colonnes s'arrondiraient en flageolant et elles se feraient de sales fractures avec des esquilles.   (*OR*, 749)

More often, awareness of freedom gives a sense of power or anguish as Mathieu, for example, meditates:

"Quoi qu'il arrive, c'est *par moi* que tout doit arriver" . . . il était libre, libre pour tout . . . il n'y aurait pour lui de Bien ni de Mal que s'il les inventait. Autour de lui les choses s'étaient groupées en rond, elles attendaient sans faire un signe, sans livrer la moindre indication.   (*OR*, 664–5)

In either case, when the dialectic of imagination and perception is suspended, the workaday functional nature of the world disappears to reveal either chaos or aesthetic order: objects lose their everyday masks of familiarity.

But Sartre's phenomenology of perception is not restricted to extreme cases, nor to purely subjective significance. On the one hand, 'le monde nous renvoie exactement, par son articulation même, l'image de ce que nous sommes . . . Nous choisissons le monde – non dans sa contexture en-soi, mais dans sa signification – en nous choisissant' (*EN*, 541). But on the other, the world necessarily appears to us already clothed in the meaning and value ascribed to it by others, and we certainly *experience* its qualities as objective: 'le jaune du citron n'est pas un mode subjectif d'appréhension du citron: il *est* le citron' (*EN*, 235, 694). 'Tout se passe comme si nous surgissions dans un univers où les sentiments et les actes sont tout chargés de matérialité, ont une étoffe substantielle, sont *vraiment* mous, plats, visqueux, bas, élevés etc' (*EN*, 696). So all that is un-covered by an analysis of these immediate, concrete categories is 'des projets très généraux de la réalité humaine' (*EN*, 706). But what is more interesting in an existential psychoanalytic perspective is individual *reactions* to what appear as universal qualities. Sartre may analyse the viscous and sugary as 'l'agonie de l'eau' (*EN*, 699), as a potential snare to consciousness, 'la mort sucrée du pour-soi' (*EN*, 701): Madame Darbédat revels in the 'chair vitreuse' of her Turkish delight, precisely *because* its sweet cloying obsequiousness symbolizes her ideal version of a docile world.[16] There are no irreducible preferences or inclinations, they all manifest certain projects towards the world: because of his desire for Marcelle, for example, Mathieu is attracted to her 'chair molle et beurreuse' (*OR*, 400), and the 'boursouflures fiévreuses' (*OR*, 408) of her breasts; Roquentin, on the other hand, is revolted by all that is soft, bloated or abundant (*OR*, 151). What is exciting for Mathieu is obscene for Roquentin (*OR*, 107), for the 'obscene' is precisely the revelation of the facticity of contingent flesh without the arousal of desire (*EN*, 472). Roquentin's project leaves little room for passive desire: he makes love with the *patronne* absent-mindedly and out of *hygiène*, his sexual fantasies leave him rigorously, and sadistic-ally, in total control (*OR*, 120). Like Boris, he is repelled by the contingency of sensuality which is, for others, precisely its appeal.

The reader, then, shares the characters' vision of the world, be it minute and closely focussed as when Roquentin watches a fly in the sunlight on the paper cloth during his lunch with the Autodidact (*OR*, 123); puzzled and naïve as when Gros Louis arrives in Marseilles (*OR*, 764, 866); 'international' through the omnipresent threat of war as Mathieu sees it whilst waiting at the station for Gomez: 'Sur la gauche, tout au bout, ce petit lac miroi-tant, au point où les rails se rejoignaient, c'était Toulon, Marseille, Port-Bou, l'Espagne' (*OR*, 964). She also shares their experience of time. It is clear from the essays of *Situations I* that Sartre considers the representation of time as a matter of primary importance for a novelist. Like value and quality, time is a human phenomenon: 'le temps universel vient au monde par le Pour-soi' (*EN*, 255). It is lived in the present, 'le Présent est pour-soi' (*EN*, 165), but this does not imply that the novel must necessarily be written in the pre-sent tense. As in the case of the 'subjective' use of the third-person form, the novel may use the past tense to convey the present: 'Le roman se déroule au présent, comme la vie. Le parfait n'est romanesque qu'en apparence; il faut le tenir pour un présent *avec recul esthétique*, pour un artifice de mise en scène' (*Sit I*, 15). This is simply another example of the essential *déloyauté* (*Sit I*, 7) of all art. In any case, as Sartre remarks, 'Ce n'est pas en changeant le temps du verbe, mais en bouleversant les techniques du récit qu'on parviendra à rendre le lecteur contemporain de l'histoire' (*Sit II*, 201). It is the *illusion* that matters: Sartre criticizes Mauriac for not even attempting to convey the awareness of time of his characters and thereby depriving the reader of the possibility of participating in their temporality: 'Dans un roman il faut se taire ou tout dire, surtout ne rien omettre, ne rien "sauter"' (*Sit I*, 48). *La Nausée* neatly sidesteps the problem by its journal form: any *raccourcis* or omissions may be attributed to Roquentin himself. By 1947, as a result, perhaps, of his own difficulties in the composition of *Les Chemins de la liberté* Sartre is less dogmatic and more cognizant of the technical problems involved in the presentation of time:

Si je ramasse six mois en une page, le lecteur saute hors du livre. Ce dernier aspect du réalisme suscite des difficultés que personne de nous n'a résolues et qui, peut-être, sont partiellement insolubles, car il n'est ni possible ni souhaitable de limiter tous les romans au récit d'une seule journée.

(*Sit II*, 237)

Nonetheless, *L'Age de raison* takes only forty-eight hours, *Le Sursis* only a week. And the actions, conversations and thoughts which are recounted give an *impression* of realistic completeness. All art is of course artifice, but a good example of the kind of illusion of reality which Sartre is advocating comes in *La Nausée*, through the juxtaposition of an extract of dialogue from *Eugénie Grandet* which Roquentin is reading in the café, and the discussion he overhears at the next table. Balzac's orderly and coherent dialogue contrasts amusingly with Sartre's stylized mimicry of the elisions and *sous-entendus* of everyday conversation:

- Dis donc, tu as vu?
- Ha, ha.
- Qu'est-ce que tu dis?
- Suzanne hier.
- . . . Qu'est-ce qu'il y a . . . tu n'aimes pas ça?
- Ce n'est pas bon.
- Ça n'est plus ça. (*OR*, 59)

It is not only at moments of lethargy or relaxation that the passing of time is felt. Despite the urgency of Mathieu's quest for money, the two days of his search are filled with the inevitable trivia that 'stories' may neglect but that everyday life cannot overcome: it is precisely when Mathieu arrives in a state of anxiety to speak to his brother that Odette wants him to pause a while and talk to her. Later, Jacques makes conversation about the weather whilst Mathieu is burning to ask for a loan (*OR*, 500). And when Mathieu is in the bell-tower waiting for the Germans, time passes for him with intolerable slowness, marked by the minute: 'trois minutes . . . sept minutes . . . dix minutes' (*OR*, 1336–41); subjective temporal experience and 'objective' or clock time are contrasted here with poignant effect. Yet the picture is resolutely anti-heroic: Mathieu's conversations with his fellow-soldiers remain entangled in the details, rivalries and pettinesses of peacetime. In the midst of firing, Pinette, white with terror, refuses to leave without Mathieu: ' "Merde alors! dit Pinette. Pourquoi que je descendrais si Delarue ne descend pas?" ' (*OR*, 1342).

Nonetheless, totally 'realistic' presentation ('tout dire') is an ideal not a real possibility; and it is perhaps in the case of interior monologue that the impossibility of doing more than create an illusion of reality is most clearly demonstrated, because it would seem at first sight an exception to prove the rule. In Sartre's view, interior monologue is not a privileged case in which the author may transcribe precisely the thoughts and feelings of his characters: psychic life may include words, but it is not composed primarily of words:

Ce n'est pas sans quelque truquage qu'on peut réduire le fleuve de la conscience à une succession de mots, même déformés . . . On peut reprocher [à l'auteur] . . . d'avoir oublié que les plus grandes richesses de la vie psychique sont *silencieuses*. (*Sit II*, 200–1)

The problem with interior monologue is that it is an attempt at a *pseudo*-realism. Literature uses language to evoke rather than to represent, it involves an inevitable and desirable stylization: 'En littérature, où l'on use de signes, il ne faut user *que* de signes; et si la réalité que l'on veut signifier est *un mot*, il faut la livrer au lecteur par d'autres mots' (*Sit II*, 200–1). Once again Sartre is emphasizing art as creation (*poesis*) and illusion rather than imitation (*mimesis*). His own technique respects, on the whole, his reservations: thoughts and feelings are described indirectly, through a mixture of processes none of which appears as an attempt at straight transcription. When Daniel decides to spare his cats, his shame precisely *prevents* him from thinking:

Il prit son canif, se baissa et coupa la ficelle. En silence: même au-dedans de lui-même il faisait silence, il avait trop honte pour parler devant soi. Il

reprit son panier et remonta l'escalier: c'était comme s'il passait en détour-
nant la tête devant quelqu'un qui le regardait avec mépris. En lui, c'était
toujours le désert et le silence. Quand il fut en haut des marches, il osa
s'adresser ses premières paroles: "Qu'est-ce que c'était que cette goutte de
sang?" *(OR,* 490)

When Daniel does, as it were, think verbally, it is a distraction from
his innermost feelings rather than an expression of them.

Quite apart from the particular problem of interior monologue,
there seems to be a tension in the Sartre of the 1940s between an
awareness of the inadequacy of language and a determination that
language can suffice for all purposes. In *Qu'est-ce que la littérature?* he strongly opposes any notion of an ineffable realm on
the grounds that it is a dangerous mystification: 'Je me méfie des
incommunicables, c'est la source de toute violence . . . notre pensée
ne vaut pas mieux que notre langage et l'on doit la juger sur la
façon dont elle en use' (*Sit II,* 305). This tension will later produce
a fascinating and complex theory of communication through con-
notation and imagination, elaborated most fully in *L'Idiot de la
famille,*[17] but for the early Sartre it remains, to some degree at
least, unresolved. It is certain that his characters feel strongly the
struggle with language and the frequent failure of expression:

Roquentin: Absurdité: encore un mot; je me débats contre des mots; là-
bas, je touchais la chose. *(OR,* 153)

Mathieu: Tout ce qui pouvait s'exprimer par des paroles, il le disait.
"Mais il n'y a pas que les paroles!" *(OR,* 398)

Words are powerful:

Daniel: L'appellerai-je Dieu? Un seul mot et tout change.   *(OR,* 907)

Pascal: Les mots lui font peur.   *(OR,* 831)

Stephen pensait "la foule française" et il était ému.   *(OR,* 748)

They are magic:

Philippe: Un autre mot aussi, suave et précieux, il ne se le rappelait déjà
plus, mais c'était le plus tendre des mots tendres, il tournoya, flamboya comme une couronne de feu et Philippe l'emporta dans son sommeil. (*OR,* 897)

But they are never powerful enough:

Daniel: De toutes ses forces il voulait se dégoûter . . . "Salaud! lâche et
comédien: salaud!" Un instant il crut qu'il allait y parvenir, mais non,
c'étaient des mots.   *(OR,* 695)

They distort:

Mathieu: C'était de l'amour. *A présent*, c'était de l'amour. Mathieu pensa: "Qu'est-ce que j'ai fait?" Cinq minutes auparavant cet amour n'existait pas: il y avait entre eux un sentiment rare et précieux, qui n'avait pas de nom. (*OR*, 461)

Mathieu: "Etre libre. Etre cause de soi, pouvoir dire: je suis parce que je le veux" . . . C'étaient des mots vides et pompeux, des mots agaçants d'intellectuel. (*OR*, 445)

And they alienate:

Odette: Elle avait eu l'air d'une perruche, une fois de plus; les mots qu'elle employait se retournaient toujours contre elle. (*OR*, 750)

They can never convey the deepest feelings:

Mathieu: Cela se passait très loin au fond de lui, dans une région où les mots n'ont plus de sens. (*OR*, 1047)

It would seem that Sartre's characters are possessed by the 'hantise du silence' which he analyses and condemns in Bataille and Jules Renard.[18] Sartre's own position, to judge from the critical essays, seems to be that language can convey thought, since language and thought create each other mutually and dialectically, but that thought itself cannot grasp entirely the complexities of events and experience; he refers to 'l'impuissance où nous sommes de *penser*, avec nos concepts, avec nos mots, les événements du monde' (*Sit I*, 103). Language is both insufficiently personal and specific, and overlaid by connotations which may conflict with my intended meaning: 'Les paroles . . . sont des actes libres et maladroits, qui disent trop et trop peu' (*Sit I*, 50). More specifically, as part of my *être-pour-autrui*, language is perpetually open to misunderstanding by others:

Le 'sens' de mes expressions m'échappe toujours . . . Autrui est toujours là, présent et éprouvé comme ce qui donne au langage son sens.(*EN*, 441)

Dès que je parle, j'ai l'angoissante certitude que les mots m'échappent et qu'ils vont prendre, là-bas, hors de moi, des aspects insoupçonnables, des significations imprévues. (*Sit I*, 219)

Language is evidently a major factor in the dialectic of freedom and non-freedom explored by the novels. Language socializes, humanizes and orders; when it breaks down, the consequence is chaos, as Roquentin discovers:

Je murmure: "c'est une banquette," un peu comme un exorcisme. Mais le mot reste sur mes lèvres: il refuse d'aller se poser sur la chose . . . Les choses se sont délivrées de leurs noms . . . je suis au milieu des choses, les innommables. Seul, sans mots, sans défenses.   (*OR*, 148)

Yet it is precisely the social aspect of language which constitutes a major aspect of its power to alienate: as Sartre later conceded to the Structuralists, we are spoken by language as much as we speak it, and the novels are particularly sensitive to the anonymity of much discourse. *Le Sursis* is constructed on the basis of a series of 'impersonal' phrases which effect the transition from one consciousness to the next: '[Milan] se répéta: "Je ne suis pas seul. Je ne suis pas seul." Daniel pensait: "Je suis seul." ' (*OR*, 723); Gros Louis in Marseilles, Philippe in Paris: 'Ils pensaient: "N'y a-t-il personne pour m'aider?" ' (*OR*, 907). In so far as it universalizes the individual and makes the subjective objective, language is bound to betray at the same time as it communicates. Mathieu responds sympathetically to the alienated and clichéd expressions of his fellow-soldiers: 'Ce sont ceux-là qui ont raison. Ils parlent par proverbe mais les mots les trahissent, il y a quelque chose dans leur tête qui ne peut s'exprimer par les mots' (*OR*, 1106). Roquentin lacks Mathieu's generosity of spirit, and ironizes at the Autodidact's expense:

Que puis-je faire? Est-ce ma faute si, dans tout ce qu'il me dit, je reconnais au passage l'emprunt, la citation? Si je vois réapparaître, pendant qu'il parle, tous les humanistes que j'ai connus?   (*OR*, 138)

Roquentin has a gift for parody and pastiche. He can take the words out of the Autodidact's mouth − ' "C'est l'Homme mûr, je suppose, que vous aimez en lui . . .?" − "Exactement", me dit-il avec défi' (*OR*, 142) − precisely because those words are so predictable. Similarly he can imagine convincingly the mentality and speeches of the right-wing *salauds* whose portraits are displayed in the museum of Bouville because they are almost interchangeable and contain no surprises:

Pacôme: Il avait toujours fait son devoir, tout son devoir, son devoir de fils, d'époux, de père, de chef. Il avait aussi réclamé ses droits sans faiblesse . . . Car un droit n'est jamais que l'autre aspect d'un devoir . . . Il disait; "Comme il est plus simple et plus difficile de faire son devoir!"   (*OR*, 102–3)[19]

It is no coincidence that *L'Enfance d'un chef* starts and ends with Lucien speaking the words of others: ' "Je suis adorable dans mon petit costume d'ange" ' (*OR*, 314): the internalization of Madame

Portier's comment about him passes through a period of conscious alienation ('"Lucien Fleurier est une grande asperge"' *OR*, 327), to become by the end a meditation on 'rights' and the phrase '"Lucien n'aime pas les Juifs"' (*OR*, 386). It would seem that the state of mind of a *chef* is one of pure alienation to society and to the language of others. In *La Nausée*, the impersonal nature of social discourse (what Heidegger refers to as *Gerede*: *parlerie* or *bavardage*) is frequently used to comic as well as satiric effect. When Roquentin, on his Sunday walk, passes a group who have just met, their voices are indistinguishable:[20]

Nous défilons devant six personnes qui se tiennent les mains: "Bonjour, monsieur, bonjour, cher monsieur comment allez-vous; mais couvrez-vous donc, monsieur, vous allez prendre froid; merci, madame, c'est qu'il ne fait pas chaud. Ma chérie, je te présente le docteur Lefrançois; docteur, je suis très heureuse de faire votre connaissance, mon mari me parle toujours du docteur Lefrançois qui l'a si bien soigné, mais couvrez-vous donc, docteur, par ce froid vous prendrez mal." (*OR*, 54)

Geneviève Idt has shown *La Nausée* to be an interweaving, almost a collage, of pastiches of other texts — from the eighteenth-century novel, satire and philosophy to historical documents, Naturalism and Surrealism.[21] More surprisingly, perhaps, it would seem also to be a prospective self-parody. When the Autodidact says portentously that it is difficult to be a man, we may suspect from the nearby reference to 'la condition humaine' that it is Malraux who is being satirized;[22] and Roquentin's reaction: 'Il me semblait qu'on n'avait qu'à se laisser aller' (*OR*, 143) is very similar to Brunet's reaction to being told he is a man by Mathieu: 'Un homme? demanda Brunet, surpris; le contraire serait inquiétant' (*OR*, 522). But in the second passage it is already less clear who is being shown up as uncomprehending and foolish. And when the Autodidact advocates action and commitment, Roquentin may think he sounds like a commercial traveller, but to the reader who knows the Sartre of the 1940s, he sounds suspiciously like a second-rate existentialist:

"La vie a un sens si l'on veut bien lui en donner un. Il faut d'abord agir, se jeter dans une entreprise. Si ensuite on réfléchit, le sort en est jeté, on est engagé. Je ne sais ce que vous en pensez, monsieur?"
"Rien," dis-je.
Ou plutôt je pense que c'est précisément l'espèce de mensonge que se font perpétuellement le commis-voyageur, les deux jeunes gens et le monsieur aux cheveux blancs.
L'Autodidacte sourit avec un peu de malice et beaucoup de solennité:
"Aussi n'est-ce pas mon avis. Je pense que nous n'avons pas à chercher

si loin le sens de notre vie."

"Ah?"

"Il y a un but, monsieur, il y a un but . . . il y a les hommes."

C'est juste: j'oubliais qu'il est humaniste.   (*OR*, 133)

The passage takes on a very different tone after the publication of *L'Existentialisme est un humanisme*; and Contat and Rybalka observe that the lecture led many to remark: 'Voilà Sartre devenu son propre Autodidacte' (*OR*, 1779). In fact, Sartre was always aware – as the ending of *L'Etre et le Néant* testifies[23] – that existentialism is as susceptible to degradation by *l'esprit de sérieux* as any other philosophy. But the similarity between the vocabulary employed by the Autodidact and that of *Qu'est-ce que la littérature?* is surely best taken as an ironic example of the alienation of language – terms which Sartre later needs to expound his philosophy have a tinge of ridicule from the outset, in part through his own efforts: exponent, ironist and satirist of linguistic alienation, he is here the biter bit.

To this extent, then, we may discern a self-deconstructing element in Sartre's literary production: parodist and proponent of commitment, action and humanism; exponent of linguistic alienation overcome in its own depiction; sceptic concerning the possibility of salvation through art, expounding his scepticism through the artistic medium. In the prose fiction, the art of writing itself reveals an ultimate faith in language, literature and human communication which is undermined but never entirely overthrown by the ostensible 'message'. It should be clear that Sartre's novels are far from being a mere simplification or popularization of his philosophical theories: they are far more complex and frequently reveal intuitions about the nature of human experience which are at odds with at least the better-known aspects of Sartre's philosophy of freedom, indeed at odds with Sartre's thinking as he has theorized it up to that point. In the case of language in particular, both *La Nausée* and *Les Chemins de la liberté* express an awareness of alienation in tension with Sartre's instinctive faith in the human potential to communicate, and which the philosophy tackles head on only at a later stage. Similarly, the weight of situation and facticity as they are lived out by the fictional characters is considerably greater in its oppressive power than the more optimistic picture given in *L'Etre et le Néant* would suggest. This alienation is not fully explored in Sartre's philosophy proper until the *Critique de la raison dialectique* in 1960. Theory and 'practice' are not in fact in conflict, but it is the literary practice which comes closer to the reality of experience as it is lived. If the early philosophy explores man's potential for freedom, the fiction explores the multiple obstacles which are encountered in even the most apparently insignificant enterprise: there are no *conversions radicales*, and perhaps Daniel's sudden decision to marry Marcelle provides, paradoxically, the best evidence of their inherent difficulty. In Daniel's case, all, superficially, is different after his marriage, but in fact nothing that matters to him has changed in the slightest. Self-punishment is no substitute for self-deliverance.

We began our examination of the novels by considering them as a literary embodiment of *l'universel singulier*. We might end by asking what in Sartre's writing took their place when he turned away from the production of fiction. The plays, of course, continued to be written up to 1965, but these, as we shall see in the next chapter, bear a somewhat different relation to Sartre's thought: dramatically and often schematically exemplary, rather than attentive to complex ambiguities. The answer, perhaps, lies in the existential biographies which focus on an individual life and its insertion into society in the domain of the real (history) rather than the imaginary (fiction). But this very distinction invites questioning: *Les Chemins de la liberté* is firmly situated in its historical context, Sartre's *Baudelaire* clearly is not. It would seem rather that the locus of the fiction/non-fiction opposition has itself shifted. The dialectic between perception and imagination, contingency and teleology, has moved onto new territory. If *La Nausée* is taken as the best early depiction of contingency, 'L'Enfance d'un chef' of fictional teleology, we may see these as continued by the politicized Sartre of the 1960s and 1970s in *L'Idiot de la famille*, his biography of Flaubert, and his own autobiography, *Les Mots*. The study of Flaubert, bringing to bear its mammoth critical apparatus taken from history, sociology, psychoanalysis, philosophy and aesthetics, was described by Sartre as a *roman vrai*, and his discussion of Gustave's infancy as a *fable*. At the same time, it is also intended to answer the serious epistemological question: 'Que peut-on savoir d'un homme aujourd'hui?' In this sense it may be seen as Sartre's response to his own hesitations concerning the novel form in 1959: 'La réalité sociale est si complexe, pour la cerner dans un roman, je ne sais pas, il faudrait tenir compte à la fois des connaissances sociologiques et psychanalytiques, traiter à la fois la société et l'individu'.[24] *Les Mots*, on the other hand, where the unsuspecting reader might expect self-knowledge to produce an interminable process of fluid self-analysis, is concise, closely structured, directed

towards an end known in advance, and a brilliant parody as
as an example of autobiography as a literary genre. At the en
his career, Sartre may be seen as attempting to break down the
barriers between truth and fiction, philosophy and literature.[25]

4

Drama: theory and practice

Sartre's theatre overlaps, but also extends beyond, his novel-writing period, stretching from *Bariona*, written and produced in a prisoner-of-war camp in 1940, to *Les Troyennes*, an adaptation of Euripides's *Trojan Women*, in 1965. It is a genre which corresponds to Sartre's purposes in a very different way from the novel, both in the contingent conditions of its production and in its essential aesthetic constitution. In the former perspective, the economic and ideological situation of the theatre in mid-twentieth-century France makes it a singularly inappropriate medium for the expression of a philosophy of self-liberation; but in the latter perspective, as a performance of action and dialogue before an audience, drama is the art-form most eminently suited to the communication of an existential world-view. Critics, however, have tended to focus on the ideological contradictions inherent in the presentation of radical committed theatre to a predominantly bourgeois audience; and indeed these contradictions have led to Sartre's drama being attacked on two very different scores. On the one hand, Sartre has been criticized by the dramatic *avant-garde*, Absurdist or Brechtian, for creating traditional, non-experimental, bourgeois theatre; on the other, he is accused by the bourgeois of writing left-wing *théâtre à thèse*, didactic, polemical and excessively political. An examination of the plays will show them to be both dramatically unconventional and politically ambiguous.

It is, of course, the economic situation of Parisian theatre which determines to a large extent the nature of its audience and the reception of its plays. Expensive and centrally located, it attracts, of necessity, primarily bourgeois support. As Sartre's success as a dramatist increased, he transferred his productions from the more unconventional direction of *Les Mouches* by Dullin in Le Théâtre de la Cité, or of *Huis clos* in the Left-Bank Vieux Colombier, to the established *boulevard* settings of Le Théâtre de la Renaissance and Le Théâtre Antoine where over half his plays were originally performed. It was not until the 1960s that Le Théâtre National Populaire staged any of his works (*Les Troyennes* in 1965, a revival of *Le Diable et le Bon Dieu* in 1968), and indeed in the 1950s Sartre seemed anxious to play down the 'popular' nature of the T.N.P. in what may perhaps be seen as a form of defensive aggression.[1] The failure of *Nekrassov* at Le Théâtre Antoine in 1955 marks the peak of Sartre's mistrust of contemporary theatre as a potential medium of radical expression. In an interview with Bernard Dort, he is openly nostalgic for the long-past *popularity* of medieval, renaissance and eighteenth-century theatre, envies the educative function of drama in the U.S.S.R., and the already politicized audience of Brecht, and concludes: 'Pour moi, maintenant, je n'ai plus rien à dire aux bourgeois' (*TS*, 74). The Algerian war was to cause him to break this vow of silence with *Les Séquestrés d'Altona* and arguably also *Les Troyennes*.

It is clear that the 'grand spectacle' productions of the boulevard theatres, emphasizing, as they invariably did, the traditional elements of the *pièce bien faite*, both enabled Sartre to speak directly to the bourgeois he was attacking and falsified at least to some extent, the 'message' of his plays. As we shall see, Sartre's theatre is not usually *à thèse*: it provokes reflection, criticism and self-criticism, it is ironic and often parodic, but its multiple possible interpretations, whilst being the condition of literature rather than propaganda, also facilitate its recuperation. Sartre always maintained that the 'objective' meaning of a work of art depends ultimately not on its author's intention but rather on its readers' or audiences' reception and interpretation, in particular in the case of a play which is recreated by the audience as a group each night rather than by individual readers. His own plays provided him with frequent examples of this phenomenon, as they seemed to escape his authorial control and lose their radical purport.

Le théâtre est tellement la chose publique, *la chose du public*, qu'une pièce échappe à l'auteur dès que le public est dans la salle. Mes pièces, en tout cas – quel qu'ait été leur sort – m'ont presque toutes échappé. Elles deviennent des *objets*. Après, vous dites: "Je n'ai pas voulu cela," comme Guillaume II pendant la guerre de 14. Mais ce qui est fait reste fait.

(*TS*, 93)[2]

The partially unpredictable metamorphosis of a play in its transition from paper to stage may have a considerable effect on its interpretation. Sometimes what Sartre, adapting Gide, calls *la part du diable*, the uncontrollable independence of the work of art, is no more noxious than the discovery that *Le Diable et le Bon Dieu* becomes, when staged, 'une pièce nocturne' (*TS*, 93), with its series of night scenes. But the transformation may be more significant.

In particular, the political meaning of a play is permanently vulnerable to what its author must feel to be misinterpretation. This aspect may, however, be used by the playwright for his own purposes: in *Bariona* the Roman envoy to Jerusalem represented the German army in the eyes of Sartre and his fellow-prisoners; the German guards interpreted the play as an attack on British colonialism (*TS*, 221). The call to revolt against Nazi occupation in *Les Mouches* escaped censorship because of its mythical disguise. At times local, temporary meanings may disappear from a text: a contemporary production of *Les Mouches* will no longer evoke the Resistance problem of reprisals against hostages which it apparently did in 1944 (*TS*, 225). New meanings will enter it: *Les Mouches* carried a very different message to post-war Germany and to wartime France (*TS*, 228–34). More seriously, the play may be 'misunderstood' from the outset: the famous 'l'enfer c'est les autres' of *Huis clos* was offered as a description of a certain kind of inauthentic human relationship, not a message of irremediable ontological pessimism (*TS*, 238). *Les Mains sales*, which was intended to pose the problem of relations between idealist intellectuals and the Communist party, was so persistently received as anti-Communist that Sartre felt obliged at one point to ban any further productions of it.

Une pièce assume un sens objectif qui lui est attribué par un public. Il n'y a rien à faire: si toute la bourgeoisie fait un succès triomphal aux *Mains Sales*, et si les communistes l'attaquent, cela veut dire qu'en réalité quelque chose est arrivé. Cela veut dire que la pièce est devenue *par elle-même* anticommuniste, objectivement, et que les intentions de l'auteur ne comptent plus.   (*TS*, 251)

But if the primacy of audience response prevents the playwright from conveying with confidence an unambiguous message, conversely other aspects of the theatrical medium make it a singularly powerful means of posing problems. Unlike a novel, a play necessarily presents characters and situations directly to its audience without the mediation of a narrator, omniscient or subjective, except by the semi-extraneous device of a prologue or chorus. Furthermore, the essentially agonistic, conflictual nature of dramatic action, in which the playwright must distribute merit and interest diversely if the play is to carry conviction, lends itself to an examination of controversies or dilemmas. *Théâtre à thèse* is thus bound to be dramatically unsatisfying, in so far as it reduces the potential complexity of conflict to a single viewpoint. In

Sartre's theoretical comments on the theatre he stresses the dialectical, problematic nature of his own productions.

Notre nouveau théâtre . . . n'est le support d'aucune "thèse" et il n'est inspiré par aucune idée préconçue. Ce qu'il tente de faire c'est d'explorer la condition dans sa totalité et présenter à l'homme contemporain un portrait de lui-même, ses problèmes, ses espoirs et ses luttes.   (TS, 61)

Je ne prends pas parti. Une bonne pièce de théâtre doit poser les problèmes et non pas les résoudre.   (TS, 247)

Je ne pense pas . . . que le théâtre soit un "véhicule philosophique" . . . Il doit exprimer une philosophie, mais il ne faut pas qu'on puisse à l'intérieur de la pièce poser le problème de la valeur de la philosophie qui s'y exprime . . . Il faut que ce soit tellement enveloppé dans l'histoire, dans le côté dramatique de l'histoire, dans son développement, qu'on ne puisse pas déclarer que la pièce est valable à partir de certains principes, ni que l'on accepte une chose et en refuse une autre.   (TS, 327)

But if Sartre's theatre is dialectical, this is not in the totalizing sense of thesis, antithesis, synthesis, but rather in the sense of testing the truth of opinions by debate. The dialectic, at least in the most successful works, remains open-ended. Since, for Sartre, the essence of the human condition is paradox and contradiction, and the only certainty in the ethical sphere is its insuperable heterogeneity, there is no way in which his conception of reality can be reduced to a neat system. Indeed, as we have seen, Sartre considers any fixed moral system to be alienating and 'immoral'. Nor does the theatre present a clash of moral absolutes, for there can be no absolutes, no categorical imperatives, if there is no way of grounding moral principles; its concern is rather the pragmatic evaluation of necessarily limited moral (and political) goods.

Very occasionally, however, Sartre's polemical zeal, or perhaps his desire to construct a satisfying dramatic conclusion, leads him to weight the scales or foreclose the dialectic: *Nekrassov* permits only the politically radical Véronique to escape ridicule, and ends in a clear victory for the Left; the Russian translation of *La Putain respectueuse* and the French film version both transform the weak and treacherous Lizzie into a stalwart heroine who eventually defends the honour of the black suspect. But this utopian optimism is absent from all Sartre's other drama: *Huis clos*, *Kean* and *Les Séquestrés d'Altona* present only anti-heroes, bad faith and negative messages. Oreste, in *Les Mouches*, may appear to be the embodiment of freedom and commitment, but he uses the language of rape, violation and possession, not that of liberation. 'Argos est à prendre . . . Je deviendrai hache et je fendrai en deux ces murailles obstinées, j'ouvrirai le ventre de ces maisons bigotes.'[3] Moreover Jupiter is no mean antagonist, and his speech is at times curiously and seductively reminiscent of *La Nausée*:

ORESTE: Les hommes d'Argos sont mes hommes. Il faut que je leur ouvre les yeux.

JUPITER: Pauvres gens! Tu vas leur faire cadeau de la solitude et de la lutte, tu vas arracher les étoffes dont je les avais couverts, et tu leur montreras soudain leur existence, leur obscène et fade existence, qui leur est donnée pour rien. (*Mouches*, 183)

Even Oreste's dramatic departure is undermined by its degree of self-satisfaction and self-congratulation. Indeed, *Les Mouches* provides a good example of a perceptible shift in meaning: Oreste clearly appeared as a heroic liberator in 1943, but to many post-war readers, including Sartre himself in later years, he seems to desert Argos in a time of crisis. A thesis play would evidently be less susceptible to reinterpretation. Again, Hoederer in *Les Mains sales* may ultimately embody Sartre's conception of compassionate political realism, but he does not survive; and the play centres on the indecisive Hugo whose final suicide, whilst clearly misguided, is given a certain heroic dignity. Similarly, Goetz may be the last-act 'hero' of *Le Diable et le Bon Dieu*, but Heinrich, Nasty and Hilda, mystified as they appear, are right at his expense, for by far the greater part of the action; and even his 'conversion' is marked by an inglorious murder and a readiness to be both 'bourreau et boucher' in a revolution that is bound to fail. Sartrean drama is essentially ambiguous, unresolved and unsynthesized.

Rather than illustrating his philosophy by means of his drama in a kind of *drame philosophique*, Sartre sees philosophy as dramatic from the outset. Existentialism implies a dynamic conception of character as a free choice not an essence; what we call 'character' is no more than 'le durcissement du choix, sa sclérose' (*TS*, 20). Sartre's novels tend to focus on the inevitable 'sclérose' of personality, his plays on the moments of choice. His theatre presents its protagonists as 'des libertés prises au piège, comme nous tous' (*Sit II*, 313), who invent themselves on the basis of their situation:

Chaque personnage ne sera rien que le choix d'une issue . . . Je m'exprimais mal, il n'y a pas d'issues à *choisir*. Une issue, ça s'invente. Et chacun, en inventant sa propre issue, s'invente soi-même. L'homme est à inventer chaque jour. (*Sit II*, 313)

Ce que le théâtre peut montrer de plus émouvant est un caractère en train de se faire, le moment du choix, de la libre décision qui engage une morale et toute une vie.   (*TS*, 20)

This is surely what Sartre means when he claims, 'Aujourd'hui je pense que la philosophie est dramatique':[4] it is a philosophy where, in the terms of *L'Etre et le Néant, faire* has precedence over *avoir* and *être*.[5]

There is nonetheless in one sense a paradox in presenting a philosophy of action-in-the-world on a stage where all is imaginary and unreal, and where, in Sartre's terms, 'acts' can only be 'gestures'. Nothing is ever achieved on stage: what is enacted is mere *répétition* (rehearsal) of a series of events which is fatal because predetermined, of a dialogue without possibility of consequence. And this is precisely a definition of what Sartre would call the inauthentic life, in which men play at being who they are – or, indeed, who they are not. But it is not only the inauthentic character who is caught up in the toils of this kind of alienation of identity. Since for Sartre man is not what he is and is what he is not, doomed never to achieve peaceful self-coincidence, he risks perpetually finding his behaviour reduced to mere role-playing as soon as he attempts to identify with his *être-pour-autrui*, or his public persona. It is perhaps this painful duality which is the most specific characteristic of Sartrean theatre: man as a useless passion.

Il s'agit de l'homme – qui est à la fois *un agent* et *un acteur* – qui produit et joue son drame, en vivant les contradictions de sa situation jusqu'à l'éclatement de sa personne ou jusqu'à la solution de ses conflits.

                                                (*Sit IX*, 12)

Agent and *acteur*, 'qui *produit* et *joue* son drame': the theatre may reduce acts to gestures by diverting their finality from the functional to the spectacular, but the gestures nonetheless represent acts: 'Les gestes au théâtre signifiant les actes, et le théâtre étant une image, les gestes sont l'image de l'action . . . Il n'y a pas d'autre image au théâtre que l'image de l'acte' (*TS*, 119).

Since theatre can present no more than the image of an act, it is the 'lieu d'illusion par excellence',[6] pure 'show', fated irremediably to reveal 'monsters' ('montrer des monstres')[7]. Sartre will make use of the inherent insubstantiality of the theatrical medium both to embody and to denounce play-acting. Hugo and Jessica cannot escape the awareness that they are permanently playing roles, whether that of the married couple, of frigid flirtatious wife, or of revolutionary assassin:

HUGO: Fais un effort, Jessica. Sois sérieuse.

JESSICA: Pourquoi faut-il que je sois sérieuse?

HUGO: Parce qu'on ne peut pas jouer tout le temps.

JESSICA: Je n'aime pas le sérieux, mais on va s'arranger: je vais jouer à être sérieuse.[8]

Jupiter, Egisthe (*Les Mouches*); Estelle (*Huis clos*); Goetz (*Le Diable et le Bon Dieu*); Nekrassov; Kean; Frantz, Joanna and *Le Père* (*Séquestrés d'Altona*) all live through their image in the eyes of others. Images of eyes (*yeux, regarder, voir, image* etc.) recur with increasing intensity and frequency in *Les Mouches*, reaching a peak in Oreste's departure when he finally succeeds in transforming himself into a mythical hero in his own eyes as well as those of the Argives and of the audience. Note the alienation of a third person narrative:

ORESTE: Vous me regardez, gens d'Argos . . . Regardez, regardez les mouches! Et puis tout d'un coup ils se précipitèrent sur ses traces. Et le joueur de flûte avec ses rats disparut pour toujours. Comme ceci.   (*Mouches*, 189–90)

Of course the uncertain status of theatrical action, which may be thematized and put to creative use, is also inescapable. Oreste's departure was probably not originally intended as dramatic self-aggrandizement; Hugo's final increase in stature as he declares himself *non-récupérable* may be seen as heroism or as false heroics depending simply on the sensitivity to rhetoric of the spectator; even Goetz's eventual conversion from pride to modesty is transformed by the dramatic process into a rhetorical heroics of modesty:[9]

GOETZ: Je leur ferai horreur puisque je n'ai pas d'autre manière de les aimer, je leur donnerai des ordres, puisque je n'ai pas d'autre manière d'obéir, je resterai seul avec ce ciel vide au-dessus de ma tête, puisque je n'ai pas d'autre manière d'être avec tous. Il y a cette guerre à faire et je la ferai.[10]

Sartre's philosophical preoccupation with play-acting (*jouer la comédie*), explored most fully in *Kean* which we shall examine later, means that the self-referential nature of his drama, the frequent allusions to its theatricality and to the illusory nature of stage, décor and character, are more than mere self-indulgent appeals to a conniving audience. If play-acting is the subject of a drama, references to it will reflect at the same time as subverting dramatic illusion. When Catherine calls Goetz a *cabotin* (*DBD*, 64)

76

or Hugo complains: 'je vis dans un décor' (*MS*, 130), the audience
may experience a brief effect of alienation, but rather than being
a simple theatrical device it is an integral part of the subject at
issue. Dramatic technique and philosophical purpose here reinforce
each other.

As will become clear when we examine his theory of literature
and commitment, Sartre has from the outset serious reservations
about the way in which art relates to the real world of politics and
history. 'L'imaginaire pur et la *praxis* sont difficilement compatibles' (*Sit II*, 324). Since the art-object – novel, play, painting
– is ultimately imaginary and unreal, it always risks distracting the
reader or spectator from her situation in the world, leading her
potentially to deny the real and escape into the realm of fantasy.
Nevertheless, the creative artist must capture the imagination of his
audience if the aesthetic experience is to take place. But since imagination and perception are for Sartre radically distinct modes of
consciousness, not susceptible of synthesis, the reader or spectator
cannot *simultaneously* engage her critical faculties (moral or
political) and participate fully in the artistic work. It is this
philosophical conception of a radical break between imagination
and perception[11] that explains Sartre's ambivalence towards the
Brechtian notion of *Verfremdungseffekt* – aesthetic alienation or
distancing of the audience. On the one hand Sartre agrees that the
traditional dramatic illusion involves a 'suspension' not only of
'disbelief' but also of criticism and judgement; but on the other, he
considers it an essential aspect of the theatrical experience. In a
sense the theatre is a particularly appropriate medium for the expression of criticism since it involves, by its nature, less identification between audience and *dramatis personae* than the novel or
cinema: in the latter genres I may see *through* the eyes of one or
more of the protagonists, in the theatre I can only ever observe the
character from outside:

Au théâtre [l'identification] est remplacé[e] par une distance absolue:
d'abord je vois de mes yeux et je reste toujours sur le même plan, à la
même place, donc il n'y a ni la complicité du roman, ni cette complicité
ambiguë du cinéma et le personnage est donc définitivement pour moi
l'autre.   (*TS*, 24–5)

In his early writings on the theatre Sartre stresses that this 'distance
infranchissable' (*TS*, 28) must not be transgressed: for this reason
he rejects certain contemporary attempts to break down the barriers between actors and audience (*TS*, 29) and appreciates rather

the *mise en abyme* technique of a play within a play, with its contrary effect of double distancing:

C'est là ce qui explique le plaisir qu'on a toujours eu à avoir un théâtre dans le théâtre . . . une distance au second degré . . . c'est alors du théâtre pur, à la seconde puissance. (*TS*, 29)

However, from the 1950s onwards Sartre's dramatic theory becomes more subtle. Whilst still agreeing with Brecht that theatre has a role of demystification, he believes this to be best obtained not by critical theatre – possible, perhaps, for Brecht's already politicized audience – but by actively *involving* the audience in the process of demystification (*TS*, 73). Ideally Sartre would wish to transcend the *montrer/émouvoir* opposition. In 1960 he explictly opposes his own 'dramatic' theatre to Brecht's 'epic' theatre which he criticizes for taking too little account of the subjective (*TS*, 149), and attempts to construct a theory of non-bourgeois dramatic theatre in which the emotional involvement of the audience is used against them in a way that precludes recuperation. This evolution in Sartre's thinking perhaps explains why we are more likely to identify with Frantz the torturer than Oreste the liberator. A theatre of example or admiration has no need of participation; in *Les Séquestrés d'Altona* the audience is, as it were, tricked into an unwilling identification with a war criminal: alienation and distance would be counter-productive in this kind of drama.

Dans *Les Séquestrés d'Altona* . . . je souhaite simplement que les scrupules de conscience et les contradictions intérieures de Frantz, poussés au plus fort, au mythe, puissent donner des moyens aux spectateurs, pendant un moment, de participer à ce Frantz, d'être lui-même. (C'est pour cela . . . que je réserve jusqu'au quatrième acte, la révélation que Frantz a torturé. C'est parce que je souhaite qu'au moment où les choses vont se dégrader et où Frantz va être en plein dans ses contradictions, je souhaite qu'alors Frantz soit le personnage auquel le spectateur participe). (*TS*, 331)

In his critical monograph on Jean Genet in 1952, Sartre describes the homosexual novelist and thief as seducing his bourgeois readers into participating in an experience of what they would normally consider 'evil' and disgusting. *Les Séquestrés d'Altona* seems to be attempting a similar seduction, though for very different purposes. Since Sartre believes art to be based on illusion and to convey truth only indirectly ('mentir pour être vrai' *Sit II*, 324), it cannot, in his view, demystify or criticize by purely direct means. It must itself 'mystify' in order to counteract an already existent generalized mystification.

Nous en revenons à Brecht. Et là je dois marquer ce qui m'en sépare. Je crois moi, profondément, que toute démystification doit être en un sens mystifiante. Ou plutôt que, devant une foule en partie mystifiée, on ne peut se confier aux seules réactions critiques de cette foule. Il faut lui fournir une contre-mystification. Et pour cela le théâtre ne doit se priver d'aucune des sorcelleries du théâtre. (*TS*, 77)

Jeanson describes this phenomenon in rather more violent language when he writes:

Si Sartre se préoccupe de fasciner et de séduire, c'est que nous sommes tous, si diversement que ce soit, en situation d'être séduits, et pour de tout autres buts que les siens; s'il nous viole c'est pour nous contraindre à nous avouer que nous sommes *déjà violés* et que nous jouissons de l'être.[12]

Sartre's views on the aims and aesthetics of his theatre, collected in *Un Théâtre de situations*, were expressed primarily in lectures and interviews, frequently in connection with his own productions or in response to specific invitations or challenges. The popularizing and sometimes polemical nature of these texts inevitably means that they tend to simplify certain philosophical and aesthetic issues, and need to be supplemented by reference to more theoretical related writings such as *L'Imaginaire*, *Saint Genet* and sections of *L'Idiot de la famille*. We will now examine briefly the recurrent themes of Sartre's dramatic theory, drawing on both the *textes de circonstance* and the more fully worked out philosophical works, and attempt to assess its impact on his theatrical practice.

In the first place Sartre rejects psychological theatre, 'le théâtre de caractères', in favour of a theatre of *situations*, on the grounds that psychological drama leaves no real room for human freedom: an essentialist view of character makes for predictable theatre, 'tout est décidé d'avance' (*TS*, 19). This does not mean that his protagonists are not individuals, but their temperaments — vain, cowardly or thoughtless — are not decisive, nor the main source of dramatic intrigue. 'Nous ne voyons pas d'intérêt à arranger d'avance les motivations ou les raisons qui forceront inévitablement [le] choix' (*TS*, 58). Empirical psychology[13] is dismissed as an abstract science which reduces man to a mechanism and removes him from his historical, moral and religious context (*TS*, 59), it is 'une perte de temps au théâtre' (*TS*, 143).[14] In consequence, Sartre's characters do not necessarily act 'consistently', and certainly not predictably — they may change radically in response to different situations. Oreste is perhaps the best early example of this kind of transformation, Goetz of a whole series of changed personae.

But Sartre characterizes his theatre as a theatre of situations as much as of liberty: 'Car la liberté n'est pas je ne sais quel pouvoir abstrait de survoler la condition humaine: c'est l'engagement le plus absurde et le plus inexorable' (*TS*, 223). It is in this sense that Sartre can situate his plays in the line of great tragedy from Aeschylus to Corneille — freedom and fatality are two sides of the same coin:

La grande tragédie, celle d'Eschyle et de Sophocle, celle de Corneille, a pour ressort principal la liberté humaine.[15] Œdipe est libre, libres Antigone et Prométhée. La fatalité que l'on croit constater dans les drames antiques n'est que l'envers de la liberté. Les passions elles-mêmes sont des libertés prises à leur propre piège. (*TS*, 19)

Conversely the freedom embodied in Sartre's drama may be envisaged as *l'envers de la fatalité*: it is an inescapable destiny. In other words, the Greek playwrights transform men's free decisions into myths; Sartre will show myths as the result of free decisions. His reworking of Aeschylus's *Oresteia* best illustrates this contention:

La tragédie est le miroir de la Fatalité. Il ne m'a pas semblé impossible d'écrire une tragédie de la liberté, puisque le Fatum antique n'est que la liberté retournée. Oreste est libre pour le crime et par-delà le crime: je l'ai montré en proie à la liberté comme Œdipe est en proie à son destin. Il se débat sous cette poigne de fer, mais il faudra bien qu'il tue pour finir, et qu'il charge son meurtre sur ses épaules et qu'il le passe sur l'autre rive . . . Oreste poursuivra son chemin, injustifiable, sans excuses, sans recours, seul. (*TS*, 223)

In a sense, Sartre's plays all embody the tragic destiny of characters 'condemned to be free', but, as we shall see, the practical implications of this 'condemnation' will change radically between 1940 and 1965.

It is already apparent that Sartre's dramatic universe is the domain of paradox, 'un monde libre *et* fatal' (*TS*, 53), rather than of *mesure* or synthesis. The same paradoxical mode will obtain within the plays themselves, exemplified in what he calls 'the conflict of rights'. If tragedy is defined as the necessity of the impossible,[16] then the attempt to resolve radically conflicting rights will always prove tragic. Once again Sartre situates himself in the lineage of Greek tragedy, but with an important modification: in contemporary theatre, opposed rights and contradictions are internalized rather than embodied in different characters:

Dans le théâtre antique, ce qui est intéressant, c'est que chaque personnage représente *un* terme de la contradiction, jamais deux. Ici, vous avez d'un côté la famille, de l'autre côté la cité . . . Ce qu'il y a de neuf aujourd'hui dans le théâtre . . . c'est que la contradiction, maintenant, peut appartenir au personnage individuellement . . . il y a des séries de contradictions intérieures au personnage.   (*TS*, 139)

Thus, to take a different example from Sartre, the human conflict between justice and mercy in the third play of Aeschylus's trilogy is projected onto the legal confrontation between Apollo and Pallas Athene, each intended to represent a facet of divine wisdom. Sartre draws from his distinction conclusions concerning not only the increased complexity of contemporary drama, but also its dialectical nature: external contradictions reflect a more static world which cannot transcend its own conflicts; the only solution implicit is a form of moderation. Internalized contradictions, on the other hand, are part of a dynamic world-view in which action is both born from the attempt to resolve conflict and creative of further contradictions: 'On change en changeant le monde et parce que le monde change' (*TS*, 141). One could of course take issue with Sartre's definitions and argue that internal contradictions may produce an initially more painful situation, but that it is ultimately less truly *tragic* in so far as the conflict-ridden protagonist is at least free to choose which pole she will eventually allow to take precedence. Sophocles's Antigone is crushed by forces entirely outside her control; Anouilh's heroine goes to her death as the result of an option which she takes freely. Sartre, however, at least in the 1940s, maintains that *fatal* disaster is less moving and less heroic (*TS*, 19). This is also why his choice of myth from Antiquity as the subject-matter of his plays is necessarily limited: Oreste may be shown as choosing his destiny, Œdipus could not.

Sartre adapted old myths for both his first and last plays: the Christian Nativity story for *Bariona*, Greek myth for *Les Mouches* and *Les Troyennes*. In the intervening years a certain ambivalence towards the use of myth may be discerned, an ambivalence which is at least partially resolved when it is recognized that the term 'myth' has both a narrow and a broader sense. Theatre, Sartre maintains, is concerned with 'truth' rather than 'reality' (*TS*, 154), universal features of the human condition rather than individual idiosyncratic contingencies:

S'il doit s'adresser aux masses, le théâtre doit leur parler de leurs préoccupations les plus générales, exprimer leurs inquiétudes sous la forme de mythes que chacun puisse comprendre et ressentir profondément. (*TS*, 61)

He distinguishes between myths and symbols, dismissing the latter as a poetic and indirect means of communication in contrast to the former, which are concrete incarnations of, for example, death, exile or love (*TS*, 62). Myth is not for Sartre an abstraction or a fiction, it is another kind of *universel singulier*: in its very specificity it corresponds to a universally experienced phenomenon: 'C'est qu'en étant le plus individuel, on est le plus universel' (*TS*, 127). If the singular *per se* escapes the domain of philosophy and is best encompassed in the novel, the theatre has a different relation again to the universal–singular dialectic. It deals with the 'global' (*TS*, 327), with, for example, a character who is neither individual nor typical but mythical, that is to say 'un personnage qui [contient], d'une façon plus ou moins condensée, les problèmes qui se posent à nous à un moment donné' (*TS*, 328). Through myth in its broad sense, theatre may, paradoxically, deal most adequately with present-day problems. This helps explain Sartre's ambivalence towards myth in its narrow sense, for, as we have already suggested, certain old myths cannot be suitably adapted to contemporary issues (*TS*, 31). On the other hand, in the case of both *Les Mouches* and *Les Troyennes*, Sartre made positive *use* of the ability of myth to obfuscate as well as to reveal: the German censors in 1943 and the French bourgeoisie in 1965 were seduced into receiving unpalatable messages about the evils of war and occupation because of their respectable Greek disguise. Sartre's primary concern is of course with the problems dealt with, not the myth that conveys them: the birth of Christ (*Bariona*), Christian Hell (*Huis clos*), even the medieval tale of Goetz (*Le Diable et le Bon Dieu*) are vehicles rather than objects of interest in their own right. The conflict of contradictory rights which is the subject of tragic drama is always a contemporary conflict, whatever its theatrical embodiment – but the dilemmas of modern society are not identical with those of the ancient world: dramatists must forge new myths, not simply rework old ones.

Antigone, dans la tragédie de Sophocle, doit choisir entre la morale de la cité et la morale de la famille. Ce dilemme n'a plus guère de sens aujourd'hui. Mais nous avons nos problèmes: celui de la fin et des moyens, de la légitimité de la violence, celui des conséquences de l'action, celui des rapports de la personne avec la collectivité, de l'entreprise individuelle avec les constantes historiques, cent autres encore.   (*TS*, 20)

It is interesting that, although written in 1947, this text describes the subject matter not only of *Les Mouches* and *Les Mains sales* but also of *Le Diable et le Bon Dieu* and *Les Séquestrés d'Altona*.

Myth, then, embodies the tension between the universal and

the particular. But this tension is not limited to the *content* of drama. It is inherent in its aesthetic constitution: simultaneously ritual and event, always the same play yet differently enacted each evening,[17] 'répétition cérémonieuse' and 'drame fulgurant' (*TS*, 175). Sartre sees the two aspects as represented by Genet and Artaud who focus on opposed poles of the dramatic experience. Sartre's own first experience of theatrical creation was in the 'privileged' collectivity of the prisoner-of-war camp in 1940. The intensity of his audience's response alerted Sartre to the 'religious' aspect of all serious drama: 'grand phénomène collectif et religieux' (*TS*, 62). And the 'sacred' nature of theatre, even in its most apparently profane manifestations, transmutes not only dramatic action but also dramatic language, which is simultaneously familiar and unfamiliar, 'quotidien *et* qui réalise la distance' (*TS*, 32). The playwright, in Sartre's view, should use everyday language, but heightened and defamiliarized by an internal tension achieved through concision, ellipsis and interruption. In the theatre even more than in the novel, language can never be 'natural':[18] attempts at realism or naturalism, in style as in stage-décor, are counter-productive and futile because based on a misconception of the aesthetic experience. Language on stage is action rather than evocation or description, and as part of the fatal, predetermined stage-process it is necessarily irreversible. Indeed dramatic language, with its special status and heightened tone, appears 'magique, primitif et sacré' (*TS*, 34), with power both to liberate and to enslave (Oreste, Jupiter), to mystify and to demystify (Goetz and Frantz), to seduce and to command (the Senator, Hoederer). Sartre describes it in terms curiously close to a definition of what linguistic philosophers since Austin have called a *performative*:[19]

Au théâtre . . . le langage est un moment de l'action . . . il est fait unique-ment pour donner des ordres, défendre les choses, exposer sous la forme de plaidoiries les sentiments (donc, avec un but actif), pour convaincre ou pour défendre ou pour accuser, pour manifester des décisions, pour des duels de paroles, des refus, des aveux, etc., bref, toujours en acte.

(*TS*, 134)

This connection between dramatic performance and performative language is evidently more than a mere verbal coincidence. But whereas in Austin's account literature cannot fulfil the conditions for what he calls a 'felicitous' performative, Sartre suggests that the language of theatre is performative *par excellence*. Of course, the performative power of drama is necessarily restricted to the imaginary realm, as Kean realizes to his cost, and the mediation between the imaginary and *praxis* is, as we shall see,[20] exceedingly problematic. Unfortunately, Sartre does not pursue the implications of his comments, although speech-act theory — and its consequences for literature — has been rethought from a Continental perspective in recent years by philosophers such as Derrida and Lyotard.[21] But what is important for an understanding of Sartre's theory of drama is his opposition to the meaningless or phatic language of, say, Ionesco and Beckett. Unlike the dramatists of the Absurd who show language as hopelessly inadequate for communication and cast doubt on the very possibility of creating meaning, Sartre retains language with all its energy at the centre of his theatre.

The persistent dualities and paradoxes at the heart of Sartrean drama — fate/freedom, distancing/participation, myth/contemporary issues, *le sacré/le quotidien* — explain many of the misunderstandings that his theatre has encountered. One of the most persistent of these is that the plays, despite their radical philosophical 'content', are traditional and even bourgeois in their 'form'. Sartre's defence has been taken up on this score by critics such as F. Jeanson,[22] R. Lorris[23] and M. Issacharoff[24] who stress the self-critical, self-destructive and even deconstructive nature of the best of his plays. What at first sight may appear to be the themes, décor and dialogue of boulevard theatre are in fact a specious and disarming illusion. The apparently conventional Second-Empire stage-set of *Huis clos* — bronze ornament, coloured sofas — is no more than a mirage masking the highly *un*conventional location: Hell. A reading of *L'Idiot de la famille* reveals that Sartre considered the Second Empire to be not only stifling and reactionary, but also the realm of dreams and illusions *par excellence* in its refusal to recognize the brutal realities of the post-1848 repression on which it was built, and its own approaching demise in the further bloodshed of the Commune and the Franco-Prussian War.[25] Similarly, the banal 'salon' dialogue is quickly shown up as no more than a hopeless attempt to postpone the moment when the intolerable truth of the situation must be recognized. Finally the 'boulevard' subject-matter of adultery, murder and marital cruelty fades away before more persistent themes of mutual alienation and the inability to be free. It has been suggested that inauthentic characters make excellent anti-heroes,[26] and *Huis clos* certainly seems to prefigure Beckett in this respect as well as in its semi-cyclical form ('Eh bien, continuons') and its initially parodic dialogue.

A similar analysis could be applied in turn to the other plays with contemporary settings. Even in *Les Mains sales*, which is the closest Sartre came to a *pièce bien faite*, the love-interest (the only 'boulevard' element) is initially undermined by the banter of Hugo and Jessica themselves, and is finally destroyed when Hugo refuses the motive of jealousy for the murder of Hoederer in favour of that of political assassination. From the point of view of form, the flash-back technique is integral to the action, not simply an easy way of providing information or sustaining suspense: Hugo is not merely recollecting his past, he is determining its significance. *La Putain respectueuse*, as Lorris has pointed out, involves an alternation of farce and realism, fluctuating between *drame réaliste* and *bouffonnerie grinçante*[27] in a disconcerting juxtaposition of audience participation and alienation. Like *Les Mains sales*, *Le Diable et le Bon Dieu* contests the bourgeois values of idealist heroism and absolute ethics by revealing them as theatrical posturing. Dramatically, it is spectacle and medieval pageant, the first scene opening with a darkened stage and an illuminated palace situated 'entre ciel et terre'. A further mix of genres may be seen in the 'farce–satire' (*TS*, 293) *Nekrassov*, which thrusts us from the outset into the patently unreal world of poetic tramps, brilliant crooks, caricaturally inadequate detectives and journalists, and impersonations of Soviet defectors. Marc Bensimon discusses the work as anti-theatre, and sees it as playing on theatrical illusion and its destruction as the 'truth' recedes ever further from grasp.[28] Some of the dialogue between Georges and Véronique (Tableau III, Sc. iii) certainly reads suspiciously like a pastiche of *Huis clos*, Georges's proposed suicide like a parody of the ending of *Les Mains sales*. Finally, in *Les Séquestrés d'Altona*, set in a pretentious German equivalent of the Second-Empire *décor* of *Huis clos*, another examination of *victimes* and *bourreaux* is played out within a wealthy bourgeois family whose masks of respectability are torn off to reveal their underlying madness, illusion and unreality. Military heroism is destroyed and consumed in Frantz's edible chocolate medals; the Eucharist is taken in the form of champagne and cake; and the cycle of *Huis clos* becomes a spiral as the fifth act returns to the Salon, but this time in readiness for a dual suicide and a new sequestration.

The philosophical interest of Sartre's theatre and the close integration of 'form' and 'content' has perhaps distracted attention from its qualities of dramatic innovation, but these are in fact considerable. In this perspective, *Kean* provides an intriguing example of self-deconstructing drama in which the theatre contests reality only to contest itself in turn in the name of reality. As we have seen already, all art for Sartre operates in the domain of the unreal and imaginary, referring perpetually to an absence (*TS*, 86), providing no more than an image of an act. This is why an elaborate stage-set is unnecessary: since a stabbing, for example, is only ever a gesture, the physical presence of a dagger will not make it any more real: it is the 'act' of stabbing that produces the dagger for the audience, not vice versa (*TS*, 131). Indeed, the 'insufficiency' of theatre may be transformed into a means of communication, and this is exploited most thoroughly by dramatists of the Absurd such as Ionesco, Beckett and Genet (*TS*, 171). *Kean* plays on the interaction of real and imaginary, life and art, *être* and *paraître* to produce a *tourniquet* (whirligig) of mutual contestation which comes down ultimately on neither side. The 'real-life' marriage which is to take place between Anna and Kean is referred to as another *comédie*; and in Sartre's version (not Dumas's) Kean's last words: 'Ah, Monseigneur, le beau mot de théâtre. Ce sera si vous voulez bien le mot de la fin',[29] are performative and self-referential. Kean is of course an ideal subject for Sartre, as the individualist Romantic actor lends himself to presentation as a self-creating existential hero. But Sartre's Kean differs from Dumas's in that he is obsessed with the *unreality* he is offering to the public. He suffers from the imaginary nature of the feelings, actions and beliefs he portrays on stage, and is 'rongé par l'imaginaire'[30] to the point where he becomes not merely a *comédien* (i.e. a professional actor) but an *acteur* (who cannot distinguish reality from illusion either on or off stage). Sartre discusses Kean in theoretical terms in *L'Idiot de la famille* where he maintains that an actor is necessarily contaminated by the unreal in so far as he uses certain aspects of his own reality as an *analogon* of the imaginary persona he is to represent.[31]

Diderot a raison: l'acteur n'éprouve pas réellement les sentiments de son personnage; mais ce serait un tort de supposer qu'il les exprime de sang-froid: la vérité, c'est qu'il les éprouve *irréellement*. Entendons que ses affections réelles − le trac, par exemple: on ''joue sur son trac'' − lui servent d'*analogon*, il vise à travers elles les passions qu'il doit exprimer . . . Son Ego réel sert lui aussi d'*analogon* à l'être imaginaire qu'il incarne . . . C'est dire que le comédien se sacrifie pour qu'une *apparence* existe et qu'il se fait, par option, le soutien du non-être.   (*IF*, I, 662–4)

The actor's choice of profession, however 'realistic' or even 'committed' in political terms, implies a greater attachment to the unreal than that of other artists, for it is he himself who provides the material to be transformed: 'Son matériau, c'est sa personne, son but: être irréellement un autre' (*IF* I, 664). He is *himself* the analogon of an aesthetic object – or, in Sartre's later terminology, a 'centre permanent, réel et reconnu d'irréalisation . . . Il se mobilise et s'engage tout entier pour que sa personne réelle devienne l'*analogon* d'un imaginaire qui se nomme Titus, Harpagon ou Ruy Blas' (*IF* I, 786–7).

In showing Kean as unable to distinguish action from acting, reality from illusion, Sartre necessarily refers perpetually not only to the illusory nature of theatrical performance, but also to the kind of play-acting which tends to undermine even our most 'serious' intentions. Since we can never *be* what we are, and there is always a gap where our freedom detaches itself from our past, our lack of substantiality may well be experienced as an anguished awareness of perpetual play-acting.[32] Sincerity and belief can never be impermeable to doubt, for they involve an impossible adherence to an unreal self-identity. *Kean* not only makes its own theatrical illusion the centre of interest, it also reveals as insubstantial the apparent 'solidity' of real life. Nevertheless, this does not doom all men to confuse the real and the imaginary: on the contrary, it is only a misunderstanding of the nature of human reality that leads man to play-act when he strives vainly to identify with a 'self' or 'ego' that is no more than an imaginary synthesis.

Bien sûr, chacun joue à être ce qu'il est. Mais Kean, lui, joue à être ce qu'il n'est pas et ce qu'il sait ne pas pouvoir être. (*IF*, I, 664)

Il ne faut absolument pas en conclure que tout le monde joue la comédie. (*Kean*, 285–6)

Like 'l'enfer c'est les autres' of *Huis clos*, 'jouer la comédie' is a measure of inauthenticity, not an ontological necessity. Kean both uses and reveals the dangers of 'envoûtement par l'imaginaire'.

Kean, Huis clos and *Les Séquestrés d'Altona* illustrate clearly what Jeanson has called Sartre's *treachery* as a playwright:

Et peut-être voit-on maintenant en quel sens le théâtre de Sartre peut tout entier être considéré comme *un théâtre de la bâtardise*. Car il trahit le Spectateur en le faisant adhérer à la dénonciation de sa propre imposture, il trahit la Société en la représentant à elle-même comme société déchirée, et pour finir il trahit le Théâtre lui-même en le contraignant à se mordre la queue.[33]

Sartre's radical conception of the work of art as created by the 'consumer' as much as by the 'producer' means that the audience will be in their turn drawn into the treacherous activity: 'Tout l'art de l'auteur est pour m'obliger à *créer* ce qu'il *dévoile*, donc à me compromettre' (*Sit II*, 110). Conversely, since the work exists through the reader or spectator it can have no deeper meaning than that which she gives it: 'l'œuvre n'existe qu'au niveau de ses capacités' (*Sit II*, 96). The problem for a subversive playwright is of course that if his 'treachery' is too evident – as was the case with *Nekrassov* – the audience may simply reject it outright; but if it is too oblique or generalized (*Huis clos*, perhaps), it may be recuperated or even ignored. And the bourgeoisie, as purveyors and recipients of the dominant (hence naturalized and transparent) ideology have, of course, immense powers of recuperation. Genet, for example, whose novels and plays celebrate 'evil' and perversion, has been fêted by his readers, who have been known to tell him that it would be an honour to have their houses burgled by him! And the outcry which greeted the aggression of Jarry's *Ubu Roi* and much Surrealist art has been transformed into complicity and approval. Nonetheless, audiences are necessarily affected by what they applaud: 'scandal' and 'heresy', even when the objects of conventional aesthetic appreciation, cannot leave the spectator with quite the same clear conscience she once had. And in the case of Sartre's more subtly provocative drama, the comment he once made on seventeenth-century literature might well apply: 'Le miroir qu'il présente modestement à ses lecteurs est magique: il captive et compromet . . . les conduites spontanées en passant à l'état réflexif, perdent leur innocence et l'excuse de l'immédiateté: il faut les assumer ou les changer' (*Sit II*, 141–2). Sartre's drama seduces its audience by an initial *appearance* of realism, but 'reality' is revealed as contaminated by illusion, and gradually or dramatically denounced as a mere web of deceit: 'Le spectateur se trouve en face de gens pris en flagrant délit de mensonges; il les découvre quêtant une réalité qui leur cache l'illusion qu'ils entretiennent'.[34] The 'lies', of course, are the stuff of their everyday lives and conversations. As we shall see,[35] this interpretation of Sartre's drama as seduction and treachery is very similar to that which he gives of Flaubert's writings in *L'Idiot de la famille*: the apparent 'realism' of *Madame Bovary* masks the true nature of Flaubert's nihilism from the bourgeois public, and Sartre describes him as playing a radically subversive role in so far as he lures his readers from the security of the real into the dangerous realm of imagination and illusion.

This essential ambiguity of Sartre's drama – committed theatre, aimed at a bourgeois audience, what Sartre himself has called 'du réalisme critique' (*TS*, 317) – may help explain his lack of popularity from the 1950s to the mid 1960s. The decade was one of polarization between the radical formal experimentation of the theatre of the Absurd on the one hand (with what Sartre considered its persistently bourgeois themes of meaninglessness and the failure of communication), and on the other the uncompromising political theatre of Brecht and his followers. Rejected by the proponents of the Absurd as too political and concerned with text rather than production, and by Brechtians as insufficiently 'distanced' and 'epic', Sartre lost his popularity as a playwright; and after the failure of *Nekrassov* in 1955 he wrote only *Les Séquestrés d'Altona* and his translation of Euripides's *Les Troyennes*. May 1968, with its dual concern for political commitment and imaginative liberation (encapsulated in the students' slogan 'l'imagination au pouvoir', 'power to the imagination') brought a brief resurgence of popularity to Sartre's theatre, marked by a revival of *Le Diable et le Bon Dieu* by the T.N.P. in September of that year, but it was too late to entice him back to his dramatic career. In tune with the mood of the 1960s, Sartre felt that the moment was no longer right for individual theatrical creation, and that he was himself too old to adapt to the demands of a collective production.[36] Moreover he had by then abandoned fiction entirely in favour of political activism and his theoretical and methodological *summa*: the study of Gustave Flaubert.

But these practical and personal considerations are in a sense contingent. There are more fundamental internal reasons for Sartre's abandonment of the theatrical medium. His plays themselves show a clear evolution away from the drama of the individual and his or her existential dilemmas (considered by the increasingly politicized Sartre as a bourgeois perspective) towards an equation of History with Fate, in which drama is replaced by necessity, free choice by inevitability, praxis by the practico-inert.[37] Sartre's disaffection with his early hero Oreste should be understood firstly in the light of changing political circumstances – what seemed a heroic liberation from Occupation in 1943 may appear an impractical gesture of unpredictable consequences in the more sober post-war period[38] – but more importantly in the light of Sartre's philosophical evolution. In 1943 Sartre described Oreste as originally *libre en conscience* and becoming, by his act, *libre en situation*. And in 1947, in a preface to a collected volume of his early plays, he wrote:

Dans n'importe quelle circonstance, dans n'importe quel temps et dans n'importe quel lieu, l'homme est libre de se choisir traître ou héros, lâche ou vainqueur . . . En face des dieux, en face de la mort ou des tyrans, une même certitude, triomphante ou angoissée, nous reste: celle de notre liberté.   (*TS*, 244–5)

Twenty years later Sartre reread his preface and dismissed his early optimism in horrified amazement: 'J'ai été proprement scandalisé . . . Quand j'ai lu cela, je me suis dit: "C'est incroyable, je le pensais vraiment!" ' (*Sit IX*, 100). In the next chapter we will examine the evolution of Sartre's thought with respect to the nature of human freedom; for the moment we will simply observe its consequences in the action of his plays which tend, of necessity, to 'dramatize' and intensify his position of the moment, and to make the gap between his early and later thinking appear almost insuperable.

Les Mains sales (1948) already stresses Hugo's conditioning rather than his freedom *from* constraint. The play confronts moral idealism with ethical pragmatism and the result is stalemate. In 1948 Sartre claimed not to be partisan: 'Je ne prends pas parti . . . Aucun de mes personnages n'a tort ni raison' (*TS*, 247–8). Public sympathy for Hugo belied Sartre's intentions, and later he explicitly repudiated the play's reception, interpreting the work as expressing an anti-idealist preference for situational ethics (*TS*, 263), and maintaining: 'C'est l'attitude de Hoederer qui seule me paraît saine' (*TS*, 249).[39]

Le Diable et le Bon Dieu (1951) presents in Goetz what Sartre has described as 'un Hugo qui se convertit . . . Rompant avec la morale des absolus, il découvre une morale historique, humaine et particulière' (*TS*, 270, 269). The play is more explicitly anti-religious than *Les Mouches*, for 'God' – or absolute Good – is revealed as radically opposed to the human, and as destructive as absolute evil: 'L'homme n'est qu'une pauvre chose lorsqu'on croit en Dieu . . . Dieu détruit l'homme aussi sûrement que le Diable' (*TS*, 269). Heinrich, Sartre maintained, was created specifically to show that in certain situations no authentic choice is possible: whether he chooses fidelity to the Church or to the poor, Heinrich cannot escape the role of traitor:

Nos pères [and Sartre should perhaps include himself at the time of *Les Mouches*] croyaient volontiers qu'on pouvait rester pur quelles que soient les circonstances. Nous savons aujourd'hui qu'il est des situations qui pourrissent jusqu'au plus intime de l'individu . . . Heinrich . . . est lui-même conflit. Et le problème, pour lui, est absolument sans solution, car il est mystifié jusqu'à la moelle. Alors dans cette horreur de lui-même, il se choisit méchant. Il peut y avoir des situations désespérées.   (*TS*, 271)

Le Diable et le Bon Dieu may be a far cry from the optimism of *Les Mouches* but, despite its emphasis on socio-historical conditioning, and its final (Marxist?) embrace of a war doomed to inevitable defeat,[40] it remains a play primarily concerned with individual destiny. The same may be said of *Nekrassov*, described by Jeanson as a hinge-play between the period of epic idealism and that of a conversion to History.[41] The strength and individuality of the major protagonist divert the play's significance from a satire of institutions to a kind of tragi-comedy which Sartre came to consider as 'une pièce à demi manquée' (*TS*, 297).

Les Séquestrés d'Altona completes Sartre's 'conversion'. It is his most pessimistic creation whose sole glimmer of hope lies in the ambiguous message of *qui perd gagne*: suicide is seen as the only possible solution in an intolerable situation: 'La torture représente l'acte radical qui ne peut être abolie que par le suicide de celui qui l'a commis.'[42] For the first time Sartre has deliberately refused to suggest any way out of personal and historical contradictions: for this reason the play leaves its audience far more uneasy than, say, *Le Diable et le Bon Dieu*: 'Si un héros à la fin se réconcilie avec lui-même, le public qui le regarde faire – dans la pièce – risque aussi de se réconcilier avec ses interrogations, avec les questions non résolues' (*TS*, 317). As we shall see, the later Sartre is no determinist, but his conception of the significance of conditioning has changed considerably. He describes Frantz's crime of torture as 'presque inévitable' (*TS*, 347): 'Il devait presque nécessairement faire ce qu'il a fait finalement' (*TS*, 347). But it is the remaining margin of liberty that is ultimately the most terrible burden, for it carries with it a concomitant responsibility: 'Son acte est d'autant plus condamnable: on peut lui trouver des explications, pas une seule excuse' (*TS*, 357). Furthermore, Frantz's situation is made intolerable not only by his crime but also by his family and its position in the capitalist world: he has been raised to be leader of an industry which has outgrown its owners (*TS*, 351). *Les Séquestrés d'Altona* is a dramatic embodiment of Sartre's attempt to synthesize the discoveries of Marx and Freud, which he will explore further in a theoretical mode in his later study of Flaubert. Family and history conspire to reduce Frantz to impotence – he is victim and prisoner of both subjective and objective contradictions (*TS*, 308). Indeed, the play shows all its protagonists subject to varying degrees of alienation: no one achieves what he or she intends. The themes of Sartre's early theatre – bad faith, conformism, loss of identity, responsibility, torture – all gain a new significance in the light of such strong historical and psychological conditioning. The play is, in a sense, a negative response to *Les Mouches*: a play of remorse, of the end of life, of a crime that cannot be claimed as one's own, of a 'commitment' enforced rather than chosen. 'Je n'ai voulu montrer que le négatif,' Sartre explained, 'Ces gens-là ne peuvent pas se renouveler. C'est la déconfiture, le crépuscule des dieux' (*TS*, 318).

As twilight of the idols, it also constitutes a pessimistic commentary on the Prometheanism of Sartre's Resistance drama where Jupiter proclaimed 'Tout ceci était prévu. Un homme devait venir annoncer mon crépuscule' (*Mouches*, 283); but the gods in question in *Les Séquestrés d'Altona* are human rather than mythological. It is the twilight of existential man himself that Sartre's later play seems to be announcing. And when he returns for the last time to myth in *Les Troyennes* the bankruptcy of a certain civilization seems complete: the tragedy is static, there is no room for freedom, religion is not merely impotent but evil. It is in this sense at the antipodes of Sartre's first incursion into religious myth with *Bariona*: in the Christmas play a God is born and with him human hope; in the later apocalyptic adaptation, gods and men are shown in the throes of total disintegration:

La pièce s'achève donc dans le nihilisme total . . . Le désespoir final d'Hécube, sur lequel j'ai mis l'accent, répond au mot terrible de Poséidon. Les Dieux crèveront avec les hommes, et cette mort commune est la leçon de la tragédie.

(*TS*, 366)

Nonetheless, *Les Troyennes*, like *Les Séquestrés d'Altona*, is perhaps less irremediably hopeless than Sartre suggests: once again the theme of *qui perd gagne* (and its grimmer correlative *qui gagne perd*) transforms even the worst defeat into a kind of human victory: the vanquished Trojans retain their dignity to the end. Hecuba's last words: 'Nous n'irons pas de notre plein gré vers l'exil et l'esclavage'[43] have the ring of defiance as much as of despair. After the death of man, there can be no further possibility of drama, but that death itself is dramatic, and Sartre's last plays show man in the throes of disaster and despair refusing to abdicate either his identity or his drive to create meaning in the face of chaos.

FRANTZ: Peut-être n'y aura-t-il plus de siècles après le nôtre. Peut-être qu'une bombe aura soufflé les lumières. Tout sera mort: les yeux, les juges, le temps − Nuit. O tribunal de la nuit, toi qui fus, qui seras, qui es, j'ai été. Moi, Frantz von Gerlach, ici, dans cette chambre, j'ai pris le siècle sur mes épaules et j'ai dit: j'en répondrai. En ce jour et pour toujours. Hein quoi?[44]

5

The later philosophy: Marxism and the truth of history

Il ne faut pas confondre le papillotement des idées avec la dialectique.

(*CRD*, 40)[1]

La vérité reste toujours à trouver, parce qu'elle est infinie . . . la vérité entière . . . est atteignable – encore que personne ne soit capable, aujourd'hui, de l'atteindre.

(*Sit X*, 148–9)

Dire la Vérité. C'est le rêve de tout écrivain vieillissant.

(*Sit IX*, 11)

Aussitôt qu'il existera *pour tous* une marge de liberté *réelle* au-delà de la production de la vie, le marxisme aura vécu; une philosophie de la liberté prendra sa place.

(*CRD*, 32)

A partir du jour où la recherche marxiste prendra la dimension humaine (c'est-à-dire le projet existentiel) comme le fondement du Savoir anthropologique, l'existentialisme n'aura plus de raison d'être. (*CRD*, 111)

Par ambiguïté, il ne faut pas entendre . . . je ne sais quelle équivoque déraison mais simplement une contradiction qui n'est pas parvenue à son point de maturité.

(*CRD*, 81)

L'autre jour j'ai relu la préface que j'avais écrite pour une édition de ces pièces – *Les Mouches*, *Huis clos* et d'autres – et j'ai été proprement scandalisé. J'avais écrit ceci: "Quelles que soient les circonstances, en quelque lieu que ce soit, un homme est toujours libre de choisir s'il sera un traître ou non." Quand j'ai lu cela, je me suis dit: "C'est incroyable; je le pensais vraiment!" . . . [J'avais] conclu que, dans toute circonstance, il y avait toujours un choix possible. C'était faux.

(*Sit IX*, 100)

Sartre's eagerness to dismiss his early philosophy of freedom as *incroyable* and *fausse* should not mislead us. It is clear from the introductory quotations to this chapter, taken in the main from *Questions de méthode*, that Sartre is capable of holding two apparently contradictory opinions simultaneously, and that there is no need to posit a volte-face over time to explain such divergences. What appears to common-sense, analytic, binary reason as paradox, self-contradiction or aporia may be recognized as the heterogeneity of different levels of truth and meaning (*CRD*, 92),

94

potentially susceptible to totalization in the light of dialectical reason (*CRD*, 74). What is less certain is whether the potential totalization could ever, in reality, be actualized. But that question must wait, at least, until the end of the present chapter. In the meantime we shall start by examining the nature and status of freedom for the later Sartre.

Already in *L'Etre et le Néant* it was clear that liberty was not a matter of an unrestricted ability to do, be or have anything that took my fancy. 'La formule "être libre" ne signifie pas "obtenir ce qu'on a voulu" ' (*EN*, 563). Other people and the world itself – or what Sartre (following Bachelard) liked to call 'le coéfficient d'adversité des choses'[2] – were always there to intervene. I was free within my situation and starting from the basis of my facticity:

Je ne suis "libre" ni d'échapper au sort de ma classe, de ma nation, de ma famille, ni même d'édifier ma puissance ou ma fortune, ni de vaincre mes appétits les plus insignifiants ou mes habitudes. (*EN*, 561)

Indeed, even my own freely chosen project constituted a *limite de fait*, if not *de droit,* to my behaviour: 'J'aurais pu faire autrement, soit, mais *à quel prix*?' (*EN*, 531). I was, moreover, condemned to be free: in other words *not* free to slough off my freedom and its concomitant responsibility. In one perspective, then, the stress on the alienation of freedom in the *Critique de la raison dialectique* may be seen as resulting from an increased awareness of the inevitable limitations imposed by situation and facticity. But the evolution in Sartre's thinking is in fact more significant than a simple change of emphasis. In the first place he no longer appears entirely happy to identify freedom and free choice. In *L'Etre et le Néant* the two were frequently assimilated: 'Pour la réalité humaine, être, c'est se choisir' (*EN*, 516). In the *Critique* freedom is a matter of *praxis*[3] rather than of choice:

Liberté, ici, ne veut pas dire possibilité d'option mais nécessité de vivre la contrainte sous forme d'exigence à remplir par une *praxis*. (*CRD*, 365)

Moreover, the dual nature of freedom in the early philosophy, according to which man was free (ontologically) through his consciousness and imagination and yet had to strive to free himself from the temptations of essentialism, bad faith, and the inert image imposed on him by other people, has further polarized by the time of the *Critique*. Man remains free on an ontological level – he still is what he is not and is not what he is – but his need (and duty) to free himself has been extended in its implications to become a historico-political mission linked to the overthrow of capitalism and the liberation of the working class. Marx has radically affected Sartre's understanding of man and the world. And so, to a lesser, and less acknowledged, extent, has Freud. We shall see later Sartre's rejection of what he considers to be the mechanistic, deterministic nature of Freudian psychology,[4] but the stress on childhood conditioning has nonetheless infiltrated his conception of freedom, to the point where in the *Critique* he can write of Flaubert that 'tout s'est passé *dans l'enfance* . . . c'est l'enfance qui façonne des préjugés indépassables' (*CRD*, 46). Indeed, one of the major preoccupations of the later Sartre, theorized in the *Critique*, explored in both theoretical and practical terms in *L'Idiot de la famille*, is precisely that of the *mediations* between society and family, macro- and microcosm, Marxist and Freudian conditioning.

D'une certaine façon nous naissons tous prédestinés. Nous sommes voués à un certain type d'action dès l'origine par la situation où se trouvent la famille et la société à un moment donné. Il est certain, par exemple, qu'un jeune Algérien né en 1935 est voué à faire la guerre. Dans certains cas, l'histoire condamne d'avance. La prédestination, c'est ce qui remplace chez moi le déterminisme: je considère que nous ne sommes pas libres – tout au moins provisoirement, aujourd'hui – puisque nous sommes aliénés. On se perd toujours dans l'enfance: les méthodes d'éducation, le rapport parents–enfant, l'enseignement, etc. – tout cela donne un moi, mais un moi perdu . . . Cela ne veut pas dire que cette prédestination ne comporte aucun choix, mais on sait qu'en choisissant on ne réalisera pas ce qu'on a choisi: c'est ce que j'appelle la nécessité de la liberté.

(*Sit IX*, 98–9)

Sartre's choice of the religious term *prédestination* is intriguing and not to be dismissed as a mere *boutade*. Predestination differs from determinism in two fundamental ways: in the first place it is teleological rather than causal, that is to say it is oriented towards the future rather than dependent on the past, a closer relative of the project than of heredity. And secondly, in so far as it has been seriously defended theologically, predestination has always been presented as an inevitable orientation for which we are nonetheless responsible. For a philosopher who, as early as 1947, could write: 'On ne fait pas ce qu'on veut et cependant on est responsable de ce qu'on est: voilà le fait' (*Sit II*, 26–7), this tragic and paradoxical Jansenist view of human destiny held an evident appeal. Sartre's sympathies are from the outset with Pascal rather than Pavlov.[5]

Sartre, then, does not really renege on his early philosophy of freedom, but rather reinterprets it and redefines it within a Marxist framework. Indeed it is clear from *L'Idiot de la famille* that certain of the theses of *L'Imaginaire* and *La Transcendance de l'Ego* have been reaffirmed rather than revised: the self remains, for example, an imaginary construct not an originary source.[6] But in other cases the shift has been radical, and it is clear that the later vocabulary has implications far beyond the window-dressing of simple reformulation. In an interview with the *New Left Review* in 1969, what sounds at first like a repetition of the definition of liberty from *Qu'est-ce que la littérature?* shifts in mid-sentence to a very different and somewhat paradoxical neo-Marxist perspective:

L'idée que je n'ai jamais cessé de développer, c'est que, en fin de compte, chacun est toujours responsable de ce qu'on a fait de lui − même s'il ne peut rien faire de plus que d'assumer cette responsabilité. Je crois qu'un homme peut toujours faire quelque chose de ce qu'on a fait de lui. C'est la définition que je donnerais aujourd'hui de la liberté, ce petit mouvement qui fait d'un être social totalement conditionné une personne qui ne restitue pas la totalité de ce qu'elle a reçu de son conditionnement. (*Sit IX*, 101–2)

And in the same interview Sartre redefines *subjectivity* in terms that bear little resemblance to his earlier analyses:

Ainsi, dans *L'Etre et le Néant*, ce que vous pourriez appeler la "subjectivité" n'est pas ce qu'elle serait aujourd'hui pour moi: le petit décalage dans une opération par laquelle une intériorisation se réextériorise elle-même en acte. Aujourd'hui de toute manière, les notions de "subjectivité" et d' "objectivité" me paraissent totalement inutiles. Il peut sans doute m'arriver d'utiliser le terme "objectivité", mais seulement pour souligner que tout est objectif. L'individu intériorise ses déterminations sociales: il intériorise les rapports de production, la famille de son enfance, le passé historique, les institutions contemporaines, puis il re-extériorise tout cela dans des actes et des choix qui nous renvoient nécessairement à tout ce qui a été intériorisé. Il n'y avait rien de tout cela dans *L'Etre et le Néant*. (*Sit IX*, 102–3)[7]

Sartre, then, became a convert to Marxism; but a convert whose initial enthusiasm quickly gave way to a critical and constructive attempt to revitalize what he believed to have become static and *sclérosé* (hidebound), and whose final position involved a disillusioned rejection of historical materialism in favour of a Maoist theory of spontaneity. It is at this politico-philosophical evolution that we must look next.

It is clear from Sartre's pre-war philosophy and fiction, from his letters to Simone de Beauvoir[8] and from her autobiography,[9] and from his own admission, that Sartre was fundamentally a-political before 1939. His increasing involvement in politics from then on is well known, culminating in his abandonment of literature in the 1960s and the polarization of his interests between the mammoth and abstruse summa of his work on Flaubert and an involvement in direct political action. This is not the place to discuss his *ad hoc* political choices, though we might bear in mind the transformation hindsight can effect on even the most courageous of stances. Sartre was not of course immune from errors of judgement, but in many cases he was simply restricted by the limited evidence of the contemporary moment; the course of history (retrospectively so clear and apparently predictable) had not yet declared itself. We shall concentrate rather on the theoretical and philosophical implications of his political writings, with particular reference to his relations with Marxism.

The war evidently instilled in Sartre an increased awareness of the pressure of history on individual lives and of the inevitability and necessity of political commitment. His involvement with the Resistance was followed by a brief participation in the newly founded R.D.R – Rassemblement Démocratique Révolutionnaire – an abortive attempt to establish a non-Communist left-wing alliance in the immediate post-war years. Sartre's discussions with David Rousset and Gérard Rosenthal, collected in *Entretiens sur la politique* (1949), which provide a record of his views at the time, demonstrate an idealistic faith in democracy and what now appears as a naïve conception of the possibility of founding a 'third force' which could remain neutral with respect to both the United States and the Soviet Union. His essay *Matérialisme et révolution*[10] of the same period is perhaps more revealing of his developing relationship with Marxism: it represents an attack on dialectical materialism and an attempt to present his own philosophy as a more human alternative to Marxism, embodying a revolutionary outlook which recognizes the creative transformative potential of free human action. But the essay is abstract and shows a relatively poor grasp of historical analysis, and a somewhat meagre knowledge of Marx, the rejection of whom is significantly modified in the 1949 version published in *Situations III*, where additional footnotes both demonstrate further reading and also distinguish the views of Marx himself from 'le néo-Marxisme stalinien' which Sartre now claims to be attacking.[11] The distinction between Marx and Marxists is one which Sartre continued to develop throughout his writings.

Les Communistes et la Paix (1952)[12] constitutes Sartre's heated response to the worst manifestations of anti-Soviet feeling in France at the height of the Cold War. It probably shows Sartre at his most pro-Communist, his most 'realistic' in the crude political sense of accepting as inevitable the means employed towards some future utopian end, and his most fatalistic. He appears to effect an identification of the French Communist Party and the interests of the working class which leaves no room for criticism of the former. His initial attack on the anti-Communist faction is of a transparent speciousness, and embodied in a rhetorical question the answer to which is only too evident:

Comment pouvez-vous croire *à la fois* à la mission historique du Prolétariat et à la trahison du Parti communiste si vous constatez que l'un vote pour l'autre? *(Sit VI, 81)*

Rhetoric seems to have replaced logic. The Communist Party is presented, quite literally, as the necessary embodiment of the Proletariat. The 'facts' of history are held to account to reveal 'dans quelle mesure le P.C. est l'expression *nécessaire* de la classe ouvrière et dans quelle mesure il en est l'expression exacte' *(Sit VI, 88)*. The Party is thus rendered incapable of transgression, for its apparent defects and errors become an inevitable consequence of the historical moment. Sartre issues a generalized and disquieting absolution: 'Ce vice incurable que vous reprochez au P.C. je me demande si ça n'est pas tout simplement la nature singulière du prolétariat' *(Sit VI, 87)*.

Sartre's opposition to the Cold War is admirable, and his insistence on the Soviet desire for peace comprehensible in the circumstances, but the identification of Marxism, the working classes, the French Communist Party and the U.S.S.R. is nonetheless unconvincing and contrives to ignore antagonisms of interest which were apparent even at the time. The essay was welcomed by the P.C.F. and attacked vigorously by many others, the best known of whom were Claude Lefort, to whose criticisms Sartre was to reply in *Les Temps modernes* (1953),[13] and Merleau-Ponty, whose devastating politico-philosophical dismantling of Sartre's argument (in *Les Aventures de la dialectique*)[14] inspired Simone de Beauvoir to retaliate by accusing Merleau-Ponty of misunderstanding Sartre's position and opposing what was merely a 'pseudo-Sartrisme'.[15] Sartre himself was later to belittle his own 'fellow-travelling' phase and to play down its importance in his evolution:

1952 n'a pas été très important. Je suis resté pendant quatre ans très proche des communistes, mais mes idées n'étaient pas les leurs, ils le savaient . . .

j'avais à peu près mes idées, je ne les ai pas abandonnées pendant que je faisais du voisinage avec les communistes; et je les ai retrouvées et développées dans la *Critique de la raison dialectique*.   (*Sit X*, 181)

In any case Sartre's honeymoon with Communism was brought to an abrupt end in 1956 with the Soviet suppression of the Hungarian uprising, and in *Le Fantôme de Staline*[16] (1956) he gives a brilliant analysis of both the contemporary political situation and its historical roots and significance. The essay acknowledges the threat Hungary posed to the authoritarian socialism of the U.S.S.R., at the same time as supporting her attempt to establish a socialist democracy, and lays the blame for the split between Hungary and the Soviets squarely at the door of the latter. Previous policy with respect to Hungary had sown the seeds for a schism: 'La surindustrialisation et la collectivisation accélérée étaient déjà criminelles' (*Sit VII*, 158). Sartre now rejects both an easy acceptance of violence and its concomitant fatalism: the Soviet intervention was *not* inevitable: 'Non, les conséquences du stalinisme n'étaient pas *fatales*: il fallait déstaliniser à temps . . . En politique, aucune action n'est inconditionnellement nécessaire' (*Sit VII*, 162, 167). Furthermore, Sartre refuses to accept that the argument from historical necessity is truly Marxist: 'On le dit marxiste; je le crois plus ancien que Marx; il se résume ainsi: "Faut ce qu'il faut" ' (*Sit VII*, 155). Nonetheless, Sartre's analysis of events makes it difficult to see just where the course of history might have been different; his argument shows with great clarity the inexorable pressures which led the U.S.S.R. to invade whilst still condemning that invasion as avoidable. It might perhaps be argued that Sartre has at last brought to his practical politics some of the paradoxical and dialectical mode of thinking previously reserved for his philosophy: 'On ne fait pas ce qu'on veut, et cependant on est responsable de ce qu'on est' (*Sit II*, 26–7).

It is in *Questions de méthode* that this mode of analysis is brought to fruition, for in it Sartre attempts a fully conscious transcendence of the antinomies of freedom and conditioning, subjectivity and history, praxis and process. Present-day Marxism is attacked as having lost touch with the complexity and subtlety of Marx's own position: 'Le marxisme s'est arrêté . . . le marxisme vivant est euristique' (*CRD*, 25, 27). But this is not to say that Marxism is dead or dying:

Cette sclérose ne correspond pas à un vieillissement normal. Elle est produite par une conjoncture mondiale d'un type particulier; loin d'être épuisé, le Marxisme est tout jeune encore, presque en enfance: c'est à peine s'il a commencé de se développer. Il reste donc la philosophie de notre temps: il est indépassable parce que les circonstances qui l'ont engendré ne sont pas encore dépassées. (*CRD*, 29)

Contemporary Marxism is lazy (*CRD*, 43), it refuses to analyse the specificity of individual events or people, and operates a reductive, mechanistic form of explanation which is satisfied when broad infra-structural economic principles have been laid bare: its concern is purely for the general, and the particular is dismissed as irrelevant. Sartre's aim is to restore to Marxist analysis an interest in the specific:

L'existentialisme considère cette [abstraction] comme une limitation arbitraire du mouvement dialectique, comme un arrêt de pensée, comme un refus de comprendre. Il refuse d'abandonner la vie réelle aux hasards impensables de la naissance pour contempler une universalité qui se borne à se refléter indéfiniment en elle-même. Il entend sans être infidèle aux thèses marxistes, trouver les médiations, qui permettent d'engendrer le concret singulier, la vie, la lutte réelle et datée, la personne à partir des contradictions *générales* des forces productives et des rapports de production . . . Valéry est un intellectuel petit-bourgeois, cela ne fait pas de doute. Mais tout intellectuel petit-bourgeois n'est pas Valéry. (*CRD*, 44–5, 44)

By 1968 Sartre had become disillusioned with Marxism in so far as it remained unwilling to accept his attempts either to ground its intelligibility or to acknowledge specificity within history. In *On a raison de se révolter* (1974),[17] we see Sartre turn to the Maoists in the hope that they will incorporate a conception of human freedom into a mode of political thinking and *praxis* which is not founded on determinism.[18] He nonetheless continues to maintain that there is, in Marx's writings themselves, especially those of the young Marx and the later *German Ideology*, a conception of freedom and subjectivity which twentieth-century theorists have contrived to ignore.[19] We shall look now, therefore, at the attempt to revivify Marxism represented by *Questions de méthode* and the *Critique de la raison dialectique*, and examine the interaction of Marxist theses of conditioning with the existential stress on liberty and subjectivity.

In a sense, the primary aim of the *Critique* is to demonstrate that men both *make* and are *made* by history. Sartre subscribes to the famous phrase of Engels: 'Les hommes font leur histoire eux-mêmes mais dans un milieu donné qui les conditionne' (*CRD*, 60). He accuses what he terms 'idealist' Marxism of neglecting the first half of the formula in favour of a facile determinism, and insists that man is simultaneously 'le produit de son propre produit' *and* 'un agent historique' (*CRD*, 61); both 'totalement conditionné' *and* able to 'réassumer ce conditionnement et en devenir responsable' (*Sit IX*, 101). Human alienation and lack of individual control over history arise not because man is *not* making history but because he is not making it alone: 'Si l'Histoire m'échappe cela ne vient pas de ce que je ne la fais pas: cela vient de ce que l'autre la fait aussi' (*CRD*, 61). We are still close here to the kind of alienation already recognized in *L'Etre et le Néant*. Sartre continues to maintain the primacy of the *project*, the specificity of human action, and man's ability to change the world.

Seul, le projet comme médiation entre deux moments de l'objectivité peut rendre compte de l'histoire, c'est-à-dire de la créativité humaine.

(*CRD*, 67–8)

Pour nous, l'homme se caractérise avant tout par le dépassement d'une situation, par ce qu'il parvient à faire de ce qu'on a fait de lui, même s'il ne se reconnaît jamais dans son objectivation. (*CRD*, 63)

If man can *never* recognize himself fully in his actions and products (his objectification), this is because of the very nature of externalization: a subject can never identify with an object even if it is entirely of his own making: this is part of the radical split between consciousness and world, nothingness and being. 'Chacun de nous passe sa vie à graver sur les choses son image maléfique qui le fascine et l'égare s'il veut se comprendre *par elle*' (*CRD*, 285). Sartre takes over Marx's distinction between simple objectification and alienation proper. For Hegel, an Idealist, the two were one and the same: 'Hegel . . . fait de l'aliénation un caractère constant de l'objectivation quelle qu'elle soit' (*CRD*, 285);[20] for Marx the former is an inevitable aspect of being-in-the-world, the latter a contingent consequence of political oppression and exploitation:

L'homme qui regarde son œuvre, qui s'y reconnaît tout entier, qui, dans le même temps, ne s'y reconnaît pas du tout . . . c'est celui-ci qui saisit . . . la nécessité comme *destin en extériorité de la liberté*. Dirons-nous qu'il s'agit d'une aliénation? Certainement, puisqu'*il revient à soi comme Autre*. Toutefois il faut distinguer: l'aliénation au sens marxiste du terme commence avec l'exploitation. (*CRD*, 285)

Nonetheless, Sartre will at times use the term alienation to cover both the results of exploitation and simple objectification; and it is as a form of alienation that he describes the inevitable transformation of *praxis* into *pratico-inerte*, of free human activity into dead structures which constitute in their objectivity further constraints and limitations:

L'activité de l'homme . . . est reflétée par le pratico-inerte, activité de l'homme retournée . . . c'est-à-dire les activités humaines en tant qu'elles sont médiées par un matériau rigoureusement objectif qui les renvoie à l'objectivité.   (*Sit IX*, 85)

La *praxis*, en effet, est un passage de l'objectif à l'objectif par l'intériorisation.   (*CRD*, 66)

Il n'est pas douteux que l'homme . . . se découvre comme *Autre* dans le monde de l'objectivité; la matière totalisée, comme objectivation inerte et qui se perpétue par inertie, est en effet un *non-homme* et même, si l'on veut, un *contre-homme*.   (*CRD*, 285)

All of man's products both reflect and distort his image in so far as they are external to him; this is as true of art as it is of economics or politics. And the interpretations and intentions of others necessarily constitute a further alienation of individual praxis. Sartre's determination to maintain constantly both terms of the liberty/alienation, praxis/practico-inert, subject/object polarities led to his being attacked from both sides as either excessively individualistic[21] or as having reneged on his earlier philosophy of freedom. To the former criticism one might reply that Sartre is well aware of the dangers of falling into bourgeois individualism, of 'le caractère suspect de robinsonnade' (*CRD*, 642) conjured up by the image of free isolated praxis. '*Il n'y a pas* d'individu isolé' (*CRD*, 642), he maintains, and we shall return to this notion later. In answer to the latter criticism one might cite *L'Etre et le Néant* with its stress on situation, facticity and *l'être pour autrui*, as well as the corresponding insistence on human freedom throughout the *Critique* where dialectical reason itself is defined as 'aventure de tous' and 'liberté de chacun': 'elle n'est que nous-mêmes' (*CRD*, 134).

The dialectical mode of thinking and presentation at times makes it difficult to determine the exact status of certain of Sartre's analyses. For example his discussion of scarcity – *la rareté* – has been variously interpreted. Scarcity is the fact of there being 'pas assez pour tout le monde' (*CRD*, 204): not enough food, money, jobs, time, or simply seats on the bus. It thus appears as a material rather than an ontological source of human conflict. Each man necessarily views every other as, ultimately, 'une menace pour sa vie' (*CRD*, 205). But what is less certain is the origin of scarcity.

Is it an objective fact, a natural phenomenon that would be alleviated or even overcome by, say, increased productivity; or is it rather subjective, a purely human interpretation of available resources which would continue whatever the quantity available? In different terms, does it reflect need or greed? The question appears important, both with respect to a final appraisal of Sartre's position in terms of optimism or pessimism, and also with respect to his particular brand of Marxism, since for Marx a non-exploitative use of surplus-value could eventually overcome scarcity. Aronson, for example, criticizes Sartre vigorously ('this terrifying picture is simply wrong', p. 254) because he believes Sartre to present scarcity as natural rather than human, and he contrasts him to his disadvantage with Marshall Sahlins[22] who recognizes that historical choice lies at the origin of scarcity. Mark Poster, on the other hand, insists (*Sartre's Marxism*, p. 55) that scarcity is presented by Sartre as human and contingent, and quotes in support passages where Sartre writes that 'la rareté . . . [n'est pas] une structure permanente . . . mais plutôt . . . un certain moment des relations humaines, toujours dépassé et partiellement liquidé, toujours renaissant' (*CRD*, 201). The disagreement arises, I believe, not so much from careless reading on the part of one or other faction of critics, as from a failure to grasp the relevance of the dialectic to Sartre's epistemology. Since there is, for Sartre, no external observer, no inhuman truth, no extra-historical human nature, 'la vérité de l'homme' is, quite simply, 'la vérité tout court' (*CRD*, 741). Scarcity is, paradoxically, a *fact* of life, not merely a matter of interpretation. It is part of 'la singularité propre de notre Histoire' (*CRD*, 201); in other words it is futile to speculate on the possibility 'pour d'autres organismes et en d'autres planètes' of 'un rapport au milieu qui ne soit pas la rareté' (*CRD*, 201). This, then, is an example of what Sartre meant when he said: 'Les notions de subjectivité et d'objectivité me paraissent totalement inutiles . . . Tout est objectif' (*Sit IX*, 102–3). Already in *L'Etre et le Néant* 'la spatialité, la temporalité, l'ustensilité etc.' (*EN*, 269) were presented as at once human and at the same time 'objective' structures of the/our world;[23] as we shall see, dialectical reason gives this initial hermeneutic position a firmer grounding.

A further example of the problem posed to common-sense reason by the dialectical method is Sartre's analysis of series and groups. The analysis is immediately comprehensible: in a series each man is interchangeable, unrelated to any other, in potential conflict rather than able to cooperate – the bus-queue is Sartre's best-known illustration, the atomization produced by secret voting by ballot-box is another. In contrast, the group involves a cooperative fusion in which the whole is more than the sum of its parts, and the individual will and praxis forms part of a larger totalization which is not a hyper-organism or a kind of super-entity, but rather a detotalized totality of a kind we shall be discussing shortly.[24] A problem appears to arise over the question of transition from one state to another: Sartre analyses different phases of the transformation of series into group and vice versa – the 'groupe en fusion', the institution etc.; what is unclear is, again, the *origin* of such transformation: is it an individual initiative or rather some kind of supra-personal impulse? But once again the question is based on false premises, dependent on a bourgeois and atomistic conception of individuality and a lack of understanding of the dialectic. In practical terms, a particular individual may, for example, have started the cry to storm the Bastille, but his identity is irrelevant: he was expressing the mood of the group and was, in a literal sense, *n'importe qui.*

Toute la dialectique historique repose sur la praxis individuelle en tant que celle-ci est déjà dialectique, c'est-à-dire dans la mesure où l'action est par elle-même dépassement négateur d'une contradiction, détermination d'une totalisation présente au nom d'une totalité future, travail réel et efficace de la matière . . . Notre problème est là: que sera *la* dialectique s'il n'y a que des hommes et s'ils sont tous dialectiques? (*CRD*, 165–6)

'Que sera *la* dialectique?' Sartre asks. It is time now to tackle this question directly rather than merely obliquely.

Sartre's title, *Critique de la raison dialectique*, is, of course, an implied reference to Kant's *Critique of Pure Reason*. But as critics such as Aronson and Poster have pointed out, there is an inherent contradiction in attempting to do for dialectical reason what Kant did for analytic reason: a *critique* is essentially analytic, dependent on a distance between subject and object, and hence incapable of dealing with the dialectic which, Sartre maintains, transcends the analytic. 'La dialectique est le contrôle de l'analyse au nom d'une totalité' (*Sit IX*, 76). The title thus becomes, like the subtitle of *L'Etre et le Néant* (*Essai d'ontologie phénoménologique*), a contradiction in terms, and doubtless part of Sartre's very attempt to get beyond the binary categories of the analytic. In a sense, of course, the question of the nature of the *critique* does not really arise: Sartre's work is unfinished, the extant section is primarily theoretical, and the interaction of analysis and synthesis which constitutes the dialectical method cannot truly be seen in practice until the *Idiot de la famille*.[25] Nonetheless, Sartre addresses the problem explicitly: he argues that the dialectic constitutes both the subject and the object, the knower and the known: 'la dialectique est une méthode *et* un mouvement dans l'objet' (*CRD*, 119). His argument is complex and its detail need not concern us here; what matters in this context is firstly that the *object* of the dialectic is not external nature but rather human history, and secondly that the *critique* of the dialectic therefore arises from the dialectic of history itself, it is in no sense imposed from outside:

Notre problème est *critique*. Et sans doute, ce problème est lui-même suscité par l'Histoire. Mais justement il s'agit d'éprouver, de critiquer et de fonder, *dans l'Histoire* et en ce moment du développement des sociétés humaines, les instruments de pensée par lesquels l'Histoire se pense, en tant qu'ils sont aussi les instruments pratiques par lesquels elle se fait. Certes, nous serons renvoyés du *faire* au *connaître* et du *connaître* au *faire* dans l'unité d'un processus qui sera lui-même dialectique.   (*CRD*, 135)

L'expérience critique . . . se fait *à l'intérieur* de la totalisation et ne peut être une saisie contemplative du mouvement totalisateur; elle ne peut être non plus une totalisation singulière et autonome de la totalisation connue mais elle est un mouvement réel de la totalisation en cours.   (*CRD*, 140)

This means that both knower and known are changed by knowledge: it is not an external abstract relationship but part of a 'totalisation en cours'. Dialectical reason shares the well-known quality Sartre likes to ascribe to micro-physics: the experimenter is part of and affects the experiment: 'la connaissance même est forcément pratique: elle change le connu' (*CRD*, 104). There is no ultimate separation between theory and practice or praxis:

La dialectique comme logique vivante de l'action ne peut apparaître à une raison contemplative; elle se découvre en cours de *praxis* et comme un moment nécessaire de celle-ci.   (*CRD*, 133)

Nous avons découvert la *praxis* individuelle comme intelligibilité plénière du mouvement dialectique.   (*CRD*, 198)

The error of contemporary Marxism is precisely to have split the two:

La séparation de la théorie et de la pratique eut pour résultat de transformer celle-ci en un empirisme sans principes, celle-là en un Savoir pur et figé.
                    (*CRD*, 25)

For Sartre, in short, 'Tout savoir est pratique' (*Sit VIII*, 456). One thing that this means, of course, is that the analytic–synthetic, regressive–progressive method which moves incessantly back and forth between object and understanding, description and explanation,[26] involves not merely a gradual increase in knowledge and clarity but a genuine hermeneutic progression: the 'circularity' of all knowledge is, paradoxically, the foundation of its validity.

In this sense analysis and synthesis are more than simply complementary activities: they are in a reciprocal relationship of mutual interdependence and implication. Their reciprocity throws a new light on the question of *mediations*: in what has come to be known as 'vulgar' Marxism of the kind Sartre is attacking in the *Critique*, the direction of influence between 'infra' and 'super' structures, economics and ideology (or culture), society and individual is all one-way: the economic base is determining. For Sartre the influence is two-way: history may make men, but men also make history. Individuals may not change the course of history if one takes a bird's-eye, inhuman perspective − what Sartre calls the *pensée de survol*, an unreal overview − but they certainly affect the way it is experienced. Sartre quotes Plekhanov speculating on the consequences of the French Revolution if Napoleon had never existed: 'en aucun cas, l'issue finale du mouvement révolutionnaire n'eût été opposée à ce qu'elle fut' (*CRD*, 85). Sartre enters into the speculation and concludes ironically:

A part *cela*, bien sûr, l'évolution eût été la même. Seulement "cela" qu'on rejette dédaigneusement au rang du hasard, c'est toute la vie des hommes.

(*CRD*, 85)

L'existentialisme refuse d'abandonner la vie réelle aux hasards impensables de la naissance pour contempler une universalité qui se borne à se refléter indéfiniment en elle-même. (*CRD*, 45)

Similarly, art, culture and ideology are not simply reflexions of economic structures, they in turn affect the structures on which they depend. The intellectual climate of an epoch is complex, multiple, ambivalent and often contradictory, it cannot be reduced to a simple reflexion of the class-struggle. Sartre takes the example of the well-known eighteenth-century myth of the Noble Savage:

Les auteurs bourgeois ont usé, par exemple, du "mythe du Bon Sauvage", ils en ont fait une arme contre la noblesse mais on simplifierait le sens et la nature de cette arme si l'on oubliait qu'elle fut inventée par la contre-réforme et tournée d'abord contre le serf-arbitre des protestants.

(*CRD*, 87)

Sartre stresses singularity, rupture, discontinuity and difference between individuals or generations over and above similarity, continuity and totality. But these 'differences' are not attributed to chance:

Nous abordons l'étude du différentiel avec une exigence totalisatrice. Nous ne considérons pas ces variations comme des contingences anomiques, des hasards, des aspects insignifiants: tout au contraire la singularité de la conduite ou de la conception est *avant tout* la réalité concrète comme totalisation vécue, ce n'est pas un *trait* de l'individu, c'est l'individu total, saisi dans son processus d'objectivation. (*CRD*, 88)

Sartre demonstrates his conception of the relationship between individual and society, man and history, with a brilliant discussion of Gustave Flaubert, later to be elaborated in over three thousand pages of dense text in *L'Idiot de la famille*. Analysis of Flaubert's writings reveals his narcissism, onanism, idealism, solitude, dependence and passivity. His family background with its petty-bourgeois contradictions is described both as origin of Flaubert's conflict and as that which he rejects by his choice of art in preference to utility:

Dépassés et maintenus, ils constituent ce que j'appellerai la coloration interne du projet; mais sa *coloration*, c'est-à-dire subjectivement son goût, objectivement son *style*, n'est pas autre chose que le dépassement de nos déviations originelles: ce dépassement n'est pas un moment instantané, c'est un long travail . . . par cette raison, une vie se déroule en spirales; elle repasse toujours par les mêmes points mais à des niveaux différents d'intégration et de complexité. (*CRD*, 71)

The discussion of Flaubert's choice or project is the synthetic or progressive movement of the dialectic; it is speculative but also verifiable:

En vérité, il s'agit d'inventer un mouvement, de le recréer: mais l'hypothèse est immédiatement vérifiable: seule peut être valable celle qui réalisera dans un mouvement créateur l'unité transversale de *toutes* les structures hétérogènes. (*CRD*, 93)[27]

Moreover, each heterogeneous structure in its turn implies the whole: 'l'exigence totalisatrice implique . . . que l'individu se retrouve entier dans *toutes* ses manifestations' (*CRD*, 89).[28] This applies both to aspects of individual experience and to the relationship between individual and society. Dialectical epistemology necessarily transcends the analytic conception of the relationship between the whole and its parts: the whole is both greater than the sum of the parts and also present implicitly in each of its parts (*CRD*, 139). Sartre expresses this neatly in the syntactically ambivalent formula *l'universel singulier*. Each individual implies, precisely *in* his singularity rather than despite it, the general structures of the universal. And he thereby also transcends the universal:

L'homme historique, par son ancrage, fait de cette universalité une situation particulière et de la necessité commune une contingence irréductible . . . l'ancrage de la personne fait de cet universel une singularité irréductible . . . Il n'est d'incarnation de l'universel que dans l'irréductible opacité du singulier . . . l'homme, irrémédiable singularité, est l'être par qui l'universel vient au monde.   (Sit IX, 173–5)

It is to Kierkegaard that Sartre turns most frequently both in the *Critique* and in *L'Universel singulier*[29] to illustrate what he understands by the relationship between singular and universal in human terms. In one sense, Kierkegaard may be seen as endorsing Marx's attack on Hegel for reducing being to knowledge, but he goes further than Marx in that he considers the specificity of lived experience to be radically heterogeneous to knowledge. It is precisely the reality of human subjectivity that escapes explanation in terms of *le savoir*:

Si rien du vécu ne peut échapper au savoir, sa *réalité* demeure irréductible. En ce sens, le vécu comme réalité concrète se pose comme *non-savoir*.
                                                              (Sit IX, 159)

In one perspective, Kierkegaard's position is ultimately untenable – he can escape History only in so far as he makes it (*Sit IX*, 179); and Kierkegaard, Sartre maintains, 'manifeste l'historialité mais manque l'Histoire' (*Sit IX*, 189). But by a further paradox it is this failure that finally redeems him; for *failure* cannot be fully accounted for by the historical process: 'Si la vie est scandale, l'échec est plus scandaleux encore' (*Sit IX*, 164). Hegel's system, Sartre argues, can cope with failure or error only by interpreting it as partial success or partial truth within the context of a developing history. But what we learn from Kierkegaard is that failure is a subjective reality which cannot be explained away as an objective *positivité relative* (*Sit IX*, 166). It is through human failure that subjectivity proves inassimilable to *le savoir objectif*. In this sense, and in this sense alone, subjectivity can be seen as an absolute:

Tout doit être relatif, en nous et en Kierkegaard lui-même, *sauf son échec*. Car l'échec peut s'expliquer mais *non se résoudre*: en tant que non-être, il a le caractère absolu de la négation – de fait la négation historique est, fût-ce au cœur d'un relativisme, un absolu.   (Sit IX, 165)

We are back on familiar ground: as a *néant*, consciousness is beyond the reach of objective knowledge: 'la subjectivité n'est *rien* pour le savoir objectif puisqu'elle est non-savoir, et pourtant l'échec montre qu'elle existe absolument' (*Sit IX*, 166). Sartre is protecting human consciousness not only from the analysis of materialism, but also from dissolution by Idealist synthesis.[30]

Of course, Sartre is not espousing Kierkegaard's position uncritically:

Marx a raison à la fois contre Kierkegaard et contre Hegel puisqu'il affirme avec le premier la spécificité de *l'existence* humaine, et puisqu'il prend avec le second l'homme concret dans sa réalité objective.(*CRD*, 21)

What Sartre does in the *Critique* is to reinterpret Kierkegaard's mystical intuitions about experience within the terms of his own rationalist enterprise. 'Kierkegaard a négligé la *praxis* qui est rationalité . . . il a dénaturé le savoir' (*Sit IX*, 189). Sartre's understanding of the notion of *non-savoir* is very different from that of the Danish theologian:

Il ne s'agit pas pour nous, comme on l'a trop souvent prétendu, de "rendre ses droits à l'irrationel" mais, au contraire, de réduire la part de l'indétermination et du non-savoir. (*CRD*, 59)

History must take account of ambiguity, not in the Kierkegaardian sense of 'je ne sais quelle équivoque déraison' but rather of 'une contradiction qui n'est pas parvenue à son point de maturité' (*CRD*, 81). Existentialism sets out to revivify Marxism by incorporating into abstract knowledge 'le non-savoir rationnel et compréhensif' (*CRD*, 107).

L'existentialisme . . . n'oppose pas, comme Kierkegaard à Hegel, la singularité irrationnelle de l'individu au Savoir universel . . . La démarche dialectique [est] . . . la réintégration de l'existence non *sue* au cœur du Savoir comme fondement. (*CRD*, 108)

Nous ne prétendons pas – comme faisait Kierkegaard – que [l']homme réel soit inconnaissable. Nous disons simplement qu'il n'est pas connu. (*CRD*, 28–9)

It seems, then, that Sartre's ultimate aim is indeed total knowledge, but that he envisages it as a future (impossible?) goal which will account for individual experience as well as universal schema:

Loin de supposer . . . que nous ne sachions rien, nous devrions à la limite (mais c'est impossible) supposer que nous savons tout. En tout cas, nous acceptons toutes les connaissances pour déchiffrer les ensembles humains qui constituent l'individu et que l'individu totalise par la façon même dont il les vit. (*CRD*, 145)

It is now time to look not merely at the nature but also at the status of Sartre's attempt to reach Truth through dialectical reason. In his preface to the *Critique* Sartre acknowledges that in *Questions de méthode* he took as already established that History and Truth are the subjects of permanent totalization, and argues that the dialectic loses its sense and reality if this is not the case. Again, on the last page of the *Critique*, he repeats that volume II will deal with the 'vrai problème de l'Histoire', that of totalization (*CRD*, 754). Sartre recognizes the present multiplicity of meanings in History but situates this with respect to a future totalization:

Ainsi la pluralité *des sens* de l'Histoire ne peut se découvrir et se poser pour soi que sur le fond d'une totalisation future, en fonction de celle-ci et en contradiction avec elle. Cette totalisation, c'est notre office théorique et pratique de la rendre chaque jour plus proche. Tout est encore obscur et, pourtant, tout est en pleine lumière: nous avons − pour nous en tenir à l'aspect théorique − les instruments, nous pouvons établir la méthode: notre tâche historique, au sein de ce monde polyvalent, c'est de rapprocher le moment où l'Histoire n'aura qu'*un seul sens* et où elle tendra à se dissoudre dans les hommes concrets qui la feront en commun.(*CRD*, 63)

At first sight this may appear categorical, but on closer examination several ambiguities remain. In theoretical terms, is the 'totalisation future' destined to remain always future, 'chaque jour plus proche', an asymptote to a truth approached but never reached? In practical terms, if the single meaning of history depends on men making it together, is this concrete unification any more possible than its theoretical counterpart? Sartre's aim is certainly not reductive: his stress on the present multiplicity of meanings (*CRD*, 69) is far stronger than that on the future totalization. And furthermore, he distinguishes explicitly between totality and totalization: the former is finished and can exist only in the imaginary (*CRD*, 138), the latter is always in the making, an act rather than the product of an act. Indeed, dialectical reason itself is defined as 'la totalisation en cours', 'activité totalisatrice' (*CRD*, 139). Moreover, the reflexivity of knowledge implied by the totalizing dialectic must make a finished 'totality' theoretically as well as practically impossible − knowledge of the totality will always intervene to modify that totality, totalization has always to take into account its own awareness of itself.[31] Sartre is clearly opposed to nihilistic relativism: the present impossibility of total Truth by no means renders partial truths impossible (*CRD*, 122). But the dialectic is envisaged in terms of a never-ending process of truth-finding, 'une totalisation qui ne s'arrête jamais' (*CRD*, 132); and even within the hypothesis of 'Une Vérité de l'Histoire' (*CRD*, 142, 152) the totalization effected is always described as without a totalizer (*CRD*, 152), and usually as a 'totalisation détotalisée' (*CRD*, 156). Sartre may seem close to Hegel when he writes:

> Alors, m'objectera-t-on, on n'a jamais rien dit de vrai? Au contraire: tant que la pensée garde son mouvement, tout est vérité ou moment de la vérité; même les erreurs contiennent des connaissances réelles . . . Le faux, c'est la mort. (*CRD*, 74)

But we must remember that, *unlike* Hegel, Sartre identifies 'la vérité de l'homme' and 'la vérité tout court' (*CRD*, 741). Volume II, intended as an attempt to found the single Truth of History – 'il tentera d'établir qu'il y a *une* histoire humaine avec *une* vérité et *une* intelligibilité' (*CRD*, 156) – was, symptomatically, destined to remain in note form. Like that of the *Morale* of the late 1940s, Sartre's other major attempt at transcending heterogeneity, the totalizing impulse of the *Critique* never got beyond the stage of an unrealized – because impossible? – dream. *L'Idiot de la famille*, in its endeavour to answer the question 'Que peut-on savoir d'un homme aujourd'hui?' is perhaps the closest Sartre ever came to realizing the project sketched in the *Critique*:

> Nous devons pouvoir, dans notre expérience régressive, utiliser *tout le savoir actuel* (au moins en principe) pour éclairer telle ou telle entreprise, tel ensemble social, tel avatar de la *praxis* . . . En tout cas, nous acceptons toutes les connaissances pour déchiffrer les ensembles humains qui constituent l'individu et que l'individu totalise par la façon même dont il les vit. Nous les acceptons parce que le rêve de l'ignorance absolue qui découvre le réel préconceptuel est une sottise philosophique aussi dangereuse que fut, au XVIIIe siècle, le rêve du "bon sauvage".[32] (*CRD*, 145)

Here Sartre makes his totalizing enterprise sound a polemical reaction against irrationalism ('l'ignorance absolue') rather than a fully grounded philosophical position. And indeed, *L'Idiot de la famille* itself leaves unanswered the same question as the *Critique*: that of the status of 'totalisations sans grand totalisateur' (*CRD*, 152, 754), 'actes sans auteur', 'constructions sans constructeur' (*CRD*, 102). It is evident that no thoroughgoing individual totalization is envisaged: what remains uncertain is the nature and indeed the possible actualization of an *impersonal* totalization.[33]

Nonetheless, despite this ultimate epistemological uncertainty, Sartre's position on several important issues has been clarified in the course of his discussion of totalization and truth. In particular, the specific nature of his humanism – or non-humanism – has been revealed and occasionally thematized. The very notion of 'actes sans auteur' should show Sartre to be light years away from the individualistic bourgeois humanism so often attributed to him in recent years by defiantly parricidal Structuralists and Deconstructionists. We have already looked at this question in relation to his early philosophy: the rethinking of project, liberty and knowledge induced by his reflections on Marx took him still further away from the notorious lecture of the mid-1940s, and refounded Roquentin's dismissal of humanism on surer grounds. 'L'humanisme est le pendant du racisme: c'est une pratique d'exclusion' (*CRD*, 702). The preface to the *Critique* made clear that one of the primary questions to which the work would address itself was: 'Y a-t-il une Vérité de l'homme?' (*CRD*, 10). And *man* certainly remains Sartre's major preoccupation in so far as he is concerned, for example, to affirm 'l'humanisme véritable de l'homme' (*CRD*, 102) in the face of 'la déshumanisation de l'homme' (*CRD*, 58) brought about by neo-Marxist idealism and determinism. But all this is far from making of Sartre a humanist in the traditional sense. Indeed well before Foucault and the Structuralists, Sartre argues that 'l'Homme n'existe pas' (*CRD*, 131);[34] the concept of man is described as an *universel singulier* forged by history and '[sans] aucun sens en dehors de *cette* aventure singulière' (*CRD*, 140). 'Le concept d'homme est une abstraction' (*CRD*, 183); 'l'homme est un être matériel au milieu d'un monde matériel' (*CRD*, 196); 'l'histoire de l'homme est une aventure de la nature' (*CRD*, 158). However, Sartre is equally far from dissolving man into the structures which traverse him:

Encore faut-il comprendre que l'Homme n'existe pas: il y a des personnes qui se définissent tout entières par la société à laquelle elles appartiennent et par le mouvement historique qui les entraîne; si nous ne voulons pas que la dialectique redevienne une loi divine, une fatalité métaphysique, il faut qu'elle vienne *des individus* et non de je ne sais quels ensembles supra-individuels. Autrement dit, nous rencontrons cette nouvelle contradiction: la dialectique est la loi de totalisation qui fait qu'il y a *des* collectifs, *des* sociétés, *une* histoire, c'est-à-dire des réalités qui s'imposent aux individus; mais en même temps, elle doit être tissée par des millions d'actes individuels.   (*CRD*, 131)

Sartre's aim is to maintain *both* poles of 'la contradiction perpétuellement résolue et perpétuellement renaissante de l'homme-producteur et de l'homme-produit, en chaque individu et au sein de toute multiplicité' (*CRD*, 158). Furthermore, just as his use of the notion of *man* is far from making of Sartre a humanist, so his use of the notion of the *individual* is far from making him an individualist. We have already seen him maintain '*il n'y a pas d'individu isolé*' (*CRD*, 642):

L'individu disparaît des catégories historiques . . . l'individu − questionneur questionné − *c'est moi* et ce n'est personne . . . Nous voyons bien comment *je* me dissous pratiquement dans l'aventure humaine.

(CRD, 142–3)

The paradox of '*je* me dissous' is close to that of *La Transcendance de l'Ego*, 'Je est *un autre*' (*TE*, 78).[35] Marx has taken over from Rimbaud as master of alienation. But Sartre is still resolutely refusing to slip into an easy acceptance of either thesis or antithesis − and furthermore his dialectic seems to remain permanently in tension without synthesis.

Just as *L'Etre et le Néant* sailed a precarious course between the Scylla and Charybdis of realism and idealism, privileging neither inert but already existent Being, nor sense-bestowing but ultimately dependent consciousness, so the *Critique de la raison dialectique* traces a path between the twin pitfalls of determinism and libertarian individualism. *L'Idiot de la famille* makes clear the debt of the later Sartre not only to Marx but also to Freud, and illustrates in practice the way in which he rejected what he saw as the determinism of both, and certainly the reductivism of many contemporary Marxists and Freudians. Sartre's desire to 'utiliser tout le savoir actuel' (*CRD*, 145) necessarily meant that rather than steer a lonely course that could be ignored as eccentric, he confronted the major philosophies and ideologies of his age head-on. It was of course this project of incorporation of others and the concomitant refusal to be assimilated himself that led Sartre to be attacked by so many different schools of thought. Even his acknowledgement of existentialism as a 'mere' ideology within Marxism −

A partir du jour où la recherche marxiste prendra la dimension humaine (c'est-à-dire le projet existentiel) comme le fondement du Savoir anthropologique, l'existentialisme n'aura plus de raison d'être.

(CRD, 111)

− is undermined by an equally unequivocal forecast earlier in the same text:

Aussitôt qu'il existera *pour tous* une marge de liberté *réelle* au-delà de la production de sa vie, le marxisme aura vécu; une philosophie de la liberté prendra sa place. (CRD, 32)

No wonder Marxists suspected that Sartre's relatively modest aim of 'revivifying' Marxism concealed the rather more radical project of a large-scale take-over bid.

And the *Critique* reveals also the foundation for Sartre's debate with the Structuralists, explicit in the main in the interviews of the 1960s and 1970s,[36] and implicit once again in the study of Flaubert. It should be clear that Sartre's insistence on maintaining in tension the dual poles of a dialectic of paradox necessarily led him to reject the one-sided nature of the so-called 'death of the Subject' (or indeed the 'death of the Author') even though he welcomed the anti-individualism of the Structuralist endeavour in so far as it was conceived as an antidote to bourgeois humanism:

> Il n'est pas douteux que la structure produit les conduites. Mais ce qui gêne dans le structuralisme radical . . . c'est que l'envers dialectique est passé sous silence et qu'on ne montre jamais l'Histoire produisant les structures. En fait la structure fait l'homme dans la mesure où l'Histoire − c'est-à-dire ici la *praxis*–processus − fait l'Histoire. (*Sit IX*, 86)

Furthermore, Sartre was in fact prepared to rethink and re-express certain of his own concepts in the light of the tenets of Structuralism, in particular with respect to language and the human psyche. In one perspective, Sartre's quarrel with Structuralism can be envisaged in terms of polemical emphasis: is man the focus or the locus of structures? The difference is perhaps less radical than either party was prepared to admit at the time. Later chapters will explore the implications of Sartre's interaction with Structuralism in the domains of literary theory, psychoanalysis and theories of language.

6

Literary theory

As an imaginative writer Sartre is fascinated by the role of imagination in the creative process. Moreover his critical, psychological and philosophical writings witness to a constant meditation on the function and status of the imaginary. In his exploration of the relationship between mind and world, the role attributed to the imagination is at least as great as that of perception: imagination is, in Sartre's view, constitutive of the 'world' as we know it. It appears, moreover, as the correlative of the freedom of human consciousness; and it is this which permits Sartre to bring his interest in art within his overriding preoccupation with human liberty and political commitment.

But Sartre's attitude to the imaginary is nonetheless ambiguous: imagination permits man to overcome his *embourbement* in reality, it allows his *pour soi* to escape the toils of the *en soi*, it is vital to any project of change; yet it can also alienate that very liberty it makes possible, leading man to deny the real and to value fantasy above reality. 'L'imaginaire pur et la *praxis* sont difficilement compatibles' (*Sit II*, 324). The ambiguity of Sartre's attitude to imagination is reflected in his literary criticism. It led him initially to establish a radical distinction between 'pure' art and 'committed' art which he spent the rest of his life trying to attenuate. His belief in the necessity for literature to be positively committed should, logically, have led him to reject those nineteenth-century writers who formed his notion of what 'pure' art should be. But if his early theory of commitment compelled him to attack works of art where the imaginary is given priority over the real, his notion of art as *dévoilement*, and the increasingly dialectical nature of his analyses, permitted him to incorporate more of the purely imaginary elements of the art-object into his aesthetic ideal, and to reveal 'pure' art as ultimately reconcilable with authentic commitment. Sartre's criticism can be seen as an increasingly complex attempt to reinterpret the semi-metaphysical intuitions about art of Romanticism and Symbolism within the terms of his own comprehensive phenomenology. The basis of Sartre's aesthetic theories is laid in his phenomenological study of the imagination, published in 1940.

An understanding of this work and its implications is essential for a proper understanding of Sartre's ideas on art. It is, moreover, in this work of psychology that many of the paradoxes of his later aesthetics originate, and we must therefore return to it from this perspective.

As we saw in Chapter 1, Sartre in *L'Imaginaire* discusses perception and imagination as two possible ways in which the mind relates to the world. Percepts and images are in no sense 'contents' of the mind; Sartre dismisses this idea as the illusion of immanence. The distinction between imagination and perception is radical; the object of perception is both real and present, and although Sartre is of course aware of the difference between simple reception of sensory stimuli and perception itself, which also involves intentions and knowledge, he nevertheless envisages perception as relatively passive. The object of the image, on the other hand, is absent: the image is unreal and depends almost totally on the spontaneity of the person imagining. Although a wide spectrum of activities is included under the heading 'imagination', from looking at a photograph or a work of art to seeing shapes in the fire, or seeking out an absent friend in a café, all of the concomitant images are, according to Sartre, essentially the same in nature, differing only in the amount of spontaneity required to evoke them. For no image can be caused, but images can be motivated: and this distinction is, as we shall see, vital to Sartre's thesis on man's freedom and on the nature of literature.

Thus imagination and perception are, Sartre thinks, two distinct modes of consciousness. The objects of these two modes of consciousness are also radically distinct, irreducible one to the other: 'Le réel s'accompagne toujours de l'écroulement de l'imaginaire, même s'il n'y a pas de contradiction entre eux, parce que l'incompatibilité vient de leur nature et non de leur contenu' (*I*, 188). On the other hand, although distinct, imagination and perception are necessarily interdependent. The act of perception implies the possibility of imagining more than can in fact be taken in by the senses. As we have seen, it is this possibility which provides the key to Sartre's conception of human freedom. But the images are potential rather than actual, and cannot be evoked simultaneously with the perception itself: 'Il y a donc dans la perception l'amorce d'une infinité d'images; mais celles-ci ne peuvent se constituer qu'au prix de l'anéantissement des consciences perceptives' (*I*, 158). Similarly imagination, although it negates the real (or perceptual) world, depends on the real as the very condition of its being:

'Une image, étant négation du monde d'un point de vue particulier, ne peut jamais apparaître que *sur fond de monde* et en liaison avec le fond' (*I*, 235).

What, then, is the status of the image in Sartre's account? This appears most clearly in his discussion of the nature of thought. Concepts, according to Sartre, can appear to the mind either reflexively as pure thought or unreflexively as images. *Le savoir pur* (*I*, 80) is defined as knowledge of abstract relations, or of a 'rule', whereas the image gives rather *un savoir dégradé* (*I*, 52). The term *dégradé* implies a hierarchy of values which seems to go from *savoir pur* down through *image* to *affectivité*. The image involves a synthesis of *savoir* on the one hand and *affectivité* on the other. The image is 'comme une incarnation de la pensée irréfléchie' (*I*, 146), it is 'une forme inférieure de pensée' (*I*, 148). Imagination is in a sense opposed to pure thought; it can never lead on to thought proper but merely to further images. For Sartre 'la pensée ir-réfléchie est une possession' (*I*, 151).

Thus *L'Imaginaire* reveals, on Sartre's part, a deep-seated mistrust of the imagination. This mistrust also underlies his analysis of the nature of reading in so far as this engages our imagination. Sartre distinguishes between two possible aspects of reading. Initially, he suggests, words must be defined as signs on the basis of which I create meanings:

Je *lis* les mots sur la pancarte . . . on dit que j'ai compris, "déchiffré" les mots. Ce n'est pas absolument exact: mieux vaudrait dire que je les ai créés à partir de ces traits noirs. Ces traits ne m'importent plus, je ne les perçois plus: en réalité, j'ai pris une certaine attitude de conscience qui, à travers eux, vise un autre objet. (*I*, 35)

As signs, words point beyond themselves to another reality. The connection between the sign and its object is purely conventional. Reading involves the transcendence of signs towards meanings. But since I cannot perceive and imagine simultaneously, any images which my reading evokes must occur outside the act of reading proper:

Les images . . . apparaissent en général en dehors de l'activité de lecture proprement dite, lorsque, par exemple, le lecteur revient en arrière et se rappelle les événements du chapitre précédent, lorsqu'il rêve sur le livre, etc. Bref les images apparaissent aux arrêts et aux ratés de la lecture. Le reste du temps, quand le lecteur est bien pris, il n'y a pas d'image mentale. (*I*, 86)

Reading can, of course, be free of images, giving us merely a *savoir signifiant* (*I*, 87). But this is not the case with literature where

118

knowledge, imagination and affectivity all come into play. Reading a novel gives us *savoir imageant* rather than *savoir pur*.

As a form of *savoir imageant* reading too involves a kind of 'possession' by the imagination:

La lecture est un genre de fascination et quand je lis un roman policier je crois à ce que je lis. Mais cela ne signifie point que je cesse de tenir les aventures de policier pour imaginaires . . . Simplement un monde tout entier m'apparaît en image à travers les lignes du livre . . . et ce monde se referme sur ma conscience, je ne peux plus m'en dégager, je suis fasciné par lui.

(*I*, 217)

Sartre compares and contrasts reading and dreaming: in dreams we are wholly possessed by the fatal world which we have imagined; in reading, on the other hand, our identification with the hero

n'est jamais complète, d'abord parce que les auteurs usent le plus souvent du "recul esthétique", ils écrivent leur livre "au passé" par exemple, etc., ce qui permet au lecteur de survoler leur personnage. En outre, la possibilité d'une conscience réfléxive est toujours présente.   (*I*, 220)

Reading can never involve us to the same extent as can a dream: 'cet état de transes . . . ne peut être entièrement réalisé dans la lecture' (*I*, 221). Moreover, Sartre suggests, such a total fascination 'nuirait . . . à l'appréciation esthétique' (*I*, 221). It is evident that for Sartre a certain distance is an essential concomitant of aesthetic pleasure, and he refers almost disparagingly to the 'genre d'intérêt passionné' (*I*, 225) which a 'lecteur naïf' may feel when reading a novel. In other words, the reader should remain aware that the novel gives her merely *un savoir imageant*, a degraded form of *savoir*. As we shall see in our examination of *Situations II*, the writer is responsible for respecting the reader's liberty in this sense, leaving her free to make her own decisions about the events or attitudes of the work. Images are essential to capture the emotional response of the reader, but they must not also capture her freedom.

Reading in turn leads us to a further aspect of Sartre's account of the imaginary: the nature of the aesthetic object. The aesthetic object is, Sartre indicates, unreal (*I*, 239). He takes in the first place the example of painting and argues that it is not the materials of the work of art, the paint on the canvas, for example, which constitute the aesthetic object. They rather form what Sartre calls an *analogon* of the image which is the aesthetic object proper, and which comes into being only through the mind of the spectator: 'Ainsi le tableau doit être conçu comme une chose matérielle *visitée* de temps à autre (chaque fois que le spectateur prend l'attitude imageante) par un irréel qui est précisément *l'objet peint'* (*I*, 240) (i.e. the absent subject of the painting). Imagination, then, is the essential element in the aesthetic experience. Sartre is categorical on this point. The paint on the canvas constitutes an *analogon* of the image which is the real domain of aesthetic appreciation. This applies not only to representational painting, where the paint directs our imagination towards the object represented, but also to abstract art; and a similar process takes place in the case of literature, music, drama, etc. The differences between these various forms of art lie, in this context, in their connection or lack of connection with the real. But in all instances, Sartre contends, the aesthetic object itself is unreal or imaginary. In the case of literature, for example, the words on the page once again serve simply as an analogon, on the basis of which the reader, like the writer, constitutes the work of art proper: 'Il va de soi que le romancier, le poète, le dramaturge constituent à travers des analoga verbaux un objet irréel' (*I*, 242).

Sartre's account of the aesthetic object aims at removing all beauty from the real world and investing it in the imaginary: 'Le réel n'est jamais beau. La beauté est une valeur qui ne saurait jamais s'appliquer qu'à l'imaginaire et qui comporte la néantisation du monde dans sa structure essentielle' (*I*, 245). Sartre's position is in part dependent on his belief in the total contingency and absurdity of the real which can never, of itself, reveal the finality or purpose which he sees as an essential element in all beauty. The notion of finality in beauty is, however, suggested rather than explicitly discussed in *L'Imaginaire*, and we shall therefore examine its implications in more detail at a later stage when we discuss Sartre's attitude to the Kantian notion of art as a *finalité sans fin*. But for the moment we must simply note an important consequence of Sartre's radical separation of perception and imagination, the real and the imaginary, contingent existence and beauty: this is the accompanying split between morality and aesthetics. 'Il est stupide de confondre la morale et l'esthétique' (*I*, 245), he states categorically. We shall see Sartre's gradual evolution away from this position in the course of the present chapter.

Sartre's reference to 'la néantisation du monde' brings us finally to an aspect of the imagination which is essential to the philosophical position of *L'Etre et le Néant* but which appears to run counter to the emphasis on imagination as fascination or possession. This is the equation of imagination with the freedom of human consciousness: 'Poser une image, c'est constituer un objet en marge de la totalité du réel, c'est donc tenir le réel à distance, s'en affranchir, en un mot, le nier' (*I*, 233). Of course, as we have seen, although imagination negates the real it is nevertheless a function of our situation in the world. It is imagination which allows us to recognize our situation, to stand back from the world and consider it *as* a world: in Sartre's terms, to totalize it. It is only through the imagination that the world can be seen in any sense as meaningful; without this faculty our consciousness would be 'totalement engluée dans l'existant et sans possibilité de saisir autre chose que de l'existant' (*I*, 237). This helps us to understand the radical distinction and yet the strict interdependence of perception and imagination:

L'imagination . . . c'est la conscience tout entière en tant qu'elle réalise sa liberté; toute situation concrète et réelle de la conscience dans le monde est grosse d'imaginaire en tant qu'elle se présente toujours comme un dépassement du réel. (*I*, 236)

Imagination, then, appears 'sur fond de monde' (*I*, 238), and reciprocally it is the imaginative potential of the mind which ensures that perception is more than a passive reception of sensory stimuli. The two modes of consciousness are never present simultaneously but are implied one by the other and are essential one to the other: 'Il ne saurait y avoir de conscience réalisante sans conscience imageante et réciproquement' (*I*, 238–9).

In *L'Imaginaire* Sartre's primary concern is to give a phenomenological account of the imagination: in so far as he discusses art it is in the context of the status of the imaginary object. Although he recognizes certain basic differences in the ways the various arts communicate an *imaginaire*, his desire to give a general account of the status of the imaginary means that these differences are seen as less important than the similarities. In *Qu'est-ce que la littérature?*, on the other hand, Sartre is anxious to isolate literature, with its possibility of commitment, from the other arts which can be broadly described as 'non-significant' in the sense that they do not convey a conceptual meaning. The work shows all the signs of being hastily written: Sartre's terminology sometimes lacks precision, and the distinctions implied are not always rigorously worked out.

Central to *Situations II* is Sartre's distinction between prose-literature, which uses signs referring the reader to something beyond themselves, and the fine arts which, even when they are representational (as in some kinds of painting, for example) concentrate rather on the sensuous qualities of the aesthetic medium itself, in so far, of course, as these are imagined not perceived:

Les notes, les couleurs, les formes ne sont pas des signes, elles ne renvoient à rien qui leur soit extérieur . . . Pour l'artiste, la couleur, le bouquet, le tintement de la cuiller sur la soucoupe sont *choses* au suprême degré; il s'arrête à la qualité du son ou de la forme, il y revient sans cesse et s'en enchante; c'est cette couleur–objet qu'il va transporter sur sa toile et la seule modification qu'il lui fera subir c'est qu'il le transformera en objet *imaginaire* . . . le peintre ne veut pas tracer des signes sur sa toile, il veut créer une chose.   (*Sit II*, 60–1)

The painter creates an art-object with which the spectator establishes a direct contact; the writer, on the other hand, creates meanings: 'L'écrivain, au contraire, c'est aux significations qu'il a affaire' (*Sit II*, 63). This difference means that whereas the writer can explicitly direct the response of his reader, the painter can only present the spectator with an object to which she is largely free to respond as she chooses:

L'écrivain peut vous guider et s'il vous décrit un taudis, y faire voir le symbole des injustices sociales, provoquer votre indignation. Le peintre est muet: il vous présente *un* taudis, c'est tout; libre à vous d'y voir ce que vous voulez. Cette mansarde ne sera jamais le symbole de la misère; il faudrait pour cela qu'elle fût signe, alors qu'elle est chose.

(*Sit II*, 62)

Sartre, then, does not believe that a painting can communicate a precise message to the spectator, though he is aware of its ability to communicate inexplicit moods and feelings: speaking of Tintoretto's *Crucifixion*, he writes:

Cette déchirure jaune du ciel au-dessus du Golgotha, le Tintoret ne l'a pas choisie pour *signifier* l'angoisse, ni non plus pour *la provoquer*; elle *est* angoisse, et ciel jaune en même temps. Non pas ciel d'angoisse, ni ciel angoissé; c'est une angoisse faite chose.   (*Sit II*, 61)

Sartre's distinction between the mode of communication of literature and the fine arts is not new; it will be familiar to anyone who has studied Baudelaire in relation to Delacroix, for example. In his journal (8 October 1822) Delacroix writes:

Quand j'ai fait un beau tableau, je n'ai point écrit une pensée . . . C'est ce qu'ils disent! . . . Qu'ils sont simples! Ils ôtent à la peinture tous ses avantages. L'écrivain dit presque tout pour être compris. Dans la peinture, il s'établit comme un pont mystérieux entre l'âme des personnages et celle du spectateur . . . L'art du peintre est autant plus intime au cœur de l'homme qu'il paraît plus matériel.[1]

But for the Romantic painter it is the 'esprits grossiers [qui] sont plus émus des écrivains que des musiciens et des peintres'.[2] Sartre, on the other hand, prefers an art-form where the artist is not dependent simply on the power of suggestion of his medium, but where he can exercise a precise control over the meaning conveyed; and he thinks that only language, by its referential nature, can permit such a degree of directional control.

Artistic creation is, Sartre argues, a two-way process. In *L'Imaginaire* he described the artist as in a sense objectifying his mental image through the creation of an analogon: in *Situations II* it is clear that he is conscious also of the reverse side of such a notion: through the creation of the work of art the artist is helped to *discover* his own idea. The full implications of the interaction between the intentional and the unintentional (Sartre adapts Gide's formula and calls this 'la part du diable') are not explored in any detail at this point. In *Situations II* Sartre is primarily concerned to show that such an interaction implies fluid possibilities of response and interpretation which, together with the lack of any means of conceptual communication, render commitment, at least as Sartre understands it at this point, impossible in the fine arts proper. Of music, for example, Sartre writes:

La signification d'une mélodie – si on peut encore parler de signification – n'est rien en dehors de la mélodie même . . . Dites qu'elle est joyeuse ou qu'elle est sombre, elle sera toujours au delà ou en deçà de tout ce que vous pouvez dire sur elle . . . On ne peint pas les significations, on ne les met pas en musique; qui oserait, dans ces conditions, réclamer du peintre ou du musicien qu'ils s'engagent? (*Sit II*, 61–3)

For all that, within *Situations II* itself we are given a foresight of the way Sartre will later commit the 'non-significant' arts, for there is a reservation attached to his claim that he has no intention of committing them: 'Non, nous ne voulons pas "engager aussi" peinture, sculpture et musique, ou, du moins, pas de la même manière' (*Sit II*, 59). The precise way in which the fine arts may be seen as committed is not discussed explicitly at this stage, but there is no reason to suppose that Sartre's remarks about the special kind of commitment open to poetry, which we shall examine shortly, are not intended to apply to the other arts also.

We must now turn to Sartre's discussion of literature in order to see how he will apply the distinctions outlined above (*sens/signification*, *signe/chose*), to language itself, using them to establish the dichotomy of prose and poetry. At first sight the dichotomy seems relatively uncomplicated: 'l'empire des signes, c'est la prose; la poésie est du côté de la peinture, de la sculpture, de la musique'

123

(*Sit II*, 63). Sartre asserts that the poet relates to words in a totally different way from the writer of prose, 'serving' them, rather than 'using' them. What is involved here is an ideal and normative definition of poetry. The poet's function is not the revelation of truth; neither is it the simple 'magical' function of nomination whereby words are used to conjure up objects: in poetry, words are objects in their own right. This means, of course, that Sartre rejects the stated aim of the Surrealists, to destroy language, as implying a misunderstanding of the nature of poetry, and indeed of their own best poetry. His definition is based upon a conception of the dual nature of the word, which can be envisaged either as a transparent means of referring us to something beyond itself, or as the object on which the imagination focusses in the aesthetic attitude. The fact that the poet adopts the second stance does not, however, mean that he is unconcerned with communication; it means simply that he will try to communicate through the material rather than the conceptual aspect of the word, using it as an image rather than as a sign: 'Sa sonorité, sa longueur, ses désinences masculines ou féminines, son aspect visuel lui composent un visage de chair qui *représente* la signification plutôt qu'il ne l'exprime' (*Sit II*, 66). Sartre will develop this notion in his later account of Flaubert's art, but his basic thesis will remain unchanged. The poet need not choose between the various meanings of a word since he is not concerned with intellectual clarity, he rather permits the different connotations to coexist: 'Florence est ville et fleur et femme, elle est ville–fleur et ville–femme et fille–fleur tout à la fois' (*Sit II*, 66). We may justifiably wonder whether echoes of Proust are sounding in Sartre's memory at this point, for he continues: 'Et l'étrange objet qui paraît ainsi possède la liquidité du *fleuve*, la douce ardeur fauve de l'*or*, et, pour finir, s'abandonne avec *décence* et prolonge indéfiniment par l'affaiblissement continue de l'*e* muet son épanouissement plein de réserves' (*Sit II*, 66). Poets use words, Sartre suggests, in much the same way as painters use colours: to create an object: 'Les mots–choses . . . s'attirent, ils se repoussent, ils se *brûlent* et leur association compose la véritable unité poétique qui est la *phrase–objet*' (*Sit II*, 67–8). Like other 'pure' artists, the poet cannot be committed, or so Sartre claims at this stage:

Sans doute l'émotion, la passion même . . . sont à l'origine du poème. Mais elles ne s'y *expriment* pas . . . les mots les prennent, s'en pénètrent et les métamorphosent . . . Comment espérer qu'on provoquera l'indignation ou l'enthousiasme politique du lecteur quand précisément on le retire de la condition humaine et qu'on l'invite à considérer, avec les yeux de Dieu, le langage à l'envers? (*Sit II*, 69–70)

The idea that the poet envisages language 'à l'envers' brings us to another aspect of Sartre's theory of poetry and one which will become increasingly important in his aesthetics: the notion of poetry as *échec*. Prosaic language usage is based on an assumption of communicability. The poet, according to Sartre, does not share this assumption; he is, in a sense, ill-adapted to language, which he envisages from outside as a barrier to true communication: 'Le poète est hors du langage, il voit les mots à l'envers, comme si . . . venant vers les hommes, il recontrât d'abord la parole comme une barrière' (*Sit II*, 65). The poet is not, however, inventing problems. Language is, Sartre believes, like all human activities, dependent on the interpretation of others for its final meaning. The poet is simply sensitive to the difficulties inherent in any attempt to communicate, and concentrates his attention on the element of failure underlying even the fullest communication: 'Il ne s'agit pas, d'ailleurs, d'introduire arbitrairement la défaite et la ruine dans le cours du monde, mais plutôt de n'avoir d'yeux que pour elles. L'entreprise humaine a deux visages: elle est à la fois réussite et échec' (*Sit II*, 86). The poet's use of language is based on the very failure inherent in all communication:

S'il est vrai que la parole soit une trahison et que la communication soit impossible, alors chaque mot, par lui-même, recouvre son individualité, devient instrument de notre défaite et receleur de l'incommunicable. Ce n'est pas qu'il y ait *autre chose* à communiquer: mais la communication de la prose ayant échoué, c'est le sens même du mot qui devient l'incommunicable pur. Ainsi l'échec de la communication devient suggestion de l'incommunicable. (*Sit II*, 86)

The apparently sophistical paradox can be explained simply in psychological terms: poetry makes use of the suggestive power of words, a power which in fact depends on a certain imprecision of meaning. In this sense a lack of intellectual clarity permits a multiplicity of poetic connotations. Sartre recognizes that poetry and prose are not radically distinct in this respect: 'Il va de soi que, dans toute poésie, une certaine forme de prose, c'est-à-dire de réussite, est présente: et réciproquement la prose la plus sèche renferme toujours un peu de poésie, c'est-à-dire une certaine forme d'échec' (*Sit II*, 87). In other words, the prose writer can never control totally the meaning of what he is saying, nor is poetry devoid of all element of conceptual communication. But if both aspects are necessarily present in all language, the writer must nonetheless choose which he will allow to predominate, for, at this stage at least, Sartre does not believe that both can be used to the full simultaneously:

Si le prosateur veut trop choyer les mots, l'*eidos* "prose" se brise et nous tombons dans le galimatias. Si le poète raconte, explique, ou enseigne, la poésie devient *prosaïque*, il a perdu la partie. Il s'agit de structures complexes, impures mais bien délimitées. (*Sit II*, 88)

As we shall see in our discussion of *L'Idiot de la famille* and of the evolution of Sartre's ideas on language, his position on this point was gradually modified. The prose/poetry distinction was not repudiated but changed its focus from a distinction between genres, to one between different forms of writing.

Sartre's identification of poetry with *l'échec* is only briefly indicated in *Situations II*, but it implies already many of the ideas which will later prove vital in his account of Genet and more especially of Flaubert. The most significant of these is the *qui perd gagne* notion, according to which failure can be seen as success on a 'higher' level. We have just seen a simple example of this in Sartre's account of the failure to communicate entailing a suggestion of the incommunicable. But Sartre is evidently already aware of more metaphysical interpretations of the idea of *qui perd gagne*, for he compares the contemporary role of poetry in recuperating failure to that performed in previous centuries by religion. Sartre's fascination with the various forms and degrees of authenticity or inauthenticity of 'loser wins' becomes increasingly apparent in his criticism and provides the key to his study of and perhaps even his eventual rehabilitation of Flaubert. Even at this stage it is the notion of *qui perd gagne* which permits him to define the special kind of commitment open to the poet: 'Le poète authentique choisit de perdre jusqu'à mourir pour gagner . . . Si donc l'on veut absolument parler de l'engagement du poète, disons que c'est l'homme qui s'engage à perdre' (*Sit II*, 86).

We can turn now from poetry and the fine arts to Sartre's discussion of committed literature itself, and his account of the nature of commitment. As we know from 'Qu'est-ce qu'écrire?' (in *Sit II*), Sartre's conception of committed literature applies to prose alone and excludes poetry; and although, in his discussion of commitment in 'Pourquoi écrire?', he makes no further reference to this distinction it must be taken as established. *L'écrivain* is then to be understood in this context as the prose writer. However, the terminology of *Situations II* is not always clearly defined. There are in fact two and perhaps even three different notions of commitment which emerge from Sartre's discussion, the first two explicit, the third implicit and more far-reaching, providing part of the basis on which he will later 'commit' arts other than literature. We shall look first, fairly briefly, at the explicit account.

The writer is, according to Sartre, *embarqué* or *engagé* in the sense of being involved in the historical and political situation of his day, whether or not he likes or even admits the fact: Balzac is implicated by his inactivity during the 1848 Revolution, just as is Flaubert during the Commune. The writer, Sartre insists, must not ignore this involvement, he must rather attempt to contribute to the establishment of social freedom and justice. In other words, he should be *engagé* also in a positive and conscious sense. This *engagement* by no means implies the reduction of the writer's role to that of mere journalist: Sartre's conception of the relevance of the historical moment is in this sense analogous to Baudelaire's notion of modernity as we find it for example in his essay on Constantin Guys:

Le beau est fait d'un élément éternel, invariable, dont la quantité est excessivement difficile à déterminer, et d'un élément relatif, circonstantiel, qui sera, si l'on veut, tour à tour ou tout ensemble l'époque, la mode, la morale, la passion. Sans ce second élément . . . le premier élément serait indigestible, inappréciable, non adapté et non approprié à la nature humaine.[3]

Baudelaire is here attempting to refute the 'professeurs–jurés d'esthétique' such as Winckelmann. Sartre is not attempting to combat neo-classical aesthetic theory, but is rather resisting the Symbolist heritage still clinging round even his own idea of literature. He emphasizes first that eternal values will in fact be reached through the temporal and relative: 'Ainsi, en prenant parti dans la singularité de notre époque, nous rejoignons finalement l'éternel et c'est notre tâche d'écrivain que de faire entrevoir les valeurs d'éternité qui sont impliquées dans ces débats sociaux ou politiques' (*Sit II*, 15). But like Baudelaire he continues: 'Mais nous ne nous soucions pas de les aller chercher dans un ciel intelligible: elles n'ont d'intérêt que sous leur enveloppe actuelle' (*Sit II*, 15). Even the vocabulary is Baudelaire's here: we are reminded of the 'enveloppe amusante . . . du divin gâteau'.[4]

The primary element of commitment, historical involvement, is, then, nothing new, nor is it in any sense propagandist. Sartre objects to both bourgeois and Communist writers, in the sense not of bourgeois or Communists who write, but rather of those who produce literature of a certain sort: exclusively analytic in the case of the bourgeois, or subordinated to utilitarian ends in the case of the Communist. Sartre's ideal literature would, he believes, flourish rather in an authentically revolutionary society:

Dans un parti authentiquement révolutionnaire [l'œuvre d'art] trouverait le climat propice à son éclosion, parce que la libération de l'homme et l'avènement de la société sans classes sont comme elle des buts absolus, des exigences inconditionnées qu'elle peut refléter dans son exigence.

(*Sit II*, 286)

The writer is, then, like all men, part of history, and responsible for the effect, direct or indirect, of his actions and therefore of his writing. Besides any deliberate and positive involvement, he is also committed in the sense that his world-view, even if apparently a-historical, itself involves a choice of perspective. If he abstains from direct political commitment he is responsible not merely for his lack of positive guidance, but also for the political implications of the imaginary universe he portrays. In this sense too, then, all writers are committed and Sartre is advising them of the necessity to be conscious of the fact.

Writers are committed also in a third and perhaps more far-reaching sense: by writing they reveal the world to their readers, and thereby change the nature of their readers' relations to that world. In Sartre's terms: 'La perception même est partiale . . . à elle seule, la nomination est déjà modification de l'objet' (*Sit II*, 110). In other words, literature necessarily transforms our non-reflexive awareness of the world into a reflexive, thetic, self-conscious awareness. The reader can no longer take the world for granted in the same passive manner as before. Literature, by its very nature, reveals the possibility of change. Of the seventeenth century, for example, Sartre writes: 'Le miroir qu'il présente modestement à ses lecteurs est magique: il captive et compromet . . . les conduites spontanées en passant à l'état réflexif, perdent leur innocence et l'excuse de l'immédiateté: il faut les assumer ou les changer' (*Sit II*, 141–2). It is an extension of this notion of art as revelation or *dévoilement* which will later allow Sartre to commit not only literature but also the fine arts, and it raises certain philosophical problems which it is worth pausing for a moment to examine briefly in their turn.

The artist for Sartre is inevitably *in* the world, and his portrait of the world must be true both to the contingency of existence and to the facts of man's relations with the world. Indeed Sartre defines his notion of the aim of art in these terms: 'Récupérer ce monde-ci en le donnant à voir tel qu'il est, mais comme s'il avait sa source dans la liberté humaine' (*Sit II*, 106). 'Tel qu'il est': in other words, in all its flux and contingency. But how can the world be revealed 'tel qu'il est' if it is modified to appear *as if* its origin were in human freedom? Moreover, Sartre is bound to be uneasy with any claim to reveal the world 'as it is' since it is man who constitutes the world as a world. Being 'tel qu'il est' is in fact fundamentally unknowable: only the human world can be known: 'Pour connaître l'être tel qu'il est, il faudrait être cet être, mais il n'y a de "tel qu'il est" que parce que je ne suis pas l'être que je connais et si je le devenais le "tel qu'il est" s'évanouirait et ne pourrait même plus être pensé' (*EN*, 270). The second half of Sartre's definition of the aim of art is equally problematic: to reveal the world 'tel qu'il est, *mais comme s'il avait sa source dans la liberté humaine*'. On a simple level, Sartre is at this point expressing within his own philosophical terms the familiar Romantic notion that aesthetic experience transcends life. And for Sartre, art transcends life because it reveals freedom, purpose and project. But the definition poses further philosophical problems. It can be argued that since Sartre has identified imagination with the freedom of the human mind, and described it as essential to our appreciation of the world as a totality, then any view of the world as a 'world' must necessarily witness to human freedom. So if 'le monde tel qu'il est' is simply the human world, it is logically identical with 'le monde . . . comme s'il avait sa source dans la liberté humaine', and Sartre's definition is a tautology. But Sartre's *mais* invites us to interpret the formula differently. It reveals, moreover, a deep-seated reservation, for it is attempting to imply more than he can in fact argue, and to credit art with an ability to reveal a world arguably inaccessible even to philosophy. An evident sleight of hand is involved. This is clearly revealed a few pages later when Sartre attempts once again to bring together the real and the imaginary, 'l'être' and 'le devoir-être':

Dans la joie esthétique, la conscience positionnelle est conscience *imageante* du monde dans sa totalité comme être et devoir-être à la fois, à la fois comme totalement nôtre et totalement étranger . . . Ecrire, c'est donc à la fois dévoiler le monde et le proposer comme une tâche à la générosité du lecteur.   (*Sit II*, 109)

Sartre, then, wants to tighten the link between art and the world. To this end he takes over the notion of *dévoilement* and its various implications and uses the term to blur the difference between his own and other more positive interpretations of the possible role of art as revelation.[5] The ambiguities of his formula suggest that he is caught between the implications of his own philosophical system on the one hand, and on the other his desire to commit all literature and ultimately all art.

There is in *Situations II* a final aspect of commitment which we have not yet discussed: this depends on the integral connection which Sartre establishes between literature and liberty. Much of Sartre's discussion, as he himself indicates, applies in fact to the fine arts also, in so far as these, like the literary work, depend on the imagination not only of their creator but also of the spectator, listener or reader. In *L'Imaginaire*, the imagination was described as constitutive of human freedom: 'c'est la conscience tout entière en tant qu'elle réalise sa liberté' (*I*, 236). For Sartre, freedom, like truth, is one: 'la liberté est une, mais elle se manifeste diversement selon les circonstances' (*Sit I*, 289); so ontological, artistic, intellectual and political freedom are inextricably linked. Whether Sartre establishes this unity as a fact or merely takes it as a supposedly incontrovertible premise will need to be examined. He can, perhaps, without much fear of contradiction, assert the interrelationship of intellectual and political freedom: 'Il y a coïncidence, non seulement entre la liberté formelle de penser et la démocratie politique mais aussi entre l'obligation matérielle de choisir l'homme comme perpétuel sujet de méditation et la démocratie sociale' (*Sit II*, 186). It is in fact the notion of liberty which provides the pivotal link between his aesthetic theories and his political or sociological beliefs. It is the key to his mistrust of excessively emotive writing, and to his belief in the necessity of a certain 'aesthetic distance': 'Dans la passion, la liberté est aliénée . . . De là ce caractère de *pure présentation* qui paraît essentiel à l'œuvre d'art: le lecteur doit disposer d'un certain recul esthétique' (*Sit II*, 99). The writer must not attempt to alienate his reader's judgement by involving her in an enforced 'participation'. On the other hand, Sartre recognizes the necessity of an emotional response, but he considers it to be of a particular nature:

Cela ne veut pas dire que l'écrivain fasse appel à je ne sais quelle liberté abstraite et conceptuelle. C'est bien avec des sentiments qu'on recrée l'objet esthétique . . . Seulement ces sentiments sont d'une espèce particulière; ils ont la liberté pour origine: ils sont prêtés. (*Sit II*, 99)

As we saw in *L'Imaginaire*, images cannot be caused but they can be motivated: we must choose to take up the imaginative rather than the purely perceptual attitude. Reading involves a free choice: the emotions and images it suggests are freely accepted and the 'suspension of disbelief' is 'willing' and chosen:

Le propre de la conscience esthétique c'est d'être croyance par engagement, par serment, croyance continuée par fidélité à soi et à l'auteur, choix perpétuellement renouvelé de croire. A chaque instant je puis m'éveiller et je le sais: mais je ne le veux pas: la lecture est un rêve libre. En sorte que tous les sentiments qui se jouent sur le fond de cette croyance imaginaire sont comme des modulations particulières de ma liberté.   (*Sit II*, 100)

It is not merely the reader whose freedom is implied by the work of art. The writer too must remain free. His freedom is closely related in Sartre's view to the 'purpose' embodied in the work of art. Sartre declares that the imagination or freedom of mind involved in the appreciation of natural beauty is unregulated, since natural beauty is simply in the eye (or mind) of the beholder. This unregulated liberty he calls *caprice*. The beauty of art, on the other hand, is willed, it is *intentionnelle*, so the spectator is assured that the beauty she recognizes is not an arbitrary construct of her own mind, it is purposeful. For Sartre this element of purpose depends on the freedom of the artist:

Si je devais soupçonner l'artiste d'avoir écrit par passion et dans la passion, ma confiance s'évanouirait aussitôt, car il ne servirait à rien d'avoir étayé l'ordre des causes par l'ordre des fins; celui-ci serait supporté à son tour par une causalité psychique et, pour finir, l'œuvre d'art rentrerait dans la chaîne du déterminisme.   (*Sit II*, 104)

Sartre's emphasis on purpose as the essential element of beauty appears in many ways as the corollary of his belief in the contingency of the natural world: only man can have purpose and in so far as a work of art may contain elements which are not fully purposeful it betrays the reader who is seeking an alternative to contingency. As we have seen, Sartre is aware of the 'part du diable' (devil's share) inherent in any art, but he considers that this too can be incorporated within the overall intention of the artist and rendered retrospectively purposeful. In the complex process of artistic creation the unintentional can be made to serve the intentional.

The 'purpose' embodied in the work of art in no way restricts the reader's freedom. Indeed the reader is rather aware of her freedom as creator of the aesthetic object. Sartre is categorical on the question of the reader's role in creation. Since the author produces only an analogon of the aesthetic object, the reader's participation is necessary if the *imaginaire* itself is to come into being:

131

Sans doute l'auteur le guide: mais il ne fait que le guider . . . En un mot, la lecture est une création dirigée . . . Ainsi, pour le lecteur, tout est à faire et tout est déjà fait; l'œuvre n'existe qu'au niveau de ses capacités.

(*Sit II*, 95–6)

The paradox of *création dirigée* parallels the paradox of *savoir imageant*: reading gives both *savoir* which can be caused, and images which can only be suggested. 'La lecture, en effet, semble la synthèse de la perception et de la création' (*Sit II*, 93). In other words, the reader does not create the conceptual meaning of the literary work, but she creates the *objet esthétique* in so far as it is always an *imaginaire* dependent on the human mind for its existence.

In one sense, then, all art, according to Sartre, is liberating. It is liberating in so far as it is negative, presenting us with an imaginary world by which we can escape our *embourbement* in reality. Art depends on the imagination, and the imagination is synonymous with the freedom of human consciousness. But this first kind of liberation involves only the subject. There is a second sense in which art can be seen as liberating. Sartre's discussion is restricted to the literary work, but the context gives us no reason to suppose that it is not applicable to the fine arts also. Literature is defined as 'l'œuvre d'une liberté totale s'adressant à des libertés plénières . . . elle manifeste à sa manière, comme libre produit d'une activité créatrice, la totalité de la condition humaine' (*Sit II*, 299). Sartre is suggesting that in so far as a work of art depends on a reader or spectator for the realization of its *imaginaire*, it is potentially a call to any man or woman, and hence, Sartre believes, to all mankind. From this theoretical position he moves on to claim that if art depends on human liberty, it must necessarily work in favour of this liberty. Sartre has made of art a kind of categorical imperative, and he uses the notion to suggest that the writer is in some sense *logically* bound to work towards a truly democratic society, all of whose members would be free to read his works and to take any action suggested by them. In this sense art becomes socially as well as psychologically liberating. Sartre is evidently struggling to identify the interests of the artist with the advancement of socialism. He appears, however, to have performed a further philosophical sleight of hand. 'Liberty' has been transformed from the ontological correlative of imagination into a practical, politico-social freedom. The distinctions have, we may suspect, been deliberately blurred for polemical reasons. Sartre is in fact trying to reinforce in the reader the notion of the artist as a political as well as a 'psychological' liberator. As a political liberator he is necessarily subversive: 'souhaitons . . . qu'il retrouve en lui-même la force de faire scandale' (*Sit II*, 52), for 'la littérature est par essence hérésie' (*Sit II*, 281). A writer, Sartre urges, must not allow his works to be 'recuperated' or incorporated into the dominant culture; or at least he must make the recuperation as difficult and therefore as productive of change as possible: 'Par la littérature, je l'ai montré, la collectivité passe à la réflexion et à la méditation, elle acquiert une conscience malheureuse, une image sans équilibre d'elle-même, qu'elle cherche sans cesse à modifier et à améliorer' (*Sit II*, 316). If the writer is subversive, the reader too is drawn into the subversive activity: 'tout l'art de l'auteur est pour m'obliger à *créer* ce qu'il *dévoile*, donc à me compromettre' (*Sit II*, 110). The reader cannot escape responsibility for her part in the *création dirigée*. This notion will acquire increasing importance in Sartre's studies of Genet and Flaubert.

Sartre has then conflated several different types of liberty and liberation in his account of art in *Situations II*. But he has established a link on various distinct levels (ontological, social, political) between art and liberty, even if these levels are not in fact interrelated in the simple manner he is attempting to imply. He has, moreover, given, at least implicitly, some indications of the basis on which he will later commit poetry and the fine arts.

The notion of commitment raises again the important question of the purpose specific to art, and this brings us to an idea which is central to Sartre's aesthetics and in particular to his conception of the function of art in the world: the notion of art as a *fin*. The idea does not change significantly in nature throughout Sartre's writings; it is important in the later critical essays on Genet and Flaubert, but it is first clearly set out in *Situations II*, where its role is vital, since without it Sartre's critical theories might be interpreted as basically anti-art.

The idea of art as an end can be interpreted on various levels, the simplest and most superficial being by opposition to any idea of art as a means to an end. Sartre rejects propaganda: he believes that true art cannot be the servant of any cause, however worthwhile:

Je dis que la littérature d'une époque déterminée est aliénée lorsqu'elle n'est pas parvenue à la conscience explicite de son autonomie et qu'elle se soumet aux puissances temporelles ou à une idéologie, en un mot lorsqu'elle se considère elle-même comme un moyen et non comme une fin inconditionnée. (*Sit II*, 190)

L'œuvre d'art, fin absolue, [s'oppose] par essence à l'utilitarisme bourgeois. Croit-on qu'elle peut s'accommoder de l'utilitarisme communiste? (*Sit II*, 286)

Art is not a means, but Sartre considers that this notion has been misunderstood and misapplied in the past, as, for example, by the art-for-art's-sake movement, according to which art must not only steer clear of utilitarianism but must deliberately set out to be useless, to become in Sartre's terms, 'la forme la plus élevée de la consommation pure' (*Sit II*, 171).

Les extrémistes souhaitent, par terreur de servir, que leurs ouvrages ne puissent pas même éclairer le lecteur sur son propre cœur, ils refusent de transmettre leur expérience. A la limite l'œuvre ne sera tout à fait gratuite que si elle est tout à fait inhumaine . . . L'imagination est conçue comme faculté inconditionnée de *nier* le réel et l'objet d'art s'édifie sur l'effondrement de l'univers. (*Sit II*, 171–2)

For Sartre, of course, imagination negates ('néantiser') the real, it cannot, in his terms, deny ('nier') it.

Sartre discusses the art-for-art's-sake movement in greater detail in *L'Idiot de la famille*, where he sees it as alienating the artist just as effectively as the bourgeois quest for profit. In *Saint Genet* he claims that the notion of art-for-art's-sake indirectly provides the bourgeois with an excuse for ignoring his own potential to effect change:

Le Juste laissera au peintre, à l'écrivain, au musicien le soin de discipliner les images; quant à lui, il se réserve *le sérieux*, c'est-à-dire le rapport originel à l'être. Beaucoup plus qu'une conception d'artiste la théorie de l'Art pour l'Art est une revendication de l'homme de Bien: "A vous les images, à moi la réalité". (*SG*, 415)

Art-for-art's-sake effects a separation between art and reality so radical that it in a sense renders the negating power of artistic creation practically harmless.

This is one interpretation of the idea of art as an end and one perversion of this interpretation. But Sartre is not content simply to state his objection. He attacks the perversion also at its very source: in the aesthetics of Kant. Kant, Sartre concedes, is 'fort sage' (*Sit I*, 99) in that he divorced art from didacticism. He rejected the subordination of art to ethical ends and introduced the idea of the separation of functions which was vital to the Romantic revolution. But Kant's theories, Sartre claims, had the effect of confining nineteenth-century aesthetics within a simple and ultimately 'inert' notion of the art-object which severed art completely from ethical activity even in the widest sense. In this way the art-for-art's-sake movement grew out of Kantianism and formed the hard-core of aesthetic doctrine in mid-nineteenth-century

France, despite the intuitions of writers like Baudelaire, Flaubert and later Mallarmé, who remained in varying degrees inassimilable to the art-for-art's-sake school.

Sartre, in *L'Imaginaire*, adopted the Kantian distinction between ethics and aesthetics: 'il est stupide de confondre la morale et l'esthétique' (*I*, 245). In its radical form such a distinction is incompatible with the notion of commitment, and whilst never explicitly repudiating his earlier statement, Sartre attempted to reinterpret it within the framework of the committed aesthetics of *Situations II*. He used the very notion of the gratuitousness of the work of art to reintroduce it into the Kingdom of Ends: 'L'œuvre d'art n'*a pas de* fin, nous en sommes d'accord avec Kant. Mais c'est qu'elle *est* une fin' (*Sit II*, 98); and he defies Kant by implication when he writes: 'L'œuvre d'art est gratuite parce qu'elle est fin absolue et qu'elle se propose au spectateur comme un impératif catégorique' (*Sit II*, 261). From a theoretical point of view, Sartre's disagreement with Kant hinges on their different ideas of the aesthetic object. Kant, according to Sartre, envisages the work of art as a more or less definitive object which is offered to the free imagination of the spectator but does not involve it in any creative way: 'Kant croit que l'œuvre existe d'abord en fait et qu'elle est vue ensuite . . . C'est oublier que l'imagination du spectateur n'a pas seulement une fonction régulatrice mais constitutive' (*Sit II*, 98, 97). For Sartre, on the other hand, the work of art is an appeal to the spectator's own creative activity to bring the aesthetic object into being: 'l'œuvre . . . n'existe que si on la *regarde* et elle est d'abord pur appel, pure exigence d'exister' (*Sit II*, 98). In this sense he is able to claim that the work of art is both 'categorical imperative' and 'fin absolue' interdependently. It can be seen that Sartre's position relies ultimately on the distinction between analogon and aesthetic object. Strictly speaking, it is the analogon which appeals to the spectator to bring the aesthetic object into being. A certain amount of unnecessary obscurity arises from the fact that Sartre sometimes compresses the two elements into a single term ('l'œuvre d'art') in order to challenge Kant with a formulation as striking as his own.

But since it involves communication between two freedoms, the categorical imperative of art cannot be regarded as merely aesthetic; so that Sartre can claim: 'au fond de l'impératif esthétique nous discernons l'impératif moral' (*Sit II*, 111). What is for Kant an incidental 'effect' of art becomes in Sartre's view its 'end'. The wheel has turned full circle. The ethical dimension has been reintroduced into art, paradoxically enough, through the very notion of the gratuitousness of art. Art becomes once again communication in the fullest sense: in responding to the categorical imperative of art, by bringing the *imaginaire* into being, the spectator or reader communicates with the artist by participating in a vision of the world seen through an individual consciousness.

Like the notion of *dévoilement*, Sartre's reflexions upon Kant play an important part in the argument of *Situations II*. It is clear nonetheless that the main thrust of *Qu'est-ce que la littérature?* can be seen to constitute a familiar 'classical' Sartre; committed literature aims to change the world: 'Je tiens Flaubert et Goncourt pour responsables de la répression qui suivit la Commune parce qu'ils n'ont pas écrit une ligne pour l'empêcher' (*Sit II*, 13). Prose can, and therefore, according to a circular polemical logic, must, be committed. Poetry, like the fine arts, cannot and must not try to teach. Twenty years later Sartre's position was equally clear: poetry performs an ethical function (*Sit IX*, 62); Flaubert is a committed writer (*Sit IX*, 14). Sartre seems to have recanted; the apparent volte-face in fact reflects a refining of his aesthetic ideas which depends ultimately on an evolution in his conception of the nature of language.

In 1947 Sartre lumbered himself with a somewhat conventional distinction between prose and poetry. Prose is committed because it communicates ideas, and all ideas can be communicated. Poetry, on the other hand, uses words as objects rather than means, that is to say, as images. Prose works through the *signification* of words, poetry through the *sens*. No true synthesis is possible because as attitudes to language the two genres are mutually antagonistic. Two crucial footnotes indicate that it is possible to see the poet as committed in a different way: precisely because of his failure to communicate conceptually, he stands outside the language, and therefore the ideology, of a bourgeois society. This is an instance of *qui perd gagne*. But this line of thought is not developed. Sartre's recognition of the poet's 'failure' to communicate in no way implies a belief in the 'ineffable'. He always rejected the Bergsonian notion that thought precedes language and is distorted by its verbal expression. His own view was that the two realms are dialectically interdependent; thought comes into being through language; language clarifies and defines thought (*I*, 112 and *EN*, 601). He never went back on this position, but after 1947, he became increasingly aware of the fact of alienation as it affects self-expression. Already in *L'Etre et le Néant*, Sartre acknowledged that language, as part of *l'être-pour-autrui*, is open to misunderstanding by others (*EN*, 441); but, he maintained, it nonetheless coincides, at its source, with thought. By 1960, in the *Critique de la raison dialectique*, the emphasis has shifted; Sartre is concerned to show how language too is part of the practico-inert whereby man's free activity, his praxis, becomes rigid and objectified, part of the external situation of both himself and other men. He no longer envisages the individual listener as the chief source of the alienation of the speaker; the very structures and semantics of language are now held responsible. Sartre has not rejected his earlier assertion of the interdependence of thought and language, but he now maintains that we are fundamentally incapable of thinking certain thoughts, which we might, in a sense, be groping towards, because language, as it is given to us, cannot provide adequate expression for them (*CRD*, 75). Our thought is not distorted *après coup* by its verbal expression, it is vitiated from the outset by the limitations of the language in which it is attempting to realize itself.

Orphée noir (1948, in *Sit III*) and *Saint Genet* (1952) appear as early explorations of the alienating power of language. The language of the white man or the bourgeois alienates the thought of the negro or the thief. Genet's alienation is an extreme example of the basic loneliness and singularity of each individual human experience. Man's inner moods and feelings are fundamentally incommunicable; the only communication which can take place is conceptual, for the very universalizing power of language which permits communication destroys the individuality of the experience expressed. Language can convey 'le savoir' but not what Sartre will later call 'le non-savoir' or 'le vécu'.[6] Even as a prose writer Genet is still using 'l'envers du langage' ('the reverse side of language'); he creates a *false* prose, based on a poetic attitude towards language, a concentration on the word itself at the expense of the objects signified (*SG*, 346). Genet, Sartre claims, is not trying to communicate but erecting a barrier of images to shield his own inwardness from the bourgeois reader.

It is perhaps in *Saint Genet* that Sartre's attitude to the possibility of communication is most pessimistic; the rationalism of *L'Etre et le Néant* has been whittled away, and the notion of another kind of communication through style, which will come to the fore in *L'Idiot de la famille*, has not yet been developed. But it is, paradoxically, this pessimistic awareness of language as practico-inert which seems to have liberated Sartre's literary criticism. Having recognized the extent of language's power to alienate, he became increasingly sensitive to the ways in which the writer succeeds in overcoming this alienation. As a result, his conception of the nature of literary communication underwent a radical transformation.

In a series of interviews and lectures given in the main in 1965–66,[7] which complement the views of the *Critique*, Sartre turns repeatedly to the theme of language as at once 'trop pauvre' and 'trop riche' (*Sit VIII*, 434): too conceptual and rigid to express the real adequately, but also overlaid by secondary connotations which may interfere with the intended meaning. Communication is distorted in two very different ways. Sartre's eventual optimism is based on his realization that the second form of distortion can be used to compensate for the first. In fact, these secondary connotations are not limited to a purely semantic level; they permeate language in all its dimensions. For example, what Sartre calls the *particularités* of any language, its specific morphological and syntactic structures (gender, word-order etc.) do not, in normal speech, draw attention to themselves, but they may at times hinder comprehension and so become, in Sartre's terms, *désinformatrices*. (A *deliberate* instance of *désinformation* is Genet's attempt to disorientate the reader through gender: 'les brûlantes amours de la sentinelle et du mannequin', *Sit VIII*, 436.) The *particularités* of a language are, so far as communication is concerned, either 'superflues ou nuisibles' (*Sit VIII*, 434). They are not merely nonsignificant, but can run counter to the speaker's (or writer's) intentions.

But it is precisely language as *désinformation*, or in more general terms the practico-inert of language, which the writer can turn to his own ends:

J'utilise des mots pour me désigner, mots auxquels, par ailleurs, mon histoire a déjà donné un autre sens et qui, d'ailleurs, à propos de l'histoire de l'ensemble du langage, ont des sens différents. A partir de là on dit qu'il n'y a pas d'adéquation, alors qu'en réalité je pense qu'un écrivain est celui qui se dit que l'adéquation se fait grâce à tout ça. C'est son travail. C'est ce qu'on appelle le style . . . Au fond, je pense que rien n'est inexprimable à la condition d'inventer l'expression. (*Sit IX*, 48–9)

Sartre's preoccupation is still with literature as commitment and communication, but the nature of this communication has changed radically: 'L'engagement de l'écrivain vise à communiquer l'incommunicable (l'être-dans-le-monde vécu) en exploitant la part de désinformation contenue dans la langue commune' (*Sit VIII*, 454).

In fact, what has happened is that Sartre's conception of the writer has changed, and this change owes something to his contact in the 1960s with *la Nouvelle Critique*. In 1965 Sartre defines 'l'écrivain contemporain' as 'le poète qui se déclare prosateur' (*Sit VIII*, 432). In other words, the communication of prose is no longer envisaged as primarily conceptual but as indirect and allusive, as was previously the case with poetry alone. Sartre, I believe, absorbed from the *Tel Quel* group certain linguistic and aesthetic insights which encouraged him to modify his early prose/poetry distinction in favour of something more subtle and which corresponded better to his own increasing awareness of the 'function' of style. For example, he evolved to the point where he found Barthes's *écrivain/écrivant*[8] distinction useful in illustrating his own conception of language as *désinformation*. But if Sartre adapts Barthes, it is in order to go beyond him: 'Je dirais, pour ma part, que ce qu'apporte une vie c'est le dépassement des deux points de vue. Je pense qu'on ne peut pas être écrivain sans être écrivant et écrivant sans être écrivain' (*Sit IX*, 46).

The key to Sartre's disagreement with *la Nouvelle Critique* lies in his view of the dialectical interdependence of *signification* and *sens*. This view was not fully developed until *L'Idiot de la famille*, but already in 1965 Sartre insisted that 'Sans signification, pas d'ambiguïté, l'objet ne vient pas habiter le mot' (*Sit VIII*, 449) and that 'Le langage . . . signifie quand même quelque chose; et c'est ça qu'on a oublié' (*Que peut la littérature?*, 117–18). Sartre came to see the literary writer as someone who uses the *signification* of words as a means to the evocation of their *sens*. In a real sense, then, *signification* is still primary, but even the prose artist is aiming to communicate something else. If Sartre continued to insist that 'le prosateur a *quelque chose à dire*' (*Sit VIII*, 437), nevertheless the nature of this *quelque chose* appears to have undergone a radical transformation since *Qu'est-ce que la littérature?*:

Ce quelque chose *n'est rien de dicible,* rien de conceptuel ni de conceptualisable, rien de signifiant . . . De là, cette phrase: "C'est de la littérature", qui signifie "Vous parlez pour ne rien dire." Reste à nous demander quel est ce *rien,* ce non-savoir silencieux que l'objet littéraire doit communiquer au lecteur. (*Sit VIII*, 437)

Sartre's *rien*, like his *néant*, has hidden depths. His terminology owes something to the vocabulary of negative theology:

Il est vrai que l'écrivain n'a fondamentalement *rien* à dire. Entendons par là que son but fondamental n'est pas de communiquer un *savoir*. Pourtant il *communique* . . . Si l'écrivain n'a *rien* à dire, c'est qu'il doit manifester *tout*, c'est-à-dire ce rapport singulier et pratique de la partie au tout qu'est l'être-dans-le-monde. (*Sit VIII*, 444–5)

The writer creates through style an *universel singulier* which expresses the individual's being-in-the-world, the subjective and objective dimensions of the real. This *rien*, which is a non-conceptual totalization, dependent ultimately on the imagination, is what Sartre means by *le non-savoir*. The task of Sartre's *écrivain* is thus defined in the 1960s and 1970s in terms almost identical with those of Jean Ricardou: 'L'écrivain n'écrit pas quelque chose . . . il écrit, voilà tout. Peut-être est-ce de cette facon également qu'il faut entendre Maurice Blanchot lorsqu'il avance que l'écrivain doit sentir, au plus profond, qu'il n'a rien *à dire*' (*Que peut la littérature?*, 94).

Sartre's notion that the *vécu* can be communicated through the *sens* of words not only altered his definition of the prose writer, it encouraged him to extend the potential commitment of the poet. In 1965, Sartre seems prepared to recognize poetry as an essential element of praxis, in so far as it is complementary to prose; in the continuous process of internalization and externalization (which is the Marxist equivalent of the bourgeois notions of subjectivity and objectivity), poetry represents 'le moment d'intériorité . . . une stase' (*Sit IX*, 62). Such a moment of reflexion has, moreover, an ethical function in so far as it involves a form of non-conceptual self-knowledge 'révélatrice de l'homme à lui-même à travers le sens' (*Sit IX*, 64). Poetry, like all art, is a form of *dévoilement*, and is committed in so far as it changes the nature of our relations to the world and ourselves: 'dévoiler c'est changer' (*Sit II*, 73). Clearly it is not simply Sartre's view of literature which has changed. This change originates in his conception of communication, which has broadened precisely to the extent that his view of human alienation has deepened, and his insight into language as alienation to the practico-inert grown more subtle. It is this fundamental re-evaluation of the nature of communication which provides the key to Sartre's rehabilitation of Flaubert: 'Le projet profond dans le *Flaubert*, c'est celui de montrer qu'au fond tout est communicable' (*Sit X*, 106). Indeed *L'Idiot de la famille* is in a sense an extended demonstration of Sartre's latest ideas on the nature of language and communication. Like Genet, Sartre argues, Flaubert is *désadapté*, alienated from language because insufficiently integrated into society through his family. As a child he envisages subjective experience and language as two distinct and irreconcilable realms: 'Vie et paroles sont incommensurables. Faute de s'exprimer *aux autres* [ses affections] restent pour lui-même inexprimables' (*IF*, I, 25). His initial alienation leads him to see language from the outside as speaking itself through men, rather than as being spoken; he ignores human intentionality, and sees only the reverse side of the communication process: 'Flaubert ne croit pas qu'*on parle: on est parlé* (*IF*, I, 623). In Sartre's view the notion of the inexpressible or the ineffable is a myth arising out of Romantic alienation; but as such it is the central problem of Flaubert's art: 'Ce problème est fondamental pour Flaubert . . . il est à la source de son Art dont le projet sera de *rendre indirectement l'indisable*' (*IF*, II, 1195–6). This is what Sartre means when he says 'Gustave . . . n'a, à la lettre, rien à . . . communiquer' (*IF*, I, 50); what he has to communicate is his personal subjective experience, *le vécu, le non-savoir.*

Moreover, in the *Idiot*, Sartre adds further to our understanding of how language can communicate *le vécu.* Briefly speaking, it is through the materiality of language, or what Sartre prefers to call the *configuration graphique* of the word. The term is somewhat loosely used, as it refers not merely to the peculiar pictorial quality which the grapheme may have, but to the 'fonction imageante' (imaging function) of words in general. In this sense it is broadly equatable with the *sens* or connotations of language. To use the terms of *L'Imaginaire*, the literary writer is one who uses the word as an analogon or image of the thing expressed. Concrete examples are few and far between in *L'Idiot*, doubtless because they would belong, logically, to the fourth volume, which never appeared, but which promised a 'formal' analysis of the text of *Madame Bovary*. In fact some of the most graphic illustrations are taken from outside Flaubert's works. Commenting on a line from Mallarmé, Sartre writes:

Si vous lisez: "perdus, sans mâts, sans mâts . . .", l'organisation poétique anime le mot: barré en croix, le *t* s'élève au-dessus des autres lettres, comme le mât au-dessus du navire; autour de lui les lettres se ramassent: c'est la coque, c'est le pont: certains – dont je suis – appréhendent dans cette lettre blanche, la voyelle *a*, écrasée sous l'accent circonflexe comme sous un ciel bas et nuageux, la voile qui s'affaisse. La négation qui s'exprime par *sans* agit surtout dans l'univers signifiant; le bateau est démâté, perdu: voilà ce que nous *apprenons.* Dans le monde obscur du sens, elle ne peut déstructurer le mot de 'mât'. Disons qu'elle le pâlit jusqu'à en faire l'*analogon* de je ne sais quel négatif de photo.   (*IF*, I, 929–30)

This is a good example of the *sens* working against or despite the *signification.* We imagine the mast which is signified as absent. In no sense can the word *mât* be said to have, in reality, the form of a ship's mast, and, moreover, as we shall see, Sartre thinks our ability to imagine that this is the case depends on our knowledge that *mât* signifies a 'mast'. But the writer's art consists in making the reader adopt an *attitude imageante* towards the words she is reading: 'En vérité le mot de mât n'a aucune ressemblance objective et réelle avec l'objet qu'il désigne. Mais l'art d'écrire, ici, consiste justement à contraindre le lecteur, de gré ou de force, à en trouver une, à faire descendre l'objet dans le signe comme présence irréelle' (*IF*, I, 930). In case our attention in the Mallarmé example should focus too exclusively on the visual aspect, Sartre reminds us that

N'importe quel mot – en dépit de son caractère conventionnel – peut avoir une fonction imageante . . . en effet il ne s'agit pas de ressemblances dues au hasard entre le matériel signifiant et l'objet signifié, mais des bonheurs d'un style qui contraint à saisir la matérialité du vocable comme unité organique et celle-ci comme la présence même de l'objet visé.

(*IF*, I, 930)

In other instances individual words may themselves evoke a succession of images independent of their context. In this case 'le graphème, par sa configuration physique et *avant tout traitement*, éveille des résonances' (*IF*, I, 931). 'Le Château d'Amboise', for example, may suggest *framboise, boisé, boiserie, Ambroisie, Ambroise* (*IF*, I, 932). These connotations are objective in the sense that they can, potentially, be apprehended by all readers. Sartre's example in *Situations II* of 'Florence, femme et fleur' (*IF*, I, 934) belongs to this category of objective connotations. But, as in the case of *Florence*, there is always the possibility that words may have subjective connotations which may be of one kind for the writer and another for the reader. Of these personal connotations Sartre writes: 'Elles constituent, chez chacun de nous, le fond singulier et incommunicable de toute appréhension du Verbe' (*IF*, I, 932). If the writer encourages these personal resonances, he will create a kind of obscure 'semi-communication' (*IF*, I, 932), which Sartre thinks is more appropriate to the comparative narcissism of poetry than to prose. The prose writer has to control and limit the personal connotations which the poet, on the other hand, may allow to proliferate both in his own imagination and in that of the reader. The 'incommunicability' Sartre refers to is, of course, not absolute. In the first instance, the subjective connotations of a word may be communicated indirectly through the objective connotations of other words used in conjunction with it; and, secondly, the 'semi-communication' of poetry is itself accepted by the later Sartre as an indispensable means of contact between two narcissisms.

The use of the connotations or the *sens* of words (whether subjective or objective) is for Sartre a language usage which implies a
preference for the imaginary and purely verbal over the real:
'Choisir la somptuosité des noms, c'est déjà préférer l'univers du
verbe à celui des choses' (*IF*, I, 934). Broadly speaking, Sartre
equates awareness of the word as a *signe* (by which he means the
word used to point beyond itself to a *signification*) with the perceptual attitude, and awareness of its materiality or *sens* with the imaginative attitude: 'Appréhender [le vocable] comme signe, c'est
une activité voisine et complémentaire de la perception. Le saisir
dans sa singularité matérielle, c'est l'imaginer' (*IF*, I, 929). Sartre's
distinction depends on the dialectic which was established first in
L'Imaginaire and which remains the fundamental insight behind all
his aesthetics: perception and imagination are radically distinct yet
totally interdependent.[9] This means that although the two aspects
of words are used simultaneously by the writer ('L'entreprise consiste à utiliser simultanément la fonction signifiante et la fonction
imageante du mot écrit', *IF*, I, 928), they cannot be present
simultaneously in the reader's mind, which passes rapidly from one
to the other: 'On ne peut obliger le discours à exercer *à la fois* la
fonction sémantique et la fonction imageante. L'écriture − et la lecture qui en est inséparable − impliquent, à ce niveau, une dialectique
subtile de la perception et de l'imagination, du réel et de l'irréel, du
signe et du sens' (*IF*, I, 934). Sartre still insists on the primary role
played by *la signification conceptuelle*: 'Il faut bien, pour présen-
tifier une Calcutta imaginaire et parée de tous les charmes de son
nom, conserver au moins un savoir rudimentaire: c'est une ville
située aux Indes, ses habitants sont indiens' (*IF*, I, 934). This is the
basis of Sartre's attack on what he considers the exclusive emphasis
of the 'critique du signifiant'. None the less, it is clear that in
Flaubert's case, *signification* remains merely a means to an end
which is 'le sens indisable': 'La forme est un langage qu'on pourrait
nommer parasitaire puisqu'il se constitue aux dépens du langage réel
et sans cesser de l'exploiter, en l'asservissant à exprimer ce qu'il n'est
pas fait pour nous dire' (*IF*, II, 1617). Communication of the *indisable* depends ultimately on the imagination: 'La matérialité non
signifiante ne peut fournir des sens que dans l'imaginaire' (*IF*, II,
1616). And, as Sartre made clear in *L'Imaginaire*, in imagining we
become ourselves imaginary:

Certes [Flaubert] ne transmet rien au lecteur réaliste sinon la fascinante
proposition de s'irréaliser à son tour. Si celui-ci, qui n'est en aucun cas l'in-
terlocuteur direct de Flaubert, cède à la tentation, s'il se fait lecteur

imaginaire de l'œuvre − il le faut, pour saisir le sens derrière les significations − alors tout l'indisable, y compris la saveur du plum-pudding, lui
sera révélé allusivement.   (*IF*, II, 2003)

We have seen enough to enable us to understand how Flaubert
communicates with his reader; it is paradoxically through the
unreal and the imaginary that the most significant communication
can take place. Flaubert exemplifies the dilemma of all art, which
can reveal the true only through creation in the domain of the
unreal. A further set of ideas would need to be developed before
we could understand how, in Sartre's view, Flaubert is 'politically'
committed in the sense of effecting change.[10] Briefly, this involves
the idea of a *mésentente* between Flaubert and his contemporary
reader, who mistakes *Madame Bovary* for a work of realism, and
is therefore tempted to give herself up imaginatively to the experience of the novel, exposing herself unwittingly to the corrosion
of Flaubert's ironical nihilism. Flaubert's use of the imagination is
a trap for the bourgeois public. His art is *dévoilement* in the sense
of demoralization: 'Le but de l'entreprise littéraire est de réduire le
lecteur au désespoir' (*IF*, III, 321). It is by the same token commitment, since, of course, 'la vie humaine commence de l'autre côté
du désespoir'.[11]

But what is more important is that Sartre has come to see the
imagination of language as the essential medium of inter-subjective
communication. It is the evolution in his ideas on the nature of
linguistic communication which has enabled him to commit writers
such as Flaubert and Mallarmé, who are now seen as communicating something less evidently universal than concepts or
ideas, but no less fundamental in human experience. An examination of *L'Idiot* shows how Sartre has absorbed into his own
rational humanism certain fundamental Romantic values: belief,
for example, in the imagination as a means of communicating and
receiving the kind of truth which is non-conceptual, or in Sartre's
terms, as the means of access to the *vécu* of another person, and
in the last analysis to the world as totalized by another project;
belief, therefore, in the human relevance of the kind of art which
does not set out directly to teach or change the world.

7

Psychoanalysis: existential and Freudian

Sartre's attitude to Freud is, from the outset, ambivalent: while recognizing the debt of existential to Freudian psychoanalysis, he is anxious to stress the differences of principle and methods. While agreeing with Freud that all human behaviour is 'significant', Sartre rejects totally both the suggestion that its source is the unconscious and the ensuing psychic determinism of Freudian theory.

But after 1943 Sartre moved increasingly closer to Freud, without always acknowledging this evolution. The reasons for this change appear to be threefold. In the first place, his own notion of human liberty underwent a considerable transformation, to the point where he could admit: 'D'une certaine façon nous naissons tous prédestinés' (*Sit X*, 98). Secondly, he significantly modified his early view of human consciousness. Thirdly, his knowledge of Lacan led him to interpret Freudian theory in a new light. *L'Idiot de la famille* provides clear evidence of this *rapprochement* with Freud.

Sartre lays out the aims and principles of existential psychoanalysis in *L'Etre et le Néant*. Existential analysis is based on the principle that man is a totality and each of his acts is therefore *révélateur* (*EN*, 656); its aim is to decipher and conceptualize the meaning of his behaviour; and it is supported, Sartre claims, by man's intuitive understanding of himself.

Le *principe* de cette psychanalyse est que l'homme est une totalité et non une collection; qu'en conséquence, il s'exprime tout entier dans la plus insignifiante et la plus superficielle de ses conduites − autrement dit, qu'il n'est pas un goût, un tic, un acte humain qui ne soit *révélateur*. Le *but* de la psychanalyse est de déchiffrer les comportements empiriques de l'homme, c'est-à-dire de mettre en pleine lumière les révélations que chacun d'eux contient et de les fixer conceptuellement.

Son *point de départ* est l'*expérience*; son *point d'appui* est la compréhension préontologique et fondamentale que l'homme a de la personne humaine . . . Sa méthode est comparative . . . c'est par la comparaison [des] conduites que nous ferons jaillir la révélation unique qu'elles expriment toutes de manière différente.   (*EN*, 656)

It is also in *L'Etre et le Néant* that Sartre makes his first reference to the regressive–progressive method which he will illustrate most fully in his work on Flaubert:

La compréhension se fait en deux sens inverses: par une psycho-analyse régressive, on remonte de l'acte considéré jusqu'à mon possible ultime – par une progression synthétique, de ce possible ultime on redescend jusqu'à l'acte envisagé et on saisit son intégration dans la forme totale.

(*EN*, 537)

In other words, behaviour and project illumine each other.

The account of Freud given in *L'Etre et le Néant* is conventional and somewhat schematic in so far as it ignores the chronological development of Freud's thought. Sartre sees the similarities between himself and Freud as dependent on the notion that all manifestations of 'la vie psychique' relate symbolically to the fundamental structures of the individual. Neither believes in 'données premières', in the sense that nothing precedes human liberty for the existentialist or personal history for the Freudian. Both consider the human being as an 'historialisation perpétuelle' and attempt to uncover the meaning, direction and transformations of this history. A further similarity follows from this: the importance of man's situation in the world:

Les enquêtes psychanalytiques visent à reconstituer la vie du sujet de la naissance à l'instant de la cure; elles utilisent tous les documents objectifs qu'elles pourront trouver: lettres, témoignages, journaux intimes, renseignements "sociaux" de toute espèce. Et ce qu'elles visent à restituer est moins un pur événement psychique qu'un couple: l'événement crucial de l'enfance et la cristallisation psychique autour de cet événement.

(*EN*, 657)

Facts of personal history are thus seen both as factors contributing to psychic evolution and as symbols of that evolution.

Both analyses, Sartre maintains, seek a fundamental pre-logical attitude which can only be reconstituted according to 'des lois de synthèses spécifiques' (*EN*, 657). The complex, he claims, is, in this respect, the Freudian equivalent of the 'choix originel'. Sartre seems to have in mind a proliferation of individual complexes of the type envisaged by some Freudians but explicitly rejected by Freud himself.[1] On the other hand, the comparison with the 'choix originel' is faithful to Freud's own specific notion of the complex as a fundamental structuring force rather than a description of a state or a merely pathogenic phenomenon (see *SE*, VII, 226).

In neither account, Sartre contends, is the subject seen as in a privileged position to undertake his own analysis.[2] Sartre recognizes the basic difference between himself and Freud over the existence of the unconscious, but emphasizes that his own notion of consciousness includes the non-rational; the 'projet fondamental' is '*vécu* [. . .] et, comme tel, totalement conscient' but it is not '*connu*' (*EN*, 658). Consciousness, then, is not necessarily knowledge. Reflexion does not reveal the original project in its pure form but rather 'le désir singulier et daté dans l'enchevêtrement touffu de sa caractéristique' (*EN*, 658). The reflecting subject may not have the instruments or techniques for isolating the choice itself which is symbolized through his behaviour, or for conceptualizing this choice. However,

Il ne s'agit point d'une énigme indevinée, comme le croient les freudiens: tout est là, lumineux, la réflexion jouit de tout, saisit tout. Mais ce "mystère en pleine lumière" vient plutôt de ce que cette jouissance est privée des moyens qui permettent ordinairement l'*analyse* et la *conceptualisation*.   (*EN*, 658).

Psychoanalysis permits the subject to know what he already in a sense 'understood'. (Sartre's distinction between formulated *connaissance* or knowledge and natural, unconceptualized *compréhension* or awareness is of great importance for his notion of *le vécu*, and we need to bear constantly in mind the specific and perhaps even idiosyncratic senses which he attributes to these two words.)[3] Analysis, whether Freudian or existential, can reveal complexes or projects only from an external viewpoint; it cannot reveal 'le projet tel qu'il est pour soi, le complexe dans son être propre' (*EN*, 659).

Sartre's analysis of the chief differences between himself and Freud is necessarily more critical; it is also less faithful to the sense of Freud's own ideas. For example, as a phenomenologist, he criticizes Freud's notion of the libido for being reductive without being a true *irréductible*, on the grounds that the notion was arrived at by contingent empirical observation rather than by phenomenological intuition, as is the case with existential liberty. The criticism is in part philosophical; but it leads Sartre to misrepresent Freud when he maintains that the libido tends to reduce the immense diversity of psychic activity to a single source. Sartre ignores the fact that Freud explicitly rejects the Jungian conception of the libido as a universal source of psychic energy, and insists throughout on its specifically sexual nature.[4]

Sartre also rejects what he sees as the mechanistic nature of traditional psychoanalytic accounts of the relations between man and his milieu:

Le milieu ne saurait agir sur le sujet que dans la mesure exacte où il le comprend; c'est-à-dire où il le transforme en situation. Aucune description objective de ce milieu ne saurait donc nous servir. · (*EN*, 660)

A consequence of this stress on individual interpretation of experience, Sartre contends, is that existential analysis eschews all theories of universal symbolism. But here too Sartre over-simplifies Freud: the kind of automatic translation ('fèces = or, pelote à épingle = sein' *EN*, 661) which he rejects appears caricatural. Freud's ideas about symbolism are complex. Some symbols, he claims, are 'universally disseminated' (at least within a particular linguistic or cultural group), but subject to 'oscillations' (*SE*, V, 684) of meaning. Others are individual and can be adequately interpreted only in the light of the personal associations they may have for a particular subject. Moreover there is no guarantee that, in dreams for example, a particular element is functioning symbolically. All this makes it impossible, in Freud's view, to establish a universally applicable decoding 'key' (*SE*, IV, 96–100).

Sartre's final objection to Freud in *L'Etre et le Néant* is that he tends to envisage consciousness as in some sense 'inhabited'. The object of analysis is, Sartre claims, one with consciousness itself, for were this not so, the subject would be unable to recognize his so-called 'unconscious' desires and impulses when they were revealed to him:

Si vraiment le complexe est inconscient, c'est-à-dire si le signe est séparé du signifié par un barrage, comment le sujet pourrait-il le *reconnaître*?
(*EN*, 661)

Sartre is returning to the topic already tackled from another angle in his discussion of *mauvaise foi*: if the unconscious and conscious are radically separated, then what is the origin of resistance to analysis, and, moreover, how is recognition of the 'complex' possible? If the conscious mind is presumed unaware of the contents of the unconscious it will not feel the need to resist analysis; moreover the unconscious is supposedly attempting to express itself and avoid the activity of the censor-mechanism. The resistance therefore must come from the censor-mechanism itself, Sartre suggests, and in this case the problem is merely displaced: if the censor does not know what it is repressing how can it perform the repression? If it *does* know its object it must also be aware of its function:

Il faut qu'elle soit conscience (d')être conscience de la tendance à refouler, mais précisément *pour n'en être pas conscience*. Qu'est-ce à dire sinon que la censure doit être de mauvaise foi? (*EN*, 91–2)

Sartre is basing his criticisms only on Freud's first topography and contriving to ignore the later writings. Freud was clearly aware of the difficulties surrounding the location of the censor, and provides various different solutions to the question, including at one point the notion of two censors (*SE*, XIV, 193). He eventually decided, around 1920, to reject the conscious/unconscious dichotomy in favour of id, ego and superego on the grounds that the term 'unconscious' should no longer be used to designate both 'a quality of what is mental' and a 'mental province' or system. He therefore restricted the term 'unconscious' to the quality, and chose the term 'id' to refer to the 'mental *region* that is foreign to the ego' (*SE*, XXI, 72). This enabled him to deal more satisfactorily with the problem of resistance to analysis:

Since . . . there can be no question but that this resistance emanates from [the patient's] ego and belongs to it, we find ourselves in an unforeseen situation. We have come across something in the ego itself which is also unconscious, which behaves exactly like the repressed . . . We recognize that the *Ucs.* does not coincide with the repressed; it is still true that all that is repressed is *Ucs.*, but not all that is *Ucs.* is repressed. A part of the ego, too – and Heaven knows how important a part – may be *Ucs.*, undoubtedly is *Ucs.* (*SE*, XIX, 17)

The question is not perhaps finally resolved, but of course Sartre's own distinction between *conscience* or *compréhension* and *connaissance* raises equally serious difficulties.

Sartre's later discussions of Freud centre chiefly on the notions of finality, the *vécu* and the unconscious. In 1966 Sartre criticizes traditional psychoanalysis for remaining on a non-dialectical level: 'Vous pouvez considérer que tout projet est une fuite mais vous devriez aussi considérer que toute fuite est un projet' (*Sit IX*, 95). In an interview with the *New Left Review* in 1969 Sartre admits that he accepts many of the facts which Freud revealed, such as 'les *faits* du déguisement et de la répression' (*Sit IX*, 105), but that he finds their expression both unacceptably mythological and also mechanistic because borrowed from the language of physiology and biology. (We might note that in 1960 Sartre referred to the mythology as 'parfaitement inoffensive' (*CRD*, 47) when he was concerned to show that psychoanalysis, with its emphasis on the individual, does not conflict with Marxism.) According to Sartre,

Freud has intuitions of the truth when he describes mental processes as part of a subjective finality, but his account of them too often degenerates into a merely mechanistic description. A serious consequence of this *syncrétisme* is the lack of a dialectical structure. Sartre means, of course, the kind of structure which permits more than an unquestioning acceptance of both an idea and its opposite with the vague explanation that 'après tout, "les opposés s'interpénètrent", (*Sit IX*, 107). A dialectical structure would, he thinks, present a far more logical and structured account of the mass of facts which can otherwise be seen as linked only loosely.

But, in fact, throughout his writings, Freud constantly stresses the 'sense', 'purpose' and intention implicit in all psychical phenomena, including neurosis: 'The symptoms of a case of neurotic illness have a sense, serve a purpose' (*SE*, XV, 239). Like Sartre, who claims that his analysis in *L'Idiot* is an example of anti-psychiatry (*Sit X*, 100), Freud too believes that neurosis can be a solution to a problem, and suggests that its 'cure' is not always desirable.[5] Furthermore, he lays the blame for neurosis as much at the door of society as of the neurotic himself:

Society has allowed itself to be misled into tightening the moral standard to the greatest possible degree, and it has thus forced its members into a yet greater estrangement from their instinctual dispositions . . . In the domain of sexuality where such suppression is more difficult to carry out, the result is seen in the reactive phenomena of neurotic disorders.

(*SE*, XIV, 284)[6]

Of course, Freud's position in this matter is less radical than Sartre's: neurosis may solve an otherwise insoluble dilemma, it may provide both 'primary' and 'secondary' gain (*SE*, XIV, 53), it may, in the case of some artists for example, be the 'reverse side' of 'other endowments' (*SE*, XVI, 414), but it is not the positive strategy envisaged by Sartre. Nonetheless, it is clear that Sartre plays down the complexity of Freud's thought, in order, perhaps, to bring his own into sharper relief.

In the same interview Sartre declares that he has replaced his old notion of *conscience* by that of *le vécu*. This change is decisive for Sartre's *rapprochement* with Freud. The term *vécu* covers several areas separated by Freudian analysis and previously included by Sartre within consciousness despite the evident conflict with the established usage of this term.[7] The *vécu*, Sartre explains,

ne désigne ni les refuges du préconscient, ni l'inconscient, ni le conscient mais le terrain sur lequel l'individu est constamment submergé par lui même, par ses propres richesses, et où la conscience a l'astuce de se déterminer elle-même par l'oubli . . . Ce que j'appelle le *vécu*, c'est précisément l'ensemble du processus dialectique de la vie psychique, un processus qui reste nécessairement opaque à lui-même car il est une constante totalisation, et une totalisation *qui ne peut être consciente de ce qu'elle est*. On peut être conscient, en effet, d'une totalisation extérieure, mais non d'une totalisation qui totalise également la conscience. En ce sens, le vécu est toujours susceptible de compréhension, jamais de connaissance.

(*Sit IX*, 108, 111)

We have here an expansion of notions previously encountered in *L'Etre et le Néant* but involving a very important reformulation: the totalization referred to is not *conscious* of what it is. The *conscience/connaissance* distinction (according to which the *vécu* was 'totalement conscient' but not 'connu', *EN*, 658) would seem to have been replaced by its counterpart, the *compréhension/connaissance* distinction. This is evidently due to the increasing flexibility of Sartre's attitude towards the unconscious, and his increasing awareness of the need to make distinctions within his own all-pervading notion of 'consciousness'. He goes so far as to say that he will discuss Flaubert's relations with 'ce qu'on appelle ordinairement l'inconscient et que j'appellerais plutôt une absence totale de connaissance doublée d'une réelle compréhension' (*Sit IX*, 110–11). The *vécu* is neither preconscious, unconscious, nor conscious: it is not *other* than these areas but rather subsumes them all. Indeed, in an interview in *Le Monde* Sartre says that the *vécu* represents for him:

L'équivalent de conscient–inconscient, c'est-à-dire que je ne crois toujours pas à l'inconscient *sous certaines formes*, bien que la conception de l'inconscient que donne Lacan soit plus intéressante.

(*Sit X*, 110–11)

And it would seem to be the Lacanian interpretation of Freud which lies at the root of Sartre's new terminology. Lacan emphasizes that side of Freud's teaching which sees language as the most important source of revelations about the unconscious, and maintains that it is Saussure's discoveries about the relation of *signifiant* to *signifié* which best illumine, retrospectively, Freud's own doctrine. For Lacan, the Freudian unconscious is embedded in language, indeed its most important manifestation *is* language in so far as this escapes the conscious control of the speaker:

L'inconscient est cette partie du discours concret en tant que transindividuel, qui fait défaut à la disposition du sujet pour rétablir la continuité de son discours conscient. Ainsi disparaît le paradoxe que présente la notion de l'inconscient, si on le rapporte à une réalité individuelle.[8]

Or, in the form in which the notion is most usually quoted: 'l'inconscient, c'est le discours de l'Autre'. This is a formulation which Sartre in 1966 accepts whole-heartedly:

Pour moi, Lacan a clarifié l'inconscient en tant que discours qui sépare à travers le langage ou, si l'on préfère, en tant que contre-finalité de la parole: des ensembles verbaux se structurent comme ensemble pratico-inerte à travers l'acte de parler. Ces ensembles expriment ou constituent des intentions qui me déterminent sans être miennes.   (*Sit IX*, 97)

Such a statement represents a radical difference from the position of *L'Etre et le Néant*.

It is true that in an interview with *L'Arc* in 1966 Sartre attacks certain elements of Lacan's teaching. He condemns, for example, the constructed nature of the Lacanian ego, and apparently rejects out of hand the Structuralist notion of a 'décentrement du sujet', according to which 'l'homme ne pense pas, il est pensé, comme il est parlé pour certains linguistes'.[9] This attack was, however, made almost inevitable by the explicit intention of the interview itself, in which Sartre was supposed to counter the Structuralists who were allegedly luring his followers from him. Sartre's real attitude to Lacan is in fact far more positive than he reveals in the 1966 interview, to precisely the extent that Lacan's real position is more subtle than the presentation that Sartre gives of it in *L'Arc*. Lacan's notion of the 'décentrement du sujet', for example, is far from being, as it is often represented, a wantonly cynical toppling of man from his pedestal. In fact Lacan, like Sartre, recognizes that if indeed 'l'homme est parlé' this is a measure of his alienation. It is while speaking of 'la folie' that Lacan tentatively suggests that

L'absence de la parole s'y manifeste par les stéréotypies d'un discours où le sujet, peut-on dire, est parlé plutôt qu'il ne parle.   (*Ecrits*, 280)

Sartre will make full use of this notion in his study of Flaubert's relations with language.

Moreover, with respect to the Ego, Sartre has himself always recognized its constructed nature, though he sees this construction as actively undertaken rather than passively undergone. In 1936 he wrote:

Cet Ego, dont Je et Moi ne sont que deux faces, constitue l'unité idéale (noématique) et indirecte de la série infinie de nos consciences réfléchies.   (*TE*, 43)

In the interview in *Le Monde* in 1971, Sartre agrees that his description of the constitution of the *moi* of Flaubert corresponds fairly closely to Lacan's own notion of the *moi* as 'une construction imaginaire, une fiction à laquelle on s'identifie après coup' (*Sit X*, 99). We may mention here a parallel between Lacan's account of the *stade du miroir* (mirror stage) in the development of the child's construction of its own ego, and Sartre's analysis of the young Gustave's experiences in front of a mirror in 'Le Miroir et le rire' and 'Le Miroir et le fétiche': 'Les miroirs le fascinent. S'il s'y surprend il sera pour lui l'objet qu'il est pour tous' (*IF*, I, 678). There are various instances in Sartre's early literary works of characters attempting to create an illusion of self-identity by observing their reflexions in a mirror (e.g. *Huis clos*, *Les Chemins de la liberté*), but this represents the first discussion in Sartre's critical writings of the role of the mirror in the process of self-objectivation; and it seems probable that Sartre's decision to afford such prominence to the notion in his account of Flaubert's 'personnalisation' depends to a large extent on his knowledge of Lacan's work. As a theoretical concept, the 'mirror stage' derives originally from a paper presented by Lacan at the International Congress of Psychoanalysis in Marienbad in 1936, the ideas of which were consequently disseminated amongst French analysts and were further developed by Lacan in 1949 in 'Le Stade du miroir comme fondateur de la fonction du Je' (*Ecrits*, 93–100). In Lacan's view, the child's sight of itself reflected in a mirror enables it to perform a socially necessary, albeit falsifying, self-unification. Lacan dates this between the sixth and eighteenth month of the infant's existence. The fact that Flaubert's fascination with mirrors continues at a later stage in his life can be explained in terms of an unsatisfactory original self-unification, for, in Sartre's account, Gustave can never identity himself fully with his *moi*, which he experiences as alienating.

In *L'Etre et le Néant* Sartre sets out his idea of the necessary conditions for a full psychoanalytic account, which should interpret not only 'les rêves, les actes manqués, les obsessions et les névroses mais aussi et surtout les pensées de la veille, les actes réussis et adaptés, le style etc.' (*EN*, 663). It is the *surtout* which has contributed to much of the Freudian outrage at the psychoanalytic elements of *L'Idiot de la famille*. In this respect also, however, Sartre is close to Lacan if not to traditional Freudians. In his reinterpretation of Freud, Lacan deliberately departs from the exclusive attention paid by traditional analysts to privileged revelations of the unconscious mind such as dreams, obsessions and parapraxes. His view of the unconscious as a symbolic discourse, repressed in one register only to appear disguised in another, leads him to propose instead a kind of analysis which concentrates just as much on the day-to-day or 'normal' aspects of a patient's life:

L'inconscient est ce chapitre de mon histoire qui est marqué par un blanc ou occupé par un mensonge: c'est le chapitre censuré. Mais la vérité peut être retrouvée; le plus souvent déjà elle est écrite ailleurs.
A savoir:
– dans les monuments: et ceci est mon corps, c'est-à-dire le noyau hystérique de la névrose où le symptôme hystérique montre la structure d'un langage et se déchiffre comme une inscription qui, une fois recueillie, peut sans perte grave être détruite;
– dans les documents d'archives aussi: et ce sont les souvenirs de mon enfance, impénétrables aussi bien qu'eux quand je n'en connais pas la provenance;
– dans l'évolution sémantique: et ceci répond au stock et aux acceptions du vocabulaire qui m'est particulier, comme au style de ma vie et à mon caractère;
– dans les traditions aussi, voire dans les légendes qui sous une forme héroïsée véhiculent mon histoire;
– dans les traces, enfin, qu'en conservent inévitablement les distorsions, nécessitées par le raccord du chapitre adultéré dans les chapitres qui l'encadrent, et dont mon exégèse rétablira le sens.   (*Ecrits*, 259)

In Lacan's view one's body, childhood memories, speech habits, style of life and personal myths constitute clues to an original neurosis which is not directly discernible but which can be seen through the distortions it imposes on the way one reconstructs one's own story. The account which *L'Idiot de la famille* seeks to provide in the 'case' of Flaubert corresponds closely to the Lacanian programme.

To assimilate the ideas of Sartre and Lacan would involve a misrepresentation of both theories, and would certainly have been rejected by both thinkers. But it is useful to point out the similarities which seem to have contributed to Sartre's *rapprochement* with Freudianism, and to have influenced the psychoanalytic dimension of *L'Idiot*. Sartre claims not to be very familiar with Lacan's work except 'à travers des lectures indirectes' (*Sit X*, 110), but, whatever the truth of this assertion, his frequent references to Lacan show that he has digested and assimilated what he has read.

In 1969, Sartre admits that his early distaste for Freud was in part due to his own Cartesian formation:

Quand on vient de passer son bachot, à dix-sept ans, après avoir reçu un enseignement fondé sur le *"Je pense, donc je suis"* de Descartes, et qu'on ouvre la *Psychopathologie de la vie quotidienne*, où l'on trouve la célèbre histoire de Signorelli, avec les substitutions, déplacements et combinaisons qui impliquent que Freud pensait simultanément à un patient qui s'était suicidé, à certaines coutumes turques et à bien d'autres choses encore . . . on a le souffle coupé. *(Sit IX*, 104)

What Sartre objected to was not simply the idea of the un-conscious, but the apparent lack of rigour and definition with which Freud handled such notions. Lacan's interpretation of Freud has the inestimable advantage in Sartre's eyes of emphasizing what can possibly be called the 'Cartesian' side of Freud's doctrines. In Lacan's view, Freudian psychoanalysis would have been un-thinkable before the birth of modern science in the seventeenth century:

Car le corrélat de la science, c'est la position cartésienne du sujet qui a pour effet d'annuler les profondeurs de la subjectivité. Souvenez-vous que Freud n'a pas hésité à rompre avec Jung lorsque celui-ci a tenté de les restaurer dans la psychanalyse. Il était absolument nécessaire que [Freud] fût un scientiste.[10]

Lacan is here referring to Jung's notion of the 'métamorphoses de la libido' which he says Freud rejected because the consequence of the accompanying idea of an archetype was to 'faire du symbole le fleurissement de l'âme' whereas for Freud the symbolic was rather *exterior* to man: 'ce n'est pas l'âme qui parle mais l'homme qui parle avec son âme' *(Ecrits*, 469).

It is an essential tenet of Sartre's philosophy that *le vécu* can be communicated; indeed he states that the 'projet profond dans le *Flaubert* c'est celui de montrer qu'au fond tout est communicable' *(Sit X*, 106). Whereas certain traditional Freudians have criticized what they see as the excessively rationalistic foundations of Sartre's analysis in *L'Idiot*, Lacan appears to share, at least in part, Sartre's assumptions of communicability. For example he speaks disparag-ingly of the

fausses pensées de la cuistrerie, quand elle arguë de l'ineffable du vécu, voire de la "conscience morbide", pour désarmer l'effort dont elle se dispense, à savoir celui qui est requis au point où justement ce n'est pas ineffable puisque ça parle, où le vécu, loin de séparer, se communique, où la subjectivité livre sa structure véritable, celle où ce qui s'analyse est iden-tique à ce qui s'articule. *(Ecrits*, 576)

In its most extreme forms the rejection by Freudians of Sartre's *L'Idiot de la famille* has been almost total ('Cet Himalaya verbal se dresse comme un barrage *contre Freud*'),[11] and Sartre's avoidance of the Freudian unconscious is compared to the 'édifices d'idées claires qu'élevaient les cartésiens face à cette "qualité occulte": l'attraction.'[12] Such an attitude is over-simple. The psychoanalysis of *L'Idiot* is quite clearly indebted to Freud: it is 'antipsychanalytique' (to use Burgelin's term) only in certain limited respects.

Sartre's analysis of Flaubert begins at infancy. Like Freud, Sartre would ideally like to possess information about 'l'allaitement, les fonctions digestives, excrétoires du nourrisson, les premiers soins de propreté, le rapport avec la mère' (*IF*, I, 51). Sartre recognizes that these early experiences are more or less directly influential in individual cases: 'il est des hommes que l'histoire a forgés beaucoup plus que la préhistoire, écrasant en eux sans pitié l'enfant qu'ils ont été' (*IF*, I, 55), but is certain that in the case of Gustave the *préhistoire* was vital.

Sartre's account of Flaubert's relations with his mother starts with a general statement of the major role of these relations in personal development:

Je rappelle les généralités: quand la mère allaite ou nettoie le nourrisson, elle s'exprime, comme tout le monde, dans sa vérité de *personne* . . . du même coup . . . par la personne même [de la mère], adroite ou maladroite, brutale ou tendre, telle enfin que son histoire l'a faite, l'enfant est manifesté à lui-même . . . Pour commencer, il intériorise les rythmes et les travaux maternels comme des qualités vécues de son propre corps . . . Sa propre mère, engloutie au plus profond de ce corps, devient la structure pathétique de l'affectivité. (*IF*, I, 57–8)

Sartre here appears to be assimilating, though not explicitly, the psychoanalytic notions of introjection and of partial objects. His synthesis is convincing, and could well be an example of what he means by the enriching of Freudianism which would result from a less purely analytic and more dialectical approach. On the other hand, however, although traditional Freudianism separates the stages of partial objects (early infancy) and of introjection of the parents to form the super-ego, most modern analysts (e.g. Fairbairn and Guntrip) envisage the latter as preceded at least by internalization of the mother at a pre-Œdipal stage. Sartre's account can therefore be seen as following contemporary trends in its assimilation of the two stages.

It is not, however, only the affectivity of the child which is dependent on the relations with the mother, but also his later aggressiveness, Sartre claims, backing up his statement by referring to the research of the American anthropologist Margaret Mead.[13] The young Flaubert is essentially passive, 'pour lui vivre est *trop fatigant*' (*IF*, I, 46), and this point is vital for Sartre's discussion of Flaubert's relations with language.[14] Sartre refers to Flaubert's inertia as his 'constitution passive', and concludes:

Ainsi de l'inertie pathétique . . . elle conservera son sens archaïque . . . conservé, dépassé, traversé de significations neuves et complexes, le sens ne peut manquer de s'altérer. Mais ces altérations *doivent être comprises*: il s'agit, en effet, de reproduire une totalisation nouvelle à partir de contradictions internes d'une totalité antérieure et du projet qui naît d'elles.

(*IF*, I, 54)

Sartre now seems to be extending the notion of *facticité* from simple givens such as race, class, sex etc. to include fundamental personal structures which cannot be changed or eradicated, but which can be variously combined, used, and interpreted, as new experiences present new possibilities of behaviour, or as new projects imply new attitudes towards the structures themselves. Moreover these structures are established extremely early, according to Sartre's present view: 'Le dur noyau sombre de ce sens est la petite enfance . . . le passé préhistorique revient sur l'enfant comme Destin' (*IF*, I, 54–5).

It is clear that Sartre has moved closer to the Freudian psychoanalytic viewpoint: in general terms in his stress on the 'Destiny' of childhood, and more particularly in his recognition of the importance of Flaubert's initial passivity for his later development. Of the pregenital stage, Freud writes:

Here the opposition between two currents, which runs through all sexual life, is already developed: they cannot yet, however, be described as 'masculine' and 'feminine', but only as 'active' and 'passive'.

(*SE*, VII, 198)

Sartre discusses the

Détermination originelle de Gustave − qui n'est *rien de plus* au départ que l'intériorisation de l'environnement familial dans une situation objective qui la conditionne du dehors et *dès avant* sa conception comme *singularité*.

(*IF*, I, 61)

The notion that the child is determined even before conception (it is named, discussed, etc.) is also to be found in Lacan (see *Ecrits*, 495), but it is, perhaps more importantly, a transposition into the realm of psychoanalysis of the sociological notion (from *Critique de la raison dialectique*) that a man's future possibilities are already sketched out for him before birth in the social possibilities of his family and in the objective structures of the world into which he will be born. The child is seen in *L'Idiot* as conditioned not merely by the restricted area of his future choices but also by his organic structure and his internalization of his mother, 'Génétrix tout entière' (*IF*, I, 61).

Gustave, then, according to Sartre, internalizes the existing family trinity 'Père – Mère – Fils Aîné'. As a baby he is seen by his mother simply as a 'recommencement des précédents' (*IF*, I, 134): he is not loved in his own right, as an individual, an end in himself. This is a factor contributing to Flaubert's feeling of inferiority. Sartre is here taking over Freud's notion that 'a child feels inferior if he notices he is not loved' (*SE*, XXII, 65). He backs up his view with an implicit reference to one of Erikson's eight stages: '[Gustave] a brûlé l'étape de la valorisation' (*IF*, I, 137). Gustave then feels he has no reason for living, for, although the individual invents his reasons in later life, this is possible, Sartre suggests, only on the basis of an early feeling of self-justification resulting from true mother-love. Discovered too soon, our contingency is not a truth but a half-truth, an 'erreur vraie' (*IF*, I, 143). Sartre's position in 1971 is a far cry from the absolute liberty propounded in *L'Etre et le Néant*. Parental love confers on the child his 'mandat de vivre' (*IF*, I, 140), an illusion of necessity, but, Sartre now argues, a necessary illusion ('une aliénation heureuse', *IF*, I, 143) if the individual in later life is to advance beyond meaninglessness to the realization that man can confer meaning on his own life. The whole process, including valorization of the child by its parents, constitutes what Sartre now calls 'la necessité de la liberté' (*IF*, I, 143).

However, Sartre's interest in mother-love is not new. Already his study of Baudelaire had discussed the way in which the infant Charles

se sentait uni au corps et au cœur de sa mère par une sorte de participation primitive et mystique; l'enfant est *consacré* par l'affection qu'elle lui porte: loin de se sentir une existence errante, vague et superflue, il se pense comme *fils de droit divin* . . . il est protégé contre toute inquiétude, il se fond avec l'absolu, il est *justifié*. (*B*, 18–19)

But the value of such a union is not made clear at this stage: phrases such as 'couple incestueux', 'fils de droit divin' and 'justifié' may sound warning notes in the reader's ears. In Sartre's notes for his monograph on Mallarmé,[15] drafted around 1952, the positive evaluation of maternal affection is more explicit. The infant's symbiotic relationship with its mother is envisaged as the primary form of both its *être-dans-le-monde* and its *Mitsein*. The child's original relation to the world is seen as passing necessarily through the mother: describing the young Stéphane's existence before his mother's death Sartre writes:

Jusqu'à six ans sa relation vécue au Tout, c'est tout simplement son amour pour sa mère. Sa Mère et le Monde ne font qu'un: l'enfant plonge ses ventouses dans la chair maternelle et pompe les sucs de la terre à travers ce corps familier . . . Le sevrage découvre à l'enfant qu'il est *un Autre* aux yeux des autres et qu'il lui faudra se couler dans la "Persona" que les adultes ont préparée à son usage; mais la tendresse de la mère en amortit les effets.   (*Mall*, 185)

Mother-love itself reduces even the pain of weaning. The child continues to see the world through his mother's eyes, and to know himself seen by her:

Il se réfugie *contre tous* dans le regard de sa mère . . . elle lui prête ses yeux . . . le monde, avec l'enfant dedans, n'est qu'une vision maternelle.
(*Mall*, 185)

Mallarmé's mother's death puts an end to the 'délivrance progressive' (*Mall*, 186) through which the child gradually comes to know himself as a separate entity, and to discover the contingency of the world to the extent of his capacity to cope with it alone. From this point onwards Stéphane is not a 'happy' child:

Les enfants heureux découvrent la plénitude comme une donnée immédiate; la négation, l'absence et toutes les formes du Néant leur apparaissent ensuite sous l'aspect des insuffisances locales, de lacunes provisoires, de contradictions volatiles; bref le Néant est postérieur à l'Etre. Mais pour cet orphelin, c'est l'inverse . . . l'enfant s'aliène à la mort d'autrui.
(*Mall*, 186)

Sartre's analysis of the young Mallarmé's *détresse*, *ressentiment*, *ennui* and *malaise*, his experience of life as *exil* and *absence*, makes it clear that he considers the poet's initiation into the bitter 'truths' of existential anguish to be both premature and harmful. But it is only since the recent publication of the *Cahiers pour une morale*, with its stress on the positive side of love as mutual valorization,[16] that it has been possible to understand the *theoretical* underpinning of Sartre's analysis of mother-love as part of the constructive side of ego-formation. *L'Idiot de la famille* confirms the presentation of maternal valorization as essential to the child's future *transcendence* of his alienation and contingency.

Sartre's analysis of the role of mother-love in *L'Idiot de la famille* may remind us of Fairbairn's notion of the central self or ego which is accompanied by both a libidinal self and a rejected self, arising from the two main aspects of the infant's early relationship with the mother (as exciting and rejecting respectively).[17] Fairbairn believes that, if the rejected self is too prominent, it leads to passivity and prevents the libidinal self from being properly assimilated into the central ego, thus resulting in a feeling of unreality as if the central ego were purely false. Flaubert is passive: he cannot distinguish knowledge from belief, for *knowing* requires an active participation in the process of verification. He is estranged from language, accepting the names of objects, but unable to internalize their active nomination. Sartre adopts Lacan's translation of the Freudian term *Unheimlichkeit* to express Gustave's unease with language:

L'*estrangement* n'a qu'une explication: il n'y a ni commune mesure ni médiation entre l'existence subjective de Gustave et l'univers des significations; ce sont deux réalités parfaitement hétérogènes dont l'une visite l'autre parfois . . . Vie et paroles sont incommensurables. (*IF*, I, 26)

It is, in Sartre's view, from Gustave's internalization of his family that his neurosis stems: contradictory and irreconcilable demands are made on him in particular by his father. Sartre's interpretation of Flaubert's crisis is finalistic. The *crise de Pont-l'Evêque* (when Flaubert fell and lost consciousness whilst driving a carriage home, after which he was permitted to abandon his law studies and stay in Croisset to write) is not caused but is, on some profound level, *intentionnelle*. However, Sartre insists that Flaubert's 'croyance organique lui masque son option passive' (*IF*, II, 1892), and goes so far as to say that when Flaubert's crisis is later repeated it is 'sans la moindre complaisance consciente de sa part' (*IF*, II, 1892). This remark illustrates again in practical terms how far Sartre has moved from his original radical position according to which all processes of the mind were *conscients* if not *connus*. Gustave's *chute* is interpreted on six different levels, coinciding in its intention at the most superficial and at the deepest level: Flaubert will obey his father and in so doing will precipitate the conflict implicit in his father's two contradictory demands: the explicit desire of Achille-Cléophas that Flaubert should lead a 'normal' bourgeois life, and the conflicting constitution of him as passive and worthless. This conflict seems a form of what Bateson[18] calls a double-bind situation, in which impossible demands made on a child result in the child's opting out of social interaction and losing confidence in the accuracy of his thought and perceptions. But whereas Bateson sees such conflict as a possible cause of schizophrenia, Sartre follows Freud in seeing the mechanism as resulting in neurosis. Freud, of course, maintained that there was a correlation between passivity and hysteria, and envisaged 'sexual passivity during the pre-sexual period' as a 'specific determinant of hysteria' (*SE*, III, 163); Sartre refers to Freud's account of hysteria to support his own view that Flaubert's symptoms are hysterical rather than epileptic (*IF*, I, 1040).

In fact it is in his account of the Pont-l'Evêque crisis that Sartre's finalism brings him closest to Freud. For example, we already find in Freud the observation that falls are frequently symptoms rather than causes of neurosis:

I can recall a number of fairly mild nervous illnesses in women and girls which set in after a fall not accompanied by any injury, and which were taken to be traumatic hysterias resulting from the shock of the fall. Even at that time I had an impression that these effects were differently connected and that the fall was already a product of the neurosis.

(*SE*, VI, 175)

Freud's further connection of the fall with sexual fantasy applies rather to women and is not of course taken over by Sartre: Flaubert is not inviting sexual violation, but he is, Sartre insists, enacting simultaneously a false death and a symbolic murder: 'Le suicide mimé de janvier 44 est, comme tant de suicides réels, un meurtre déguisé' (*IF*, II, 1908–9). It is, in fact, an imaginary parricide. Sartre makes use of Freud's notion of a symbolic father (Moses) whom, before his crisis, Flaubert had never succeeded in distinguishing from his real father, Achille-Cléophas: 'Jamais père empirique n'a été plus proche du père symbolique et n'a contribué si fort à le personnaliser' (*IF*, II, 1893). By confronting the two, the crisis succeeds in separating the real and the symbolic, but the real father nonetheless remains 'la contestation radicale de Gustave' (*IF*, II, 1899). Despite his passive defiance of his father, Flaubert is only partially liberated from him: it is only the death of Achille-Cléophas himself, two years after the crisis, that frees Gustave from this domination, and Sartre describes him living his father's death in January 1846 as a real deliverance. The parallel with Freud is clear in this respect also: liberation from the father is, in Freud's view, often made possible only by the real death of the parent:

A physician will often be in a position to notice how a son's grief at the loss of his father cannot suppress his satisfaction at having at length won his freedom. (*SE*, IV, 257)

It is in connection with Sartre's account of Flaubert's juvenilia that the most serious conflicts with Freudian analysis arise. A major problem lies in the fact that Sartre is analysing written texts which he sees as providing 'la confidence la plus étrange, la plus aisément déchiffrable: on croirait entendre un névrosé parlant "au hasard" sur le divan du psychanalyste' (*IF*, I, 8). For Flaubert, Sartre claims, 'écrire . . . c'est se défouler' (*IF*, I, 954). Indeed, he analyses Flaubert's writings as if they were dreams, applying to them the Freudian categories of symbolization, condensation and displacement. Freudian critics are of course irritated firstly by the assumption that written texts *reveal* in the same way as oral communication, and more importantly by Sartre's claim that they are 'aisément déchiffrable[s]'. The claim is a necessary consequence of Sartre's rejection of a separate unconscious mind, for if all is ultimately accessible to the conscious mind, then problems of interpretation are considerably reduced. Sartre's aim of thoroughgoing totalization also goes against the grain of Freudian analysis: totalization can be possible only if there are no 'failles dans le savoir',[19] no 'ruptures', no 'trous',[20] whereas Freudian analysis is based on these very lacunae, the identification of which is the first step in the psychoanalytic 'cure'.[21]

Even within his own terms, Sartre's analysis of the juvenilia can perhaps be criticized on methodological grounds. He states categorically that

l'œuvre ne révèle *jamais* les secrets de la biographie: elle peut être simplement le schème ou le fil conducteur qui permet de les découvrir dans la vie elle-même. (*CRD*, 91)

His analysis of the juvenilia would seem to be unfaithful to his own criteria, for the notions of parricide and of Flaubert's hatred of his brother Achille are derived almost entirely from the early works. But this is another issue.

Sartre's interpretation of the juvenilia as an example of what Freud would call a 'family romance' (*SE*, IX, 237ff.) raises one final question concerning his *rapprochement* with Freud: this centres on Gustave's relations with his mother. According to Sartre, Madame Flaubert rarely appears except to be excused of all blame for Gustave's suffering, since this blame is relegated in its entirety to his father. The Freudian analyst Marthe Robert and the critic Claude Burgelin both remark on the absence of any reference to an Œdipal situation in Sartre's interpretation. A truly Freudian analysis would, in Burgelin's opinion, have examined

La façon dont, à travers l'histoire de l'individu, ont été symbolisées un certain nombre de relations fondamentales. Comment la triangulation des rapports enfant – figure paternelle – figure maternelle est vécue symboliquement, comment donc a été résolue la crise de l'Œdipe ou quels conflits sa non-résolution a fait naître, ce sont là toutes questions que Sartre refuse de poser. En ce sens, son ouvrage est le plus anti-psychanalytique qui soit. Dans la structuration de la personnalisation de Flaubert qu'il propose, la relation œdipienne est totalement absente.[22]

Sartre has of course admitted Flaubert's parricidal wishes, though, according to Robert, he is mistaken in believing that Flaubert was 'trop imaginaire et surtout trop conformiste pour aller jamais au bout de son idée'.[23] Robert's feeling of dissatisfaction is evidently due to Sartre's apparent failure to draw any Œdipal consequences from the parricidal wish. We may suspect a *parti pris* on Sartre's part, especially when we look at the juvenilia themselves and note that he explains an attempted rape (of Adèle by Djalioh in *Quidquid Volueris?*[24]) as representing Flaubert's ambivalent sexual feelings towards Elisa Schlésinger, whom Sartre recognizes as a mother figure, without drawing any further conclusion. Even more startling is Sartre's interpretation of what he calls the 'cycle maternel' (*IF*, I, 698), in which mother–son incest is linked to parricide, as evidence not of any sexual desire of Gustave for his mother, but rather of his passivity and the imaginary nature of his sexual life:

J'ai insisté sur ces différents thèmes 'maternels' pour montrer la *problématique sexuelle* du jeune garçon: il comprend obscurément que sa mère *n'est plus* la moitié active de l'androgyne dont il est la moitié passive. Elle l'a été, pourtant, illusoirement: marquant sur lui son empreinte, elle l'a condamné pour toujours à n'avoir qu'une vie sexuelle *imaginaire*.

(*IF*, I, 703)

Similarly in his analysis of Flaubert's *Saint Julien*, in which the future saint murders both his parents while they are asleep in his own conjugal bed, Sartre's final interpretation is in terms of a generalized genocide and of the complexities of the *qui perd gagne* schema. He does, however, mention here, for the first time, the parallel with the Œdipus myth, which he now relates retrospectively to others of Flaubert's early works. Julien's rage when he thinks his wife is sleeping with another man is described as

l'écho d'une fureur lointaine, dont nous avons trouvé les traces dans beaucoup de ses premières œuvres, "un homme couché dans le lit de ma mère", aspect classique de l'Œdipe.   (*IF*, II, 1901)

The notion is explored no further, however, and it is once again the element of parricide rather than that of incest which is stressed.

Moreover, Sartre accepts the traditional interpretation of the dream related in Chapter 4 of *Mémoires d'un fou* as a dream of castration, while adding the rider that 'le mot "castration" n'est pour moi que l'expression des faits *dans un certain discours*' (*IF*, II, 1545), in order to defend himself against any accusation of promoting what he sees as the reductive side of Freudian mythology. But his own interpretation of the accompanying dream of Gustave's mother drowning as her son lies looking down on her, unable to save her, must surely appear insufficient:

Madame Flaubert est punie par où elle a péché: elle s'enfonce, réclamant la protection d'un fils qu'elle n'a su ni protéger . . . ni rendre tel qu'il la protège un jour . . . l'assouvissement est complet quand le fils *condamne à mort* sa mère.   (*IF*, I, 703)

Sartre does not explore the link between water and sexuality, although his own paraphrase of the dream makes the symbolism clear: 'Sa mère *est devenue fleuve*; elle était debout à ses côtés, elle s'étale au-dessous de lui, plate et couchée' (*IF*, I, 702).

We are therefore driven to ask why Sartre has apparently chosen to ignore, or at least to minimize, all evidence of an Œdipal situation in Flaubert's childhood. The two possibilities which spring first to mind can, in the light of what has been said about Sartre's changed attitude to Freud, be dismissed at once. Sartre's account of Flaubert's development in *L'Idiot* could easily have assimilated the Œdipus complex without creating an impression of imbalance or excessive dependence on Freud: indeed in this respect Sartre simply appears not to draw the evident conclusions from his own analysis. Neither can the reasons for the omission lie in the implicit fatalism of the notion – Sartre's view of man has been able to incorporate progressively more deterministic elements without losing its stress on some form of freedom, and the Œdipus complex is unlikely to prove unassimilable in this respect either. Moreover, Sartre does make use of the notion in his account of Alfred le Poittevin who, he says, 'vit une certaine situation œdipienne de deux manières à la fois' (*IF*, I, 1001) (i.e. 'anorexie'/'ataraxie'). A third supposition is perhaps more fruitful: namely that Sartre is once again taking account of modern developments in psychoanalytic theory, which has become, since 1930, progressively more aware of the importance of the pre-Œdipal relationship with the mother, and thus has tended to regard the Œdipus complex as a psychic structure itself requiring interpretation in terms of earlier conflicts, rather than as a primary source of neurosis.[25] This would explain why Sartre does not attempt to account for Flaubert's *earliest* constitution in terms of the Œdipus complex, but it does not fully account for the omission of such an explanation of later stages of Flaubert's development.

We must conclude ultimately that Sartre's apparent omission of any serious consideration of the Œdipus complex in *L'Idiot* is a result of his concern to give an existential analysis of Flaubert's subjectivity rather than a clinical categorization of his 'complexes'. The notion of an Œdipus complex can easily be merely reductive, a peg on which to hang a variety of differing situations and thus avoid a detailed account of the individual situation itself.[26] As Sartre said in 1969:

On peut tout tirer du complexe d'Œdipe . . . les psychanalystes . . . s' arrangent pour y trouver n'importe quoi, aussi bien la fixation à la mère, l'amour de la mère, que la haine de la mère – selon Mélanie Klein.

(*Sit IX*, 106)

There is in *L'Idiot* as a whole a systematic refusal to rely on categorization as a means of explanation. Sartre is unwilling, for example, to define Flaubert as a homosexual 'par cette raison d'abord que notre parti pris de nominalisme nous interdit les classifications' (*IF*, I, 686). It is in the same spirit that he claims to make no definitive decision as to whether Flaubert's crisis was hysterical or epileptic:[27] 'On admet aujourd'hui que certaines épilepsies ont pour origine l'hystérie. Alors, pour serrer les faits de plus près, nous serons franchement nominalistes' (*IF*, II, 1786). Sartre's apparent rejection of the Œdipus complex can thus be seen as a refusal to rely on Freudian terminology, rather than as a thoroughgoing rejection of the notion itself, since the notion can often be sensed between the lines of Sartre's account. In 1969 Sartre declared:

Je suis entièrement d'accord sur les *faits* du déguisement et de la répression, en tant que faits. Mais les *mots* de "répression", "censure", "pulsion" – qui expriment à un moment une sorte de finalisme et, le moment suivant, une sorte de mécanisme – je les rejette. (*Sit X*, 105)

We may surmise that his attitude to the Œdipus complex is very similar: his phenomenological standpoint can accept the findings of Freudian psychoanalysis as processes but not as explicative categories. And it is, in the last analysis, this attitude which both defines and limits Sartre's *rapprochement* with Freud.

8

Biography and autobiography:
The discontinuous self

Sartre's four thousand pages of biographical studies have repeatedly been set off by critics against his dismissive remarks on biography in *La Nausée*, and seen as revealing either inconsistency or at least a change of heart.[1] Such an interpretation is indicative of both a partial reading of the novel, and a simplification of Sartre's biographical project itself. Roquentin becomes disillusioned with his study of Monsieur de Rollebon precisely because it is, as he himself senses, the *wrong kind* of biography. Sartre's studies of Baudelaire, Genet and Flaubert (and, of course, himself) amongst others, are of a very different nature, and indeed are not biographies in the ordinary sense of the word at all. 'Que peut-on savoir d'un homme aujourd'hui?' (*IF*, I, 7): the question would be trivial if it applied primarily to the *facts* of a man's life. Roquentin's comments on the Marquis could well be repeated by Sartre thirty years later with respect to Flaubert:

L'homme commence à m'ennuyer. C'est au livre que je m'attache, je sens un besoin de plus en plus fort de l'écrire – à mesure que je vieillis, dirait-on.   (*OR*, 19)

Je ne comprends plus rien à sa conduite. Ce ne sont pas les documents qui font défaut: lettres, fragments de mémoires, rapports secrets, archives de police. J'en ai presque trop, au contraire. Ce qui manque dans tous ces témoignages, c'est la fermeté, la consistance.   (*OR*, 18)

Eh bien, oui: il a pu faire tout ça, mais ce n'est pas prouvé: je commence à croire qu'on ne peut jamais rien prouver. Ce sont des hypothèses honnêtes et qui rendent compte des faits: mais je sens si bien qu'elles viennent de moi, qu'elles sont tout simplement une manière d'unifier mes connaissances . . . J'ai l'impression de faire un travail de pure imagination.   (*OR*, 19)

Je l'avoue: c'est une fable. Rien ne prouve qu'il en fut ainsi. Et, pis encore, l'absence de ces preuves . . . nous renvoie, même quand nous fabulons, au schématisme, à la généralité . . . l'explication réelle, je peux m'imaginer, sans le moindre dépit, qu'elle soit exactement le contraire de celle que j'invente.   (*IF*, I, 139)

But, unlike Roquentin, Sartre embraces the paradoxes of an attempted yet always impossible totalization of the fragmentary, and acknowledges the extent to which he himself is implicated in the 'story' he tells. His purpose is critical, epistemological and political rather than narrowly academic. His committed method involves historical and psychological interpretation, not factual or hagiographic reporting. If *L'Idiot* is a *fable* it is to the extent that all truth, and more especially truth about men, is human. But to acknowledge the situated nature of truth is not, of course, to espouse idealist subjectivism: truth may be historical (or trans-historical)[2], not eternal; this does not mean that objectivity (albeit perspectival) is impossible. In *Saint Genet*, Sartre is scathingly dismissive of the subjectivism of bourgeois idealism:

C'est le cercle vicieux de tout scepticisme . . . Bien sûr . . . quels que soient les instruments qu'il emploie, finalement c'est avec *ses* yeux que l'expérimentateur constate les résultats de l'expérience. Mais si l'objectivité, dans une certaine mesure, est déformée, elle est aussi bien *révélée* . . . Mais dira-t-on le critique est créature historique et ses jugements sont relatifs à l'époque. C'est vrai, mais on aurait tort de confondre l'historisme et le subjectivisme idéaliste de nos habiles. Car, s'il est vrai que le critique, créature de l'histoire, ne met au jour que la signification de Mallarmé *pour notre époque*, il est vrai aussi que cette signification est objective.

(*SG*, 622, n. 1)

And as we saw in Chapter 5, Sartre's conception of the nature of truth and the (im)possibility of totalization is extremely complex.

In a sense it could be argued that all Sartre's biographies – and, indeed, his autobiography also – are a contribution to a continuing epistemological enquiry into the relations between man and the world, and to an ethical enquiry into the nature of freedom. But it is the ethical preoccupation which predominates in the earlier works. The study of Baudelaire sets out explicitly to contest the platitude that the poet 'n'a pas eu la vie qu'il méritait' (*B*, 17). 'Si, au contraire des idées reçues, les hommes n'avaient jamais que la vie qu'ils méritaient?' (*B*, 18), Sartre asks rhetorically. He describes Baudelaire as a mere rebel, not a true revolutionary, and interprets his *vertige* and *sensation du gouffre* as intuitions of his radical freedom (*B*, 48) which he flees in the hope of thereby reducing his responsibility for himself (*B*, 84). Baudelaire's Satanism is interpreted as an attempt to have his cake and eat it: to retain the stability of the theocratic order whilst rebelling against it: 'la mauvaise foi est encore de la foi' (*B*, 101) is Sartre's *boutade*. And his conclusion seems unequivocal: 'Le choix libre que l'homme fait de soi-même s'identifie absolument avec ce qu'on appelle sa destinée' (*B*, 245). But at other moments he is more *nuancé*, and it is clear that freedom is not envisaged as the almost disembodied ability to change at any moment which certain of his more polemical pronouncements would suggest:

Sa [i.e. Baudelaire's] mauvaise foi est si profonde qu'il n'en est plus le maître.   (*B*, 103)

Baudelaire, sans retour possible, a choisi de ne pas choisir.   (*B*, 147)

We may be reminded of the discussion of a change of project in *L'Etre et le Néant*: 'j'aurais pu faire autrement, soit, mais *à quel prix*?' (*EN*, 531).

Sartre's intention in his preface to Baudelaire's *Ecrits intimes* was to give a picture of the poet as a totality, a unique and unified whole, consistent even within apparent inconsistency, because motivated by an original choice rather than determined by chance events over which he had no control. He set out therefore to make use of biographical data, not in the disparate and haphazard manner of previous critics, but rather in order to draw from it clues to Baudelaire's basic option, and verification of that option once it was discovered. In this sense the analysis already follows the broad lines of the progressive–regressive method first referred to by Sartre in *L'Etre et le Néant* in the context of an analysis of the nature of *compréhension*,[3] the kind of understanding which implies empathy and intuition of human intentions:

Est compréhensible toute action comme projet de soi-même vers un possible . . . Et la compréhension se fait en deux sens inverses: par une psycho-analyse régressive on remonte de l'acte considéré jusqu'à mon possible ultime – par une progression synthétique, de ce possible ultime on redescend jusqu'à l'acte envisagé et on saisit son intégration dans la forme totale.   (*EN*, 537)

Psychoanalysis thus forms part of the regressive analysis to be eventually totalized within a broader perspective. But in the essay on Baudelaire itself the contextualization of the poet's project and achievement is minimal, at least in a historical sense. It is not until *L'Idiot de la famille*, in conjunction with Sartre's reassessment of Gustave Flaubert, and in the light of a paradoxically more comprehensive and liberal Marxism, that the focus shifts from Baudelaire's moral inauthenticity to the *positive* side of his project and a concomitant reappraisal of his poetic innovation.

In a sense, the biographical purpose of *Saint Genet, comédien et martyr* is simply a more explicit and expanded version of that of the *Baudelaire*: to explore the interaction of man and society in the perspective of a philosophy of freedom which transcends the determinism of both psychoanalysis and Marxism:

Montrer les limites de l'interprétation psychanalytique et de l'explication marxiste et que seule la liberté peut rendre compte d'une personne en sa totalité, faire voir cette liberté aux prises avec le destin, d'abord écrasée par ses fatalités puis se retournant sur elles pour les digérer peu à peu, prouver que le génie n'est pas un don mais l'issue qu'on invente dans les cas désespérés, retrouver le choix qu'un écrivain fait de lui-même, de sa vie et du sens de l'univers jusque dans les caractères formels de son style et de sa composition, jusque dans la structure de ses images, et dans la particularité de ses goûts, retracer en détail l'histoire d'une libération: voilà ce que j'ai voulu; le lecteur dira si j'ai réussi. (*SG*, 645)

Sartre's avowed desire to show the *limits* of psychoanalysis and Marxism necessarily means that his study is neither very Freudian nor very Marxist. Indeed, although he gives more space to Genet's childhood than he did to Baudelaire's, the analysis concentrates on Genet's adoption by a peasant family and his later return to Mettray Reformatory, with scant mention of the implications of his separation from his mother in early infancy, except for the brief speculation that deprivation of maternal intimacy rendered him permanently ill at ease with his body and physical life (*SG*, 15). We saw in the last chapter Sartre's hostility to the psychoanalytic catch-all, the *complex*, and here this is manifested obliquely in his espousal of a Bachelardian[4] rather than a Freudian interpretation of Genet's sexuality. For Genet, sex is a ritual of submission and self-abasement rather than sensual pleasure: 'Bachelard parlerait à son propos du "complexe d'Icare" ' (*SG*, 127). Similarly, Genet's 'dream of stone' (*rêverie pétrifiante*) is explained in terms of the Bachelardian 'complexe de Méduse' and its source is situated not in the steely glance of the Father, but − *pace* Freud − in the petrifying look of the Just Man: 'C'est le regard du Juste qui l'a d'abord pétrifié' (*SG*, 330). Sartre is evidently determined to carry out a phenomenological description of Genet's imagination rather than a Freudian psychoanalysis of his 'unconscious'.

Furthermore, the progressive − regressive method outlined in *L'Etre et le Néant* and redefined in *Questions de méthode* still concentrates, in *Saint Genet*, primarily on only one side of the supposedly dialectical interaction between man and history:

Nous définirons la méthode d'approche existentialiste comme une méthode régressive–progressive et analytico-synthétique; c'est en même temps un va-et-vient enrichissant entre l'objet (qui contient toute l'époque comme significations hiérarchisées) et l'époque (qui contient l'objet dans sa totalisation). (*CRD*, 94)

The object (Genet) is exhaustively analysed; the epoch, the inter-war years, hardly appears in Sartre's study. Sartre shows the child Genet becoming a thief in splendid isolation from any real social conditioning: he steals in an attempt to counteract his anguish and worthlessness; he is called a *voleur* and defiantly internalizes the label as an expression of his identity. 'Cela s'est passé ainsi ou autrement' (*SG*, 26): the 'facts' may be irrelevant, but in any case the explanation is metaphysical rather than economic. *Saint Genet* concentrates on Genet himself, not on his objective situation, and this is why Sartre later criticized his study as inadequate despite its length. 'Il est évident que l'étude du conditionnement de Genet par les événements de son histoire objective est insuffisante, très très in-suffisante' (*Sit IX*, 114). Although Sartre lays more stress on the formative influence of Genet's background than in the case of Baudelaire, it is nonetheless clear that he is still concerned with the free choice Genet made within his situation at the expense of an equally detailed account of that situation itself, which alone could enable us to judge the extent of Genet's area of choice, or the extent to which his liberty dominated his conditioning. Sartre is anxious to show the limitations of a rigid Marxism which claims to have *explained* a man once it has situated him in a broad historical framework – 'Valéry est un intellectuel petit-bourgeois, cela ne fait pas de doute. Mais tout intellectuel petit-bourgeois n'est pas Valéry' (*CRD*, 44) – but *Saint Genet* errs rather by over-emphasizing the singularity of the individual and underestimating the importance of his historical context.

Where Sartre is perhaps closest to achieving his aim is in his account of Genet's decision to become a writer. Already in *Qu'est-ce que la littérature?*, in answer to his own question, 'Pourquoi écrire?', Sartre replied:

Chacun a ses raisons: pour celui-ci l'art est une fuite; pour celui-là un moyen de conquérir. Mais on peut fuir dans un ermitage, dans la folie, dans la mort; on peut conquérir par les armes. Pourquoi justement *écrire*, faire par *écrit* ses évasions et ses conquêtes? (*Sit II*, 89)

Saint Genet is Sartre's first concerted attempt to discover why one individual author chose writing rather than any other activity as a way of resolving his personal problems. *Les Mots* and *L'Idiot de*

170

la famille will later share the same focus of attention. Sartre examines Genet's evolution in the different domains of sexuality, social interaction and art in a fascinating account which reveals the common move as that from passivity to activity: initial masturbator, he becomes first a passive, then an active homosexual; lonely orphan, he internalizes the ostracization of society and determines to become the evil (thief) he has been labelled; dreamy and sensitive adolescent, he will concretize his fantasies in a form of writing which becomes, in Sartre's view, the ultimate political act. Genet's 'perverted' erotic descriptions will be rendered palatable and indeed enticing to the reader by their formal beauty: caught in the aesthetic trap, the bourgeois will be seduced into a complicity which is demoralizing in a positive sense, since it undermines values which have been self-righteously assumed without question.[5] Sartre presents Genet as 'un des héros de ce temps' (*SG*, 661). His defence of his works is, paradoxically and controversially, on the grounds of the moral utility they may have within the terms of existential humanism: helping us work towards a more authentic personal life and a better society.[6] There are two sides to this provocative assertion. In the first place Genet has some, if not all, the qualities of an existential hero – he is utterly lucid, he affirms his own values in the face of society, he disrupts the bad faith of the bourgeois, and he finds his own highly successful way out of a seemingly impossible dilemma. But more importantly, Genet turns the tables on the reader who might set out to judge him: through Genet we experience a life of 'vice' from the inside, we enter his world rather than its being revealed from the outside as alien and unrelated to us. Genet imposes upon us the subjectivity of the homosexual traitor and thief, and forces us to recognize an aspect of humanity which we might prefer to ignore or deny: he brings us face to face with our failure to be fully human:

Puisque la relation sociale est ambiguë et comporte toujours une part d'échec . . . puisque toute parole rapproche par ce qu'elle exprime et isole par ce qu'elle tait . . . puisque nous échouons sans cesse à communiquer, à aimer, à nous faire aimer et que chaque échec nous fait éprouver notre solitude . . . puisque nous sommes, en tout état de cause, d'*impossibles nullités*, il faut écouter la voix de Genet, notre prochain, notre frère . . . S'il est encore temps, par un dernier effort, de réconcilier l'objet et le sujet, il faut, ne fût-ce qu'une fois et dans l'imaginaire, réaliser cette solitude latente qui ronge nos actes, nos pensées . . . Aujourd'hui il s'agit de faire apparaître le sujet, le coupable, cette bête monstrueuse et misérable que nous risquons à tout moment de devenir; Genet nous tend le miroir: il faut nous y regarder. (*SG*, 660–2)

In a sense, perhaps, this passage may give us further clues to the reasons behind Sartre's choice of three writers so apparently uncommitted as Baudelaire, Genet and Flaubert. All three are solitary, misanthropic, anti-bourgeois *par excellence* (in theory if not in life-style) and, like Sartre himself, *contestataires* in so far as they reject ready-made values without creating an alternative *system* with which to replace them. But, by the *qui perd gagne* reversal, therein lies their moral and political utility. It is their very lack of conventional commitment which protects them from the *esprit de sérieux* and forces the reader to glimpse in their works intuitions of the kind of nihilism which disrupts comfortable assumptions of a stable moral order. Baudelaire is least radical in this respect; Genet has been elevated to a paradoxical sainthood. We shall look now at the eventual fate of Gustave Flaubert.

In Flaubert's case Sartre himself has addressed the question of his choice of subject. His reasons are various, ranging from the personal: 'J'ai eu le sentiment d'un compte à régler avec lui' (*IF*, I, 8) to the psychoanalytic: 'le témoignage de Flaubert sur lui-même – cette confession boudeuse et déguisée, nourrie de cette haine de soi . . . est une chose exceptionnelle' (*Sit IX*, 117–18); the aesthetic: 'Flaubert représente . . . l'opposé exact de ma propre conception de la littérature: un désengagement total et la recherche d'un idéal formel qui n'est pas du tout le mien' (*Sit IX*, 116–17); and the socio-historical: 'à travers tout cela, il est possible de poser la question: "Quel était le *monde social imaginaire* de la rêveuse bourgeoisie de 1848?" ' (*Sit IX*, 118–19). Furthermore, behind these reasons for the choice of Flaubert, lies the deeper project of the study *per se*, which is, as already indicated, epistemological and methodological:

Le projet profond dans le *Flaubert* c'est celui de montrer qu'au fond tout est communicable et qu'on peut arriver, sans être Dieu, en étant un homme comme un autre, à comprendre parfaitement, si on a les éléments qu'il faut, un homme. (*Sit X*, 106)

This profoundly optimistic statement perhaps belies the subtlety of Sartre's discussion of knowledge and communication in *L'Idiot*, where, although a humanist attitude still prevails, the categorical and over-confident rationalism of *L'Etre et le Néant* has been left far behind. As we saw in a previous chapter,[7] it is now *le non-savoir* and *le vécu* that Sartre is primarily concerned to investigate.

Moreover, his aim of totalizing all available information concerning Flaubert does not preclude his recognition of the problematic nature of such an undertaking:

> Rien ne prouve, au départ, que cette totalisation soit possible et que la vérité d'une personne ne soit pas plurale; les renseignements sont fort différents de *nature* . . . Ne risquons-nous pas d'aboutir à des couches de significations hétérogènes et irréductibles? Ce livre tente de prouver que l'irréductibilité n'est qu'apparente.　　　　　　　　　　(*IF*, I, 7)

Rather than merely showing the *limits* of psychoanalysis and Marxism, Sartre's enterprise is this time more ambitious: it is to *incorporate* those disciplines within a broader anthropological project. *L'Idiot* is therefore both more Marxist and more Freudian than either of the two earlier biographies.

It is also, as we saw in Chapter 6, a practical and theoretical response to Structuralist conceptions of language in its stress on the dialectic between *signifiant* and *signifié*, and between alienation and self-expression. In a sense, Flaubert provides Sartre with a test-case, since he himself 'ne croit pas qu'*on parle: on est parlé*' (*IF*, I, 623). For Sartre, this is only half the picture: 'l'homme ne peut "être parlé" que dans la mesure où il parle − et inversement' (*IF*, II, 1977). He describes our thought as 'toujours déviée, toujours reprise et gouvernée puis déviée encore − ainsi de suite à l'infini' (*IF*, I, 623). Gustave's 'mauvais rapport initial au langage' (*IF*, I, 20) is both caused by his 'constitution passive' and also chosen in 'une option secrète pour l'inarticulé' (*IF*, I, 26). He is seen as suffering from 'une mauvaise insertion . . . dans l'univers linguistique, cela revient à dire: dans le monde social, *dans sa famille*' (*IF*, I, 21). Sartre's account concentrates first on the determining factors of the family situation: not only does he interrogate the final years of Flaubert's life to illumine his childhood choices and attitudes, but also the regressive analysis takes him back to Gustave as a suckling, and he even regrets having no knowledge of the foetus's life in the uterus. His account necessarily mixes objective fact and pure speculation: considerable weight is given for example to an isolated allusion to Flaubert's slowness in learning to read (hence the work's striking title) which is interpreted as evidence of his alienation from practical language, and indeed from all praxis. Gustave is described as a passive, apathetic, over-protected infant: nurtured but not loved by his mother, an early disappointment to his father: middle child and younger son, he is second best on all scores. Personal characteristics which Sartre would previously have represented as part of a freely chosen project, are now interpreted as ineradicable structures of the infant's facticity: apathy, for example, 'est d'abord la famille vécue au niveau psychosomatique le plus élémentaire − celui de la respiration, de la succion, des fonctions digestives, des sphincters − par un organisme *protégé*' (*IF*, I, 54). But such structures form the basis of individual evolution and transformation, they orientate personal development rather than determining character:

Gustave assume [l'apathie] pour en faire une conduite plus évoluée et pour lui assigner une fonction nouvelle: l'action passive devient tactique . . . Conservé, dépassé, traversé de significations neuves et complexes, le sens ne peut manquer de s'altérer.   (*IF*, I, 54)

The relation between freedom and conditioning is described in terms of a dialectic of chance and necessity: as individuals we make ourselves on the basis of structures and circumstances so personal that we cannot but take them for granted as constituting our 'self', rather than envisage them as limitations to a freedom which would otherwise be both unsituated and disembodied:

Cette dialectique de la chance et de la nécessité se réalise librement et sans gêner personne dans la pure existence de chacun . . . Ce que nous cherchons ici, nous, c'est l'enfant chanceux, la rencontre d'un certain corps et d'une certaine mère . . . ces déterminations élémentaires, loin de s'ajouter ou de s'affecter l'une l'autre en extériorité, sont immédiatement inscrites dans le champ synthétique d'une totalisation vivante.   (*IF*, I, 60–1)

Gustave, then, is described in terms of his relations with a mother who does not valorize him sufficiently, and a father who prefers his elder brother Achille. As we saw in the last chapter, Sartre's analysis appears to sketch an Œdipal situation − albeit stressing the parricidal wishes rather than the incestuous desires of Gustave − but it studiously eschews Freudian terminology in a way that must remind us of Sartre's *parti-pris* of nominalism (*IF*, II, 1786), and his refusal to allow jargon to replace explanation and interpretation.

But if Sartre's account incorporates certain elements that we associate with Freud, it also runs insidiously counter to much that Freudians hold most dear. There is, of course, no *evidence* concerning Gustave's babyhood, merely Sartre's hypothetical reconstructions.[8] Reading − the subject of the first section of the work − is far from being the major concern of traditional Freudian psychoanalysts, even those such as Jacques Lacan whose interest centres on language. Furthermore, Sartre's evidence is of course all drawn from written material – Flaubert's correspondence, juvenilia etc. – which Freudians might admit as additional data but which would not be considered any kind of substitute for the patient's oral self-revelation. Sartre's attitude to the relationship between a man and his works is itself complex. On the one hand the writer necessarily reveals himself in his works (*IF*, I, 894), on the other 'l'œuvre ne révèle *jamais* les secrets de la biographie' (*CRD*, 91).[9] Finally, the interpretation of the crisis at Pont-l'Evê-que in 1844 seems, as Sartre himself indicates, indebted to anti-psychiatry rather than psychoanalysis proper: 'L'analyse de la névrose, c'est de l'antipsychiatrie; j'ai voulu montrer la névrose comme solution à un problème' (*Sit X*, 100).[10] His analysis is finalistic; the crisis is described as a strategy which would eventually allow Flaubert to fulfil his ambition of becoming an artist. Sartre is rejecting causal explanation in favour of phenomenological description and interpretation in terms of intentionality. He envisages the meaning of the crisis as polyvalent: Flaubert, caught in a double bind,[11] made to feel worthless yet expected to live a 'normal' bourgeois life, turns the tables on his father by 'obeying' him in a literal sense which runs entirely counter to his father's explicit wishes. Sartre interprets Flaubert's fatal decision to drive the carriage home on six levels:

Ainsi, en allant du plus clair au plus complexe, nous pourrions déceler, à la racine de son activité, plusieurs niveaux intentionnels: 1° Obéir à son père, coûte que coûte. 2° Se faire dans la rage l'artisan de son destin bourgeois en complicité avec ceux qui le lui ont assigné. 3° Dompter la révolte obscure qui gronde, faute de pouvoir l'assumer dans une action négative. 4° Se réfugier dans ce rôle d'agent qui l'absorbe pour oublier la résistance qui s'organise et pour laisser le champ libre à la croyance, bref, courir à la mort dans l'innocence. 5° Exaspérer cette résistance passive dans la mesure même où le rôle d'agent – ici, la conduite de la voiture – symbolise l'activité générale qu'on lui impose et qu'il ne peut supporter. 6° Plus profondément encore: restituer, à la faveur de circonstances pro-pices, et condenser dans un moment si court qu'il puisse la vivre tout en-tière, la situation d'ensemble dans laquelle il se débat depuis son adolescence de manière à susciter en lui une réponse globale à ses prob-lèmes, bref mettre en présence *par la soumission absolue et partiellement jouée* les deux volontés contradictoires de l'Autre – celle du bourgeois Achille-Cléophas qui lui assigne un destin bourgeois, celle du Père sym-bolique qui l'a condamné au néant – et les laisser (ou les faire) s'entre-dévorer. (*IF*, II, 1825–6)

Flaubert's *chute* is considered as his response to impossible and contradictory demands. It is also an option in its own right, for it symbolizes a refusal of *praxis* and a choice of the *aesthetic*:

> S'il tombe à Pont-L'Evêque, c'est donc à la fois *contre* la Destinée et *pour* l'Art. (*IF*, II, 1914)

> Ne serait-ce pas *pour renaître Artiste* que Gustave a rompu les amarres qui le retenaient à la vie immédiate? (*IF*, II, 1918)

The *chute* is both 'une réponse tactique et négative au père' and 'une réponse stratégique et positive à la question posée par la necessité et l'impossibilité, pour Gustave, d'être Artiste' (*IF*, II, 1920). However, the *positive* side of the strategy is never explored by Sartre in any detail: the progressive – regressive method does not follow an order predictable to those more familiar with chronological biography or thematic criticism, and the full explanation of Flaubert's crisis as a form of artistic self-liberation (not simply in the practical sense of finding time to write, but in a deeper and more symbolic sense) would have been part of the study of *Madame Bovary* which Sartre never completed:

> La maladie de Gustave exprime dans sa plénitude ce qu'il faut bien appeler sa liberté: ce que cela veut dire, nous ne pourrons l'entendre qu'à la fin de cet ouvrage, après avoir relu *Madame Bovary*. (*IF*, II, 2136)[12]

Sartre's incorporation of Freud and Marx involves much more than mere juxtaposition of psychoanalytic and historical analysis. What is analysed on one level as intimate family problems, reappears on another as endemic to a whole society in transition. Internalized contradictory parental demands reflect, of necessity, social disorder. Flaubert internalizes his historical situation precisely through the mediations of his family. His personal structures are formed by what Marx would call introjected conflict. The objective socio-historical conflicts are closely paralleled by the 'double-bind' family contradictions just referred to. Flaubert internalizes conflicts already present in his father's situation and life-style. Achille-Cléophas is himself a product of contradictory elements: as a member of the *classe moyenne* under Louis XVIII, certain of his interests are served by the very monarchical system which excludes him from participation in the elections. Furthermore, the *classe moyenne* itself is torn by internal contradictions, and Achille-Cléophas envelops the latent conflict of industrialists and ex-émigrés: doctor and atheist on the one hand, royalist provincial on the other. And the Flaubert family is further split: feudal in Sartre's terms rather than conjugal (or democratic), it adapts the old notion of hierarchy to a form of bourgeois individualism, which ratifies and valorizes its members according to their position in it, whilst appearing to base its judgements on merit. As younger son Gustave is made to *feel* fundamentally unworthy. This is, of course, the historical correspondence of Madame Flaubert's non-valorization of her infant son. Sartre describes the Flaubert family as fifty years behind the times, and suggests that this *hystérésis* will make of Gustave a *névrosé* and thereby a great writer.

The detail of Sartre's sociological and historical analysis is fascinating, but we can look now only at its methodological implications. The neurosis produced in Gustave by the internalization of conflict both within and between his parents (father a scientist and atheist, mother religious and reactionary) is seen as triple: personal, historical and artistic. In summary, Flaubert's generation is doomed *historically* to neurosis because it cannot face the implications of its participation in the bloody suppression of the 1848 revolution. It can save its self-image only by turning its back resolutely on events (in a willed blindness) or by inauthentically blaming forces beyond its control (such as Fate or History). Furthermore, the generation is doomed *artistically* to neurosis because it cannot satisfy the implicit demands made on it by the art which it has already internalized and taken as its model. The anti-bourgeois poetic stance of the Romantic generation lies uneasily on the shoulders of its sons, post-Romantic bourgeois *par excellence*, and can be lived out only in an imaginary fashion. Flaubert's generation may try to *feel* part of an aristocratic élite, they cannot ever equal the social status of Chateaubriand, Lamartine, Vigny or Musset. The three neuroses are thus linked through class: not only is the objective historical neurosis which follows the 1848 revolution a result of the self-hatred of the bourgeois who attempt to hide the shame of their own status; *l'art-névrose* also depends on the inability of the bourgeois as bourgeois to satisfy demands internalized from previous art; and Flaubert's own personal neurosis is finally revealed in its objective dimension as an imaginary rejection of his bourgeois property-owning status (*IF*, II, 1971). But Sartre's remarks on the interconnection of the subjective and objective domains are brief and do not entirely satisfy his proposed aims. It is clear that the fourth volume was intended to explore the interaction further, and explain the implications of the way in which Gustave fulfils the demands of the reading public paradoxically *because* his own neurosis pre-dates, chronologically, the abortive revolution (1848) which it nonetheless reflects and symbolizes:

Quand l'assouvissement dépasse de loin le scandale – comme ce fut le cas pour *Madame Bovary* – il faut comprendre *à la fois* qu'il y a *malentendu* (nous verrons dans le 4ème tome Gustave étiqueté réaliste et hurlant sa rage) et que, sous ces erreurs d'interprétation, lecteurs et auteur se découvrent synchrones. (*IF*, III, 33)

It is this 'misreading'[13] of Flaubert by his public, this historical gap (*hystérésis*) between the subjective and objective neuroses, this diachronic slippage which explains both Flaubert's *succès de scandale* and the nature of his commitment. On one level Sartre can speak of Flaubert's 'désengagement total', on another of his 'engagement sur un second plan que j'appellerai politique, malgré tout . . . Prendre l'univers comme un tout, avec l'homme dedans, en rendre compte du point de vue de néant, c'est un engagement profond' (*Sit X*, 112). Flaubert is, perhaps, a test-case of Sartre's theory of literary commitment. Like all artists he communicates with his readers through the imagination, through the *sens* as much as the *signification* of language: 'Mis entre parenthèses, le monde et le langage ne sont réels ni l'un ni l'autre: tous deux sont des imaginaires; on rend l'image des choses par des images–mots' (*IF*, II, 1999). As we saw in a previous chapter, the reader must herself become imaginary and unreal if she is to reach the *indisable* which is conveyed through the non-utilitarian side of language.[14] The public which acclaims Flaubert as a realist is thus exposed to a nihilism of the imagination which it has no means of evading if it is to read his works at all: 'S'il se fait lecteur imaginaire de l'œuvre – il le faut, pour saisir le sens derrière les significations – alors tout l'indisable . . . lui sera révélé allusivement' (*IF*, II, 2003).

To use Sartre's own earlier terminology, Flaubert's art is committed in so far as it is *dévoilement*. It reveals the world to its readers, a world based on hatred and misanthropy, a world where nothingness eats away at the heart of being, the very world in fact which its readers are trying not to see. Unwittingly, perhaps – but as in the case of Genet, Sartre is more concerned with effect than intention – Flaubert, anti-realist *par excellence*, seduces and demoralizes his public. His masterpiece, *Madame Bovary*, has no immediate political effect, it is even misunderstood in the sense that its particular message (the bourgeois is evil) is generalized ('le pire est toujours sûr'), but it is all the more insidious for its apparent harmlessness. Flaubert is communicating with his public in the domain of the unreal: he is luring his readers from the comfortable security of *being* and exposing them to the deeper terror and reality of *non-being*. A false notion which extends the solidity of being to human values and intentions is at the base of bourgeois *mauvaise foi* for Sartre. Any writing which will undermine this pernicious and mystifying attempt at self-justification must necessarily be committed in the fullest sense of the term.

It has become clear that Sartre's biographies are far from being mere academic exercises or traditional critical or historical accounts. They form part of his continuous tussle with literature, both as a necessarily ambivalent product of the imagination and as a cultural institution. Starting with Roquentin's famous 'Il faut choisir: vivre ou raconter' (*OR*, 48), and ending with Sartre's abandonment of literature in favour of political activism in the 1960s and 1970s, the questions of *Qu'est-ce que la littérature?* – 'Qu'est-ce qu'écrire?', 'Pourquoi écrire?', 'Pour qui écrit-on?' – continue to reverberate through the whole of his career.

And it is this focus which provides far more fruitful links between Sartre's biographies and his autobiography than the psychoanalytic or factual similarities which critics have delighted in exploring. Like Baudelaire, Sartre may have hated his stepfather; over-protected like Flaubert, he may not have developed any aggression (*IF*, I, 136); and of course his refusal to admit such parallels – 'je ne pense pas qu'il y ait un intérêt à dire que je me découvre dans Flaubert . . . j'ai très peu de points communs avec Flaubert' (*Sit X*, 103) – can be interpreted as *dénégation*.[15] Biographers and would-be psychoanalysts have had a field-day finding connections of all sorts between Sartre and his objects of study. But the most evident similarity is also by far the most productive of interest: all are *writers*, all maintain an uneasy, even aggressive, relationship with their (bourgeois) reading public and the institution of literature itself. It is in this perspective that we shall turn now to an examination of *Les Mots*, Sartre's 'adieu à la littérature' (*Sit X*, 94).

To the reader familiar with Sartre's style and evolution, and even more acutely to the reader familiar with *L'Idiot de la famille*, *Les Mots* appears at first surprisingly out of line. It is highly literary, condensed, apparently traditional in its presentation of childhood, and reveals Sartre's 'free choice' to be a writer as a veritable vocation. The increasing complexity of the biographies, from Baudelaire through Genet to Flaubert, seems to have given way in the autobiography to a linear and teleological account of a destiny. Just when Sartre has most material at his disposal, most information and insight (privileged or not)[16] into the 'case' in question, his account is most schematic. Just when he could be expected to experience personally the fluidity, contingency and intangibility of selfhood, the self appears as defined and ultimately totalizable. In contrast to the massive and often ponderous debate with Marx and Freud in *L'Idiot*, *Les Mots* seems flippant and even trivial.

It may also appear incoherent: is the bitterness, violence and rushed allusiveness of the last few pages a discordant coda, a last-minute attempt to salvage the myth of freedom from the wreckage of predestination? Or does the work as a whole demand a rather different reading? We will look now at the apparent discrepancy between Sartrean theory and the textuality of *Les Mots* and attempt to account for the disjuncture.

Sartre's philosophical positions, from *La Transcendance de l'Ego* through to the *Critique de la raison dialectique* all militate against a closed picture of the self. As we have seen, the self is presented as a fiction created by and external to consciousness, transcendent product rather than originary source. And if the *Critique* does not elaborate this description it is because it is both taken for granted and also left behind in the later stress on the group rather than the individual, and on the materiality of experience. Furthermore, introspection is doomed to failure: it can meet only emptiness, uncover only what it has already determined; as an imaginary synthesis the self cannot be discovered, for imagination is impoverished to the extent that it can find in the image only what it has first put there. The 'richesses de la vie psychique' are a mere optical illusion.

Illusion, too, is the appearance of finality endemic in a retrospective account. *Les Mots* is written like a *récit* not a *roman*:[17] 'Le récit se fait au passé . . . le récit explique: l'ordre chronologique . . . dissimule à peine l'ordre des causes' (*Sit I*, 15–16). *Les Mots* recounts Sartre's childhood in the very way Roquentin rejected in *La Nausée*:

Pour que l'événement le plus banal devienne une aventure, il faut et il suffit qu'on se mette à le *raconter* . . . Quand on raconte la vie, tout change; seulement c'est un changement que personne ne remarque: le preuve c'est qu'on parle d'histoires vraies. Comme s'il pouvait y avoir des histoires vraies; les événements se produisent dans un sens et nous les racontons en sens inverse. On a l'air de débuter par le commencement . . . Et en réalité c'est par la fin qu'on a commencé.   (*OR*, 48–9)

It is, moreover, Roquentin's imaginary autobiography that he uses to illustrate his thesis. And Sartre is far from having forgotten his comments, for he reiterates them within the text of *Les Mots* itself: 'Mon grand-père m'avait élevé dans l'illusion rétrospective . . . Reconnue, cette erreur d'optique ne gêne pas: on a les moyens de la corriger' (*M*, 168–9).[18] We have analysed Sartre's attempts at correcting the retrospective illusion in *La Nausée* and *Les Chemins de la liberté*.[19] *Les Mots* seems rather to revel in it, and indeed to reproduce it systematically.

Of course, the *Critique*, *L'Idiot* and Sartre's later interviews have taught us the extent to which man is predestined: not simply unable to escape his class, nation and family,[20] but actually 'voué à un certain type d'action dès l'origine' (*Sit X*, 98); his freedom defined as the little gap (*décalage*) between internalization and externalization (*Sit IX*, 102). But the gap remains, it is explored and exploited in the cases of Genet and Flaubert, a hole in the heart of being through which genius can be invented. In *Les Mots*, however, the *décalage* between conditioning and freedom may seem to approach zero. But artistic creation is envisaged by Sartre, at least where *others* are concerned, as an apparently privileged and non-determined form of activity: why, then, should what saves Jean and Gustave seem to damn Jean-Paul?

To some extent Sartre is simply being hard on himself. 'Je n'ai pas d'empathie pour moi-même. On a toujours un peu de sympathie ou d'antipathie dans les rapports à soi . . . On adhère à soi' (*Sit X*, 103). Sartre does not claim to be entirely free from narcissism, defined as

une certaine manière de se contempler réflexivement, de s'aimer . . . un rapport constant à soi, soi n'étant pas d'ailleurs exactement le soi actif qui parle, qui pense, qui rêve, qui agit, mais plutôt un personnage fabriqué à partir de lui.   (*Sit X*, 198)

Je ne crois pas que le rapport juste de soi avec soi doit être un rapport d'amour. Je pense que l'amour est le vrai rapport de soi avec les autres. A l'inverse, ne pas s'aimer, se blâmer constamment, se détester, empêche tout autant la pleine possession de soi.   (*Sit X*, 199)

If *Les Mots* is free from self-love, it does not appear so free from self-hatred: antipathy dominates sympathy, at least where the writer's relation to his former adult self is concerned. And Sartre's comments on the limits of autobiography, which he links to those of self-analysis, certainly lead the reader to ask again what is the role and status of *Les Mots*: 'je ne crois pas qu'il y ait intérêt à faire ce travail sur soi-même. Il y a d'autres manières de se chercher' (*Sit X*, 104–5).

Just as *L'Idiot de la famille* was described as a 'roman vrai', so *Les Mots* is 'un roman auquel je crois' (*Sit X*, 146). And despite Sartre's expressed reservations – 'Il est impossible de totaliser un homme vivant' (*Sit X*, 105) – *Les Mots* represents an attempt at totalization:

> Il s'agissait, par le biais d'une fiction vraie – ou d'une vérité fictive – de reprendre les actions, les pensées de ma vie pour essayer d'en faire un tout.
>
> (*Sit X*, 148)

In a sense, as we have seen, all truth is fictive: 'la vérité reste toujours à trouver parce qu'elle est infinie' (*Sit X*, 148); the problem is, however, particularly acute where truth about the self is concerned. As both subject and object of enquiry the self is necessarily transformed by its own investigation. In the *Plaidoyer pour les intellectuels* Sartre defines the intellectual's task as an attempted resolution of the contradictions which the current ideology has imposed on him: 'Il enquête d'abord *sur lui-même* pour transformer en totalité harmonieuse l'être contradictoire dont on l'a affecté' (*Sit VIII*, 401). Like the intellectual, 'monstrueux produit de sociétés monstrueuses' (*Sit VIII*, 401), the child too, be it Gustave or Jean-Paul, is a 'monster' alienated by the contradictory if implicit demands of an uneasy society internalized through the mediation of his family. 'J'étais un enfant, ce monstre qu'ils fabriquent avec leurs regrets' (*M*, 72). But when social contradiction is internalized, or 'naturalized', *authentic* attitudes and behaviour may in their turn *appear* contradictory. And an analysis of this sort is one of the explicit objects of *Les Mots*:

> De reprendre les actions, les pensées de ma vie pour essayer d'en faire un tout, en regardant bien leurs prétendues contradictions et leurs limites, pour voir si c'était bien vrai qu'elles avaient ces limites-là, si l'on ne m'avait pas forcé à considérer telles idées comme contradictoires alors qu'elles ne l'étaient pas.
>
> (*Sit X*, 148)

In this sense it is society which forms the object of enquiry as much as the 'self'. The autobiographer cannot analyse himself without simultaneously analysing the world in which he lives:

> L'objet spécifique de son enquête est double, en effet: ses deux aspects sont inverses l'un de l'autre et complémentaires; il faut qu'il se saisisse lui-même dans la société en tant qu'elle le produit . . . D'où un perpétuel renversement: renvoi de soi au monde et renvoi du monde à soi. (*Sit VIII*, 402)

His object is dual and ambiguous; his enquiry is reflexive and self-critical:

La véritable recherche intellectuelle . . . implique un passage de l'enquête par la singularité de l'enquêteur . . . la pensée . . . doit se retourner sans cesse sur elle-même, pour se saisir toujours comme *universalité singulière*, c'est-à-dire singularisée secrètement par les préjugés de classe inculquées dès l'enfance alors même qu'elle croit s'en être débarrassée et avoir rejoint l'universel. (*Sit VIII*, 403–4)

Autobiography thus becomes *auto-poesis* or self-transformation as much as self-description: 'L'intellectuel tente de *se* modifier dans sa sensibilité aussi bien que dans ses pensées' (*Sit VIII*, 406); 'Je fus amené à penser systématiquement contre moi-même' (*M*, 211–12). *Les Mots* enacts what it describes. It is an 'autobiographical act'.

Why then does Sartre's autobiography take such an apparently finalistic and orderly form? It is indeed as if he were putting Roquentin's early dream into practice: 'J'ai voulu que les moments de ma vie se suivent et s'ordonnent comme ceux d'une vie qu'on se rappelle' (*OR*, 50). But Roquentin is not fooled: 'Autant vaudrait tenter d'attraper le temps par la queue' (*OR*, 50). And neither, we may be sure, is Sartre. If he prefers the autobiography with its *récit suivi*, its 'histoire systématique de la personnalité', its totalization and temporal closure, to the self-portrait evoking rather the *vide* and *absence à soi*, 'ce rien [qui se mue] en pléthore',[21] it is, primarily, because this suits his polemical purpose. Like Genet and Flaubert, Sartre is constructing a *piège à cons* to trap the bourgeois. Just as Gide's autobiography lulls its readers into a false sense of security with its conventional opening line: 'Je naquis le 22 novembre 1869'[22] the better to assault them later with its avowal of homosexuality, so *Les Mots* uses chronology, analysis and pseudo-naïve anecdote to disguise an often vicious attack on these very bourgeois conventions and their concomitant blindness to the role of ideology, dialectics and the interplay of liberty and situation, freedom and necessity.

If the force of the polemic in *Les Mots* is so often overlooked it is, needless to say, precisely because of its ambivalent nature: like (Sartre's reading of) *Madame Bovary*, it appears at first sight an innocuous and traditional tale, only to subvert the reader's assumptions by surreptitiously exposing her to a particularly corrosive form of nihilism. It has been suggested[23] that the destined reader of *Les Mots* is dual: the bourgeois public on the one hand, and left-wing anti-bourgeois radicals such as Nizan (posthumously) on the other. In this sense it is simultaneously attack and *mea culpa*: Sartre is a judge–penitent,[24] both condemning his past and at the same time pleading extenuating circumstances (*M*, 153). This duality can be seen on several levels, most strikingly perhaps in the text's stylistic effects. Sometimes the tone changes mid-sentence, from a literary effeteness to a crude virulence designed to win the approval of iconoclastic political allies, and smack the unsuspecting bourgeois between the eyes. Speaking of his lack of desire to attain *l'âge de raison*, for example, Sartre writes: 'Pour moi, avant d'être voué, je grandissais dans l'indifférence: la robe prétexte, je m'en foutais' (*M*, 198). Or again: 'Qu'il restât au moins un clerc vivant pour continuer la besogne et fabriquer les reliques futures. Sales fadaises: je les gobai sans trop les comprendre' (*M*, 151). The 'gentle reader' is not treated with gentleness. At other times a single phrase invites two conflicting interpretations. 'Je devins traître et je le suis resté' (*M*, 199): the naïve reader's instinctive recoil from treachery is to be put in question by the increasing valorization of infidelity throughout the paragraph, to the point where it becomes clear that constancy can only ever be to a dead self. A superficially easy text conceals considerable problems of interpretation. The reader who follows Mamie's advice – 'Glissez, mortels, n'appuyez pas' (*M*, 213) – will miss the point and be disconcerted rather than demystified.[25]

Philippe Lejeune argues convincingly that the apparent chronological development of the text conceals a dialectical structure: the two sections *Lire* and *Ecrire* are overlapping (1909–14, 1912–15) rather than sequential; anecdotes are drawn freely from within the period of childhood to illustrate the necessity of Jean-Paul's evolution without respect for sequence. Karl's lectures on humanism are reactivated two years after their delivery to explain Sartre's latest conception of his literary vocation; events are used to illumine attitudes they post-date as if childhood formed some kind of eternal present. It is the overall design that matters, not the temporal order. But the anachronisms are far from evident: *Ecrire* in particular has the appearance of a strictly sequential narrative. The reader is reassured by the illusion of chronology which implies a 'natural' chain of cause and effect with which she is familiar. The progressive – regressive method, despite its rigorous grounding in the 'higher' truth of dialectics, is disturbing. Its *va-et-vient* between analysis and synthesis implies a risk of error which a straightforward temporal account seems to bypass. But the risk is of course merely the reverse of a chance – the possibility of a truth which chronology can never attain. In the text in question the effect is striking: that of a logical and temporal *necessity* which both assuages the reader's desire for meaning, and throws it into question by its very excess. The teleological and totalizing structure of the text has been seen as a form of self-protection[26] on Sartre's part, a refusal to allow any alternative explanation which might undermine his own. What this interpretation overlooks entirely is the subversive force of the last few pages in particular, where the irony seems to achieve an almost infinite regression of unstable signification.

For irony is of course the key to a proper interpretation of *Les Mots* at the level of meaning, just as parody is the key at the level of form. And the irony and parody have three main objects of attack. Firstly, a parody of traditional autobiography, with a ferocious irony at the expense of bourgeois family life and beliefs and a second-level methodological critique of interpretations of the individual which either ignore the dialectic between man and society, as in the case of bourgeois biography, or else reduce it to a causal chain which leaves no room for freedom, as in the case of a vulgar Marxism or a naïve Structuralism. Secondly, we find a parody of Freudian psychoanalysis which has too frequently been taken at face value. And thirdly, a parody of literary style with a concomitant ironizing of the very institution of literature.

Like all good autobiographies, Sartre's begins with a family tree, but the speed and apparent frivolousness of the tone are less familiar:

En Alsace, aux environs de 1850, un instituteur accablé d'enfants consentit à se faire épicier. Ce défroqué voulut une compensation: puisqu'il renonçait à former les esprits, un de ses fils formerait les âmes; il y aurait un pasteur dans la famille, ce serait Charles. Charles se déroba, préféra courir les routes sur la trace d'une écuyère. On retourna son portrait contre le mur et fit défense de prononcer son nom. A qui le tour? August se hâta d'imiter le sacrifice paternel: il entra dans le négoce et s'en trouva bien. Restait Louis, qui n'avait pas de prédisposition marquée: le père s'empara de ce garçon tranquille et le fit pasteur en un tournemain. Plus tard Louis poussa l'obéissance jusqu'à engendrer à son tour un pasteur, Albert Schweitzer, dont on sait la carrière. (*M*, 11)

All the stock ingredients are present: names, professions, children, character sketches. But the ellipsis of the very first sentence disconcerts: money (or its lack) is of course the missing, unmentionable link. And the grocer has other delusions of grandeur: no longer a primary-school teacher, he considers himself *défroqué* and, in a near zeugma, wishes on one of his sons the vocation he himself never had: 'puisqu'il renonçait à former les esprits, un de ses fils formerait les âmes . . . ce serait Charles'. Charles prefers to become a black sheep. 'A qui le tour?' Auguste follows in the footsteps of his shopkeeper father. 'Restait Louis' − who goes so far as to sire a *pasteur* in his turn . . . But where is Sartre in this family romance? We could as well be reading a novel for the first few pages. *Je* appears on the fourth page, but he is still the undefined narrator. *Moi*, Jean-Paul, comes in to ratify his story only a couple of pages later. The attack on Church and family is bitter, and made palatable only by the speed and humour of the delivery. Grandfather Charles translates dirty jokes for his straitlaced wife 'par charité chrétienne' (*M*, 12); Louise profits from her headaches to avoid her marital duties; their daughter Anne-Marie is taught to tone down her qualities and beauty, and be bored. Charles's cruel vulgarity, Louise's cynical scepticism combine to all but kill their daughter's spirit. Sartre continues to relate his tale with the same racy mixture of black humour and stylish impropriety: his uncle Joseph is also marked for life by his parents' defects: 'pris entre le mutisme de l'un et les criailleries de l'autre, il devint bègue' (*M*, 16). Sartre's father marries his mother and dies. Jean-Paul himself tries to follow suit: 'je m'appliquai, moi aussi, à mourir: d'entérite et peut-être de ressentiment' (*M*, 16). This time the syllepsis cannot entirely mask the seriousness of intent. Sartre's father is a long time a-dying: when he finally makes it, Jean-Paul recovers his health and his mother.

'Familles, je vous hais,' writes Gide. 'Je déteste mon enfance et tout ce qui en survit' (*M*, 140), Sartre claims in his turn. In fact his hatred seems to exclude his mother and to be at its most virulent towards his father-figures.[27] 'Il n'y a pas de bon père, c'est la règle' (*M*, 19). The pseudo-naïveté of Sartre's psychoanalytic *boutades* should not deceive us. The space accorded to sexuality in *Les Mots* has been almost systematically underestimated by critics accustomed to veiled or explicit self-revelation rather than to analysis or criticism. If Sartre spares us his 'mauvaises habitudes'[28] it is because he has larger issues in hand.

The psychoanalytic dimension of *Les Mots* is pervasive and operates on several different levels. When these are conflated by critics an inevitable distortion and confusion arise. None of Sartre's comments is entirely ironic or totally straightforward, but the spectrum between the two poles is wide, from *boutades* on the one hand to serious opposition to Freud on the other. If the *boutades* −

'je n'ai pas de Sur-moi' (*M*, 19); 'la prompte retraite de mon père m'avait gratifié d'un "Œdipe" fort incomplet' (*M*, 25) – are read as naïve allegiance to Freud, Sartre appears both ignorant and inconsistent.[29] He refers to the 'verdict d'un éminent psycho-analyste' (*M*, 19) as a quip rather than as a *caution* (security), which is not, of course, to say that there is no narcissistic fascination with what analysis might produce if applied to his 'case'. A missing super-ego and an incomplete Œdipus complex are hardly subjects for self-congratulation in the Freudian canon. In the schema of *Les Mots* they are the necessary conditions for the continual childhood paradise (*M*, 31) that Jean-Paul enjoys 'loin des hommes et contre eux' (*M*, 185).[30] The lack of a super-ego is subordinated to a more existen-tial comment on aggression and violence: 'Pas de Sur-moi, d'accord, mais point d'agressivité non plus. Ma mère était à moi, personne ne m'en contestait la tranquille possession: j'ignorais la violence et la haine, on m'épargna ce dur apprentissage, la jalousie' (*M*, 25). We are reminded again of Sartre's acceptance of 'les *faits* du déguise-ment et de la répression' (*Sit IX*, 105) and his refusal of the *terms* with their implicit mechanism and finalism.[31]

Similar in nature to the *boutades*, though formally the converse, are the anecdotes which call out provocatively for a Freudian inter-pretation which they never receive. Louise's taste for stories of honeymoon rape (*M*, 14), the grand-paternal habit of relegating sex to procreation and silence ('Charles . . . lui fit quatre enfants par surprise', *M*, 14; 'le docteur Sartre . . . de temps à autre, sans un mot, l'engrossait', *M*, 15) are mentioned but never explored. Most striking in this respect perhaps is Sartre's *faux-naïf* comment on his uncle Emile: 'Il m'intrigue; je sais qu'il est resté célibataire mais qu'il imitait son père en tout, bien qu'il ne l'aimât pas' (*M*, 14). A few lines later, in an apparent non-sequitur, the true nature of this mysterious filial imitation becomes apparent: 'il adorait sa mère . . . il la couvrait de baisers et de caresses puis se mettait à parler du père, d'abord ironiquement puis avec rage' (*M*, 14). Œdipus is never mentioned, but Emile has evidently carried his identification with the father to the point of sharing permanently the paternal object of desire: an incestuous love that explains the celibacy to which Sartre alludes without explicit comment.

Thirdly, we find nods and winks in the direction of a psycho-analytic reading of *Les Mots* itself. Like Baudelaire,[32] Sartre dreams of a 'jeune géante', his mother: 'de moi-même, je la pren-drais plutôt pour une sœur aînée' (*M*, 21). Twenty pages later we learn of his fascination with fraternal incest, but before we can make the link Sartre has made it for us: 'Dérivation? Camouflage de sentiments interdits? C'est bien possible. J'avais une sœur aînée, ma mère' (*M*, 48), and has even provided a footnote listing the occurrences of this type of incest in his fiction. It is in this spirit that Sartre recounts his dream of Madam Picard's bare bottom (*M*, 92),[33] or refers to his grandfather or father as Moses (*M*, 97, 134); in this spirit too that he gestures towards a psychoanalytic reading of his childhood fantasies of being an inconsolable widower: 'Un veuvage, une plaie inguérissable: à cause, à cause d'une femme,[34] mais non point par sa faute; cela me permettait de repousser les avances de toutes les autres. A creuser' (*M*, 158). It is as if Sartre had already performed the analysis his text invites, and somehow gone beyond it. These passages have, of course, been seen as a form of self-protection, and even as an unconvincing attempt to suggest a liquidated Œdipus complex,[35] but this interpretation is too simple. In the last example (*M*, 158) Sartre is clearly far from claiming a resolved Œdipus which would permit 'l'accès aux autres femmes'.[36] The passages should be read rather as an ostentatious indifference to Freudian psychoanalytic interpretations.[37]

In a somewhat different category are the less clear-cut allusions to genital or anal eroticism associated with reading. Charles's books are phallic – 'pierres levées . . . menhirs, boursouflées . . . couvertes de veinules noires' (*M*, 37). Louise's are lying down ('couchés') (*M*, 38); the two copies of Mérimée's *Colomba* are differentiated by their virginity or its lack: no look has ever deflowered the one, the other is 'un sale petit bouquin brun et puant . . . c'était Mérimée humilié' (*M*, 59). Sartre's fantasy of himself as a book involves being opened, spread out, stroked: 'Je me laisse faire et puis tout à coup je fulgure, j'éblouis . . . je suis un grand fétiche maniable et terrible' (*M*, 164). Josette Pacaly has psychoanalysed such passages in terms of an anal fixation, etc.; it is hard to believe that they have not been composed deliberately for the purpose. This does not, of course, necessarily make them unfit objects for analysis, but it certainly changes its nature: as Sartre himself points out, even the deliberate ignoring of psychoanalysis is today far from naïve (*Sit IX*, 122–3).

More interesting, perhaps, if less amusing, are Sartre's own serious analytic comments which situate his views in an oblique oppositional relation to those of Freud. The first, and recurrent, example concerns his father's terminal illness, which led to the early weaning of the infant Jean-Paul. Far from proclaiming the benefits of such a weaning as critics have persistently maintained,[38] Sartre rather expresses the pain and trauma which it elicited. The baby nearly dies in consequence: 'je profitais de la situation . . . sans la chance de cette double agonie, j'eusse été exposé aux difficultés d'un sevrage tardif' (*M*, 17) can surely only be interpreted as cruelly ironic. 'Sevré de force à neuf mois,' Jean-Paul may not feel the last snip at the umbilical cord but this is because of *fièvre* and *abrutissement*: his world is one of nightmare and hallucination, and when he is reunited with his mother he no longer recognizes her: 'Je reprenais connaissance sur les genoux d'une étrangère' (*M*, 17). In a sense his father's death entailed the symbolic death of his mother also. The price of his freedom would seem to have been a high one: it certainly made the infantile paradise of union with the mother particularly difficult to forgo. In Freudian terms the young boy's *castration* is in a sense both deferred and repeated: enacted by his grandfather (in the paternal role) when his curls are cut off, its effect (the ensuing ugliness of Jean-Paul, his separation from his mother, and, paradoxically, his masculinization, *M*, 84) is not fully realized until his adolescence, when his mother marries again. Sartre's stepfather is very much the absent presence to whom the text alludes, but who is never admitted within its pages. Jean-Paul's discovery of his ugliness and Anne-Marie's remarriage, are the violent, and half-hidden, end of a childhood idyll (*M*, 211).

But the *writing* which they symbolically inaugurate in fact began earlier with the first, less radical, expulsion from Paradise. Sartre describes the whole of his literary production as originating in the unhappy consciousness which it masks: 'l'appétit d'écrire enveloppe un refus de vivre' (*M*, 161). His analysis of the connection between writing and the death-wish deserves some attention: superficially Freudian, it receives an existential interpretation — the flight from life is at the same time itself a project. Like that of Genet and Flaubert, Sartre's imagination produces effects in the real world:

La mort était mon vertige parce que je n'aimais pas vivre: c'est ce qui explique la terreur qu'elle m'inspirait . . . Nos intentions profondes sont des projets et des fuites inséparablement liés: l'entreprise folle d'écrire pour me faire pardonner mon existence, je vois bien qu'elle avait, en dépit des vantardises et des mensonges, quelque réalité: la preuve en est que j'écris encore, cinquante ans après. Mais si je remonte aux origines, j'y vois une fuite en avant, un suicide à la Gribouille; oui, plus que l'épopée, plus que le martyre, c'était la mort que je cherchais.   (*M*, 162–3)

It is perhaps tempting to try to psychoanalyse Sartre at this point;

this is not our intention. What matters here is rather the implications of his insistence on the *ambivalence* of behaviour as both flight and project, imaginary and real, caused and chosen. And this is surely Sartre's most serious point in his implicit dialogue not only with Freud but also with Marx: however forceful the factors of early childhood may appear, they never determine entirely what will be made of them. Sometimes Sartre seems to hesitate on this point, elsewhere the text is explicit:

L'enchaînement paraît clair: féminisé par la tendresse maternelle, affadi par l'absence du rude Moïse qui m'avait engendré, infatué par l'adoration de mon grand-père, j'étais pur objet, voué par excellence au masochisme si seulement j'avais pu croire à la comédie familiale. Mais non . . . le système m'horrifia . . . Je me jetai dans l'orgueil et le sadisme. (*M*, 97)

Or again, 'Enfant soumis, j'obéirais jusqu'à la mort mais à moi' (*M*, 146). Conditioned to obedience and masochism, Jean-Paul opts for an independent sadism.[39] At times Sartre seems to stress the freedom we are familiar with from the early philosophy: 'Croit-on que les enfants ne choisissent pas leurs poisons eux-mêmes?' (*M*, 170); 'Les enfants ont les pères qu'ils méritent' (*M*, 189); at others the dialectic of liberty and conditioning takes over in a kind of whirligig. This seems to be the key to an interpretation of the last few pages: an interminable *va-et-vient* between freedom and necessity:

Je fuyais, des forces extérieures ont modelé ma fuite et m'ont fait.(*M*, 208)

Truqué jusqu'à l'os et mystifié . . . J'ai changé . . . Je suis un homme qui s'éveille, guéri d'une longue, amère et douce folie.   (*M*, 211–12)

Du reste, ce vieux bâtiment ruineux, mon imposture c'est aussi mon caractère: on se défait d'une névrose, on ne se guérit pas de soi. Usés, effacés, humiliés, rencoignés, passés sous silence, tous les traits de l'enfant sont restés chez le quinquagénaire.   (*M*, 213)

Pardaillan m'habite encore. Et Strogoff.[40] Je ne relève que d'eux qui ne relèvent que de Dieu et je ne crois pas en Dieu. Allez vous y reconnaître. Pour ma part je ne m'y reconnais pas.   (*M*, 213)

Rather than unwittingly self-revealing, or crassly misinterpreted, Sartre's offerings to the Freudian critic should be read as part of the continuing debate between a philosopher of freedom and one of the major sources of twentieth-century determinism. And in a sense, of course, *Les Mots* – like *L'Idiot de la famille* but in a different register – must be a test-case. A textual trap, provocatively inviting a teleological, psychoanalytic or determinist reading, how far is it in fact determined by what it ironically describes? To what extent can Sartre master the reading that attempts to master him? Or, in more familiar terms, what is the status of a literary farewell to literature?

'Le sens du style dans *Les Mots*, c'est que le livre est un adieu à la littérature: un objet qui se conteste soi-même doit être écrit le mieux possible' (*Sit X*, 94). *Les Mots* is certainly Sartre's most literary work: stylish, condensed and polished, it is, on a superficial reading, the one that conforms most closely to the norms of the literary canon. But it is precisely the closeness of the conformity, coupled with the disconcerting juxtaposition of high-flown and popular language, which makes the reader suspect that more is going on than at first meets the eye. *Les Mots* is a farewell to literature in a particularly strong sense: its ingredients constitute a semi-collage of parodic elements; it is parasitic on those very texts it desires most fiercely to deny and demystify, and like all parasites it both undermines and at the same time depends on its hosts. A close stylistic analysis would be needed to show precisely how much of the text can be read in this manner.[41] But the deliberately and explicitly intertextual nature of the work is nonetheless clear. And it points to a further aspect of Sartre's dialogue with Structuralism. Jean-Paul's relations to language – *les mots* – may appear to determine his relations with the world, 'Je prenais les mots pour la quintessence des choses' (*M*, 121), but this is part of the 'longue, amère et douce folie' (*M*, 212) from which he eventually awakens. Similarly, the child's writing may start as 'plagiat délibéré' (*M*, 121), the pleasure (*M*, 125) of composition finally liberates him both from literary imitation and also from play-acting. 'Je suis né de l'écriture' (*M*, 130) should be read not only as indicating Sartre's dependence on writing but also his self-creation through the act of writing: 'Je suis né de l'écriture: avant elle, il n'y avait qu'un jeu de miroirs; dès mon premier roman, je sus qu'un enfant s'était introduit dans le palais de glaces' (*M*, 130). Not that Sartre can be seen here as subscribing to an individualist thesis – far from it, he is *spoken* not only by his grandfather: 'la voix de mon grand-père . . . je ne l'écouterais pas si ce n'était la mienne' (*M*, 140), but also by the myriad voices of the world: 'le monde usait de moi pour se faire parole. Cela commençait par un bavardage anonyme dans ma tête' (*M*, 183). But his attitude to his own alienation is, as we have seen, highly ambivalent, and hovers between ferocious rejection –

'Je déteste mon enfance et tout ce qui en survit' (*M*, 140) – and a lucid resignation to the inevitable: 'Que reste-t-il? Tout un homme, fait de tous les hommes et qui les vaut tous et que vaut n'importe qui' (*M*, 214). Nonetheless the complexity of the last few pages cannot disguise the bitterness of Sartre's ironic attack, and our concern finally will be with its self-reflexive nature.

In the guise of a *récit d'enfance* Sartre launches a polemical attack on bourgeois ideology, mediated, in the case of the child, through the members and institutions of the family. Freud's *roman familial* is travestied in Sartre's *comédie familiale* in which the cosseted and over-protected Jean-Paul is depicted as an actor always playing to the gallery, and in particular to Karl in his role as grandfather and high priest of the literary canon. Precocious and spoilt ('je vivais au-dessus de mon âge', *M*, 61), Jean-Paul, as infant prodigy and juvenile lead, has to hide his taste for garish comics, and spend considerable time self-consciously rehearsing his role: inventing pearls of childish wisdom or carefully prepared 'improvisations' to delight his elders. Only when he misjudges his audience or misses a cue does the emptiness of his behaviour impinge on him with any force. His response is then to retreat into inverted narcissism, and pull ugly faces at himself in front of a solitary mirror (*M*, 94). But his attack on himself as product of such a family is as virulent as that on the family that produced him: 'Vermine stupéfaite, sans foi, sans loi, sans raison ni fin je m'évadais dans la comédie familiale' (*M*, 81). 'J'avais la larme facile et le cœur dur' (*M*, 96). In a piece of grating self-parody, Sartre writes of his own complacency: 'On m'adore, donc je suis adorable' (*M*, 26).[42]

And the criticism embraces not only the young Jean-Paul but the Sartre of *La Nausée* and *L'Etre et le Néant*, and, at least in an interrogative mode, the author of *Les Mots* also. The last few pages of text explain their own vertiginous retreat into irony and reflexivity: self-totalization is a necessary *and* impossible task: 'autant vaudrait tenter d'attraper le temps par la queue' (*OR*, 50). Sartre is happy to confess his faults and errors: he is exposing only a past, dead, self, 'une dépouille inerte' (*M*, 201), and is delighting in 'le plaisir de me sentir un enfant qui vient de naître' (*M*, 201); 'Je pense que je ferais mieux aujourd'hui et *tellement* mieux demain' (*M*, 202). If Sartre belittles the complexity of *La Nausée* and reduces to absurdity the theses of *L'Etre et le Néant* – 'j'exposai gaîment que l'homme est impossible' (*M*, 211) – it is to emphasize his present lucidity. 'J'ai changé' (*M*, 211): Sartre refers to the quicklime which dissolved his earlier self, 'La chaux vive où l'enfant merveilleux s'est dissous' (*M*, 211); we are reminded again of the comment in *L'Etre et le Néant* on the possibility of change: 'J'aurais pu faire autrement, soit; mais *à quel prix?*' (*EN*, 531). The price in Sartre's case seems to have been great.

But even this bitter celebration of change is too conclusive. Sartre is not fooled by his own perverse and sardonic optimism: 'Naturellement je ne suis pas dupe: je vois bien que nous nous répétons' (*M*, 202), and this realization is in its turn interpreted, self-consciously and ironically, as progress. Sartre even suspects himself, as present narrator one must assume, of playing at loser-wins, and the phrase points clearly to the unstable *tourniquets* which paradox and reflexivity inevitably produce. The anti-individualistic humanism of the last few lines, so different from the 'humanisme de Prélat' (patriarchal humanism) (*M*, 60) of Karl, and indeed from the naïve humanism which Sartre's detractors[43] have attributed to him in recent years, should still not be read as Sartre's last word. A farewell to literature, the literary finale provides a rhetorical conclusion which, in philosophical terms, subverts its own closure. Jean-Paul may live entirely in and through language, but *Les Mots* becomes the literary act which both depicts and ironizes the child's linguistic alienation, producing in practice the *décalage* between determining forces and creative action which is described in theory in the studies of Genet and Flaubert. Even as he rejects literature, Sartre reaffirms the ability of the text (and indeed the subject) to elude the totalization threatened by his Marxist, Freudian and Structuralist opponents. In extra-textual terms also, the threat of achieving closure is further deferred: a threat which would constitute an instance of 'winner loses', for self-totalization must remain an unrealized ideal if existential 'death' is to be averted. Sartre comments in an interview contemporary with the publication of *Les Mots*:

Si je n'ai pas publié cette autobiographie plus tôt et dans sa forme la plus radicale, c'est que je la jugeais excessive. Il n'y a pas de raison de traîner un malheureux dans la boue parce qu'il écrit. D'ailleurs, entre-temps, je m'étais rendu compte que l'action aussi a ses difficultés et qu'on peut y être conduit par la névrose.

On n'est pas plus sauvé par la politique que par la littérature.[44]

Sartre's self-treachery disavows in turn its own product.

9

A contemporary perspective: Qui perd gagne

Current disaffection with Sartre in French philosophical circles is almost total. Certain rare voices in the Structuralist and Post-Structuralist movements have taken up his defence,[1] but these have generally been drowned in the cacophony of polemical criticism to which Sartre's views have been subjected. The aggression may well be considered a form of self-defence; the global rejection of Sartre is a necessary but transitional stage in the assessment of a major thinker. Indeed, the insistent repudiation of his influence by his successors can only be interpreted as a form of intellectual *dénégation*.

The preceding analyses of Sartre's ideas should have made clear the sense in which he is a precursor and indeed a founder of certain contemporary philosophical tenets, tenets which are perhaps in danger of becoming the current *idées reçues* rather than contestatory scandals subverting doxa and ideology. The decentred subject, the 'death of man', the paradoxes of *qui perd gagne* and of 'différance', the rejection of Hegelian dialectics and the recognition of the impossibility of ultimate synthesis – such notions are more commonly associated with Lacan, Lévi-Strauss, Foucault, Derrida and Lyotard than with Sartre, but a close reading of *La Transcendance de l'Ego*, *L'Etre et le Néant*, *Saint Genet*, *Critique de la raison dialectique* and *L'Idiot de la famille* in particular, shows them to have been, at least in part, of Sartre's making. Sartre may be cursorily dismissed at present for his 'humanism',[2] and derided for translating the Heideggerian *Dasein* as *la réalité humaine*. (Nonetheless, Derrida recognizes that the phrase was intended as an anti-metaphysical, anti-substantialist neutralization of 'toutes les présuppositions qui constituaient depuis toujours le concept de l'unité de l'homme',[3] and even admits that 'le *Dasein*, s'il *n'*est *pas* l'homme n'est pourtant *pas autre chose* que l'homme'.)[4] Sartre's strategic importance in helping to liberate French philosophy from the stranglehold of bourgeois individualism and idealism has largely been ignored. This willed blindness to all but Sartre's best-known theses has involved a repression of some of the most interesting and controversial of his

194

positions; little serious attention has been paid in recent years to the rejection of humanistic individualism in *La Nausée*, the insistence on the self as an imaginary construct and an unrealizable limit in *La Transcendance de l'Ego*, the refusal of human nature in *L'Etre et le Néant* and of Man in the *Critique de la raison dialectique* – 'l'Homme n'existe pas' – or to the radically post-Heideggerian nature of his epistemology.[5]

It would be interesting to explore in detail the relationship between Sartre's ideas and those of the currently more popular thinkers just referred to. Sartre himself discussed the parallels between his conception of the formation of the ego and that of Lacan;[6] he engaged in a debate with Lévi-Strauss over the nature of dialectical and analytic reason and the status of 'thinking' in primitive peoples.[7] In a different perspective, Lyotard[8] and Derrida[9] have insisted on their opposition to what they see as the Hegelian tendency of Sartrean dialectics, and to the persistence of his humanism, in particular where language is concerned. More positively Barthes[10] and Deleuze[11] have both declared their debt to Sartre's philosophy, whilst maintaining a certain distance from it, the former with respect to the imaginary and the imagination, the latter in connection with the nature of perception and the common constitution of the world.

But these explorations would certainly take us far beyond the scope of the present study. What I should like, nonetheless, to attempt in this final chapter is an exemplary examination of Sartre's relations with one of the most radical of contemporary philosophers, Jacques Derrida, with a view to establishing certain intriguing similarities between vital aspects of the thought of the two men, as well as suggesting what might be the reasons underlying Derrida's almost too vehement rejection of Sartre's early philosophy.[12]

In *L'Etre et le Néant* Sartre is concerned, like Derrida twenty years later, with questioning the identification of Being and presence. In the wake of Heidegger and Husserl he rejects the 'common-sense' Aristotelian view of time as a series of 'nows':

Ces trois prétendus "éléments" du temps: passé, présent, avenir, ne doivent pas être envisagés comme une collection de "data" dont il faut faire la somme – par exemple comme une série infinie de "maintenant" dont les uns ne sont pas encore, dont les autres ne sont plus – mais comme des moments structurés d'une synthèse originale. (*EN*, 150)

And whilst taking over the Hegelian paradox of time as 'the being which, in that it *is*, is *not*, and in that it is *not*, *is*'[13] to apply to the present (and moreover to consciousness): 'En tant que présent il n'est pas ce qu'il est (passé) et il est ce qu'il n'est pas (futur)' (*EN*, 168), he refuses the Hegelian conclusion that 'only the present is'.[14] For Sartre 'le présent n'est pas' (*EN*, 168); it is *néant* rather than *être* (*EN*, 164–5). It is difficult to see how Sartre can be said to exemplify what Derrida describes as the persistent metaphysical identification of Being and presence, since in Sartre's argument 'l'en-soi ne peut être présent' (*EN*, 165), 'être *là* n'est pas être *présent*' (*EN*, 166), 'le présent est précisément cette négation de l'être, cette évasion de l'être en tant que l'être est *là* comme ce dont on s'évade' (*EN*, 167). It is of course true that for Sartre the present and presence come into the world through the *pour soi*, but it is in his view a misunderstanding of the nature of the *pour soi* which lies at the heart of the misunderstanding involved in the 'common-sense' view of time: 'L'instant présent émane d'une conception réalisante et chosiste du Pour-soi' (*EN*, 168), 'Le Pour-soi n'a pas d'être parce que son être est toujours à distance' (*EN*, 167).

Sartre's analysis of 'la présence à soi' of the *pour soi* clearly anticipates Derrida's deconstruction of Husserl's *Logical Investigations* in *La Voix et le phénomène* (1967). Derrida sets out to demonstrate that Husserl's own analyses undermine his insistence on the notion of self-identity: 'l'identité du vécu présent à soi dans le même instant'.[15] To this end, Derrida concentrates on Husserl's discussions of time and of interior monologue and concludes that the phenomenologist cannot maintain consistently the self-coincidence of the present or presence in either sphere:

Si le présent de la présence à soi n'est pas *simple*, s'il se constitue dans une synthèse originaire et irréductible, alors toute l'argumentation de Husserl est menacée en son principe. (*VP*, 68)

This is precisely Sartre's argument in the first chapter of Part II of *L'Etre et le Néant*. 'Présence à soi' is defined as 'une façon de *ne pas être sa propre coïncidence*, d'échapper à l'identité' (*EN*, 119). It is not *plénitude*, not 'la plus haute dignité d'être' (*EN*, 119). Sartre cites Husserl as evidence that even the most determined philosopher of presence cannot entirely overcome the reflexivity implicit in all consciousness. Presence is precisely what prevents identity: 'S'il est présent à soi, c'est qu'il n'est pas tout à fait soi' (*EN*, 120). Consciousness is always elsewhere, 'à distance de soi' (*EN*, 120): 'C'est l'obligation pour le pour-soi de n'exister jamais que sous la forme d'un ailleurs par rapport à lui-même' (*EN*, 121).

Presence then, in Derrida's sense, can be attributed neither to the *en soi* nor to the *pour soi*. Sartre never maintains, as Derrida asserts, that consciousness is a form of *L'Etre*. Even in the conclusion to *L'Etre et le Néant* where he is anxious to avoid an insurmountable dualism of *en soi* and *pour soi* and considers the question of the 'being' of the *pour soi* in so far as it is *néantisation* (*EN*, 716), the paradoxical nature of the formulations surely problematizes Being in a way far removed from Derrida's assertion that for Sartre 'l'être en-soi et l'être pour-soi étaient *de l'être*' (*Marges*, 137). The *pour soi* is not Being in any recognizable sense of the term: 'le Pour-soi n'a d'autre réalité que d'être la néantisation de l'être' (*EN*, 711–12); it is like 'un trou d'être au sein de l'Etre' (*EN*, 711), 'il fonde perpétuellement son néant d'être' (*EN*, 713); 'Son être n'est jamais donné . . . puisqu'il est toujours séparé de lui-même par le néant de l'altérité; le pour-soi est toujours en suspens parce que son être est un perpétuel sursis' (*EN*, 713). Sartre ultimately refuses to answer the question of whether it is 'plus profitable à la connaissance' (*EN*, 719) to consider Being as having two dimensions (*pour soi* and *en soi*) or if the old duality (consciousness/being) is preferable. Such questions, he argues, are metaphysical, not ontological. Nonetheless, the whole intention of the work is to insist 'contre Hegel . . . que l'être *est* et que le néant *n'est pas*' (*EN*, 51).

Derrida has frequently acknowledged that metaphysical discourse is inescapable even by those who attempt to deconstruct it. Of Heidegger, for example, he writes: 'Il reste que l'être qui n'est rien, qui n'est pas un étant, ne peut être dit, ne peut se dire que dans la métaphore ontique' (*Marges*, 157). But in the case of Sartre, Derrida focusses on selected terminology of existentialism and contrives to ignore its real emphasis on negation. His rejection of Sartre's humanism relegates Sartre's own critique of humanism in *La Nausée* to a footnote (*Marges*, 138). Such a representation of his predecessor's thinking not surprisingly brings in its wake a refusal to recognize basic analogies between Sartre's philosophy and his own. Derrida's insistence that 'la chose même se dérobe toujours' (*VP*, 17), that there is no 'perception pure' (*VP*, 136), no original experience of reality that precedes the sign, is less far removed from Sartre's notion that it is meaningless even to try to imagine 'l'être tel qu'il est' (*EN*, 270) than a simple view of the two thinkers might at first suggest. Moreover it would be possible to argue that Derrida's notion of *différance*, whilst being radically impersonal and intended as a means of deconstructing consciousness – that cornerstone of humanism – is in fact clearly related to consciousness in the Sartrean sense. The relationship can be traced through at least three of the meanings of *différance*: firstly as a deferring and a non-coincidence; secondly as differentiation; and thirdly as producer of differences and ultimately of meaning. In the fourth sense, that of ontico-ontological difference, *différance* could also be seen as analogous to consciousness in so far as it makes possible the difference between *l'Etre* and *l'étant*, Being and beings. But the analogy need not be carried into such abstract realms: what is important here is rather the way in which Derrida's descriptions of *différance*, *trace*, etc. appear to be based on the same paradoxical logic as Sartre's definition of the *pour soi*: 'la trace *n'est rien*',[16] '*la trace elle-même n'existe pas*',[17] 'la différance *n'est* pas, n'existe pas' (*Marges*, 6).

These parallels, which cannot be pursued here, are more than mere analogies: they are keys to Derrida's attitude to Sartre, for they point to a fundamental mode of recuperative transformation which tempts both thinkers whilst being repudiated by them. This is the transformation effected by the principle of *qui perd gagne*, loser wins, and represented in its inauthentic form, in the view of both Sartre and Derrida, by negative theology and Hegelian dialectics.

Sartre's own attitude to negative theology is severely critical and tends to misrepresent and distort it.[18] There are, of course, evident parallels between the mystical conception of God, exemplified for instance by Plotinus, and the transcendent *néant* of human consciousness. But Sartre never recognizes these – on the contrary, throughout his writings, when discussing the notion of God, he resolutely considers only the Scholastic conception of absolute Being: even the God of the mystics is designated as positivity. It is evident that Sartre is familiar with the paradoxes of the negative tradition in theology: in *Saint Genet*, for example, he dismisses as part of 'la sophistique du Non' (negative sophistry), as conservative rhetoric, the writings of Saint John of the Cross and Eckhart, in which God's absence is transformed into a higher kind of presence, death into life. And in *L'Idiot de la famille* Sartre refers frequently to 'cette théologie négative qui nous empoisonne encore aujourd'hui et fonde l'*être* de Dieu sur son absence de toute réalité' (*IF*, III, 180). It represents, in Sartre's view, a kind of religious bad faith, 'un christianisme *d'après l'athéisme* qui cherche à tourner la défaite en victoire' (*Mall*, 180).

Sartre's objections to negative theology are the same as his objections to Hegel: it is a sophistical reaffirmation of Being parading as negation, 'la négation universelle équivaut à l'absence de néga-tion' (*Mall*, 194). Of Saint Teresa's mysticism Sartre writes: 'pour elle, comme pour Hegel, la négation de la négation fait sauter nos limites et devient affirmation' (*SG*, 235); 'le dépassement conserve ce qu'il nie' (*SG*, 236). In fact he sees negative theology as a primitive version of an unacceptable dialectic positing an ideal syn-thesis beyond the tragic contradictions of human experience. Sar-tre's attack on Hegel is three-pronged: through the ontology of *L'Etre et le Néant* where he insists 'ce qu'il faut rappeler ici contre Hegel, c'est que l'être *est* et que le néant *n'est pas*' (*EN*, 51); through Marxism in the *Critique de la raison dialectique*, for Marx, according to Sartre, never tried to dissolve the reality of human initiative in the welter of historical process; and finally in 'L'Universel Singulier' where he argues that from Kierkegaard we learn that failure is a subjective reality which cannot be explained away as an objective 'positivité relative' (*Sit IX*, 166). It is through failure that human subjectivity proves inassimilable to *le savoir objectif*. It becomes clear that there are in Sartre's view two ver-sions of success through failure or *qui perd gagne*. The one, con-demned, tries to recuperate failure as success in another dimension, i.e. in the future or on a different level of attainment. The other, his own version of salvation through defeat, sees the possibility of failure as proof of the freedom of human consciousness from the deterministic process. Sartre, then, is unavoidably aware of the parallels between his own version of salvation through failure and religious patterns of thought. But he believes his own conception of the process to be unimpeachable because based on a resolutely non-recuperative ontology.

Derrida's objections to negative theology and to Hegel are iden-tical to Sartre's. Negative theology is not truly negative – God's being is denied in order to attribute to Him a higher kind of essence. Like Sartre, Derrida quotes Eckhart as an example of what he calls onto-theology:

Quand j'ai dit que Dieu n'était pas un être et était au-dessus de l'être, je ne lui ai pas par là contesté l'être, au contraire, je lui ai attribué un être plus élevé.[19]

The negative *moment* of the Hegelian dialectic is precisely that: a moment that will be transcended. Hegel dissolves difference in the eventual unity of being and non-being, presence and absence. Der-rida refers repeatedly to the inescapability of the *Aufhebung*, or speculative dialectic, and poses the question: 'Que serait un négatif qui ne se laisserait pas relever?' (*Marges,* 126). Philosophy, in Derrida's view, necessarily recuperates negativity: 'Le langage philosophique, dès qu'il parle, récupère la négativité – ou l'oublie, ce qui est la même chose – même lorsqu'il prétend l'avouer, la reconnaître' (*ED,* 55). Like Sartre, Derrida takes Kierkegaard[20] as exemplary of the ever-renewed, ever-frustrated attempt to elude deathly absorption into *le Savoir Absolu.* And like Sartre he criticizes certain contemporary thinkers for their inadequate attempts to deal with individual specificity, defined negatively, in terms of absence and failure, of 'erreur pathétique' (*ED,* 255), 'le néant au cœur de la parole, le "manque de l'être" ' (*ED,* 255). The attempt to evade dialectical totalization by preserving the negativity of the negative is, as Derrida recognizes, a form of 'loser-wins' thinking, a strategy of *qui perd gagne* which is explicitly intended to escape recuperation: 'Contrairement à l'interprétation métaphysique, dialectique, "hégélienne", du mouvement économique de la différance, il faut admettre un jeu où qui perd gagne et où l'on gagne et perd à tous les coups' (*Marges,* 21). But as Derrida is also aware, his own anti-philosophical, anti-metaphysical, antilogocentric paradoxes may thereby run the risk of being interpreted as sophisticated forms of negative theology:

Les détours, les périodes, la syntaxe auxquels je devrai souvent recourir, ressembleront, parfois à s'y méprendre, à ceux de la théologie négative. Déjà il a fallu marquer *que* la différance *n'est pas,* n'existe pas . . . et nous serons amenés à marquer aussi tout *ce qu'*elle *n'est pas,* c'est-à-dire *tout*; et par conséquent qu'elle n'a ni existence ni essence. Elle ne relève d'aucune catégorie de l'étant, qu'il soit présent ou absent. Et pourtant ce qui se marque ainsi de la différance n'est pas théologique, pas même de l'ordre le plus négatif de la théologie négative, celle-ci s'étant toujours affairée à dégager, comme on sait, une supra-essentialité par-delà les catégories finies de l'essence et de l'existence, c'est-à-dire de la présence, et s'empressant toujours de rappeler que si le prédicat d'existence est refusé à Dieu, c'est pour lui reconnaître un mode d'être supérieur, inconcevable, ineffable. Il ne s'agit pas d'un tel mouvement et cela devrait se confirmer progressivement.   (*Marges,* 6)

Derrida returns frequently to the question and is constantly at pains to prevent his *logique paradoxale* from slipping into the recuperative mode[21] exemplified by the 'ruse inépuisable' (*Marges,* 339) of the Hegelian *Aufhebung. Différance* is precisely an attempt to elude the *Aufhebung:* 'S'il y avait une définition de la différance, ce serait justement la limite, l'interruption, la destruction de la relève hégélienne *partout* où elle opère'.[22] But this emphatic repudiation of Hegel and of negative theology does not in practice save Derrida from the temptations of transformation and recuperation. *Différance*, as has been frequently noted by critics, tends to become the origin it denies and displaces.[23] Truth, dismissed, reappears in a new form:

La disparition de la vérité comme présence, le dérobement de l'origine présente de la présence est la condition de toute (manifestation de) vérité. La non-vérité est la vérité. La non-présence est la présence. La différance, disparition de la présence originaire, est *à la fois* la condition de possibilité et la condition d'impossibilité de la vérité.[24]

As Sartre has already demonstrated, *qui perd gagne* is a slippery *tourniquet* which cannot remain entirely uncontaminated by its own transformative logic. His resistance to negative theology, to most forms of 'loser wins' and to Hegel, is exacerbated by an awareness of such modes of thinking as dangers and temptations into which his own philosophy might fall. Derrida's rejection of these modes of thought, and of Sartre's own, has, I would suggest, the same source. In both thinkers, paradoxical logic is valiantly protected against the pitfalls of recuperative dialectics: the lapses of both reveal not so much their inadequacy as the voracity of the philosophical hydra against whom they are doing battle.

Derrida is, of necessity, more cognizant of Sartre's vulnerability to the seductions of totalization than of his own. Nonetheless, there is a serious misrepresentation involved in the current attempt to assimilate Sartre's unresolvable *tourniquets* and aporias to a version of Hegelian synthesis. It can perhaps best be explained as a form of philosophical parricide, or, in other words, as part of that very antithetical mode of thinking his critics are most anxious to reject. But the parricide may ultimately prove Sartre's salvation: if the vogue for existentialism in the 1940s led all but the most dedicated student to a facile, simplifying view of its tenets, its current *lack* of popularity is already leading to a reappraisal of its philosophical contribution and originality.[25] Sartre's unsynthesized dialectics are being taken with renewed seriousness, while the one-sided reaction against humanism, the subject, the individual and History is losing a little of the prestige it had in the 1960s and 1970s. In the end, Sartre's survival as a major philosopher may perhaps depend on the operation of his own transformative 'law' for converting failure into success. *Qui perd gagne.*

Notes

1. The early philosophy

1 See below p. 20, and pp. 23–4 for a discussion of these terms.
2 See Chapter 5 for an explanation of these terms.
3 See *La Transcendance de l'Ego*, 1972, pp. 19, 79 (henceforth *TE*).
4 The reference in the English edition is to *The Critique of Pure Reason*, tr. N. K. Smith, 1980, p. 152. Sartre quotes accurately but attempts to give the 'doit pouvoir' ('must be able') a more contingent sense than Kant's argument would support.
5 See below p. 10.
6 Henceforth *E*.
7 Most readers will probably find Sartre's argument more convincing if they substitute love for hatred in this example.
8 Collected in *Situations I*, 1947, pp. 29–32 (henceforth *Sit I*).
9 For the epistemological basis of this position see above pp. 1–2, and below pp. 17–19.
10 See below, Chapter 7.
11 In another sense, of course, Sartre comes close to the Romantic position in this dissociation of consciousness and sentiment or emotion.
12 See below p. 24.
13 *L'Imagination*, 1969 (first edition 1936), p. 140 (henceforth *Im*).
14 In *La Transcendance de l'Ego* Sartre will suggest that this 'mise entre parenthèses de l'attitude naturelle' (*Im*, 140) may be less difficult and miraculous than it seems in Husserl. If, as Sartre believes, there is *no* transcendental ego, then the attempt to put a personal self into brackets may simply involve an anguish-producing return to an original pre-egoic freedom rather than the almost incomprehensible relinquishing of a permanent inhabitant of consciousness (*TE*, 84).
15 Sometimes referred to as eidetic intuition.
16 *L'Imaginaire*, 1940, p. 14 (henceforth *I*).
17 See below pp. 18–19.
18 Michel Foucault later expresses the same disquiet when he objects that psychology contrives to ignore human 'ambiguity', man's empirico-transcendental status. See *Les Mots et les choses*, 1966, pp. 329–33.
19 See below p. 15.
20 See R. Aronson, *Jean-Paul Sartre. Philosophy in the World*, 1980, p. 48.
21 By Aronson, p. 45.
22 See Chapters 6 and 8.

23 *L'Etre et le Néant*, 1943, p. 12 (henceforth *EN*).
24 Technically speaking, there is a semantic slippage here between 'being' and 'world': the significance of the two terms will be explained shortly. See below pp. 17–18 and Chapter 9, p. 197.
25 See preceding note.
26 Whether this be the abstraction involved in Kant's attempt to discover the conditions of possibility of experience, or that of Husserl's phenomenological reduction.
27 Sartre's italics.
28 See my 'Sartre and negative theology', *Modern Language Review* 76, (1981), pp. 549–55; and below, Chapter 9.
29 See also *EN*, 33, 121.
30 See *EN*, 121.
31 Objections are always possible to the detail of Sartre's examples (does he expect the waiter to engage in an interesting conversation rather than bring the coffee?), but their general import is quite clear.
32 See above pp. 14–15.
33 See Chapter 2 for a different perspective.
34 See *EN*, 391: 'Ma finitude est condition de ma liberté.'
35 See Chapter 7.
36 See B. Pascal, *Pensées*, no. 90. (Brunschvicg 337) in *Œuvres complètes*, 1963, p. 510.

2. Notes for an ethics

1 *Prescription* is itself another example of the same change in meaning – a *claim* founded on *usage*.
2 Real name of Pierre Victor who collaborated with Sartre and Philippe Gavi in *On a raison de se révolter*, 1974.
3 *Sartre. Un film réalisé par A. Astruc et M. Contat*, 1977, p. 103.
4 B. Lévy, *Le Nom de l'homme, dialogue avec Sartre*, 1984.
5 In his *life* he was always prepared to make bold *ad hoc* moral and political choices.
6 *Situations II*, 1948, p. 299 (henceforth *Sit II*). See also Chapter II of *Qu'est-ce que la littérature?*, 'Pourquoi écrire?'
7 See below, Chapter 6, for a further discussion of this question.
8 In the terms of contemporary British philosophy, Sartre might be accused of 'mentioning' Kant's concepts rather than 'using' them.
9 In *L'Etre et le Néant* he describes Kant as the first great moral philosopher to substitute an ethics of action for an ethics of 'being' (*EN*, 507).
10 *L'Existentialisme est un humanisme*, 1964, p. 70 (henceforth *EH*).
11 H. J. Paton, *The Moral Law, Kant's Groundwork of the Metaphysic of Morals*, 1981, p. 84 (henceforth *Groundwork*).
12 *Groundwork*, 91.

13 *Saint Genet, comédien et martyr*, 1952, p. 652 (henceforth *SG*).

14 See I. Kant, *Critique of Practical Reason*, translated by L. White Beck, 1956, p. 74 (henceforth *CPR*).

15 See M. Contat and M. Rybalka, *Les Ecrits de Sartre*, 1970, p. 132.

16 *Groundwork*, 96.

17 See *EN*, 517–18 and my Chapter 1, p. 22. Kant himself is not entirely consistent on this point. In the *Groundwork* he suggests that the will could be alienated by listening to sensuous inclination or desire; but according to the third antinomy such a mediation should be impossible.

18 *Cahiers pour une morale*, 1983, p. 485 (henceforth *C*). See also p. 147: 'La liberté qui soutient pour Kant l'impératif catégorique est nouménale donc liberté *d'un autre* . . . Elle est projection de l'Autre dans le monde nouménal.' And compare 'Détermination et liberté' (1964) in *Les Ecrits de Sartre*, ed. Contat and Rybalka, pp. 735–45: 'Le devoir . . . est un ordre donné par quelqu'un d'autre, et qui conserve pour l'agent ce caractère d'altérité' (p. 740).

19 See S. Körner, *Kant*, 1972, p. 153.

20 Though it is more complex than this in the case of the body, as we have already seen. See above, Chapter 1, p. 20.

21 Sartre's relationship to Kantian ethics, like his relationship to Hegel in other spheres, seems to reveal what Harold Bloom would call 'an anxiety of influence'.

22 In fact, Kant himself argued that his ethical formulations did *not* depend on a Divine Being but rather themselves provided evidence of His existence: morality as proof of God, rather than God as guarantor of morality; but Sartre is not alone in finding this argument unconvincing.

23 See *Groundwork*, p. 31.

24 See also 'Détermination et liberté', in *Les Ecrits de Sartre*, where Sartre refers to the 'tu dois, donc tu peux' as 'rassurant' (p. 736).

25 See *C*, p. 541. Sartre's attitude to the paradoxes of Christian theology seems also to reveal an 'anxiety of influence'. He reproaches it for a spurious kind of negative theology in which absence is redefined as presence, failure as success etc., in a series of inversions which have evident parallels in his own ontology. (See above, Chapter 1, pp. 15–16 and below, Chapter 9, for a fuller discussion of the issues involved.)

26 In *Réflexions sur la question juive*, 1946, Sartre examines the problem of the Jew's self-image in the face of anti-semitism, and concludes that to be authentic he must accept and affirm his Jewishness rather than attempt an alienating integration with the Gentile community.

27 See also *C*, 128.

28 *SG*, 70.

29 Sartre's later attitude to Marx is very different, as we shall see, but for the moment he tends to assimilate Marx to Hegel: 'L'idée de *la fin de la préhistoire* ne change rien au problème' (*C*, 438).

30 We shall see when we look at Sartre's later philosophy that this notion of a never-totalized History is part of an anti-Hegelian conception of

the dialectic of truth, a rejection of 'une Histoire où l'altérité est reprise par l'unité'. (*C*, 55). See Chapter 5.

31 We shall return to the question of biography as fable in Chapter 8.

3. The novels

1 'La temporalité chez Faulkner', *Sit I*, 66.

2 Nor the logocentric philosophy repudiated by Derrida (see below, Chapter 9).

3 *Situations II*, 1948, p. 251 (henceforth *Sit II*).

4 See Chapter 8.

5 See below, Chapter 6.

6 See G. J. Prince, *Métaphysique et technique dans l'œuvre romanesque de Sartre*, 1968, p. 46.

7 *La Nausée* in *Œuvres romanesques*, 1981, pp. 48–50 (henceforth *OR*).

8 See *Sit I*, 15 and 33–4.

9 See *Sit II*, 256.

10 See *Sit II*, 109 and *SG*, 419.

11 For Sartre, of course, 'la nature sans les hommes', like 'l'être tel qu'il est' is strictly unimaginable (see Chapter 1, p. 18).

12 And which some of the plays, in focussing on dramatic moments of genuine choice, also encourage.

13 The question of abortion is perhaps a good example of Sartre's refusal to come to categorical ethical conclusions. Considered criminal by Church and State in the 1940s, promoted as a feminist issue by Simone de Beauvoir, fervently wished for by Mathieu, abortion does not appear as necessarily in Marcelle's own best interests (though Sartre's attitude to her – like Mathieu's – could nonetheless be criticized as singularly unsympathetic).

14 See *EN*, 656: 'D'autre part, la pure et simple description empirique ne peut nous donner que des nomenclatures et nous mettre en présence de pseudo-irréductibles.'

15 It has received one: see J. Pacaly, *Sartre au miroir*, 1980, p. 127.

16 'La Chambre', *Le Mur*, *OR*, 234.

17 See below, Chapter 6.

18 'Un nouveau mystique', and 'L'homme ligoté. Notes sur le *Journal* de Jules Renard', *Sit I*.

19 See *SG*, 39.

20 Here Sartre's technique prefigures that of Nathalie Sarraute, whose 'anti-roman', *Portrait d'un inconnu*, he reviews with favour in *Sit IV*.

21 G. Idt, *La Nausée: analyse critique*, 1971.

22 Rieux, in Camus's *La Peste*, would be another (anachronistic) contender.

23 See Chapter 1, p. 25.

24 Maria Craipeau, 'Interview avec Jean-Paul Sartre', *France-Observateur*, 10 September 1959, p. 5.
25 See Chapter 8.

4. Drama: theory and practice

1 See 'Théâtre populaire et théâtre bourgeois' in *Un Théâtre de situations*, ed. M. Contat et M. Rybalka, 1973, pp. 68–80 (henceforth *TS*).
2 I have not indicated by name which of the numerous brief articles and interviews collected in *TS* are the subject of quotation. Immediate access to the page reference seemed more useful.
3 *Les Mouches*, 1943, p. 140 (henceforth *Mouches*).
4 'Les Ecrivains en personne', interview with M. Chapsal, *Situations IX*, p. 12 (henceforth *Sit IX*).
5 See 'Avoir, faire et être', *EN*, 507–708.
6 R. Lorris, *Sartre dramaturge*, 1975, p. 11.
7 See F. Jeanson, *Sartre par lui-même*, 1955, p. 100.
8 *Les Mains sales*, 1948, Tableau III, Scene i, p. 75 (henceforth *MS*).
9 See Jeanson, p. 101.
10 *Le Diable et le Bon Dieu*, 1951, p. 241 (henceforth *DBD*).
11 Explored most fully in theoretical terms in *L'Imaginaire*; see my Chapter 6.
12 Jeanson, p. 110.
13 See Chapter 1, pp. 7–8.
14 See also *TS*, 19: 'Si la psychologie gêne, au théâtre, ce n'est point qu'il y ait trop en elle: c'est qu'il n'y a pas assez.'
15 The exclusion of Racine is significant.
16 Lorris (p. 82) quoting V. Jankélévitch: 'Il y a tragédie toutes les fois que l'impossible au nécessaire se joint' (from *L'Alternative*, 1938, p. 150).
17 Of course, the same duality applies to all art in so far as it depends on the spectator's imaginative response to the 'analogon', but it is clearest in the case of drama and music which depend on a fresh performance for their realization. See below, Chapter 6. Derrida has dealt interestingly with the 'duality' of drama in his essay on Artaud, 'La Parole soufflée' in *L'Ecriture et la différence*, 1967.
18 See Chapter 3, p. 62.
19 See J. L. Austin, *How To Do Things With Words*, 1962. At its most simple, a performative is a speech act which literally enacts what it relates: e.g. 'I name this ship Britannia', 'I declare this meeting open.'
20 See Chapter 6.
21 See, for example, J. Derrida, 'Signature, événement, contexte' in *Marges de la philosophie*, 1972; and J.-F. Lyotard, *La Condition postmoderne*, 1979, and *Le Différend*, 1983.
22 *Sartre par lui-même*, 1955.

23 *Sartre dramaturge*, 1975.
24 *Sartre et la mise en signe*, 1982, pp. 56–67.
25 See 'Névrose et programmation chez Flaubert: le Second Empire', *L'Idiot de la famille*, III, 1972 (henceforth *IF*, III).
26 Lorris, p. 81.
27 Lorris, p. 119. The latter phrase is Simone de Beauvoir's, taken up by Sartre.
28 M. Bensimon, '*Nekrassov* ou l'anti-théâtre', *French Review* 31 (1957). pp. 18–26.
29 *Kean*, 1973, p. 185.
30 *L'Idiot de la famille*, I, 1971, p. 662 (henceforth *IF*, I).
31 The analogon is the real material from which the art object is created, e.g. the paint on the canvas. For a fuller explanation, see Chapter 6.
32 Haunting Hugo, for example.
33 Jeanson, *Sartre par lui-même*, p. 99.
34 Lorris, p. 348.
35 Chapter 8.
36 See *TS*, 11.
37 See Chapter 5.
38 His disaffection probably also reflects his revised view of the historical importance of the Resistance.
39 But see above (p. 72) for Sartre's insistence that despite his *intentions* the play has become *objectively* anti-Communist.
40 See R. Wilcocks, 'Thomas l'obscur', in *Obliques*, 18–19 (1979), pp. 131–5, for an interesting discussion of the play in this light: 'La pièce est une tragédie dans la mesure où il n'y a pas d'issue. Elle est Marxiste dans la mesure où elle révèle et déchiffre la nécessité historique de cette lutte vouée à un échec' (p. 135).
41 See Jeanson, *Sartre par lui-même*, p. 165.
42 Jean Lacroix, 'Le Séquestré d'Altona condamné à un deuxième suicide', *Paris-Presse*, 29 April 1966. Quoted by Lorris, p. 278.
43 Euripide, *Les Troyennes*, adaptation de J.-P. Sartre, 1965, p. 125.
44 *Les Séquestrés d'Altona*, Livre de Poche, 1967, p. 382.

5. The later philosophy

1 *Critique de la raison dialectique* (précédé de 'Questions de méthode'), 1960, p. 40 (henceforth *CRD*).
2 See, for example, *EN*, 462.
3 The Marxist term for constructive action.
4 See Chapter 7.
5 See also *Sit II*, 251: 'Nous sommes donc jansénistes parce que l'époque nous a faits tels.'
6 See also *Sit X*, 99–100.

7 As usual, Sartre exaggerates the difference between his present and former positions.

8 *Lettres au Castor et à quelques autres*, 2 vols, 1983.

9 S. de Beauvoir, *La Force de l'âge*, 1960.

10 Collected in *Situations III*; written in 1946, revised 1949.

11 See Aronson, *Jean-Paul Sartre . Philosophy in the World*, 1980, p. 120; and Contat and Rybalka, *Les Ecrits de Sartre*, p. 149.

12 Reprinted in *Situations VI. Problèmes du Marxisme*, I, 1964 (henceforth *Sit VI*).

13 Reprinted in *Situations VII*, 1965, pp. 7–93 (henceforth *Sit VII*).

14 Gallimard, 1955.

15 'Merleau-Ponty et le pseudo-Sartrisme', *Les Temps modernes* (June–July 1955), 114–15.

16 Reprinted in *Sit VII*, 144–307.

17 Ph. Gavi, Sartre, P. Victor, *On a raison de se révolter*, 1974.

18 See p. 100, for example.

19 See p. 260 and pp. 344–5.

20 In fact this is a simplification. Hegel *does* recognize historical alienation.

21 See for example Aronson, p. 269, and M. Poster, *Sartre's Marxism*, 1979, p. 79.

22 M. Sahlins, *Stone Age Economics*, 1972.

23 See Chapter 1, pp. 17–18.

24 See below, pp. 111–2.

25 Ronald Aronson had access to the notes for volume II of the *Critique*, which he utilized for his chapter on 'Individualist Social Theory' (in *Jean-Paul Sartre . Philosophy in the World*). A reconstruction of volume II, and a new annotated edition of volume I, appeared early in 1986, too late for consideration in the present study.

26 See *CRD*, 42.

27 We may be reminded here of Lévi-Strauss's criteria for establishing the validity of his structural myth-models. See *Anthropologie structurale*, 1958, p. 306.

28 Compare *EN*, 656, and see above, Chapter 3, p. 47.

29 Sartre's contribution to the U.N.E.S.C.O. conference (1966) on Kierkegaard, reprinted in *Sit IX*.

30 See my 'Sartre and negative theology', *M.L.R* 76 (1981), and below, Chapter 9.

31 See *Sit IX*, 111.

32 A more recent opponent of the 'dangerous' notion of 'le réel préconceptuel' is Jacques Derrida (see Chapter 9).

33 For a discussion of this aspect of *L'Idiot de la famille* see my *Sartre's Theory of Literature*, 1979, Chapter V, pp. 125–43.

34 See Foucault, *Les Mots et les choses* (especially Chapter IX, 'l'homme et ses doubles').

35 See also: 'Ce que le pour-soi manque, c'est le soi . . . le soi est individuel' (*EN*, 132–4).
36 See for example the essays of *Sit IX* and *X* and 'Jean-Paul Sartre répond', in *L'Arc*, 30 (1966), pp. 87–96.

6. Literary theory

1 E. Delacroix, *Journal*, ed. A. Joubin, 1980, p. 29.
2 *Ibid.*
3 C. Baudelaire, 'Le Peintre de la vie moderne', *Œuvres complètes*, 1961, p. 1154.
4 *Ibid.*
5 See my *Sartre's Theory of Literature*, Chapter II.
6 For a discussion of *le vécu* see Chapter 7, pp. 150–1.
7 'Jean-Paul Sartre' in *Que peut la littérature?* (1965); 'L'Ecrivain et sa langue' (1965), in *Sit IX*; 'L'Anthropologie' (1966) in *Sit IX*; 'Jean-Paul Sartre répond', in *L'Arc* 30 (1966); 'Sartre par Sartre' (1970) in *Sit IX*; *Plaidoyer pour les intellectuels* (1972), being lectures given in Tokyo and Kyoto, 1965, reprinted in *Sit VIII*.
8 For the *écrivain* writing is an end in itself, for the *écrivant* it is an instrument. See 'Ecrivains et écrivants' in *Essais critiques* (1964).
9 See *I*, 156–8 and 235–6.
10 See 'Les Ecrivains en personne', *Sit IX*, 14, and 'Sur *L'Idiot de la famille*', *Sit X*, 112.
11 *Mouches*, Act III, Scene ii, p. 183.

7. Psychoanalysis: existential and Freudian

1 See, for example, *The Standard Edition of the Complete Psychological Works of Sigmund Freud*, translated and edited by J. Strachey, 24 vols, XIV, 29–30 (henceforth *SE*).
2 For Freud's increasing reservations about the efficacy and indeed the possibility of self-analysis see *SE*, I, 271; XIV, 20–1; XV, 19.
3 See below, pp. 150–1. See also R. Goldthorpe, *Sartre: Literature and Theory*, 1984, p. 88 and p. 230 for an account of Sartre's debt to German thinkers in his conception of *compréhension*.
4 See *SE*, XVI, 413; XVIII, 90 and 244.
5 See *SE*, VII, 43; XI, 150; XVI, 382.
6 See also *SE*, IX, 177–205; XXI, 57–147.
7 See above, p. 147. See also Goldthorpe, Chapter 6, for an interesting discussion of Sartre's notion of *le vécu*.
8 J. Lacan, *Ecrits*, 1966, p. 258.
9 'Jean-Paul Sartre répond', pp. 91–2.
10 'Sartre contre Lacan', *Figaro Littéraire*, 29 December 1966, p. 4.

11 C. Burgelin, 'Lire *L'Idiot de la famille?*', *Littérature*, 6 May 1972, p. 115.

12 C. Mouchard, 'Un Roman vrai', *Critique*, 27 (II), 1971, p. 1048.

13 *IF*, I, 58.The reference is probably to *Sex and Temperament in Three Primitive Societies*, 1935.

14 See above, p. 141.

15 Published in *Obliques: Sartre Inédit*, 18–19, directed by M. Sicard, pp. 169–97 (henceforth *Mall*).

16 See above, Chapter 2, pp. 38–9.

17 See W. R. D. Fairbairn, *Psychoanalytic Studies of the Personality*, 1952.

18 G. Bateson *et al.*, 'Towards a Theory of Schizophrenia', *Behavioural Sciences* I (1956), pp. 251–63.

19 See Burgelin, 'Lire *L'Idiot de la famille?*', p. 115.

20 See Mouchard, 'Un Roman vrai', p. 1042.

21 Indeed, some lacunae may remain even after analysis – see *SE*, V, 525.

22 Burgelin, 'Lire *L'Idiot de la Famille?*', p. 114.

23 M. Robert, 'Le Tribunal ou l'analyse', *Le Monde*, 2 July 1971, p. 16.

24 In Flaubert, *Œuvres complètes*, 1964, vol. I.

25 See C. Rycroft, *A Critical Dictionary of Psychoanalysis*, 1968, reprinted 1972, p. 106; and J. Laplanche and J.-B. Pontalis, *Vocabulaire de la psychanalyse*, 1967, pp. 323–4.

26 Freud's own misgivings about the widespread misuse of the term 'complex' in a loose and merely descriptive sense have been already referred to (p. 146). Nonetheless, he considered the Œdipus complex to be universal and probably phylogenetically transmitted.

27 In fact, Sartre prefers to interpret it as hysterical in so far as this implies a greater element of choice on Flaubert's part.

8. Biography and autobiography

1 See, for example, M. Scriven, *Sartre's Existential Biographies*, 1984, p. 38.

2 See *SG*, 623.

3 See Goldthorpe, p. 88 and p. 230 for a discussion of *compréhension* (*Verstehen*).

4 Bachelard's phenomenological studies of poetic imagery were known and admired by Sartre. See my *Sartre's Theory of Literature*, p. 71.

5 See above, p. 43 and p. 144 and below, pp. 178–9.

6 See Lévy, *Le Nom de l'homme*, pp. 59–87, for an interesting and controversial alternative reading of *Saint Genet*. See also above, pp. 44–5 for a more detailed analysis of the ethical implications.

7 Chapter 6, pp. 138–41.

8 This is not in itself necessarily un-Freudian. Freud's notions of

childhood were almost all elaborated on the basis of revelations of adult patients.

9 For a fuller discussion of this subject see my *Sartre's Theory of Literature*, pp. 112–15. Also see above, Chapter 7, p. 162.

10 The notion of antipsychiatry originated with R. D. Laing and David Cooper, who were influenced by Sartre's existentialist approach to human problems; and it has since been practised by others as diverse as Aaron Esterton and Gregory Bateson in England, Franco Basaglia in Italy and Roger Gentis in France. It depends on the belief that madness is not an illness but rather an intelligible response to an intolerable situation; and it attempts to break down the hierarchy implicit in the doctor–patient relationship.

11 See above, p. 160–1.

12 Already in the *Critique* Sartre had used Flaubert to illustrate the progressive–regressive method. There, too, his nervous crises are given a positive interpretation which is suggested but never explained: 'Le mouvement qui va de l'enfance aux crises nerveuses est . . . un dépassement perpétuel de ces données; il aboutit, en effet, à l'engagement littéraire de Gustave Flaubert' (*CRD*, 72).

13 To use Harold Bloom's term (in *A Map of Misreading*, 1975).

14 See Chapter 6.

15 The Freudian notion that excessive protests prove precisely that which the subject wishes to deny ('Methinks the lady doth protest too much'). See Freud, 'Negation' ('Die Verneinung') in *SE*, xix, 233–9.

16 See *TE*, 69 and my Chapter 1, p. 3.

17 See Chapter 3, p. 48.

18 *Les Mots*, 1963 (henceforth *M*).

19 See Chapter 3, pp. 49–51.

20 See *EN*, 501 and my Chapter 5, p. 95.

21 M. Beaujour, *Miroirs d'encre, rhétorique de l'autoportrait*, 1980, p. 9.

22 A. Gide, *Si le grain ne meurt*, 1954, p. 7.

23 P. Lejeune, *Le Pacte autobiographique*, 1975, p. 206.

24 Camus's term for Clamence, 'hero' of *La Chute*.

25 There is an interesting interpretation of this phrase in *EN*, 673: 'De là le fameux conseil: "Glissez, mortels, n'appuyez pas", qui ne signifie pas "Devenez superficiels, n'approfondissez pas", mais, au contraire: "Réalisez des synthèses en profondeur, mais sans vous compromettre,"' In this sense, of course, Mamie's advice is good.

26 See Lejeune, p. 231.

27 We might note that Sartre makes the same observation of Flaubert. Also that his mother was still alive when *Les Mots* was published.

28 Cf. Gide, *Si le grain ne meurt*, p. 8.

29 See Pacaly, *Sartre au miroir*, p. 69.

30 See G. Idt, 'Des *Mots* à *L'Enfance d'un chef*' in *Sartre et la mise en signe*, ed. Issacharoff, p. 22.

31 See above, p. 165.
32 'La Géante', *Œuvres complètes*, p. 21.
33 Also, perhaps, as a reworking in the comic mode of J.-J. Rousseau's traumatic confession (*Confessions*, Book III). *Les Mots* exposes others rather than the self.
34 The echo of Verlaine forms part of a multiplicity of parodic intertextual allusions. See below, p. 191.
35 See Pacaly, p. 90.
36 *Ibid.*
37 It was in a similar spirit that Sartre was prepared for his private correspondence to become public property after his death.
38 See, for example, Pacaly, p. 67.
39 Of course, Freudians could interpret this inversion as 'reaction formation' on Sartre's part. But such interpretations, which apparently verify Freudian hypotheses, even when their truth is least in evidence, form part of what Sartre rejects as the syncretic and non-dialectical nature of psychoanalytic theory. See above, pp. 149–50.
40 Heroes of children's adventure stories.
41 J. Lecarme ('*Les Mots* de Sartre; un cas limite de l'autobiographie?', *Revue d'histoire littéraire de la France* 75, no. 6 (1975), pp. 1047–61) briefly analyses parodies of Victor Hugo (*L'Art d'être grand-père*), R. Rolland, Alain, Valéry, Gide, J. Benda, Giraudoux, A. France, and indeed Sartre himself. Autobiography → Autoparody.
42 See 'Une idée fondamentale de la phénoménologie de Husserl: l'intentionnalité', *Sit I*, 29–32. (See Chapter 1, p. 4).
43 Even by someone as brilliant as Jacques Derrida who should know better! See Chapter 9.
44 Interview with J. Piatier, *Le Monde*, 18 April 1964.

9. A contemporary perspective

1 See below: Barthes, Deleuze; also Dominique Grisoni, 'Sartre: de la structure à l'histoire', in *Politiques de la philosophie* (contributions by Chatelet, Derrida, Foucault, Lyotard, Serres), ed. D. Grisoni, 1976.
2 See, for example, J. Derrida, 'Les Fins de l'homme', in *Marges de la philosophie*, 1972, and J.-F. Lyotard, *Tombeau de l'intellectuel*, 1984.
3 *Marges*, p. 136.
4 *Marges*, p. 151.
5 See, in particular, Chapters 1 and 5 for a discussion of these issues.
6 See *Sit X*, 100 and above, Chapter 7.
7 See *Sit IX*, 75–8, and C. Lévi-Strauss, *La Pensée sauvage*, 1962, 324–57.
8 See, for example, *Discours, Figure*, 1971 (reprint 1978), pp. 33–4. What Lyotard has to say about prose and poetry in this work has

evident analogies with Sartre's own analyses, though he does not acknowledge these (compare p. 287, note 4, and pp. 316–26).

9 See 'Tympan' and 'Les Fins de l'homme' in *Marges*, and *Glas*, 1974.

10 See, for example, *La Chambre claire*, 1980, which is dedicated 'En hommage à *L'Imaginaire* de Sartre'.

11 See 'Michel Tournier et le monde sans autrui', Appendix II to *Logique du sens*, 1969; and *Dialogues* (with Claire Parnet) 1977, pp. 18–19: 'Et Sartre n'a jamais cessé d'être ça, non pas un modèle . . . mais un peu d'air pur, un courant d'air . . . C'est stupide de se demander si Sartre est le début ou la fin de quelque chose. Comme toutes les choses et les gens créateurs, il est au milieu.'

12 Derrida entirely ignores the development of Sartre's thought and his unequivocal rejection of 'humanist individualism' and 'metaphysics' in *CRD*. He focusses solely on *EN*.

13 G. W. F. Hegel, *Philosophy of Nature*, I, edited and translated by M. J. Petry, 1970, Section 258, pp. 229–30.

14 *Ibid.*, Section 259, p. 235.

15 *La Voix et le phénomène*, 1967, p. 67 (henceforth *VP*).

16 J. Derrida, *De la grammatologie*, 1967, p. 110.

17 *Ibid.*, p. 238.

18 I have discussed this elsewhere (*M.L.R.*, 1981) and will simply refer briefly now to some points of interest relevant to the present debate.

19 Derrida, *L'Ecriture et la différence*, 1967, p. 398 (henceforth *ED*).

20 See *ED*, 162–4.

21 See, for example, *Grammatologie*, p. 191; *ED*, p. 91.

22 *Positions*, 1972, p. 55.

23 See, for example, *Grammatologie*, p. 96.

24 Derrida, *La Dissémination*, 1972, p. 194.

25 The recent issue of *Yale French Studies* no. 68 (1985), *Sartre after Sartre*, bears clear witness to this reappraisal amongst Anglo-American critics. See, in particular, the articles by F. Jameson, P. Wood, R. Aronson and D. Gross.

Translations

(The translations are keyed by page and listed in order of occurrence.)

Chapter 1

3   'It must be possible for the "I think" to accompany all my representations.'

'There is no *I* on the unreflexive level.'

'The ego only ever appears when one is not looking at it . . . by nature the Ego is fleeting.'

'So the intuition of the Ego is a perpetually deceptive mirage.'

'the death of consciousness'

4   'How could I have done that!'

5   'the digestive philosophy of empirico-criticism, of neo-kantianism'

'Consciousness and the world are given together: external in essence to consciousness, the world is, in essence, relative to it.'

'conscious of itself non-thetically'

'it is to this extent, and only to this extent, that one can say of an emotion that it is not sincere'

'the qualities intended in objects are apprehended as true'

'If we love a woman, it is because she is lovable.'

'Emotion is endured. We cannot get out of it as we wish, it exhausts itself but we cannot stop it.'

'bewitched, overwhelmed, by our own emotion'

6   the "seriousness" of emotion'

'One can stop running away; one cannot stop trembling.'

'My hands will remain frozen.'

'Consciousness is not limited to projecting affective meanings onto the world around it: it *lives* the new world which it has just constituted.'

'on the one hand an object in the world, and on the other the immediate lived experience of consciousness'

The origin of emotion is a *spontaneous*, *lived* degradation of consciousness in the face of the world.'

'The spontaneity of consciousness should not be imagined as meaning that it is always free to deny something at the very moment of positing it.'

'Consciousness is moved by its emotion, it intensifies it.'

214

'Liberation has to come from purifying reflexion or from a total disappearance of the emotional situation.'

7 'Phenomenology is a description of the structures of transcendental consciousness, based on the intuition of the essences of those structures.'

8 ' "that which indicates itself"; that of which the reality is precisely the appearance'

'So Husserl can take advantage of the absolute proximity of consciousness to itself, from which psychologists had not wished to profit.'

9 'The method is simple: to produce images in ourselves, to reflect on those images, to describe them, that is to say to attempt to determine and classify their distinctive characteristics.'

'The psychological sciences . . . study human consciousness indissolubly linked to a body and confronting a world . . . Phenomenological reflexion . . . tries to grasp essences. That is to say it starts by putting itself from the outset in the domain of the universal.'

10 'revived sensible impression'

'a naïve reification',

'these corroborations will never permit us to go beyond the realm of the probable'

11 'illusion of immanence'

'In fact the expression "mental image" is confusing. It would be better to say "consciousness of Pierre-in-an-image" or "imaging consciousness of Pierre".'

'essential poverty'

'imaging consciousness posits its object as a nothingness'

'I see nothing at all.'

'A perceptual consciousness *appears to itself* as passive.'

'plenitude', 'richness'

'I always *perceive* more than and *differently* from what I see.'

12 'degraded knowledge', 'pure knowledge'

'unreflecting knowledge'

'I do not see them in spite of myself, I produce them.'

'But, you might reply, at least the vomiting is undergone. Yes, certainly, to the extent that we undergo our irritations, our obsessions . . . It is a spontaneity which escapes our control. But . . . we became moved, carried away, we vomited *because of nothing*.'

'consciousness is in a sense its own victim'

'The imaginary object is unreal . . . to affect these unreal objects I must split myself in two and become unreal.'

'The unreal can be seen, touched, smelt only unreally. Conversely it can act only on an unreal being.'

13 'The images that we have of Annie will become increasingly banal.'

'The feeling became *degraded*, because its richness and inexhaustible depth came from its object.'

'the unreal object . . . will conform far more to our desires than Annie ever did'

'artificial', 'ossified'

'To posit the world as a world or to "nihilate" it is one and the same thing.'

'One must consider that the act of positing the world as a synthetic totality and the act of "stepping back" from the world are one and the same act.'

'bogged down in the world', 'pierced by the real', 'totally engulfed by the existent and with no possibility of grasping anything other than the existent'

'it is consciousness in its entirety in so far as it realizes its freedom'

'situated in the world'

'The imaginary always appears "against the background of the world", but conversely any awareness of the real as a world implies a hidden movement of transcendence towards the imaginary.'

14 'consciousness in its entirety in so far as it realizes its freedom'

'The phenomenon does not point, over its shoulder, to a true being which would be the absolute. What it is, it is absolutely, for it is revealed *as it is*.'

15 'Being is . . . it overflows and grounds the knowledge we have of it.'

22 'being-in-the-world'

'The being through which Nothingness comes into the world must be its own Nothingness. And by this we must understand not a nihilating act which would require in its turn a grounding in Being, but an ontological characteristic of the Being required. It remains to be discovered in what delicate and exquisite region of Being we may find the Being which is its own Nothingness.'

'delicate and exquisite'

'consciousness experiences itself as nihilation of its past being'

'being which is its own nothingness'

'a being which is what it is not and is not what it is'

16 'I *am* not he who I will be.'

'at the limit of self-coincidence . . . the self fades away to leave room for identical being'

'If it is present to itself, that is because it is not entirely itself.'

'Its being is always at a distance.'

'a useless passion'

'It is in anguish that man becomes conscious of his freedom, or, if you prefer, anguish is the mode of being of freedom as consciousness of being.'

'Anguish is . . . the reflexive apprehension of freedom by itself.'

17 'it is what it is not'

'it is not what it is'

'transcendent givens'

'There is ethical anguish when I consider myself in my original relationship to values . . . anguish is the opposite of the spirit of seriousness which understands values as issuing from the world and which resides in the reassuring and reifying substantiation of values.'

'It is, it is in itself, it is what it is.'

18 'To know being as it is, one would have to be that being, but there is an "as it is" only because I am not the being that I know, and if I were the "as it is" would disappear and could no longer even be thought.'

'the *pour soi* must be the nothingness through which "there is" being'

'It remains to be explained how the sudden arrival of the *pour soi* in being can mean that there is a *whole* and some *individual elements*.'

'"There is" being because I am the negation of being, and worldliness, spatiality, quantity, instrumentality, temporality come into being only because I am the negation of being . . . The world is human.'

'a world of tasks'

'The *pour soi* . . . is temporality . . . but . . . in the unreflexive mode it discovers temporality in being, that is to say, outside itself.'

19 'the world *appears* to me as objectively articulated'

'universal time comes to the world through the *pour soi*'

'universal temporality is objective'

'I apprehend being-with-others as an essential characteristic of my being.'

'a relation of being to being'

'The essence of relations between consciousnesses is not *Mitsein*, it is conflict.'

'I am he through whom *there is* a world.'

Like me, the other 'creates space and time'.

'The other presents himself . . . as the radical negation of my experience, because he is someone for whom I am not a subject but an object.'

217

20 'The other is first of all the permanent flight of things towards a goal . . . which escapes me . . . he has stolen the world from me.'

'We cannot perceive the world and simultaneously grasp a look which is fixed upon us.'

'Being seen constitutes me as a being without defence against a freedom which is not my freedom.'

'he *through whom* I gain my objectivity'

'unkind, jealous or pleasant'

'that through which things are revealed to me'

'I am my body to the extent that I *am*; I *am not* my body to the extent that I am not what I am; it is through my nihilation that I escape it. But that does not mean that I make of it an object.'

'the *facticity* of the *pour soi*'

'All this − in so far as I go beyond it in the synthetic unity of my being-in-the-world − is *my body* as the necessary condition for the existence of a world and as the contingent realization of that condition.'

'alienated and impossible to grasp'

21 'ugly or beautiful'

'The Other *looks* at me, and, as such, he holds the secret of my being, he knows what I am.'

'triple destructibility'

'deception', 'infinite regression'

'In consequence, love as a fundamental mode of being-for-others has in its being-for-others the seeds of its own destruction.'

'respect for the freedom of others is an empty expression'

'By simply existing, I impose a factual limit on the freedom of the Other . . . charity, *laisser-faire*, tolerance . . . are personal projects which commit me and commit the other when he assents to them.'

'So original sin is my arrival in a world inhabited by the other, and, whatever my subsequent relations with him may be, they will only be variations on the original theme of my guilt.'

'I am condemned to be free . . . we are not free to stop being free.'

22 'such a clear-cut duality is inconceivable at the heart of psychic unity'

'Either man is entirely determined (which is unacceptable, particularly because a determined consciousness . . . is no longer consciousness) or else man is entirely free.'

'Voluntary deliberation is always rigged. How, in fact, could I weigh up grounds and motives when it is I who give them their weight before any deliberation and by my very choice of self? . . . When I deliberate, the die is cast.'

'This in no way means that I am free to stand up or sit down, to go in or out, to run away or to face danger, if one understands by freedom a pure, capricious, unlawful, gratuitous, incomprehensible contingency. Certainly, each of my acts, even the smallest, is entirely free . . . but this does not mean that it can be *anything at all*, nor even that it is unpredictable.'

'the motive can be understood only by the end'

'the ultimate and initial project'

23 'fundamental choice' is 'non-positional'

'There is no character − there is only a project of oneself.'

'This does not mean that I *must necessarily* stop, but just that I can refuse to stop only by a radical conversion of my being-in-the-world, that is, by a sudden metamorphosis of my initial project, that is, by another choice of myself and my aims. This transformation is, moreover, always possible.'

'I could have acted differently, of course, but at what cost?'

'There can be a free *pour soi* only as committed in a resisting world.'

'So I am never free except in situation.'

'it is a *relationship of being* between a *pour soi* and the *en soi* which it nihilates.'

'When I am born I take my place, but I am responsible for the place I take.'

'We choose the world − not its *en soi* contexture, but its meaning − when we choose ourselves.'

'freedom is the awareness of my facticity'

'Every choice . . . implies elimination and selection; every choice is a choice of finitude.'

'Finitude is an ontological structure of the *pour soi* which determines freedom . . . to be finite, in effect, is to choose oneself.'

24 'In this sense [we] are born several, and make ourselves one.'

'There has been no constraint . . . I have had no excuse . . . I am responsible for everything, in effect, apart from my responsibility itself.'

'useless passion'

'factual limits'

'constraint'

'at will', '"To be free", does not mean "to obtain what one wanted." '

'Ontology cannot itself formulate moral precepts.'

25 'So it comes to the same thing to get drunk alone or to lead a nation.'

'the being through whom values exist'

'Is it possible . . . for freedom to take itself as a value in so far as it is the source of all value? . . . A freedom which wills itself as freedom is in effect a being-which-is-not-what-it-is and which-is-what-it-is-not who chooses, as an ideal mode of being, being-what-it-is-not and not being-what-it-is. It chooses not to *possess* itself but to flee itself, not to coincide with itself, but always to be at a distance from itself . . . Is it a matter of bad faith or of another fundamental attitude? And can one *live* this new aspect of being?'

'subsequent work'

Chapter 2

27 'Ontology cannot itself formulate moral precepts.'

'Morality takes place in an atmosphere of failure.'

'Basically I wrote two Moral treatises: one between '45 and '47 – totally mystified – that was the 'Morale' that I thought I could produce as a sequel to *L'Etre et le Néant* – I've a pile of notes for it, but I've abandoned them; and then notes from around '65, for another 'Morale' concerned with the problem of realism and the problem of morality. On that occasion I could have completed a book, but I didn't.'

28 'Is it possible for freedom to take itself as a value in so far as it is the source of all value? . . . A freedom which wills itself freedom, is, in fact, a being which . . . chooses not to possess itself but to flee itself, not to coincide with itself but to be always at a distance from itself.'

29 'the work of a total freedom addressing itself to plenary freedoms'

'The work of art *has no end*, we agree with Kant on that point. But that is because it *is* an end.'

'The work of art is gratuitous because it is an absolute end and presents itself to the spectator as a categorical imperative.'

'At the heart of the aesthetic imperative we can detect the moral imperative.'

30 'I construct the universal when I choose myself.'

'The man who commits himself . . . is . . . a legislator choosing at the same time as himself the whole of humanity.'

'If we could all be – in a perfect simultaneity and reciprocity – objects and subjects at one and the same time, each for the others and each by the others . . . or if, as in the Kantian City of Ends, we were simply subjects recognizing one another as subjects, the barriers between us would come down.'

31 'Values are vague . . . and always too broad for the particular concrete case.'

'Principles that are too abstract fail to define action . . . There is no way of judging. The content [of an action] is always concrete and therefore unpredictable; it always involves invention.'

'The only thing which matters is to know if the invention is carried out in the name of freedom.'

32 'Duty is the Other at the heart of Will.'

33 'While one believes in God it is permissible to *do* Good in order to *be* moral . . . for in *practising* charity we serve only men, but in *being* charitable we serve God . . . But when God dies the Saint is no more than an egoist . . . Morality must be transcended towards a goal other than itself. Give a drink to someone who is thirsty, not for the sake of giving a drink nor in order to be good but to quench thirst. Morality suppresses itself as it posits itself, it posits itself as it suppresses itself.'

'Morality: permanent conversion.'

'Immorality of morality.'

'Ethics must be historical.'

'The problem of collaboration versus resistance: here is a concrete moral choice. Kantianism teaches us nothing on the subject.'

34 'Morality takes place in an atmosphere of failure.'

'Problem: I am suspicious of instant morality, it involves too much bad faith and all the half-heartedness of ignorance. But at least it has this characteristic essential to morality − spontaneity, subordination to its object . . . Reflexion suppresses bad faith and ignorance, but the object is relegated to the ranks of the inessential.'

'Since absolute knowledge is impossible, morality must be conceived as taking place, in principle, in ignorance.'

'you must, therefore you can'

'obligation implies that you are not caught in the mesh of determinism'

'There is then a confidence in human freedom which regards it as if it were the freedom of God. That is to say, absolute creative freedom.'

'It is in and through that failure that each of us must shoulder his moral responsibilities.'

35 'If it is irrelevant whether one is in good or bad faith because bad faith takes possession of good faith and slips in at the very origin of its project, this does not mean that one cannot escape radically from bad faith. But this involves a self-renewal by the corrupted being which we will call authenticity, and the description of which would be out of place here.'

'These considerations do not exclude the possibility of an ethics of deliverance and salvation. But this can be achieved only after radical conversion which we cannot discuss here.'

'The essence of relations between consciousnesses is not *Mitsein*, it is conflict.'

'Love is conflict.'

'Pleasure entails the death and the failure of desire.'

'Hatred, in its turn, is a failure.'

'So we can never get out of the circle.'

'I cannot, in fact, *experience* this alienation without at the same time recognizing the other as transcendence. And, as we have seen, this recognition would have no meaning were it not a free recognition of the freedom of the other. So, I can only apprehend the other as freedom in the free project of apprehending him as such . . . and the free project of *recognition* of the other is not distinct from the free assumption of my being-for-others . . . There is no circle: but by the free assumption of this being-alienated which I experience, I suddenly make the transcendence of the other exist for me as such.'

36   'It is because human reality *is not enough* that it is free' (my italics).

'la réflexion non complice': untranslatable; approximates to 'pure reflexion'.

'Failure can lead to conversion.'

'conversion . . . is a virtual possibility in all oppressed people'

'conversion . . . can be born from the perpetual failure of every attempt of the *pour soi* to *be*'

'conversion . . . is born from the failure of *réflexion complice*'

37   'Sincerity was ruled out because it focussed on what I *am*. Authenticity focusses on what I want . . . It is the refusal to define myself by what I am (Ego), but rather by what I want (that is to say by my enterprise itself).

'In *réflexion complice* I give water so that my Self may be charitable.'

'It is this simultaneous dual aspect of the human project, gratuitous at its heart and consecrated by being taken up reflexively, which makes of it *authentic existence*.'

'We must love the fact that we might not have existed; that we are *de trop* etc. . . . For the authentic man . . . greatness . . . derives necessarily from misfortune or contingency. It is because man is perspective, finitude, contingency and ignorance that he constitutes a world.'

'The more multiple the world is for me who lose myself so that this multiplicity exists, the richer I am.'

38   'Sadism and Masochism are the revelation of the Other. They have

meaning – like, indeed, the conflict between consciousnesses – only before conversion. If we have assumed the fact of being both freedom and an object for others (e.g. the authentic Jew) there is no longer any ontological reason to remain at the level of conflict. I *accept* my being-object and I go beyond it. But there can still be historical reasons.'

'reciprocal recognition'

'unpredictable freedom'

'We create ourselves by giving ourselves to the Other . . . So I must lose myself in order to find myself.'

'True freedom *gives* . . . it recognizes other freedoms through their gifts . . . true freedom makes itself an *opportunity* for other freedoms.'

'The *pour soi* and the Other; the gift. In sacrifice I am, and I give preference to the other. I prefer what I do not prefer. But I *am* my gift to the other. Joy.'

'Besides, what is opposed to negation (as judgement) is in fact affirmation. But what corresponds to nihilation as its derivative is rather *creation*.'

'There is no love without that sado-masochistic dialectic of enslavement of freedoms which I have described. No love without a deeper recognition and a reciprocal understanding between freedoms (dimension which is missing in *L'Etre et le Néant*).'

39 'The Ego is *in order to lose itself*: that is the Gift. Reconciliation with destiny is generosity. In a classless society it can also be love, that is to say the confident project that freedoms valorized as such and willed as such will take up and transform my work and thereby my Ego which then loses itself in the absolute dimension of freedom.'

'It follows that my freedom is the sole foundation for values, and that *nothing*, absolutely nothing, justifies my adopting this or that value, this or that scale of values.'

'Method: values mask freedom at the same time as alienating it. A classification of values must lead up to freedom. Classify values in an order such that freedom becomes increasingly apparent. At the top: generosity.'

'A hierarchy of values showing that they approach freedom asymptotically. The lowest values crush freedom under *Being*: Purity, innocence, race, sincerity. The intermediary values: the notion of life as an objectification of transcendence: nobility, virility, sexual values and once again *race*. Social values: The Other as product of the project and as external solicitation of the project. Already the idea of creation comes in.'

Nation, society etc., SACRIFICE. Values of *subjectivity*: passion, pleasure and the present moment, criticism and the demand for proof, responsibility, creation, generosity. This hierarchy leads us to see — like a light beyond the summit of generosity — freedom itself.'

40   'the lowest values'

'the values of *subjectivity*'

'reconciliation with Destiny'

'Through reflexion, I consent to be human; that is to say, by committing myself to an adventure which is very likely to finish badly, I transform my contingency into a *Passion*.'

'constitution of a freedom which takes itself as its own end'

'One cannot carry out conversion *on one's own*. In other words, morality is possible only if everyone is moral.'

41   'The meaning of conversion: a rejection of alienation.'

'Conversion is a virtual possibility for all oppressed people.'

'The suppression of alienation must be universal. Impossibility of being moral alone.'

History will *always* be alienated . . . However, if we imagine a Utopia where each person treats the other as an end, that is to say, takes the other's enterprises as an end, we can imagine a History where alterity is subsumed within unity . . . Historical revolution depends on moral conversion. It is utopian because the conversion of everyone at once, which is always possible, is the least likely combination (because of the variety of situations). So it is important to equalize people's situations in order to make that combination less unlikely, and to give History a chance to get beyond pseudo-History.'

'Rimbaud wanted to change life; Marx, Society.'

'Hence a problem: History ↔ ethics. History implies ethics (without universal conversion evolution or revolutions have no sense). Ethics implies History (there is no morality possible without systematic action on the situation).'

42   'The end of History would be the advent of Ethics. But this advent cannot be brought about from within History . . . moreover, morality is not a fusion of consciousnesses in a single subject, but the acceptance of the detotalized Totality and the decision within this recognized inequality to take as a concrete end each consciousness in its concrete singularity (and not in its Kantian universality).'

'All ethics suppose the end of History (or rather the end of History

[is] the advent of the reign of ethics). But the end of History is also death.'

'*True* (concrete) morality: to prepare for the Kingdom of Ends by a revolutionary, finite and creative politics.'

'Reversal: that the Kingdom of Ends lies precisely in preparing for the Kingdom of Ends.'

'*It is not possible* for the revolutionary not to violate moral laws.'

'a dead end'

'a structure of slavery'

'In *impossible* cases the choice of Good tends to reinforce the impossibility, we must choose Evil in order to find Good.'

'immorality of morality'

'It took place in this way or in another . . . It makes no difference.'

'a vertiginous word'

43   'Evil is the Other.'

'Evil is the unity of all his impulses to criticize, to judge, to reject, in so far as he refuses to *recognize* them, to see in them the normal exercise of his freedom . . . Good men forged the myth of Evil by depriving human freedom of its positive power and reducing it to its negative aspect alone.'

'So any Ethics which is not presented explicity as *impossible today* contributes to the mystification and alienation of men. The "moral problem" arises from the fact that Ethics is *for us* at once inevitable and impossible.'

'It is the law . . . which creates sin.'

'pure contradiction'

'Act in such a way that society always treats you as an object, a means, and never as an end, as a person. Act as if the maxim of each of your acts had to serve as a rule in a den of thieves.'

44   'true morality'

'the ethics of praxis'

'joint enterprise'

'the free call which a creative freedom addresses to all other freedoms'

'prayer for the good use of Jean Genet'

'There is failure whenever there is action . . . There is failure when the end is not achieved . . . Any triumph is a failure. I no longer recognize my end.'

45   'Good without Evil is Parmenidian Being, that is to say Death.'

Chapter 3

46   'novelistic technique always reflects the novelist's metaphysics'

'I should say that we are all metaphysical writers . . . for metaphysics is not a sterile discussion of abstract notions outside experience, it is a living attempt to embrace from within the human condition in its totality.'

'To embrace *from within* the human condition.'

47   'man is a totality . . . consequently, he expresses the whole of himself in the most insignificant and superficial of his actions'

'in the work of art, each partial structure relates in various ways, to various other partial structures and to the total structure'

48   'To write is to reveal the world . . . it is certainly the final aim of art: to recuperate this world by showing it as it is, but as if it had its source in human freedom.'

'This soft clay, traversed by undulations which have their cause and their end outside themselves, this world without a future, where everything is chance encounter, where the present comes like a thief, where events are naturally recalcitrant to both thought and language, where individuals are accidents, pebbles in the clay, for whom the mind fabricates, retrospectively, general headings.'

'The novel takes place in the present, like life . . . in a novel the die is not cast beforehand, for the characters in a novel are free. The die is cast before our very eyes; our impatience, our ignorance, our waiting are the same as those of the hero. The *récit* (short story), on the other hand . . . takes place in the past. But the *récit* gives explanations: chronology − the order of life − hardly masks causality − the order of understanding; the event does not move us, it is half way between a fact and a rule.'

49   'characters in a novel are free'

'the die is not cast'

'For the most trivial event to become an adventure we must simply recount it to somebody . . . We have to choose: to live or to recount . . . When we're living, nothing happens. The scenery changes, people come and go, and that's all. There are never any beginnings . . . There's no end either . . . Monday, Tuesday, Wednesday. April, May, June. 1924, 1925, 1926.

That's living. But once we recount a life, everything changes . . . Events happen one way and we recount them backwards. We seem to be starting at the beginning: "It was a beautiful autumn evening in 1922. I was a solicitor's clerk at Marommes.'' And in fact we've begun at the end. The end is there, present and invisible, it's the end which gives those few words the pomp and value of a beginning . . . for us, the fellow is already the hero of the story . . . And we have the impression that the hero lived all the details of that night like omens, like promises . . . We forget that the future wasn't yet there; the fellow was walking around in a night without portents which offered him a jumble of humdrum riches, and he didn't choose between them.'

'the die is cast'

'the novel fades away before your eyes'

'He must conceal his choice by purely aesthetic means, by constructing *trompe–l'œil* and – as always where art is concerned – lie in order to express the truth.'

50 'We have to choose: to live or to recount.'

'In the middle of the rue Vercingétorix, a tall fellow grabbed Mathieu by the arm; a policeman was patrolling up and down on the other pavement. "Give me something, gov'ner, I'm hungry." His eyes were close together, his lips were thick, and he smelt of booze.'

'a vague feeling of regret'

'A train blew its whistle and Mathieu thought "I am old." '

51 'Their destiny had faded away, time had started to flow again haphazardly and aimlessly; the train was going along aimlessly, out of habit . . . "It's just like the day after a bank-holiday," Mathieu thought, with a pang of anguish.'

'a free dream'

'feeling of security'

'To write is simultaneously to reveal the world and to propose it as a task to the reader's generosity . . . The realists' mistake was to think that the real disclosed itself to contemplation, and that, consequently, an impartial picture was possible. How could it be possible, when perception itself is partial, when the simple act of naming already modifies its object? . . . The whole of the author's art lies in making me *create* what he *reveals*, and thereby compromising me.'

'this soft clay, traversed by undulations . . . this world without a future, where everything is chance encounter'

52 'And if I am shown this world with all its injustices, it is not so that I may contemplate them coolly, but so that I can bring them alive with my indignation . . . and generous indignation entails the vow

to bring about change . . . at the heart of the aesthetic imperative we perceive the moral imperative.'

'insipid flesh blooming and quivering in an abandoned fashion'

'People who live socially active lives have learnt to see themselves, in mirrors, very much as they appear to their friends. I have no friends: is that why my flesh is so naked? One might say — yes, one might say nature without man.'

'I exist because I think . . . if I exist *it's because* I loathe existing. It is I, *it is I* who drag myself out of the nothingness I aspire to.'

'Now, when I say "I" it sounds hollow to me . . . and suddenly the I fades, fades away and finally goes out. Lucid, still and deserted, the consciousness is immured; it perpetuates itself. It is no longer inhabited . . . But it *never* forgets itself . . . it is a consciousness of being a consciousness which forgets itself . . . There is consciousness of this body walking slowly along a dark road . . . There's consciousness of all that and consciousness, alas! of consciousness. But no one is there to suffer and wring his hands and feel sorry for himself.'

53 'The statue seemed to me unpleasant and stupid and I was aware that I was dreadfully bored. I couldn't understand what I was doing in Indo-China.'

'I am no longer writing my book on Rollebon; it's all over, I *can't* write it any more . . . The great Rollebon affair has come to an end, like a great passion.'

'He had stood up; he was going to say to her, "I love you." He faltered a little and said clearly, "Well, it's true, I no longer love you." He was still listening to the phrase, quite amazed, a long while after it had been said.'

54 'Daniel was split in two . . . he thought of Mathieu with a kind of pride — "It's *I* who am free," he said to himself. But it was an impersonal kind of pride, for Daniel was no longer a person . . . Suddenly he felt that he was just one man again. Only one. A coward. A fellow who loved his cats and didn't want to dump them in the water. He took his penknife, bent down and cut the string. In silence: even deep inside him there was silence, he was too ashamed to talk in front of himself. He picked up the basket again and went back up the steps.'

'Do you want your characters to live? Make them free. It's not a matter of definition, still less of explanation . . . but simply *presenting* unpredictable passions and actions . . . [characters in novels] . . . have personalities, but it's only in order to escape from them; free over and above their natures, if they give in to their natures it's still freely. They can let themselves be dragged down by their physical systems, but they will never be merely mechanical.'

'No more characters: the heroes are freedoms caught in a trap, like all of us.'

'The man who is condemned to be free must still free himself . . . This progression of the free man towards his freedom is the paradox of freedom, and it is also the theme of my book . . . a description of the aporias of freedom . . . Mathieu personifies that total freedom which Hegel calls terrorist freedom and which is really a counter-freedom . . . Mathieu is the freedom of indifference, abstract freedom, freedom for nothing . . . Brunet embodies the *esprit de sérieux* which believes in intelligible transcendent values, inscribed in the heavens . . . Brunet is a militant who wastes his freedom.'

55 'A discreet insuperable nausea permanently reveals my body to my consciousness.'

'Desire compromises me . . . in sexual desire consciousness seems to have grown thick . . . the slightest desire is already overwhelming . . . Heavy and swooning, consciousness slips towards a languor rather like sleep.'

'Boris became aware that he desired Lola and was pleased: desire soaked up depressing thoughts. As it did all other thoughts.'

'Soon she groaned and Boris said to himself, "That's it. I'm going to pass out." A thick wave of desire spread from his loins to the nape of his neck. "I don't want to," Boris thought, gritting his teeth. But he suddenly felt as though he was being lifted up by his neck, like a rabbit, he let himself go on Lola's body and was reduced to a flushed whirl of sensual pleasure.'

'He locked his entrails, his bowels shut like a fist, he no longer felt his body . . . All his longings, all his desires were wiped out, he felt clean and crisp.'

'He is afraid of the huge wave of desire which suddenly overwhelms him, a desire to live, a desire to love, a desire to caress white breasts.'

'the inertia of his flesh'

56 'that guilty flower'

' "The bastard, he did that to me, he forgot himself inside me like a kid who soils his sheets." '

'clammy dream'

'The body started to walk again, dragging its feet, heavy and hot, with shivers and burning sensations of anger in its throat and stomach.'

'Since we were *situated*, the only novels we could dream of writing were novels of *situation*, without internal narrators or omniscient

229

witnesses; in short, if we wanted to give an account of our time, we had to update our novelistic technique by moving from Newtonian mechanics to generalized relativity; to populate our books with consciousnesses that were half lucid and half benighted, some or other of whom we perhaps might feel an affinity for, but none of whom would have a privileged viewpoint either on events or on itself; to present creatures whose reality would be the tangled and contradictory web of judgements which each would form about all the others – including himself – and all would form about him, and who would never be able to decide from within if the changes in their destinies came from their own efforts, from their mistakes, or from the inevitable course of the universe.'

57 'there are no tastes, mannerisms or human acts which are not revealing'

'the essential task is hermeneutic, that is to say one of deciphering, fixing and conceptualizing'

58 'the very stuff of things'

'totally stuck in the existent'

'When the voice broke the silence, I felt my body harden and the Nausea faded away . . . I too have had real adventures. I can't recall any detail of them, but I can sense the rigorous succession of circumstances . . . I've had women, I've fought other blokes, and I could never go back, any more than a record can turn backwards. And *where* was all this leading me? To this very moment, to this bench, in this bubble of light humming with music.'

'we have to choose, to live or to recount'

'vile pulp'

'grotesque, pig-headed, gigantic . . . things'

'being as it is'

59 'contemporary philosophy has established that meanings are also immediate givens . . . This is the human world the right way up.'

'necessary being, *ens causa sui*'

'Everything had started to fall, he had seen houses as they really were – frozen in mid-fall . . . a few kilos more and the fall would begin again; the columns would sag and bend and develop nasty splintered fractures.'

'"Whatever happens it's *through me* that it must come about" . . . he was free, free for everything . . . there would be no Good or Evil for him unless he invented them himself. Things were grouped around him, they were waiting without making any sign, without giving the slightest direction.'

'the world, by its very articulation, reflects back to us exactly the image of what we are ... We choose the world − not its *en soi* contexture, but its meaning, when *we choose ourselves*.'

'The yellow of the lemon is not a subjective mode of apprehending the lemon: it *is* the lemon.'

'It is as if we arrived in a universe where feelings and acts are all charged with materiality, have a substantial stuff, are *really* soft, flat, viscous, low, elevated, etc.'

60   'very general projects of human reality'

'the mortal agony of water'

'the sugary death of the *pour soi*'

'lacklustre flesh'

'soft, buttery flesh'

'feverish swellings'

'On the left, right at the end, that tiny shimmering lake where the rails joined together, that was Toulon, Marseilles, Port-Bou, Spain.'

'universal time comes to the world through the *pour soi*'

'the Present is *pour soi*'

'The novel takes place in the present, like life. The perfect tense only appears to be novelistic; it must be considered a present *with aesthetic distance*, an artifice of production.'

61   'It is not by changing the tense of the verb, but by disrupting the techniques of the *récit*, that we will succeed in making the reader feel contemporaneous with the story.'

94   'In a novel one must keep silent or say everything, in particular miss nothing out, "skip over" nothing.'

94   'If I sum up six months in one page the reader leaps out of the book. This last aspect of realism creates difficulties that none of us has resolved, and which, perhaps, are partially insoluble, for it is neither possible nor desirable to limit all novels to the account of a single day.'

'I say, did you see that?'

'Ha, ha.'

'What did you say?'

'Suzanne yesterday.'

'. . . . What's the matter . . . don't you like it?'

'It's not nice.'

'It's not the same.'

62   'three minutes . . . seven minutes . . . ten minutes'

' "Hell," said Pinette. "Why should I go down if Delarue isn't going?" '

'It is not without some trick effects that one can reduce the flow of

231

consciousness to a succession of words, even distorted . . . One can reproach [the author] . . . with having forgotten that the greatest riches of psychic life are *silent*.'

'In literature, where signs are used, one must *use only* signs; and if the reality one wants to express is *a word*, one must transmit it to the reader by other words.'

'He took his penknife, bent down and cut the string. In silence: even deep inside him there was silence, he was too ashamed to talk in his own presence. He picked up his basket again and went back up the steps: it was as if he was turning his head away and going past someone who was watching him with contempt. In his heart there was still the desert and silence. When he was at the top of the steps, he dared to address his first words to himself. "What was that drop of blood?"'

63 'I distrust ineffable ideas, they are the source of all violence . . . Our thought is not worth any more than our language and we must judge it according to the use it makes of language.'

Roquentin: 'Absurdity: another word; I am struggling with words; over there I touched the thing itself.' Mathieu: 'Everything that words could express, he would say. "But there are not just words!"' Daniel: 'Would I call it God? One single word and everything changes.' Pascal: 'Words frighten him.' 'Stephen thought "the French crowd" and felt moved.'

Philippe: 'Another word too, soft and precious, he could no longer remember it, but it was the tenderest of tender words, it spun round, flared like a crown of fire, and Philippe carried it with him into his slumber.'

Daniel: 'With all his strength he wanted to feel disgust for himself . . . "Bastard! coward and deceiver; bastard." For a moment he thought he was going to succeed, but no, they were mere words.'

64 'It was love. *Now* it was love. Mathieu thought: "What have I done?" Five minutes before the love didn't exist, there was a rare and precious feeling between them which had no name.'

'"To be free. To be *ens causa sui*, to be able to say: I am because I will it . . ." They were empty, pompous words, irritating intellectual's words.'

Odette: 'Once again she'd looked like a gas bag; the words she used always turned back against her.'

Mathieu: 'It was happening far away, deep inside him, in a place where words have lost their meanings.'

'our inability to think, with our concepts, with our words, the events of the world'

'The words we speak . . . are free, clumsy acts, which say too much and too little.'

'The "sense" of my expressions always escapes me . . . the Other is always there, present and experienced as what gives language its sense.'

'As soon as I speak, I have the distressing certainty that the words are escaping me, and that they will take on, over there, outside me, an appearance I never dreamt of, unforeseen meanings.'

65 'I murmur "it's a bench", rather like an exorcism. But the word stays on my lips: it refuses to go and settle on the thing . . . things have freed themselves of their names . . . I am in the midst of unspeakable things. Alone, without words, without any defence.'

'[Milan] repeated to himself: "I'm not alone. I'm not alone." Daniel thought: "I'm alone."'

'They thought: "Is there no one to help me?"'

'They are the ones who are right. They speak in clichés but their words betray them, there is something in their heads which can't be expressed in words.'

'What can I do? Is it my fault if in everything he says to me, I recognize, as he speaks, borrowings and quotations. If I see reappearing, while he's talking, all the humanists I've known?'

'"It's the mature Man, I suppose, that you like in him . . .?" — "Exactly," he replied warily.'

Pacôme: 'He had always done his duty, his entire duty, his duty as a son, a husband, a father, a leader. He had also insisted firmly on his rights . . . for a right is only ever the reverse side of a duty . . . He would say, "How much simpler and harder it is to do one's duty." '

'"I'm adorable in my little angel's outfit."'

66 '"Lucien Fleurier is a big bean-pole."'

'"Lucien doesn't like Jews."'

'We pass by six people who are holding hands. "Good morning, *monsieur*, good morning, *cher monsieur*, how are you; do put your hat on again, *monsieur*, you'll catch cold; thank you, *madame*, it's certainly not very warm. Darling, may I introduce Doctor Lefrançois; Doctor, I'm very pleased to meet you, my husband is always talking to me about Doctor Lefrançois who looked after him so well, but do please put your hat on again, Doctor, in this cold weather you'll catch a chill."'

'I always thought you only had to let yourself go.'

' "A man?" Brunet asked with surprise, "the opposite would be worrying." '

'"Life has a meaning if we care to give it one. We must start by acting, by throwing ourselves into a project. If afterwards we pause to reflect, the die is cast, we are already committed. I don't know what you think about that, *monsieur*?" "Nothing" I say. Or rather I think that it's exactly the kind of lie that the commercial-traveller, the two young people, and the gentleman with white hair are always telling themselves. The Autodidact smiles with a little malice and a good deal of solemnity. "That's not my view — I don't think that we have to look so far for the meaning of our lives." — "Ah?" — "There is a goal, *monsieur*, there is a goal . . . there is mankind." Of course, I was forgetting he's a humanist.'

67　'There's Sartre turned into his own Autodidact.'

68　'What can we know of a man today?'

'Social reality is so complex that to delimit it in a novel — I don't know — one would have to take account of both sociological and psychoanalytic knowledge, and deal with both society and the individual at the same time.'

Chapter 4

71　'As far as I'm concerned, I've now no longer anything to say to the bourgeois.'

'The theatre is such a public affair . . . that a play escapes its author as soon as the audience is in the auditorium. My plays, in any case — whatever their fate — have almost all escaped me. They become *objects*. Afterwards you say, "That wasn't what I intended", like William the Second (Kaiser Wilhelm) during the 14–18 War. But what's been done remains done.'

'a nocturnal play'

72　'Hell is other people'

'A play acquires an objective meaning bestowed on it by an audience. Nothing can be done: if all the bourgeois consider *Les Mains sales* a great success, and the Communists attack it, this means that in reality something has happened. It means that the play has become *of itself* objectively anti-Communist, and that the author's intentions no longer count.'

73　'Our new theatre . . . is not a medium for expressing a "thesis", and is not inspired by any preconceived idea. What it's trying to do is to explore the whole human condition and to present contemporary man with a portrait of himself, his problems, his hopes and his struggles.'

'I don't take sides. A good play should pose problems not solve them.'

'I don't think . . . that the theatre is a "philosophical vehicle" . . . It should express a philosophy, but one mustn't be able to pose the problem of the value of that philosophy within the play itself . . . It should be so bound up in the story, in the dramatic side of the story, in its development, that one cannot state that the play is worthwhile given certain principles, nor that one accepts one aspect of it and rejects another.'

74 'Argos must be taken . . . I will become an axe and I'll cleave these obstinate city walls, I'll burst open the stomach of these bigoted houses.'

'Oreste: The men of Argos are my men – I must open their eyes. Jupiter: Poor people! You're making them a present of solitude and conflict, you're going to tear away the covers I put over them, and you'll suddenly show them their existence, their obscene, insipid existence, which is given them for nothing.'

'executioner and butcher'

'the hardening of choice, its sclerosis'

'freedoms caught in a trap, like all of us'

'Each character will be no more than the choice of a solution . . . I expressed myself badly, there are no solutions to *choose*. A solution has to be invented. And each of us, by inventing his own solution, invents himself. Man has to be invented afresh every day.'

75 'The most moving thing the theatre can show is a character in the making, the moment of choice, of free decision which commits an ethic and an entire life.'

'Today I consider that philosophy is dramatic.'

'It is . . . man – who is simultaneously *an agent* and *an actor*, producing and acting out his drama, living through the contradictions of his situation until his personality is shattered or his conflicts are resolved.'

'Gestures in the theatre signify acts, and since the theatre is an image, gestures are the image of the action . . . There is no other image in the theatre except the image of the act.'

'place of illusion *par excellence*'

76 'Hugo: Make an effort, Jessica. Be serious.
Jessica: Why should I be serious?
Hugo: Because we can't play-act all the time.
Jessica: I don't like being serious, but we'll work something out. I shall pretend to be serious.'

'Oreste: You are watching me, people of Argos . . . look, watch the flies. And then suddenly they rushed after him. And the pied-piper and his rats disappeared for ever, like this.'

'Goetz: I will horrify them because I have no other way of loving them, I will give them commands because I have no other way of obeying, I will remain alone with the empty sky above my head because I have no other way of being with all men. There is this war to wage, and I will wage it.'

77 'I live in a stage set.'

'The purely imaginary and praxis are hard to reconcile.'

'In the theatre [identification] is replaced with an absolute distancing: in the first place I see with my own eyes, and I remain always on the same level and in the same place, so there is neither the complicity of the novel, nor the ambiguous complicity of the cinema, and the character is therefore, for me, definitively the other.'

'insuperable distance'

78 'That's what explains the pleasure we have always experienced at seeing theatre within theatre . . . distancing at a further remove . . . that's pure theatre, raised to the second power.'

'In *Les Séquestrés d'Altona* . . . I simply hope that Frantz's qualms of conscience and internal contradictions, pushed to extremes, to a mythical level, may momentarily give the audience the means of identifying with Frantz, of being Frantz. (That's why . . . I keep for the fourth act the revelation that Frantz has tortured. It's because I hope that at the point where things are getting worse and where Frantz is deeply enmeshed in his contradictions, I hope that by then Frantz will be the character with whom the spectator identifies.)'

'lie so as to be true'

'We come back to Brecht. And here I must make clear how I differ from him. Personally, I am quite convinced that any demystification must, in a sense, be mystifying. Or rather that, in the face of a partly mystified crowd of people, one cannot rely solely on the critical reactions of that crowd. They must be provided with a counter-mystification. And for that reason the theatre should not deprive itself of any theatrical magic.'

79 'If Sartre is concerned to fascinate and seduce, it's because we are all in our various ways being seduced, and for purposes quite different from his; if he rapes us it is in order to force us to admit that we have *already been raped* and that we take pleasure in it.'

'everything is decided beforehand'

'We don't see the interest in organizing in advance the motives or the reasons which will force [the] choice in an inevitable fashion.'

'a waste of time in the theatre'

80 'For freedom isn't some kind of abstract power to remain outside the human condition: it is the most absurd and most inexorable commitment.'

'Great tragedy – that of Aeschylus and Sophocles, that of Corneille – has human freedom as its main motivating force. Œdipus is free. Antigone and Prometheus are free. The fatality that we think we see in the drama of Antiquity is only the reverse side of freedom. Passion itself is freedom caught in its own trap.'

'Tragedy is the mirror of Fatality. I didn't think it impossible to write a tragedy of freedom because the Fatum of the ancients is only the other side of freedom. Orestes is free for his crime and beyond his crime: I showed him a prey to freedom as Œdipus is a prey to his destiny. He struggles against the iron fist, but he has to kill in the end, and to shoulder his murder and carry it over to the other bank . . . Orestes will follow his path, unjustified, with no excuse, with no way out, alone.'

'In the theatre of Antiquity, what's interesting is that each character represents *one* pole of the contradiction, never two. Here you have on the one hand the family, on the other the City State . . . What's new today in the theatre . . . is that now contradiction can belong to one individual character . . . there are several series of contradictions within one character.'

81 'We change when we change the world and because the world changes.'

'If the theatre is to address the masses it must speak to them of their most general concerns, and express their anxieties in the form of myths which everyone can understand and experience profoundly.'

82 'It is by being the most individual that one is the most universal.'

'a character who [contains] within himself, in a more or less condensed fashion, the problems we are facing at any given moment'

'Antigone, in Sophocles's tragedy, has to choose between the ethic of the City State and the ethic of the family. This dilemma hardly has any sense today. But we have our own problems: that of means and ends, of the legitimacy of violence, of the consequences of action, of the relationship between the individual and the collective, between the individual enterprise and historical constants, and hundreds more.'

83 'great collective religious phenomenon'

'everyday and yet distanced'

'magic, primitive and sacred'

'In the theatre . . . language is a moment in the action . . . it is made uniquely to give orders, forbid things, express feelings in the form of a plea (so with an active aim), to convince or defend or accuse, to indicate decisions, for verbal duels, refusals, confessions etc. . . . in short, it is always active.'

85 'between sky and earth'

'Ah, Monseigneur, the splendid theatrical phrase. If you are willing, it will be our last word.'

'eaten away by the imaginary'

'Diderot is right: the actor does not really experience the sentiments of the character he plays, but it would be wrong to assume that he expresses them in *sang-froid*, the truth is that he experiences them *in an unreal fashion*. By which we mean that his real feelings — stage-fright, for example, one "plays on one's stage-fright" — serve as an *analogon* for him, he uses them as a base for the passions he has to portray . . . His real Ego also serves as an *analogon* for the imaginary being he is playing . . . which means that the actor sacrifices himself so that an *appearance* may have existence, and that he choses to make himself the support of non-being.'

87 'His raw material is himself, his aim: to be another in an unreal mode.'

'a permanent, real, recognized centre of irrealization. . . . He mobilizes and commits himself entirely so that his real self may become the *analogon* of an imaginary person called Titus, Harpagon or Ruy Blas.'

'Of course, each of us plays at being what he is. But Kean plays at being what he is not and what he knows he cannot be.'

'We absolutely must not conclude that everyone is play-acting.'

'Hell is other people'

'play-acting'

'And perhaps we may now see how Sartre's theatre as a whole may be considered a *theatre of bastardy*. For he betrays the Spectator by making him accept the denunciation of his own deception, he betrays Society by representing it as divided against itself, and in the last analysis he betrays the Theatre itself by forcing it to bite its own tail.'

88 'All the author's art lies in making me *create* what he *reveals*, so in compromising me.'

'the work exists only at the level of his abilities'

'The mirror it presents modestly to its readers is magic: it captivates and compromises . . . spontaneous behaviour, as it becomes reflexive, loses its innocence and the excuse of immediacy: we must either assume it or change it.'

'The spectator finds himself facing people caught in the act of lying: he discovers them in search of a reality which will hide from them the illusion they are fostering.'

89 'critical realism'

'In whatever circumstances, at whatever time, and in whatever place, man is free to choose himself as traitor or hero, coward or conqueror . . . In the face of the gods, in the face of death or tyrants, one single certainty, triumphant or anguished, remains to us: that of our freedom.'

90 'I was absolutely scandalized . . . when I read that, I said to myself "It is incredible. I really thought that!" '

'I don't take sides . . . None of my characters is right or wrong.'

'It's only Hoederer's attitude which seems sound to me.'

'a Hugo who is converted . . . Breaking with ethical absolutism he discovers a specific historical and human morality.'

'Man is but a paltry thing if one believes in God . . . God destroys man as surely as the Devil.'

'Our fathers were quite ready to believe that one could remain pure whatever the circumstances. We know today that there are situations which corrupt even the individual's inmost heart . . . Heinrich . . . is conflict personified. And the problem, for him, is absolutely without solution, for he is mystified to the marrow. So in his horror of himself, he chooses to be evil. Desperate situations do exist.'

91 'a near failure'

'Torture represents the radical act which can be abolished only by the suicide of him who committed it.'

'If the hero is eventually reconciled with himself, the audience which is watching him acting − in the play − also risks reconciling itself with its interrogations and its unresolved questions.'

'almost inevitable'

'He had almost necessarily to do what he eventually did.'

'His act is all the more blameworthy: we can find explanations for him, but not a single excuse.'

92 'I wanted to show only the negative aspects. These people can't renew themselves. It's the downfall, the twilight of the gods.'

'All this was foreseen. A man was to come to announce my twilight.'

'The play concludes in total nihilism . . . The final despair of Hecuba, which I emphasized, corresponds to Poseidon's terrible words. The gods will die with men, and this common death is the moral of the tragedy.'

'We will not go of our free will to exile and slavery.'

'Frantz: Perhaps there will be no more centuries after ours. Perhaps a bomb will have blown out the lights. Everything will be dead: the eyes, the judges, time − Night. O tribunal of night, you who were, who will be, who are, I existed. I, Frantz von Gerlach, here in this room, I took the century on my shoulders and I said: I will answer for it. Today and for ever. Eh?'

Chapter 5

94 'One must not confuse the flickering of ideas with the dialectic.'

'Truth always remains to be found, because it is infinite . . . the whole truth . . . is attainable − although no one is capable, today, of attaining it.'

'To speak the Truth. That's the dream of all aging writers.'

'As soon as a margin of *real* freedom beyond the production of his life exists *for everyone* Marxism will have had its day; a philosophy of freedom will take its place.'

'From the time when Marxist research takes the human dimension (i.e. the existential project) as the foundation for anthropological Knowledge, existentialism will have no further *raison d'être*.'

'By ambiguity, one must not understand . . . some kind of equivocal unreason, but simply a contradiction which has not reached its full maturity.'

'The other day I reread the preface I wrote for an edition of some plays − *Les Mouches*, *Huis clos* and others − and I was truly scandalized. I had written this: "Whatever the circumstances, in whatever place, a man is always free to choose whether or not he will be a traitor." When I read that, I said to myself, "It's incredible. I really thought that!" . . . [I had] concluded that, in all circumstances, a choice was always possible. I was wrong.'

'incredible' and 'false'

95 'The phrase "to be free" does not mean "to obtain what one wanted".'

'the coefficient of adversity of things'

'I am not "free" to escape the lot of my class, my nation, my family, nor even to increase my power or my wealth, nor to conquer my most insignificant desires or my habits.'

'I could have acted differently, of course, but at what cost?'

'For human reality, to be is to choose oneself.'

'Freedom, here, does not mean possibility of choice, but the necessity of living constraint, that is, of fulfilling a demand through a *praxis*.'

96 'Everything happened *in his childhood* . . . it's childhood that moulds insuperable prejudices.'

'In a sense we are all born predestined. We are destined to a certain kind of action from the outset by the situation of our family and society at a given time. It is certain, for example, that a young Algerian born in 1935 is fated to take part in the war. In some cases, history condemns us beforehand. Predestination is what, for me, replaces determinism: I consider that we are not free — at least provisionally, today — because we are alienated. We always lose ourselves in our childhood: the methods of upbringing, the parent–child relationship, education etc. — all this produces a self, but it is a lost self . . . This does not mean that predestination does not involve any element of choice, but we know when we choose that we will not achieve what we have chosen: that is what I call the necessity of freedom.'

'We do not do what we want and nonetheless we are responsible for what we are: that is the fact of the matter.'

97 'The idea that I have never ceased developing is that, in the last analysis, each of us is always responsible for what has been made of him — even if he can do no more than assume that responsibility. I believe that a man can always make something of what has been made of him. That is the definition I would give today of freedom, the little movement which makes of a totally conditioned social being a person who does not reproduce in its entirety what he received from his conditioning.'

'So, in *L'Etre et le Néant*, what you might call "subjectivity" is not what it would be for me today: the little gap in an operation by which what has been internalized is re-externalized as an act. Today, in any case, the notions of "subjectivity" and "objectivity" seem to me entirely useless. Of course I may happen to use the term "objectivity", but only in order to emphasize that everything is objective. The individual internalizes his social determinants: he internalizes the relations of production, the family of his childhood, the historical past, contemporary institutions, then he re-externalizes all that in acts and choices which necessarily refer us to everything that has been internalized. There was none of that in *L'Etre et le Néant*.'

98 'Stalinist neo-Marxism'

99 'How can you believe *simultaneously* in the historical mission of the Proletariat and in the treachery of the Communist Party if you observe that the former votes for the latter?'

'to what extent the Communist Party is the *necessary* expression of

241

the working class, and to what extent it is the exact expression of it'

'The incurable vice with which you reproach the C.P. – I wonder if it is not quite simply the particular nature of the Proletariat.'

'1952 was not very important. I remained very close to the Communists for four years, but my ideas were not theirs, and they knew it . . . I had more or less my own ideas, I didn't abandon them while I was on friendly terms with the Communists; and I rediscovered and developed them in the *Critique de la raison dialectique*.'

100   'Over-industrialization and accelerated collectivization were already criminal.'

'No, the consequences of Stalinism were not inevitable: they should have destalinized in time . . . in politics, no action is unconditionally necessary.'

'It's said to be Marxist; I think it's older than Marx; it can be summed up as follows: "What will be, will be."'

'We do not do what we want, and nonetheless we are responsible for what we are.'

'Marxism has come to a halt . . . living Marxism is heuristic.'

'This sclerosis does not correspond to a normal process of aging. It is produced by a specific world-wide set of circumstances; far from being exhausted, Marxism is still young, almost in its infancy; it has hardly begun to develop. So it remains the philosophy for our time: we cannot go beyond it because we have not yet gone beyond the circumstances which gave rise to it.'

101   'Existentialism considers this abstraction to be an arbitrary limitation of the dialectical movement, a cessation of thought, a refusal to understand. Existentialism refuses to abandon real life with its unbelievable accidents of birth in order to contemplate a universality which is limited to an indefinite reflexion upon itself. It intends – without being unfaithful to Marxist theses – to discover the mediations which permit the engendering of the concrete and singular, of life, of real and specific historical conflict, of the individual, on the basis of the *general* contradictions of productive forces and relations of production . . . Valéry is a petty-bourgeois intellectual, there is no doubt about that. But not every petty-bourgeois intellectual is Valéry.'

'Men make their history themselves, but in a given milieu which conditions them.'

102   'the product of his own product'

'a historical agent'

'totally conditioned'

'reassume this conditioning and become responsible for it'

'If History escapes me this is not because I am not making it: it is because the other is also making it.'

'Only the project as mediation between two moments of objectivity can account for history, that is to say for human creativity.'

'For us, man is characterized above all by his overcoming of a situation, by what he manages to make of what has been made of him, even if he never recognizes himself in his objectification.'

'Each of us spends his life engraving on things his baleful image which fascinates him and leads him astray if he tries to understand himself through it.'

'Hegel . . . considers alienation a constant characteristic of any kind of objectification.'

'The man who looks at his work, who recognizes himself entirely in it, who, at the same time, does not recognize himself in it at all . . . is the man who grasps . . . necessity as *the destiny of freedom externalized*. Shall we say that this involves alienation? Certainly, because *he comes back to himself as Other*. However, we must make a distinction: alienation in the Marxist sense of the term begins with exploitation.'

103 'The activity of man . . . is reflected by the practico-inert, the reverse side of man's activity . . . that is, by human activities in so far as these are mediated by a rigorously objective material which directs them back to objectivity.'

'*Praxis*, in effect, is a passage from the objective to the objective through internalization.'

'There is no doubt that man . . . discovers himself as *Other* in the world of objectivity; totalized matter, as an inert objectification which perpetuates itself by inertia, is in effect a *non-man*, and even, if you like, a *counter-man*.'

'the suspicious similarity to Robinson Crusoe's mission'

'*There is no* isolated individual.'

'the adventure of all'

'the freedom of each'; 'it is simply ourselves'

'a threat to his life'

104 'scarcity . . . [is not] a permanent structure . . . but rather . . . a certain moment of human relations, always overcome and partially liquidated, always reborn'

'the truth of man'

'truth itself'

'the specific singularity of our History'

'for other organisms on other planets'

243

'a relationship to the environment which is not one of scarcity'

'The notions of subjectivity and objectivity seem to me completely useless . . . Everything is objective.'

'spatiality, temporality, instrumentality etc.'

105 *'The whole historical dialectic depends on individual praxis in so far as this is already dialectical,* that is to say, to the extent that action is of itself the negating overcoming of a contradiction, the determination of a present totalization in the name of a future totality, the real and efficient work of matter . . . This is our problem: what will *the* dialectic be if there are only men and if they are all dialectical?'

'The dialectic is the control of analysis in the name of a totality.'

106 'the dialectic is a method *and* a movement in the object'

'Our problem is critical. And, doubtless, the problem is itself provoked by History. But it is precisely a matter of testing, criticizing and founding, *in History* and at this point in the development of human societies, the instruments of thought with which History thinks itself, in so far as these are also the practical instruments with which History makes itself. Of course, we will be referred back and forth from *doing* to *knowing* and from *knowing* to *doing* in the unity of a process which will itself be dialectical.'

'The critical experience . . . takes place *within* the totalization and cannot be a contemplative grasping of the totalizing movement; nor can it be a singular and autonomous totalization of the totalization it knows, but it is a real movement of the ongoing totalization.'

'knowledge itself is inevitably practical, it changes the known'

'The dialectic, as the living logic of action, cannot appear to contemplative reason; it is disclosed in the course of *praxis* and as a necessary moment of it.'

'We have discovered individual *praxis* as the plenary intelligibility of the dialectical movement.'

'The separation of theory and practice had as its result to transform the latter into an empiricism without principles, the former into a pure, frozen abstract knowledge.'

'All knowledge is practical.'

107 'In no circumstances would the final outcome of the revolutionary movement have been the opposite of what it was.'

'Apart from *that*, of course, the evolution would have been the same. Only "that", which is contemptuously relegated to the ranks of chance, is all human life.'

'Existentialism refuses to abandon real life with its unbelievable accidents of birth to contemplate a universality which is limited to an indefinite reflexion upon itself.'

'Bourgeois writers have, for example, made use of the "myth of the Noble Savage", they have made it into a weapon against the nobility, but we would simplify the meaning and nature of that weapon if we forgot that it was invented by the Counter-Reformation and turned at first against the *servum arbitrium* [slave will] of the Protestants.'

108 'We begin our study of the differential with a totalizing intention. We do not consider these variations as anomic contingencies, accidents, insignificant aspects: on the contrary, the singularity of the conduct or the conception is, *above all*, the concrete reality as a lived totalization, it is not a *characteristic* of the individual, it is the whole individual, grasped in his process of objectivation.'

'Overcome and preserved, they constitute what I would call the internal colouring of the project; but its colouring, that is to say subjectively its taste, objectively its *style*, is nothing other than the overcoming of our original deviations: this overcoming is not a single moment, it is a long endeavour . . . for this reason, a life goes by in spirals; it always passes by the same places, but at different levels of integration and complexity.'

'In fact, it is a matter of inventing a movement, of recreating it: but the hypothesis is immediately verifiable: it can be valid only if it realizes, in a creative movement, the transverse unity of *all* the heterogenous structures.'

'the totalizing requirement implies . . . that the individual is to be found in his entirety in *all* manifestations of him'

109 'Historical man, by his anchorage, makes from this universality a particular situation, and from this common necessity an irreducible contingency . . . the anchorage of the individual makes from this universal an irreducible singularity . . . There is no incarnation of the universal except in the irreducible opacity of the singular . . . man, irremediable singularity, is the being through whom the universal comes into the world.'

'If nothing of lived experience can escape knowledge, its *reality* remains irreducible. In this sense, lived experience as a concrete reality is posited as *non-knowledge*.'

'manifests historiality but misses History'

'If life is scandal, failure is even more scandalous.'

'Everything must be relative, in us and in Kierkegaard himself, *except his failure*. For failure can be explained but not resolved: as non-being, it has the absolute characteristic of negation — in fact, historical negation is, albeit at the heart of a relativism, an absolute.'

110 'subjectivity is *nothing* for objective knowledge since it is non-knowledge, and yet failure shows that it exists absolutely'

'Marx is right in opposition to both Kierkegaard and Hegel, because he affirms with the former the specificity of human *existence*, and because with the latter he takes account of concrete man in his objective reality.'

'Kierkegaard neglected *praxis* which is rationality . . . he distorted knowledge.'

'It is not a matter for us, as has too often been claimed, of "giving the irrational its rights", but, on the contrary, of reducing the element of indeterminacy and non-knowledge.'

'some kind of equivocal unreason'

'a contradiction which has not reached its point of maturity'

'rational, comprehensive non-knowledge'

'Existentialism . . . does not oppose — like Kierkegaard to Hegel — the irrational singularity of the individual to universal Knowledge . . . The dialectical process [involves] . . . the reintegration of non-known existence at the heart of Knowledge as its foundation.'

'We do not claim — as Kierkegaard did — that the real human being is unknowable. We simply say that he is not known.'

'Far from assuming . . . that we know nothing, we should almost (but it is impossible) assume that we know everything. In any case, we accept all types of knowledge in order to decipher the human structures which constitute the individual, and which the individual totalizes by the very way he lives them.'

111   'true problem of History'

'So the plurality *of meanings* of History can only be discovered and posited for itself on the basis of a future totalization, in function of it and in contradiction with it. It is our theoretical and practical task to bring this totalization nearer each day. Everything is still obscure, and yet, everything is entirely clear: we have — to remain on the theoretical level — the instruments, we can establish the method: our historical task, at the heart of this polyvalent world, is to bring closer the time when History will have *only one meaning* and when it will tend to be dissolved in the concrete men who make it together.'

'totalizing activity'

'a totalization without end'

112   'a [single] Truth of History'

'detotalized totalization'

'So, someone may object, have we never said anything true? On the contrary, while thought is still in motion, everything is truth or moment of truth; even errors contain real knowledge . . . what is false is death.'

'the truth of man'

'truth itself'

'it will attempt to establish that there is a *single* human history with a *single* truth and a *single* intelligibility'

'What can we know of a man today?'

'We must be able, in the regressive phase of our experimentation, to use *all present-day knowledge* (at least in principle) to throw light on such and such an enterprise, social structure, or embodiment of *praxis* . . . In any case, we accept all types of knowledge in order to decipher the human structures which constitute the individual and which the individual totalizes by the very way he lives them. We accept them because the dream of absolute ignorance discovering the pre-conceptual real is a philosophical stupidity as dangerous as was, in the eighteenth century, the dream of the "Noble Savage".'

'totalizations without a grand totalizer', 'acts without an author', 'constructions without a constructor'

113 'Humanism is the counterpart of racism: it is a practice of exclusion.'

'Is there a Truth of man?'

'the true humanism of man'

'the dehumanization of man'

'Man does not exist'

'[with] no meaning outside *this* singular adventure'

'The concept of man is an abstraction.'

'man is a material being in the midst of a material world'

'the history of man is an adventure of nature'

'Still we must understand that Man does not exist: there are people who are entirely defined by the society to which they belong and by the historical movement which carries them in its wake; if we do not want the dialectic to become another divine law, a metaphysical fatality, it must come *from individuals* and not from some kind of supra-individual structures. In other words, we come across this further contradiction: the dialectic is the law of totalization which means that there are *collectivities*, *societies* and *one* history, that is to say realities which are imposed on individuals; but at the same time it must be woven out of millions of individual acts.'

'the perpetually resolved and perpetually renewed contradiction between man-as-producer and man-as-product, in each individual and at the heart of each multiplicity.'

114 *'there is no isolated individual'*

247

'The individual disappears from historical categories . . . the individual – questioned questioner – *is I*, and is no one . . . we can see clearly how *I* am dissolved practically in the human adventure.'

'*I* am dissolved'

'I is *an other*'

'utilize all contemporary knowledge'

'Starting from the day when Marxist research takes the human dimension (that is to say the existential project) as the foundation of anthropological Knowledge, existentialism will no longer have any *raison d'être*.'

'As soon as a margin of *real* freedom beyond the production of his life exists *for everyone*, Marxism will have had its day; a philosophy of freedom will take its place.'

115   'There is no doubt that the structure produces behaviour. But what is wrong with radical Structuralism . . . is that the reverse side of the dialectic is passed over in silence, and History is never shown producing structures. In fact the structure makes man to the extent that History – that is to say, in this case, the process of *praxis* – makes History.'

Chapter 6

116   'The purely imaginary and *praxis* are hard to reconcile.'

117   'The real is always accompanied by the collapse of the imaginary, even if there is no contradiction between them, because the incompatibility comes from their nature and not their content.'

'So there is in perception the beginning of an infinity of images; but these can be constituted only at the cost of annihilating the perceptual consciousnesses.'

118   'An image, being the negation of the world from a particular point of view, can only ever appear against the background of the world, and in relation to that background.'

'like an incarnation of unreflecting thought'

'an inferior form of thought'

'unreflecting thought is a possession'

'I *read* the words on the notice . . . one says that I have understood, "deciphered" the words. That is not absolutely right: it would be better to say that I have created them on the basis of the black characters. These characters no longer matter to me, I no longer perceive them: in reality, I have taken up a certain attitude of consciousness which, through them, aims at another object.'

'Images . . . appear in general outside the activity of reading proper, when, for example, the reader goes back and remembers the events of the previous chapter, when he day-dreams over the book etc. In short, images appear in the pauses and failures of the reading process. The rest of the time, when the reader is absorbed, there is no mental image.'

119 'Reading is a type of fascination, and when I read a detective novel I believe what I am reading. But this in no way implies that I stop considering the detective's adventures as imaginary . . . Simply a whole imaginary world appears to me through the lines of the book . . . and this world encloses my consciousness, I can no longer get free of it, I am fascinated by it.'

'is never complete, in the first place because authors usually make use of "aesthetic distance", they write their book "in the past tense" for example etc., which allows the reader to remain outside the character. Moreover, the possibility of a reflexive consciousness is always present.'

'this state of trance . . . can never be fully realized in reading'

'would be harmful . . . to aesthetic appreciation'

'type of passionate interest'

'naïve reader'

'So the painting must be conceived of as a material thing *visited* from time to time (each time the spectator takes up the imaginary attitude) by an unreal which is precisely the *object painted*.'

120 'It goes without saying that the novelist, the poet and the playwright constitute an unreal object through verbal analoga.'

'The real is never beautiful. Beauty is a value which could only ever be applied to the imaginary and which entails the nihilation of the world in its essential structure.'

'It is stupid to confuse morality and aesthetics.'

'To posit an image is to constitute an object in the margins of the totality of the real, it is thus to hold the real at a distance, to free ourselves from it, in a word, to deny it.'

121 'totally stuck in the existent and with no possibility of grasping anything other than the existent'

'Imagination . . . is the whole of consciousness as it realizes its freedom; every real and concrete situation of consciousness in the world is pregnant with the imaginary in so far as it is always presented as a transcendence of the real.'

'against the background of the world'

'There can be no realizing consciousness without an imagining consciousness and vice versa.'

249

122 'The notes, the colours, the shapes are not signs, they refer to nothing external to them . . . for the artist, the colour, the scent, the tinkling of the spoon on the saucer are *things* in the fullest sense; he pauses before the quality of the sound or the shape, he comes back to it ceaselessly and is enchanted by it; it is this colour–object that he will transport onto his canvas and the only change he will make it undergo is to transform it into an *imaginary* object . . . the painter does not want to trace signs on his canvas, he wants to create a *thing*.'

'The writer, on the contrary, is concerned with meanings.'

'The writer can guide you and if he describes a hovel, can make you see in it the symbol of social injustices, and provoke your indignation. The painter is dumb: he presents you with *a* hovel, that is all; it is up to you to see in it what you wish. This garret will never be the symbol of poverty; for that it would need to be a sign, whereas it is a thing.'

'This yellow gash in the sky above Golgotha, Tintoretto did not choose it to *signify* anguish, nor yet to provoke it: it *is* anguish, and yellow sky at the same time. Not sky of anguish, nor anguished sky: it is anguish made into a thing.'

'When I have produced a beautiful painting, I have certainly not written down a thought . . . That's what they say! . . . How simple they are! They take all the advantages away from painting. The writer says almost everything in order to be understood. In painting, a kind of mysterious bridge is established between the souls of the figures and that of the spectator . . . The painter's art is all the closer to the heart of man for appearing more material.'

'crude minds who are more moved by writers than by musicians and painters'

123 'the devil's share'

'The meaning of a melody − if one can still speak of meaning − is nothing outside the melody itself . . . Whether you say it is joyful or sombre, it will always be beyond or short of anything you can say of it . . . We do not paint meanings, we do not put them to music: who would dare, in these conditions, demand of the painter or musician that they be committed?'

'No, we do not want to "commit also" painting, sculpture and music, or, at least, not in the same way.'

'The empire of signs is prose; poetry is on the side of painting, sculpture, music.'

124 'Its sound, its length, its masculine or feminine endings, its visual aspect create a physical appearance which represents meaning rather than expresses it.'

'Florence is town and flower and woman, it is town–flower and town–woman and girl–flower at one and the same time.'

'And the strange object which thus appears possesses the liquidity of *fleuve* (river), the soft wild ardour of *or* (gold), and finally, gives itself up with *décence* (decency), and prolongs indefinitely by the continued fading of the mute *e* its radiance full of reserve.'

'Word–things . . . attract each other, repel each other, *burn* each other, and their association creates the real poetic unity which is the *phrase–object*.'

'Doubtless emotion, even passion . . . are at the origin of the poem. But they are not *expressed* in it . . . Words take them up, are penetrated by them, and transform them . . . How could we hope to provoke the indignation or political enthusiasm of the reader, when, precisely, we are withdrawing him from the human condition and inviting him to consider, with the eyes of God, the reverse side of language?'

125 'The poet is outside language, he sees the other side of words, as if . . . coming towards men, he first met speech as a barrier.'

'It is, moreover, not a matter of arbitrarily introducing defeat and ruin into the course of the world, but rather of having eyes only for them. The human enterprise has two faces: it is simultaneously success and failure.'

'If it is true that speech is treachery and that communication is impossible, then each word, of itself, conceals its individuality, becomes an instrument of our defeat and concealer of the incommunicable. It is not that there is *something else* to communicate: but prose communication having failed, it is the very meaning of the word which becomes the pure incommunicable. So the failure of communication becomes the suggestion of the incommunicable.'

'It goes without saying that, in all poetry, a certain kind of prose, that is to say of success, is present: and reciprocally, the driest prose always contains a little poetry, that is, a certain kind of failure.'

126 'If the prose writer fusses too much over his words, the *eidos*, "prose", breaks down and we descend into nonsense. If the poet recounts, explains or teaches, poetry becomes *prosaic*, he has lost the battle. It is a matter of complex structures, impure but clearly delimited.'

'The authentic poet chooses to lose to the point of death in order to win . . . So if we absolutely must speak of the poet's commitment, let us say that he is the man who commits himself to losing.'

127 'The beautiful is made up of an eternal, invariable element, whose quantity is exceedingly hard to determine, and a relative, circumstantial element, which can be, if you like, in turn or all at once, epoch, fashion, morality, passion. Without this second element . . . the first element would be indigestible, imperceptible, ill-adapted and inappropriate to human nature.'

'So, by participating in the singularity of our time, we eventually rejoin the eternal, and it is our task as writers to give a glimpse of the eternal values which are implicated in these social and political debates.'

'But we are not concerned with seeking them in an intelligible heaven, they are interesting only in their present-day dress'.

'the amusing dress . . . of the divine cake'

128 'In an authentically revolutionary party [the work of art] would find a favourable climate for its creation, because the liberation of mankind and the advent of the classless society are, like it, absolute goals, unconditional demands which it can reflect in its own demand.'

'Perception itself is partial . . . the simple act of naming already modifies its object.'

'The mirror which it modestly presents to its readers is magic: it captivates and compromises . . . when spontaneous behaviour becomes reflexive it loses its innocence and the excuse of immediacy: we must assume it or change it.'

'To recuperate this world by showing it as it is, but as if it had its source in human freedom.'

129 'To know being as it is, we would have to be that being, but there is an "as it is" only because I am not the being that I know, and if I were, the "as it is" would disappear and could no longer even be thought.'

'In aesthetic pleasure, positional consciousness is an *imaginary* consciousness of the world in its totality as simultaneously what it is and what it should be, at once entirely ours and entirely foreign . . . So, to write is at once to reveal the world and to propose it as a task to the generosity of the reader.'

130 'it is the whole of consciousness as it realizes its freedom'

'freedom is one, but it manifests itself differently according to the circumstances'

'There is a coincidence not only between the formal freedom of thought and political democracy, but also between the material obligation to choose man as perpetual subject of meditation and social democracy.'

'In passion, freedom is alienated . . . Hence the characteristic of *pure presentation* which seems essential to the work of art: the reader must have at his disposal a certain aesthetic distance.'

'This does not mean that the writer appeals to some kind of abstract conceptual freedom. It is indeed with feelings that the aesthetic object is recreated . . . only these feelings are of a particular kind; they have their origin in freedom: they are lent.'

131 'The distinctive feature of aesthetic consciousness is that it is belief by commitment, by oath, belief continued out of fidelity to oneself and to the author, a perpetually renewed choice to believe. At any moment I can wake up, and I know it: but I do not want to: reading is a free dream. So that all the feelings which are played out against the background of that imaginary belief are particular modulations of my freedom.'

'If I were to suspect the artist of having written out of passion and in the throes of passion, my trust would immediately fade away, for it would serve no purpose to have backed up the causal order by the order of ends; the latter would be supported in turn by a psychic causality and, ultimately, the work of art would go back into the chain of determinism.'

132 'Without doubt the author guides him: but he only guides him . . . In short, reading is directed creation . . . So, for the reader, everything remains to be done and everything is already done; the work exists only at the level of his abilities.'

'Reading . . . seems to be the synthesis of perception and creation.'

'the work of a total freedom addressing plenary freedoms . . . it manifests, in its own way, as a free product of a creative activity, the totality of the human condition'

133 'let us hope . . . that he finds within himself the strength to create a scandal'

'literature is essentially heresy'

'Through literature, as I have shown, the collectivity attains reflexion and meditation, it acquires an unhappy consciousness, an unbalanced image of itself that it ceaselessly attempts to modify and improve.'

'the whole of the author's art is to force me to *create* what he *reveals*, and thereby to compromise me'

'I consider that the literature of a particular period is alienated when it has not reached an explicit consciousness of its autonomy and submits itself to temporal powers or to an ideology, in short when it envisages itself as a means and not as an unconditioned end.'

'The work of art, absolute end, [is opposed] in its essence to bourgeois utilitarianism. Do you believe that it can adapt to Communist utilitarianism?'

134 'the highest form of pure consumption'

'The extremists hope, for fear of being useful, that their works cannot even enlighten the reader about his own heart, they refuse to transmit their experience. Ultimately, the work will not be completely gratuitous unless it is completely inhuman . . . Imagination is conceived of as an unconditional faculty of *denying* the real, and the art-object is built upon the collapse of the universe.'

'The Just Man will leave to the painter, the writer and the musician the task of keeping images in order: as for him, he keeps for himself what is serious, that is to say the original relationship to being. Rather than being the conception of artists, the theory of art-for-art's-sake is a claim put forward by the Good Man: "Images are yours, reality is mine."'

'very wise'

135 'it is stupid to confuse morality and aesthetics'

'The work of art *has no end*, we are in agreement with Kant over that. But that is because it *is* an end.'

'The work of art is gratuitous because it is an absolute end and it proposes itself to the spectator as a categorical imperative.'

'Kant believes that the work exists first in fact and that it is seen subsequently . . . That is to forget that the spectator's imagination has not only a regulatory but a constitutive function.'

'the work . . . exists only if it is *looked at*, and it is first of all pure appeal, pure demand for existence'

'absolute end'

'at the heart of the aesthetic imperative we discern the moral imperative'

136 'I hold Flaubert and Goncourt responsible for the repression which followed the Commune because they did not write a line to prevent it.'

138 'too poor' and 'too rich'

'the burning loves of the sentry and the model' [Here sexual identity and grammatical gender are at odds.]

'superfluous or harmful'

'I use words to refer to myself, words to which, in another context, my history has already given another meaning and which, moreover, with respect to the history of the language as a whole, have different meanings. For this reason it is said that language is inadequate and inappropriate, whereas in reality I think that a writer is someone who says to himself that appropriateness is achieved thanks to all that. That's his job. That's what we call style . . . Basically, I think that nothing is inexpressible provided we invent its expression.'

'The writer's commitment aims to communicate the incommunicable (lived being-in-the world) by exploiting the element of disinformation contained in ordinary language.'

139   'contemporary writer' as 'the poet who calls himself a prose writer'

'I should say, for my part, that what life brings is the overcoming of the two points of view. I believe that one cannot be an *écrivain* without being an *écrivant* or an *écrivant* without being an *écrivain*.'

'Without meaning there is no ambiguity, the object does not come to inhabit the word.'

'Language . . . does mean something; and that is what has been forgotten.'

'the prose-writer has *something to say*'

'This something *is nothing sayable*, nothing conceptual or conceptualizable, nothing which signifies . . . Hence the phrase "that's just empty words" ("C'est de la littérature"), which means "You're speaking with nothing to say." We must now ask ourselves what is this *nothing*, this silent non-knowledge which the literary object must communicate to the reader.'

'It is true that the writer has basically *nothing* to say. We should understand by that that his fundamental aim is not to communicate abstract *knowledge*. Nonetheless he does *communicate* . . . If the writer has nothing to say, it is because he must manifest *everything*, that is to say the singular and practical relationship of the part to the whole which is being-in-the-world.'

140   'The writer does not write something . . . he writes, that's all. Perhaps it is also in this way that we should understand Maurice Blanchot when he suggests that the writer must feel, in his inmost self, that he has nothing *to say*.'

'the moment of interiority . . . a stasis'

'revealing of man to himself through sense'

'to reveal is to change'

'The fundamental project in the *Flaubert* is that of showing that in the end everything is communicable.'

'Life and words are incommensurable. For want of being expressed *to others* [his feelings] remain inexpressible for himself.'

141   'Flaubert does not believe *that we speak:* we are spoken.'

'This problem is fundamental for Flaubert . . . it is at the source of his art whose project will be to *render indirectly the unsayable*.'

'Gustave . . . has, literally, nothing to . . . communicate.'

'If you read: "perdus, sans mâts, sans mâts . . ." ["lost, without masts, without masts"], the poetic organization animates the word: like a cross, the *t* rises up above the other letters, like the mast above

255

the ship: around it the letters cluster − that is the hull, that is the deck: some people − and I am one − sense in that white letter, the vowel *a*, crushed under the circumflex accent as if under a low cloudy sky, the sail which is sagging. The negation which is expressed by *sans* (without) is active particularly in the universe of meaning: the ship is mastless, lost: that is what we *learn*. In the obscure world of sense, it cannot destructure the word "mast". Let us say that it makes it fade to the point of becoming the *analogon* of some kind of photographic negative.'

142 'In fact the word *mast* has no real objective similarity to the object it refers to. But the art of writing, in this case, consists precisely in forcing the reader, like it or not, to find one, to make the object come down into the sign as an unreal presence.'

'Any word − irrespective of its conventional character − can have an imaging function. . . in fact it is not a matter of chance similarities between the signifying material and the object signified, but of the felicities of a style which forces one to grasp the materiality of the words as an organic unity, and that unity as the very presence of the object referred to.'

'the grapheme, by its physical configuration and *before any treatment*, arouses resonances'

'They constitute, for each of us, the singular and incommunicable basis of any awareness of the Word.'

143 'To choose the sumptuousness of names is already to prefer the verbal universe to that of things.'

'To grasp [the word] as a sign is an activity related and complementary to perception. To grasp it in its material singularity is to imagine it.'

'The enterprise consists in using simultaneously the signifying function and the imaging function of the written word.'

'We cannot force the text to exercise *simultaneously* the semantic function and the imaging function. Writing − and reading which is inseparable from it − implies, on this level, a subtle dialectic of perception and imagination, real and unreal, sign and sense.'

'conceptual meaning'

'We must, if we are to make present an imaginary Calcutta clothed in all the charms of its name, conserve at least a rudimentary knowledge: it is a town in India, its inhabitants are Indian.'

'meaning'

'Form is a language that could be called parasitic because it is constituted at the expense of real language and without ceasing to exploit it, by forcing it to express what it is not made to say to us.'

'the unsayable'

'The non-significant materiality can provide meanings only in the imaginary.'

'Certainly [Flaubert] transmits nothing to the realist reader apart from the fascinating invitation to become in his turn unreal. If he – who is in no circumstances Flaubert's direct interlocutor – gives in to the temptation, if he becomes the *imaginary* reader of the work – he must, to grasp the sense behind the meanings – then all the un-sayable, including the flavour of the plum-pudding, will be revealed to him allusively.'

144   'The goal of the literary enterprise is to reduce the reader to despair.'

'human life begins the other side of despair'

Chapter 7

145   'In a sense we are all born predestined.'

'The *principle* of this psychoanalysis is that man is a totality and not a collection; that, in consequence, he expresses himself in his entirety in the most insignificant and superficial of his actions – in other words, there is no taste, mannerism or human act which is not *revealing*. The *goal* of this psychoanalysis is to decipher man's empirical behaviour, that is to say, to cast light on the revelations which the behaviour contains and to conceptualize them.'

'Its *point of departure* is *experience*; its *support* is the fundamental preontological understanding which man has of the human person . . . Its method is comparative . . . it is by comparing examples of behaviour that we will bring to light the unique revelation which they all express in different ways.'

146   'Understanding takes place in two opposed directions: by a regressive psychoanalysis we move up from the act under consideration to my ultimate possibility – by a synthetic progression we come back down from that ultimate possibility to the act being examined and grasp its integration in the total form.'

'psychic life'

'primary givens'

'perpetually developing in time (history)'

'Psychoanalytic investigations aim to reconstitute the subject's life from his birth to the moment of the cure: they use all the objective documents they can find: letters, witnesses, diaries, "social" information of all sorts. And what they try to restore is not so much a pure psychic event as a pair: the crucial event of childhood and the psychic crystallization around that event.'

'the laws of specific syntheses'

'original choice'

147   'fundamental project' is *'lived* . . . and, as such, totally conscious' but it is not *'known'*

'the specific, dated desire in the complex tangle of its characteristic nature.'

'It is not a matter of an unsolved riddle, as the Freudians believe: everything is there, in the light, reflexion has access to everything, grasps everything. But this "mystery in broad daylight" comes rather from the fact that the access enjoyed is deprived of the means which usually permit *analysis* and *conceptualization*.'

'the project as it is for itself, the complex in its own being'

148   'The environment can act on the subject only to the exact extent that he understands it; that is, transforms it into a situation. So no objective description of this environment could be of any use to us.'

'faeces = gold, pin-cushion = breast'

'If the complex really is unconscious, that is, if the sign is separated from the thing signified by a barrier, how could the subject *recognize* it?'

149   'It must be consciousness (of) being conscious of the tendency to regress, but precisely *in order not to be conscious of it.* What does this mean but that the censor must be in bad faith?'

'You may consider that every project is a flight but you must also consider that every flight is a project.'

'the *facts* of disguise and repression'

'perfectly inoffensive'

150   'after all, "opposites interpenetrate each other" '

'designates neither the refuges of the pre-conscious nor the unconscious, nor the conscious, but the area in which the individual is constantly swamped by himself, by his own riches, and where consciousness is shrewd enough to determine itself by forgetting . . . What I call the *vécu* is precisely the whole of the dialectical process of psychic life, a process which remains necessarily opaque to itself for it is a constant totalization, and a totalization *which cannot be conscious of what it is.* One may be conscious, in fact, of an external totalization, but not of a totalization which also totalizes consciousness. In this sense the *vécu* is always susceptible of understanding, never of knowledge.'

151   'totally conscious' but not 'known'

'what is usually called the unconscious and what I would prefer to call a total absence of knowledge accompanied by a real understanding'

'The equivalent of conscious–unconscious, that is to say that I still do not believe in the unconscious *in certain forms*, although the conception of the unconscious given by Lacan is more interesting.'

'The unconscious is that part of concrete discourse in so far as it is transindividual, which is not available to the subject to enable him to re-establish the continuity of his conscious discourse. This entails the disappearance of the paradox presented by the notion of the unconscious when it is related to an individual reality.'

152 'the unconscious is the discourse of the Other'

'As far as I'm concerned, Lacan has clarified the unconscious as a discourse which separates through language, or, if you prefer, as a counter-finality of speech: verbal structures are organized as a structure of the practico-inert through the act of speaking. These structures express or constitute intentions which determine me without being mine.'

'decentring of the subject'

'man does not think, he is thought, as he is spoken for certain linguists'

'The absence of speech is manifested by the stereotypes of a discourse where the subject, one might say, is spoken rather than speaking.'

'This Ego, whose two faces are the I and the Me, constitutes the ideal (noematic) indirect unity of the infinite series of our reflecting consciousnesses.'

153 'an imaginary construction, a fiction with which one identifies afterwards'

'Mirrors fascinate him. If he surprises himself in one he will be, for himself, the object he is for everyone else.'

'dreams, failed acts, obsessions and neuroses, but also and especially the thoughts of waking life, well-adjusted and successful acts, style, etc.'

154 'The unconscious is that chapter of my history which is marked by a blank space or occupied by a lie; it is the censored chapter. But the truth can be found; most often it is already written elsewhere. That is to say: in monuments: and this is my body, that is, the hysterical core of neurosis where the hysterical symptom exhibits the structure of a language and is deciphered like an inscription which, once collected, can without serious loss, be destroyed; in archival documents also: and these are the memories of my childhood, equally impenetrable when I do not know where they come from; in semantic evolution: and this corresponds to the stock and meanings of the vocabulary particular to me, and to my life-style and character; in traditions, too, even in the legends which in a heroic form carry my history; in the traces of truth finally, that are inevitably conserved in the distortions necessitated by the linking of the adulterated chapter with the sur- rounding chapters, and whose meaning my exegesis will re-establish.'

'through indirect reading'

'When you have just taken your *baccalauréat*, at the age of seventeen, after receiving an education based on the "*I think therefore I am*" of Descartes, and you open the *Psychopathology of Everyday Life*, where you find the famous story of Signorelli, with the substitutions, displacements and combinations which imply that Freud was thinking simultaneously of a patient who had committed suicide, of certain Turkish customs, and of many other things besides . . . your breath is taken away.'

'For the correlative of science is the Cartesian position of the subject, the effect of which is to nullify the depths of subjectivity. Remember that Freud did not hesitate to break with Jung when the latter tried to restore them to psychoanalysis. It was absolutely necessary that [Freud] was a scientist.'

'metamorphoses of the libido'

'to consider the symbol as the flowering of the soul'

'It is not the soul which speaks but man who speaks with his soul.'

'the deepest project in the *Flaubert* is that of showing that fundamentally everything is communicable'

'false thoughts of priggish pedantry, when it uses the ineffableness of lived experience or even "morbid consciousness" to undermine the effort from which it is dispensing itself: i.e. the effort which is required at the point where precisely it is not ineffable because it speaks, where experience, far from separating, is communicated, where subjectivity reveals its true structure, in which what is analysed is identical to what is articulated'

'This verbal Himalaya stands as a barrier *against Freud*'

156 'edifices of clear and distinct ideas which the Cartesians constructed in the face of that "occult quality": attraction'

'breast-feeding, the digestive and excretory functions of the infant, the first attempts at toilet-training, the relationship to the mother'

'there are men who have been made far more by history than by their pre-history, crushing in them pitilessly the child they once were'

'I shall recapitulate some general truths: when a mother feeds or changes her baby, she is expressing herself, as everyone does, in her truth as a *person* . . . by the love . . . and by the very person [of his mother], adroit or clumsy, rough or tender, such, finally, as her history has made her, the infant is revealed to himself . . . To begin with, he internalizes the maternal rhythms and tasks as the lived qualities of his own body . . . His own mother, engulfed in the depths of his body, becomes the pathetic structure of his affectivity.'

157 'for him, living is *too tiring*.'

'So, as for his pathetic inertia . . . it will retain its archaic sense . . . conserved, overcome, traversed by new and complex meanings, the sense cannot fail to be modified. But these modifications *must be understood*: it is a matter of reproducing a new totalization on the basis of the internal contradictions of a previous totality and the project which arises from them.'

'The hard dark kernel of this sense is infancy . . . the pre-historic past comes back to the child like a Destiny.'

'Original determinants of Gustave − which are *no more* at the outset than the internalization of the family environment in an objective situation which conditions them externally and *before* his conception as a *singularity*.'

158   'the whole Genetrix'

'Father–Mother–Elder Son'

'renewal of the previous infants'

'[Gustave] missed out the stage of valorization'

'true error'

'mandate to live'

'a fortunate alienation'

'the necessity of freedom'

'felt himself united with the body and heart of his mother through a sort of primitive, mystical participation: the child is *consecrated* by the affection she bears towards him: far from feeling himself to have a wandering, vague, superfluous existence, he thinks of himself as *son by divine right* . . . he is protected against all anxiety, he is one with the absolute, he is *justified*'

'incestuous couple', 'son by divine right' and 'justified'

159   'Until the age of six, his lived relationship to the Whole is quite simply his love for his mother. His Mother and the World are one: the child plunges his suckers into the maternal flesh and sucks up the juices of the earth through her familiar body . . . Weaning reveals to the infant that he is *an Other* in the eyes of others and that he will have to mould himself to the "Persona" that adults have prepared for his use; but his mother's tenderness softens the effects of this.'

'He takes refuge *from everyone* within his mother's look . . . She lends him her eyes . . . the world, with the child in it, is only a maternal vision.'

'progressive deliverance'

'Happy children discover plenitude as an original given; negation, absence and all the forms of Nothingness appear to them afterwards as local insufficiencies, provisional lacunae, fleeting contradictions:

in short Nothingness is posterior to Being. But for this orphan, it is the opposite . . . the child is alienated in the death of another.'

'distress, resentment, boredom and unease, exile, absence'

160   'His *estrangement* has only one explanation: there is neither common ground nor mediation between Gustave's subjective existence and the universe of meanings; they are two perfectly heterogeneous realities which occasionally meet . . . Life and speech are incommensurable.'

'intentional'

'organic belief masks from him his passive choice'

'without the slightest conscious connivance'

'conscious', 'known', 'fall'

161   'The mimed suicide of January 1844 is, like so many real suicides, a murder in disguise.'

'Never has the empirical father been closer to the symbolic father nor has contributed so strongly to characterize him.'

'the radical contestation of Gustave'

162   'the strangest and most easily decipherable confidence: one would think one was listening to a neurotic speaking "at random" on the analyst's couch'

'writing . . . is a means of self-release'

'easy to decipher'

'gaps in knowledge', 'breaks', 'holes'

'The work *never* reveals the secrets of the biography: it can simply be the schema or vital thread which allows us to discover them in the life itself.'

163   'The way in which, through the individual's personal history, a certain number of fundamental relations were expressed symbolically. How the triangular relationship child–paternal figure–maternal figure is lived out symbolically, how the Œdipal crisis was resolved or what conflicts its non-resolution gave rise to, these are all questions that Sartre refuses to ask. In this sense, his work is the most anti-psychoanalytic possible. In the structuration of Flaubert's personalization which he puts forward, the Œdipal relation is entirely absent.'

'too imaginary and above all too conformist ever to carry his idea through to its conclusion'

'maternal cycle'

'I have emphasized these different "maternal" themes to demonstrate *the sexual problematic* of the young boy: he understands obscurely that his mother *is no longer* the active half of the androgyne of which he is the passive half. She was once, however, in an illusory fashion: making her mark on him, she condemned him for ever to have only an imaginary sexual life.'

'the echo of a far-off fury whose traces we found in many of his early works: "a man sleeping in my mother's bed", the classic image of the Œdipus complex'

164 'the word "castration" is for me only the expression of facts *within a certain discourse*'

'Madame Flaubert's punishment fits her crime: she sinks down, calling for protection from a son she was able neither to protect . . . nor to make such that he could one day protect her . . . satisfaction is complete when the son *condemns* his mother *to death*.'

'His mother *has become a river*: she was standing at his side, she stretches out beneath him, lying flat.'

'lives a certain Œdipal situation in two different ways simultaneously' (i.e. 'anorexia'/'ataraxia')

165 'One can derive anything from the Œdipus complex . . . psychoanalysts manage to find anything in it, fixation on the mother, love for the mother, just as much as hatred of the mother – according to Melanie Klein.'

'primarily because our bias towards nominalism forbids us to classify'

'It is recognized today that some forms of epilepsy are hysterical in origin. So, to study matters more closely, we will be explicitly nominalist.'

'I am entirely in agreement as to the *facts* of disguise and regression, as facts. But as for the *words* "regression", "censor", "drive" – which express at one moment a sort of finalism, and the next moment a sort of mechanism – I reject them.'

Chapter 8

166 'What can we know about a man today?'

'The man is beginning to bore me. It's the book I'm attached to, I feel an increasingly strong need to write it – as I get older, one might say.'

'I no longer understand anything about his behaviour. It's not that the documents are lacking: letters, fragments of memoirs, secret reports, police records. On the contrary, I have almost too many of them. What's lacking in all these pieces of evidence is firmness and consistency.'

'Well, yes: he may have done all that, but it isn't proved: I'm starting to think that nothing can ever be proved. They are reasonable hypotheses which account for the facts: but I'm so strongly aware that they come from me, that they are quite simply a way of unifying my knowledge . . . I've the impression of creating a work of pure imagination.'

'I admit it: it is a fable. Nothing proves that things were like that. And, worse still, the absence of proof . . . means that, even when we are constructing the fable, we have to fall back on the schematic, on generalities . . . I can imagine, without the slightest vexation, that the real explanation is exactly the opposite of the one I am inventing.'

167 'It is the vicious circle of all scepticism . . . Of course . . . whatever instruments he uses, it is in the end with *his* eyes that the experimenter observes the results of the experiment. But even if objectivity is to some extent distorted, it is also still *revealed* . . . But, someone will object, the critic is a historical creature and his judgements are relative to his time. That is true, but it would be wrong to confuse historicism and the subjective idealism of our pundits. For, if it is true that the critic, as a creature of history, only ever brings to light Mallarmé's meaning *for our time*, it is also true that that meaning is objective.'

'did not have the life he deserved'

'What if, contrary to received wisdom, men only ever had the lives they deserved?'

'dizziness', 'sensation of the abyss'

'bad faith is still faith'

'quip'

'The free choice that a man makes of himself is absolutely identifiable with what we call his destiny.'

168 'Baudelaire's bad faith is so deep-rooted that he is no longer master of it.'

'Baudelaire, with no possibility of reversal, chose not to choose.'

'I could have acted differently, of course, but *at what cost*?'

'Any action is comprehensible as a project of oneself towards a possible goal. And understanding takes place in two opposed directions: by a regressive psychoanalysis we move up from the act under consideration to my ultimate possibility – by a synthetic progression, we come back down from that ultimate possibility to the act being examined and we grasp its integration in the total form.'

169 'To show the limits of psychoanalytic interpretation and of Marxist explanation and that only freedom can account for a person in his totality, to show this freedom battling with destiny, first crushed by

264

the components of its fate, then turning back on them to digest them gradually, to prove that genius is not a gift but the solution invented in desperate cases, to discover the choice a writer makes of himself, of his life and of the meaning of the universe right down to the formal characteristics of his style and composition, right down to the structure of his images and the specific nature of his tastes, to trace in detail the history of a self-liberation: this is what I wanted to do; the reader will say whether I succeeded.'

'Bachelard would speak in his case of an "Icarus complex".'

'It is the look of the Just Man which first turned him to stone.'

'We will define the existentialist method as a regressive–progressive, analytic–synthetic method; it is an enriching movement back and forth between the object (which contains the whole epoch in the form of hierarchized meanings) and the epoch (which contains the object in its totalization).'

'It took place in this way, or in another.'

'It is clear that the study of Genet's conditioning by the events of his objective history is inadequate, extremely inadequate.'

'Valéry is a petty-bourgeois intellectual, there is no doubt about that. But not every petty-bourgeois intellectual is Valéry.'

'Every writer has his reasons: for one art is an escape; for another a means of conquest. But one can escape to a hermitage, take flight into madness, into death; one can conquer by arms. Why specifically *write*, use *writing* to carry out one's escapes and conquests?'

171 'one of the heroes of our time'

'Since social relations are ambiguous and always involve an element of failure . . . because all speech draws us closer by what it expresses and isolates us by what it keeps silent . . . since we ceaselessly fail to communicate, to love, to make ourselves loved, and every failure makes us feel our solitude . . . since we are, in any case, *impossible nonentities*, we must listen to the voice of Genet, our neighbour, our brother . . . If there is still time, by a final effort, to reconcile the object and the subject, we must – if only once and in the imaginary – realize that latent solitude which gnaws away at our acts and our thoughts . . . Today it is a matter of bringing to light the subject, the guilty one, that monstrous and impoverished beast that we risk becoming at every moment; Genet offers us the mirror, we must look at ourselves in it.'

172 'I had the impression of a score to settle with him.'

'Flaubert's account of himself – that sullen disguised confession, fed on his self-hatred – is something exceptional.'

'Flaubert represents . . . the exact opposite of my own conception of literature: a total non-commitment and the search for a formal ideal, which is not mine at all.'

'Finally, *through* all that, it is possible to ask the question: "What was the *imaginary social world* of the dreamy bourgeoisie in 1848?"'

'The underlying project in the *Flaubert* is that of showing that ultimately everything is communicable and that one can succeed, without being God, whilst being a man like any other, to understand perfectly — if one has the necessary facts — a man.'

173 'Nothing proves at the outset that this totalization is possible and that the truth of a person is not plural; the pieces of information are very different in *nature* . . . Do we not risk ending up with layers of heterogeneous and irreducible meanings? This book attempts to prove that the irreducibility is only apparent.'

'does not believe that *we speak: we are spoken*'

'man can "be spoken" only to the extent that he speaks and vice versa'

'always diverted, always recaptured and controlled then diverted again — and so on interminably'

'bad initial relationship with language'

'passive constitution'

'a secret choice of the inarticulate'

'a bad insertion . . . into the linguistic universe, which comes down to saying: into society, *into his family*'

174 'is in the first place the family experienced at the most elementary psychosomatic level — that of breathing, sucking, the digestive functions, the sphincters — by a *protected* organism'

'Gustave assumes [his apathy] to make it into a more highly developed form of behaviour and give it a new function: passive action becomes a tactic . . . Preserved, overcome, traversed by new and complex meanings, its sense cannot fail to change.'

'This dialectic of chance and necessity comes about freely without troubling anyone in the pure existence of each of us . . . What we are seeking here is the child of chance, the meeting of a certain body and a certain mother . . . these elementary determinants, far from being added together or affecting each other externally, are immediately inscribed in the synthetic field of a living totalization.'

175 'the work *never* reveals the secrets of the biography'

'The analysis of the neurosis is a piece of anti-psychiatry; I wanted to reveal the neurosis as a solution to a problem.'

'So, if we go from the most evident to the most complex, we can uncover at the root of his activity several levels of intentionality: (1) To obey his father, whatever the cost. (2) To make himself, in his fury, the author of his bourgeois destiny in complicity with those who assigned it to him. (3) To overcome the obscure revolt that is brewing, for want of being able to assume it in a negative action. (4) To take refuge in the absorbing role of agent in order to forget the resistance which is being organized and to leave the field free for belief; in short, to rush to his death innocently. (5) To exasperate this passive resistance, to the precise extent that the role of agent — here, driving the carriage — symbolizes activity in general which is being imposed on him and which he cannot stand. (6) At a still deeper level: to restore, thanks to propitious circumstances, and to condense in a moment so brief that he can live it in its entirety, the whole situation he has been struggling with since his adolescence, in such a way that it arouses in him a global response to his problems; in short, to confront, *by his absolute and partially acted submission*, the two contradictory demands of the Other — that of the bourgeois Achille-Cléophas who assigns him a bourgeois destiny, and that of the symbolic Father who has condemned him to nothingness — and let them (or make them) devour each other.'

176 'If he falls at Pont-L'Evêque, it is simultaneously *against* Fate and *for* Art.'

'Is it not in order *to be reborn an Artist* that Gustave has broken the moorings that held him to immediate reality?'

'a tactical and negative response to his father'

'a strategic and positive response to the question posed by the necessity and the impossibility for Gustave of being an Artist'

'Gustave's illness expresses in its fullness what we must call his freedom: what this means can be understood only at the end of this work, after rereading *Madame Bovary*.'

177 'historical disjunction', 'neurotic'

178 When the satisfaction goes far beyond the scandal — as was the case with *Madame Bovary* — we must understand *both* that there has been a *misunderstanding* (we will see in the fourth volume Gustave labelled a realist and shouting with fury) and that, beneath these errors of interpretation, readers and author find themselves contemporaries.'

'total lack of commitment'

'commitment on a second level that I will call political, despite everything . . . To take the universe as a whole, with man in it, and account for it from the point of view of nothingness is a profound commitment.'

'Bracketed off, neither the world nor language are real: both are imaginary objects; one renders the image of things with word–images.'

'If he makes himself the imaginary reader of the work — he must, to grasp the sense behind the meanings — then all the unsayable . . . will be revealed to him allusively.'

'the worst is always certain'

179 'We have to choose: to live or to recount.'

'What is writing?' 'Why write?' 'For whom does one write?'

'I don't think there is any point in saying that I recognize myself in Flaubert . . . I've very few points in common with Flaubert.'

'farewell to literature'

'the riches of the life of the psyche'

'The *récit* is told in the past . . . the *récit* explains: the chronological order . . . hardly masks the causal order.'

'For the most trivial event to become an adventure we must simply *recount* it to somebody . . . Once we recount a life, everything changes; but it's a change that nobody notices: the proof is that we speak of true stories. As if there could be any true stories; events happen one way and we recount them backwards. We seem to be starting at the beginning . . . And in fact we've begun at the end.'

181 'My grandfather had brought me up in the retrospective illusion . . . Recognized, this optical error is not troublesome: it can be corrected.'

'destined to a certain type of action from the outset'

'I have no empathy for myself. There is always a bit of sympathy or antipathy in our relations to ourselves . . . We adhere to ourselves.'

'a certain way of contemplating oneself reflexively, of loving oneself . . . a constant relationship with oneself, the self being, moreover, not exactly the active self which speaks, thinks, dreams, acts, but rather a character created from that starting point'

'I don't believe that the proper relationship of self with self should be a love-relationship. I think that love is the true relationship between the self and others. However, not loving oneself, constantly blaming oneself, hating oneself, prevents just as effectively the full possession of oneself.'

'I don't think there's much point in doing this work on oneself. There are other ways of trying to find oneself.'

182 'a novel I believe in'

'It is impossible to totalize a living man.'

'It was a matter of taking the actions and thoughts of my life and, by means of a true fiction − or a fictive truth − trying to make a whole of them.'

'truth always remains to be found because it is infinite'

'His enquiry is directed first of all *into himself* in order to transform into a harmonious totality the contradictory being which he has been allotted.'

'monstrous product of monstrous societies'

'I was a child, that monster they fabricate with their regrets.'

'To take up the actions and thoughts of my life and try to totalize them, looking carefully at their supposed contradictions and limitations, to see if it was really true that they had those limits, or if I had not been forced to consider certain ideas as contradictory when they were not.'

'The specific object of his enquiry is dual, in fact: its two aspects are the inverse one of the other and are complementary; he must understand himself within society in so far as it produces him . . . Whence a perpetual reversal, back and forth from the self to the world and from the world to the self.'

183 'True intellectual research . . . involves enquiry passing through the singularity of the enquirer . . . thought must turn back ceaselessly upon itself and always grasp itself as a *singular universality*, that is, secretly made singular by the class prejudices inculcated since childhood although he believes himself to be rid of them and to have attained the universal.'

'The intellectual tries to modify *himself* in his sensibility as well as in his thoughts.'

'I was led to think systematically against myself'

'I wanted the moments of my life to follow each other and be ordered like those of a life remembered.'

'One might as well try to catch time by its tail.'

'systematic history of the personality'

'this nothing which becomes a plethora'

'I was born on 22 November 1869'

184 'As for me, before I was dedicated, I grew up in indifference: I didn't give a damn about the *toga praetexta*.'

'At least one living cleric should remain to carry on the task and manufacture future relics. Absolute rubbish: I swallowed it without really understanding it.'

'I became a traitor and have remained one.'

'Glide, mortals, don't delve deeply.'

185 'In Alsace, around 1850, a schoolteacher burdened with children resigned himself to becoming a grocer. This unfrocked cleric wanted some compensation: since he was renouncing the formation of minds, one of his sons should form souls; there would be a pastor in the family, it would be Charles. Charles ran away, preferring to roam the roads in pursuit of a riding mistress. His portrait was turned to face the wall and no one was allowed to mention his name – whose turn next? Auguste hastily imitated the paternal sacrifice: he went into trade and did very well. That left Louis, he had no pronounced predisposition: his father took hold of this peaceful boy and made him a pastor in a trice. Later Louis carried obedience to the point of fathering – in his turn – a pastor, Albert Schweitzer, whose career is well known.'

186 'out of Christian charity'

'caught between the silence of the one and the scolding of the other, he developed a stutter'

'I tried to die myself, too, of enteritis and perhaps of resentment.'

'Families, I hate you.'

'I hate my childhood and all that survives of it.'

'There are no good fathers, that is the rule.'

187 'I have no super-ego'

'my father's sudden withdrawal had favoured me with a very incomplete "Œdipus" '

'verdict of an eminent psychoanalyst'

'far away from men and against them'

'No super-ego, perhaps, but no aggression either. My mother was mine, no one challenged my tranquil possession of her; I had no knowledge of violence or hatred, I was spared the harsh apprenticeship of jealousy.'

'the *facts* of disguise and repression'

'Charles . . . sprung four children on her', 'Doctor Sartre . . . from time to time, without speaking a word, made her pregnant'

'He fascinates me; I know he remained a bachelor but imitated his father in everything, although he did not like him.'

'He adored his mother . . . he would smother her with kisses and caresses then start to speak about his father, at first ironically and then angrily.'

'young giant'

'on my own, I should have taken her rather for an elder sister'

188 'Diversionary tactic? A camouflage for forbidden emotions? It is quite possible. I had an elder sister, my mother.'

'Widowerhood, an incurable wound: because, yes, because of a woman, but not through her fault; this allowed me to reject the advances of all the others. To be investigated.'

'access to other women'

'erect stones . . . menhirs, swollen . . . covered in small black veins'

'a dirty little book, brown and smelly . . . it was Mérimée humiliated'

'I put myself in their hands and then suddenly I light up, I am dazzling . . . I am a great and terrible fetish in their hands.'

189 'I benefited from the situation, without the lucky coincidence of this double death-agony I should have been exposed to the difficulty of a late weaning.'

'Forcibly weaned at nine months'

'I regained consciousness on the lap of a stranger.'

'my appetite for writing covers up a refusal to live'

'Death intoxicated me because I did not like life: that is what explains the terror with which it filled me . . . Our deepest intentions are an inextricable web of projects and means of escape: I can see clearly that the mad enterprise of writing so that my existence should be forgiven me had, despite the boasting and lies, some reality; the proof is that I am still writing today, fifty years later. But if I go back to the beginning I can see a flight forward and a rash suicide; yes, more than epic conquest, more than martyrdom, it was death I was seeking.'

190 'The sequence seems clear: made feminine by my mother's tenderness, insipid by the absence of the severe Moses who had fathered me, conceited by my grandfather's adoration, I was a pure object, destined above all to masochism if only I could have believed in the family comedy. But no . . . the system horrified me . . . I threw myself into pride and sadism.'

'Docile child, I would obey to the death, but obey myself.'

'Do you think that children do not choose their own poisons?'

'Children have the fathers they deserve'

'I fled; external forces moulded my flight and made me.'

'A fraud down to my bones, and mystified . . . I have changed . . . I am a man who is waking up, cured of a long, bitter-sweet madness.'

'Moreover, this old ruined construction, my imposture, is also my character: one gets rid of a neurosis, one is never cured of oneself.

Worn, faded, humiliated, driven into a corner and passed over in silence — all the characteristics of the child have survived in the fifty-year-old man.'

'Pardaillan still inhabits me. And Strogoff. I depend only on them who depend only on God and I do not believe in God. Try to unravel that. For my part I am completely lost.'

191 'The point of the style of *Les Mots* is that the book is a farewell to literature: an object which contests itself should be as well-written as possible.'

'I took words to be the quintessence of things'

'long bitter-sweet madness'

'deliberate plagiarism'

'I was born of writing'

'I was born of writing; before that, there was only a play of reflexions; after my first novel I knew that a child had entered the hall of mirrors.'

'I would not listen to my grandfather's voice if it were not my own.'

'the world used me to express itself. It began with an anonymous chattering in my head.'

192 'I hate my childhood and all that remains of it'

'What is left? A whole man, made of all men, worth all of them, and any one of them worth him.'

'I lived beyond my age'

'Stupefied vermin, faithless, lawless, without reason or aim, I took refuge in the family comedy.'

'I wept easily and my heart was hard.'

'I am adored, therefore I am adorable.'

'one might as well try to catch time by its tail'

'an inert corpse'

'the pleasure of feeling like a child who has just been born'

'I think I would do better today and *so much* better tomorrow.'

'I have cheerfully explained that man is impossible'

'I have changed'

'the quicklime in which the wonder-child was dissolved'

193 'I could have acted differently, of course, but *at what cost*?'

'Naturally, I am not fooled; I see clearly that we repeat ourselves.'

'If I did not publish this autobiography earlier and in its more radical form, it was because I judged it to be excessive. There is no reason to drag a poor man through the mud because he writes.

Moreover I had realized in the meantime that action too has its difficulties, and that one can be led to it by neurosis. One is not saved by politics any more than by literature.'

Chapter 9

194 'all the presuppositions which have always constituted the concept of the unity of man'

'*Dasein*, if it is *not* man, is still not *anything other* than man'

195 'Man does not exist'

'These three so-called "elements" of time: past, present, future, must not be considered as a collection of "data" to be added together — for example as an infinite series of "nows" of which some are not yet and others are no longer — but as structured moments of an original synthesis.'

196 'as present it is not what it is (past) and it is what it is not (future)'

'the present is not'

'the *en soi* cannot be present'

'to be there is not to be present'

'the present is precisely this negation of being, this escape from being in so far as being is *there* as something one escapes'

'The present moment emanates from a realizing and reifying conception of the *pour soi*.'

'The *pour soi* has no being because its being is always at a distance.'

'the self-presence'

'the identity of lived experience instantaneously present to itself'

'If the present of self-presence is not *simple*, if it is constituted in an originary irreducible synthesis, then all Husserl's argument is threatened in its principle.'

'self-presence'

'a way of *not coinciding with oneself*, of escaping identity'

'the highest dignity of being'

'If it is present to itself, that means it is not completely itself.'

'at a distance from itself'

'The *pour soi* is obliged never to exist except as an elsewhere in relation to itself.'

197 'being *en soi* and being *pour soi* were *both being*'

'the *pour soi* has no other reality than being the nihilation of being' 'a hole in being at the heart of Being'

'it is perpetually founding its nothingness-of-being'

'its being is never *given* . . . since it is always separated from itself by the nothingness of otherness; the *pour soi* is always in suspense, because its being is a perpetual postponement'

'more profitable to knowledge'

'against Hegel . . . that being *is* and nothingness *is not*'

'The fact remains that the being (*être*) which is nothing, which is not a being (*étant*) cannot be spoken of, cannot speak itself, except in the ontic metaphor.'

'the thing itself is always elusive'

'pure perception'

'being as it is'

198 'the trace *is nothing*', '*the trace itself does not exist*', '*différance is not*, does not exist'

'that negative theology which still poisons us today and founds God's *being* on his lack of all reality'

'a *post-atheistic* christianity which tries to transform defeat into victory'

199 'universal negation is equivalent to the absence of negation'

'for her, as for Hegel, negation of negation bursts our limits and becomes affirmation', 'overcoming preserves what it denies'

'what we must bear in mind here against Hegel is that being *is* and nothingness is not'

'relative positivity'

'When I said that God was not a being and was above being, I was not thereby contesting His being, on the contrary, I was attributing to Him a higher being.'

'What would be the status of a negative which could not be transcended?'

200 'Philosophical language, as soon as it speaks, recuperates negativity − or forgets it, which comes to the same thing − even when it claims to affirm it, to recognize it.'

'pathetic error', 'nothingness at the heart of speech, the "lack of being" '

'Contrary to the metaphysical, dialectical "Hegelian" interpretation of the economic movement of *différance*, we must recognize here a game of loser wins, where one wins and loses every time.'

'The detours, periods and syntax to which I will often have to resort will resemble those of negative theology, sometimes to the point of seeming indistinguishable from them. We have already felt it necessary to emphasize that *différance is not*, does not exist . . . and we will be led to emphasize also all *that* it *is not*, and that is to say, everything; and consequently that it has neither existence nor essence. It belongs to no category of being, either present or absent. However, this description of *différance* is not theological, not even of the most negative order of negative theology which has always striven to reveal – as we know – a super-essentiality beyond the finite categories of essence and existence, that is to say of presence, and is always quick to remind us that if the predicate of existence is refused to God, it is in order to recognize in him a superior, inconceivable, ineffable mode of being. There is no such procedure here, as will be progressively borne out.'

'inexhaustible ruse'

'If there was a definition of *différance*, it would be precisely the limiting, the interruption, the destruction, of the Hegelian dialectic *everywhere* it operates.'

201   'The disappearance of truth as a presence, the elusiveness of the present origin of presence is the condition of every (manifestation of) truth. Non-truth is truth. Non-presence is presence. *Différance*, the disappearance of originary presence, is *at once* the condition of possibility and the condition of impossibility of truth.'

Notes

202   'bracketing off of the natural attitude'

203   'My finitude is the condition of my freedom.'

204   'The freedom which, for Kant, underpins the categorical imperative is noumenal and thus the freedom of *another* . . . It is the projection of the Other into the noumenal world.'

'the idea of the *end of pre-history* makes no difference to the problem'

205   'a History where alterity is subsumed with unity'

'Duty . . . is an order given by someone else, and which retains for the agent this characteristic of alterity.'

'you must therefore you can' as 'reassuring'

'nature without man' like 'being as it is'

'Moreover, pure and simple empirical description can only give us labels and present us with pseudo-irreducibles.'

206   'If psychology is troublesome in the theatre, it is not because there is too much in it: it is because there is not enough.'

'There is tragedy every time the impossible is joined with the necessary.'

207   'The play is a tragedy to the extent that there is no solution . . . It is Marxist to the extent that it reveals and deciphers the historical necessity of this struggle doomed to fail.'

'We are therefore Jansenists because the times have made us so.'

209   'what the *pour soi* is lacking is the *soi* . . . the *soi* is individual'

211   'The movement which goes from childhood to the nervous crises is . . . a perpetual overcoming of these givens: it leads, in fact, to the literary commitment of Gustave Flaubert.'

'Hence the famous advice: "Glissez, mortels, n'appuyez pas", which does not mean "Become superficial, do not go into anything too deeply", but, on the contrary "Synthesize in depth, but without compromising yourself."'

213   'And Sartre never stopped being that − not a model . . . but a breath of fresh air, a breeze . . . It's stupid to ask if Sartre is the beginning or the end of something. Like all creative things and people he's in the middle.'

Bibliography

Place of publication of all French texts Paris, publisher Gallimard unless otherwise indicated.

Sartre's works

Editions cited: I have tried to use readily available editions, usually the original edition except in the following cases: *Les Mots*: Folio edition cited; the novels and short stories: single-volume Pléiade *Œuvres romanesques* (1981) cited; the plays: paperback editions cited; *La Transcendance de l'Ego*: Vrin reprint cited.

La Transcendance de l'Ego, Esquisse d'une description phénoménologique, first published in *Recherches philosophiques*, 1936, reprinted in edition by Sylvie le Bon, Vrin, 1965.
L'Imagination, Alcan, 1936 (reprint P.U.F., 1969)
La Nausée, 1938
Le Mur, 1939
Esquisse d'une théorie des émotions, Hermann, 1939
L'Imaginaire, Psychologie phénoménologique de l'imagination, 1940
Les Mouches, 1943 (Livre de Poche, 1971)
L'Etre et le Néant, Essai d'ontologie phénoménologique, 1943
Huis clos, 1945 (Livre de Poche, 1971)
L'Age de raison, 1945
Le Sursis, 1945
L'Existentialisme est un humanisme, Nagel, 1946
Morts sans sépulture, Lausanne, Marguerat, 1946 (Livre de Poche, 1966)
La Putain respectueuse, Nagel, 1946 (Livre de Poche, 1946)
Réflexions sur la question juive, P. Morihien, 1946 (Collection, 'Idées', 1961)
Les Jeux sont faits, Nagel, 1946 (Methuen, 1974)
Situations I: essais critiques, 1947
Baudelaire, 1947
Les Mains sales, 1948
Situations II: Qu'est-ce que la littérature?, 1948
L'Engrenage, Nagel, 1948
La Mort dans l'âme, 1949
Situations III, 1949
Entretiens sur la politique (avec D. Rousset et G. Rosenthal), 1949
Le Diable et le Bon Dieu, 1951
Saint Genet, comédien et martyr, 1952
Kean, 1954 (O.U.P., 1973)
Nekrassov, 1956 (Folio, 1973)

BIBLIOGRAPHY

Les Séquestrés d'Altona, 1960 (Livre de Poche, 1967)
Critique de la raison dialectique, précédé de Questions de méthode, I, Théorie des ensembles pratiques, 1960
Les Mots, 1963 (Folio, 1972)
Situations IV: Portraits; *V: Colonialisme et néo-colonialisme*; *VI: Problèmes du marxisme, I*, 1964
Situations VII: Problèmes du marxisme, II, 1965
Les Troyennes (Euripide, Les Troyennes, adaptation francaise de J.-P. Sartre), 1965
'Jean-Paul Sartre', *Que peut la littérature?*, Union Générale d'Editions, 1965, pp. 107–27
'Sartre contre Lacan', *Figaro littéraire* (29 December 1966), p. 4
'Jean-Paul Sartre répond', *L'Arc*, 30 (1966), pp. 91–2
L'Idiot de la famille, G. Flaubert de 1821 à 1857, vols I & II, 1971
L'Idiot de la famille, vol. III, 1972
Situations VIII: Autour de '68; *IX: Mélanges*, 1972
Un Théâtre de situations, ed. M. Contat and M. Rybalka, Collection 'Idées', 1972
On a raison de se révolter (discussions avec Ph. Gavi et P. Victor), 1974
Situations X: Politique et autobiographie, 1976
Sartre. Un film réalisé par A. Astruc et M. Contat, 1977
Œuvres romanesques, Pléiade, 1981
Les Carnets de la drôle de guerre, 1983
Letters au Castor et à quelques autres, 1983
Cahiers pour une morale, 1983
Le Scénario Freud, 1984
Critique de la raison dialectique, vol. II (inachevé), L'Intelligibilité de l'Histoire, 1985

Books and articles referring to Sartre

Arnold, A. J. and Piriou, J. P., *Genèse et critique d'une autobiographie: 'Les Mots' de Jean-Paul Sartre*, Archives des Lettres Modernes, 1973
Aronson, R., *Jean-Paul Sartre. Philosophy in the World*, New Left Books, London, 1980
Barnes, H., *Sartre*, Quartet Books, 1973
    Sartre and Flaubert, University of Chicago Press, 1981
Beauvoir, S. de, 'Merleau-Ponty et le Pseudo-Sartrisme', *Les Temps modernes* (June–July 1955), 114–15
    La Force de l'Age, 1960
    La Force des Choses, 1963
    Tout Compte fait, 1971
    La Cérémonie des adieux suivi de Entretiens avec Jean-Paul Sartre, 1981
Bensimon, M., 'Nekrassov ou l'anti-théâtre', *French Review 31* (1957), pp. 18–26

Burgelin, C., 'Lire *L'Idiot de la famille*?', *Littérature* (6 May 1972), pp. 111–20

Caws, P., *Sartre*, Routledge & Kegan Paul, London, 1979

Cohen-Solal, A., *Sartre 1905–1980*, 1985

Colombel, J., *Sartre ou le parti de vivre*, 1981

Contat, M. and Rybalka, M., *Les Ecrits de Sartre*, 1970

Craipeau, M., 'Interview avec Jean-Paul Sartre', *France-Observateur* (10 September 1959)

Danto, A., *Sartre*, Fontana Modern Masters, London, 1975

Derrida, J., 'Les Fins de l'homme' in *Marges*, Minuit, 1972

Desan, W., *The Marxism of Jean-Paul Sartre*, Anchor Books, New York, 1965

Fell, J., *Emotion in the Thought of Sartre*, New York, Columbia University Press, 1965

Heidegger and Sartre, Columbia University Press, New York, 1979

Fretz, L., 'Humanistic foundation of Sartrean ethics'; Appendix (pp. 235–70) to *Het Individualiteitsconcept in Sartres Filosofie*, Delft University Press, 1984

Goldthorpe, R., *Sartre: Literature and Theory*, C.U.P., Cambridge, 1984

Grisoni, D. (ed.), *Politiques de la philosophie*, Grasset, 1976

Hayman, R., *Writing Against . A Biography of Sartre*, Wiedenfeld and Nicolson, London, 1986

Howells, C., *Sartre's Theory of Literature*, M.H.R.A., 1979

'Sartre and the commitment of pure art', *British Journal of Aesthetics* 18, no. 2, (1978)

'Sartre and Freud', *French Studies* 33 (1979)

'Sartre and the language of literature', *Modern Language Review* 74, no. 3 (1979)

'Sartre and negative theology', *Modern Language Review* 76, no. 3, (1981)

'Sartre and Derrida: Qui perd gagne', *Journal of the British Society for Phenomenology* 13, no. 1 (1982)

'Sartre, esquisse d'une théorie de la lecture', *Etudes Sartriennes*, II–III (*Cahiers de sémiotique textuelle 5–6*) Paris, 1986

'Sartre and Levinas' in *Levinas*, Warwick Studies in Philosophy and Literature, Routledge & Kegan Paul (forthcoming 1988)

Idt, G., *La Nausée: analyse critique*, Hatier, Profil d'une œuvre 18, 1971

Issacharoff, M. (ed.), *Sartre et la mise en signe*, Klincksieck and French Forum, Paris and Lexington, 1982

Jeanson, F., *Le Problème moral et la pensée de Sartre,* Seuil, 1947

Sartre par lui-même, Seuil, 1955

Sartre, (Les Ecrivains devant Dieu), Desclée de Brouwer, 1966

Sartre dans sa vie, Seuil, 1974

Jolivet, R., *Sartre, ou la théologie de l'absurde*, Fayard, 1965

King, T. M., *Sartre and the Sacred*, University of Chicago Press, Chicago and London, 1974

König, T. (ed.), *Sartres Flaubert Lesen: Essays zu Der Idiot der Familie*, Rowohlt, 1980

La Capra, D., *A Preface to Sartre*, Methuen, London, 1979

Lacroix, J., 'Le Séquestré d'Altona condamné à un deuxième suicide', *Paris-Presse* (29 April 1966)

Lecarme, J., '*Les Mots* de Sartre: un cas limite de l'autobiographie?', *Revue d'histoire littéraire de la France*, 75, no. 6 (November–December 1975), pp. 1047–61

Lejeune, P., *Le Pacte autobiographique*, Seuil, 1975
Je est un autre, Seuil, 1980

Lévy, B., *Le Nom de l'homme, dialogue avec Sartre*, Verdier, 1984

Lorris, R., *Sartre dramaturge*, Nizet, 1975

Manser, A., *Sartre, a Philosophic Study*, Athlone Press, London, 1966

Mehlman, J., *A Structural Study of Autobiography*, Cornell University Press, Ithaca and London, 1974

Morot-Sir, E., *Lire aujourd'hui 'Les Mots' de Jean-Paul Sartre*, 1975

Mouchard, C., 'Un roman vrai', *Critique*, 27 (II) (1971) pp. 1029–49

Murdoch, I., *Sartre, Romantic Rationalist*, Bowes and Bowes, Cambridge, 1953

Pacaly, J., *Sartre au miroir*, Klincksieck, 1980

Poster, M., *Sartre's Marxism*, Pluto Press, London, 1979

Prince, G., *Métaphysique et technique dans l'œuvre romanesque de Sartre*, Droz, Geneva, 1968

Robert, M., 'Le Tribunal ou l'analyse', *Le Monde* (2 July 1971), p. 16

Scriven, M., *Sartre's Existential Biographies*, Macmillan, London, 1984

Silverman, H., and Elliston, F. (eds), *Jean-Paul Sartre: Contemporary Approaches to his Philosophy*, Duquesne University Press, 1980

Verstraeten, P., *Violence et éthique, esquisse d'une critique de la morale dialectique à partir du théâtre politique de Sartre*, 1972
(ed.), *Autour de J.-P. Sartre: Littérature et Philosophie*, 1981

Whitford, M., *Merleau-Ponty's Critique of Sartre's Philosophy*, French Forum, Kentucky, 1982

Wilcocks, R., 'Thomas l'obscur', *Obliques*, 18–19, pp. 131–5

Obliques, Sartre, 18–19, 1979
Obliques, Sartre et les Arts, 24–5, 1981
Yale French Studies, Sartre after Sartre, no. 68, 1985

Other Works

Austin, J. L., *How to do Things with Words*, O.U.P., Oxford, 1962

Bachelard, G., *L'Eau et les rêves*, J. Corti, 1943
L'Air et les songes, J. Corti, 1943

Barthes, R., *Essais critiques*, Seuil, 1964
La Chambre claire, Seuil, 1980

BIBLIOGRAPHY

Bateson G. *et al.*, 'Towards a Theory of Schizophrenia', *Behaviourial Science*, I (1956), pp. 251–63

Baudelaire, C., *Œuvres complètes*, Pléiade, 1961

Beaujour, M., *Miroirs d'encre, rhétorique de l'autoportrait*, Seuil, 1980

Bloom, H., *The Anxiety of Influence*, O.U.P., Oxford, 1973
A Map of Misreading, O.U.P., Oxford, 1975

Delacroix, E., *Journal*, Plon, 1932, reprint 1980

Deleuze, G., *Logique du sens*, Minuit, 1969
(with C. Parnet), *Dialogues*, Flammarion, 1977

Derrida, J., *La Voix et le phénomène*, P.U.F., 1967
L'Ecriture et la différence, Seuil, 1967 (Points, 1979)
De la grammatologie, Minuit, 1967
Marges de la philosophie, Minuit, 1972
La Dissémination, Seuil, 1972
Positions, Minuit, 1972
La Carte postale, Aubier-Flammarion, 1980

Descombes, V., *Le Même et l'Autre*, Minuit, 1979

Fairbairn, W. R. D., *Psychoanalytic Studies of the Personality*, Tavistock Publications, London, 1952

Fingarette, H. *Self-deception*, Routledge and Kegan Paul, London and New York, 1969

Flaubert, G., *Œuvres complètes*, Seuil, 1964

Foucault, M., *Les Mots et les choses*, 1966

Freud, S., *The Standard Edition of the Complete Psychological Works of Sigmund Freud*, 24 vols, translated and edited J. Strachey, Hogarth Press, London, 1953–74

Genet, J., *Œuvres complètes*, vol. II, 1951

Gide, A., *Si le grain ne meurt*, Folio, 1954

Hegel, G. W. F., *La Phénoménologie de l'esprit*, translated J. Hyppolite, Aubier, 1941
Philosophy of Mind, translated W. Wallace, 1894, reprint, O.U.P., Oxford, 1971
Science of Logic, translated W. H. Johnson and L. G. Struthers, London, 1951
Philosophy of Nature, translated M. J. Petry, Allen & Unwin, London, 1970

Heidegger, M., *Being and Time*, translated J. Macquarrie and E. Robinson, 1962, reprint, Blackwell, Oxford, 1967
Poetry, Language, Thought, translated A. Hofstradten, London, 1971

Husserl, E., *Ideas*, translated W. R. Boyce Gibson, Allen & Unwin, London, 1967
Logical Investigations, translated J. N. Findlay, Routledge & Kegan Paul, London, 1970

Jankélévitch, V., *L'Alternative*, Alcan, 1938

Kant, I., *Critique of Judgement*, translated J. Meredith, O.U.P., Oxford, 1911

BIBLIOGRAPHY

Critique of Pure Reason, translated Norman Kemp Smith, Macmillan, London, 1980

The Moral Law, Kant's Groundwork of the Metaphysic of Morals, translated H. J. Paton, Hutchinson, London, 1981

Critique of Practical Reason, translated L. White Beck, Indianapolis, 1956

Körner, S., *Kant*, Penguin, Harmondsworth, 1972

Lacan, J., *Ecrits*, Seuil, 1966

Laplanche, J. and Pontalis, J.–B., *Vocabulaire de la psychanalyse*, P.U.F, 1967

Lévi-Strauss, C., *Anthropologie structurale*, Plon, 1958
La Pensée sauvage, Plon, 1962
Le Cru et le cuit, Plon 1964

Lyotard, J.-F., *Discours, Figure*, Klincksieck, 1971, reprint 1978
La Condition postmoderne, Minuit, 1979
Le Différend, Minuit, 1983
Tombeau de l'Intellectuel, Galilée, 1984

Mallarmé, S., *Œuvres complètes*, Pléiade, 1945

Mead, M., *Sex and Temperament in Three Primitive Societies*, Routledge & Kegan Paul, London, 1935

Merleau-Ponty, M., *Phénoménologie de la perception*, 1945
Sens et non-sens, Nagel, 1948
Signes, 1960

Nietzsche, F., *Genealogy of Morals*, translated F. Golffing, Anchor Books, New York, 1956
Beyond Good and Evil, translated R. J. Hollingdale, Penguin, Harmondsworth, 1973
Twilight of the Idols, translated R. J. Hollingdale, Penguin, Harmondsworth, 1968

Pascal, B., *Œuvres complètes*, Seuil, 1963

Rousseau, J.-J., *Confessions*, Garnier, 1957

Rycroft, C., *A Critical Dictionary of Psychoanalysis*, Penguin, Harmondsworth, 1972

Index